T0398109

The Challenges for Russia's Politicized Economic System

During the early 2000s the market liberalization reforms to the Russian economy, begun in the 1990s, were consolidated. But since the mid-2000s economic policy has moved into a new phase, characterized by more state intervention with less efficiency and more structural problems. Corruption, weak competitiveness, heavy dependency on energy exports, an unbalanced labour market, and unequal regional development are trends that have arisen and which, this book argues, will worsen unless the government changes direction. The book provides an in-depth analysis of the current Russian economic system, highlighting especially structural and institutional defects, and areas where political considerations are causing distortions, and puts forward proposals on how the present situation could be remedied.

Susanne Oxenstierna holds a doctorate in Economics and is Deputy Research Director at the Swedish Defence Research Agency, FOI.

Routledge Contemporary Russia and Eastern Europe Series

The Challenges for Russia's Politicized Economic System

Edited by Susanne Oxenstierna

Routledge
Taylor & Francis Group

London and New York

First published 2015
by Routledge
2 Park Square, Milton Park, Abingdon, Oxon, OX14 4RN

and by Routledge
711 Third Avenue, New York, NY 10017

Routledge is an imprint of the Taylor & Francis Group, an informa business

British Library Cataloguing in Publication Data
A catalogue record for this book is available from the British Library

Library of Congress Cataloging in Publication Data

[CIP data]

ISBN: 978-1-138-79662-1 (hbk)
ISBN: 978-1-315-75778-0 (ebk)

Typeset in Times New Roman
by Sunrise Setting Ltd, Paignton, UK

Contents

Figures

Tables

Contributors

Ruta Aidis is Senior Fellow at the Center for Entrepreneurship and Public Policy (CEPP), School of Public Policy, George Mason University; VP, Research and Business Development, The GEDI Institute; and President and CEO, ACG Inc. Dr Aidis specializes in comparative entrepreneurship development, institutions, gender and public policy.

Clifford G. Gaddy is Senior Fellow at the Brookings Institution, Washington, DC, and Senior Scientific Advisor of the Center for Research on International Financial and Energy Security (CRIFES) at Pennsylvania State University.

Vladimir Gimpelson is Director of the Centre for Labour Market Studies and Professor at the Higher School of Economics in Moscow. He specializes in labour market developments in transition countries with a special focus on Russia. Among his multiple publications is the book *The Russian Labour Market Between Transitions and Turmoil* (Rowman & Littlefield 2001).

Barry W. Ickes is Professor and Associate Head of the Department of Economics and Director of CRIFES at Pennsylvania State University, and Non-resident Senior Fellow at the Brookings Institution, Washington, DC.

Irina Ilina is Professor at the Department of Regional Studies at NRU-HSE and Director of the Institute of Regional Studies and Urban Planning at HSE. She is former Deputy Mayor of Moscow.

Rostislav Kapeliushnikov is Chief Researcher at the Institute of World Economy and International Relations, the Russian Academy of Sciences, in Moscow and Deputy Director of the Centre for Labour Market Studies at the Higher School of Economics in Moscow. Among his publications is the book *The End of the Russian Model of the Labour Market?* (2009).

Masaaki Kuboniwa is Professor at the Institute of Economic Research, Hitotsubashi University in Tokyo. He received his PhD from Hitotsubashi University and has an Honorary Doctorate from the Central Economics and Mathematics Institute (TsEMI), Russian Academy of Sciences. He is Executive Officer of the Association for Comparative Economic Studies.

Carol Scott Leonard is Professor and holds the Department Chair of the Higher School of Economics in Moscow as well as being Emeritus Fellow of St Antony's College, Oxford. She is also a member of the Presidential Academy of the National Economy and Public Administration and is the author of *Privatization in Transition in Russia in the Early 1990s* (Routledge 2013).

Robert W. Orttung is Associate Research Professor of International Affairs and Assistant Director of the Institute for Russian, European, and Eurasian Studies at the Elliott School of International Affairs at George Washington University. He is also a visiting fellow at the Center for Security Studies at the Swiss Federal Institute of Technology in Zurich. He is managing editor of *Demokratizatsiya: The Journal of Post-Soviet Democratization* and co-editor of the *Russian Analytical Digest*.

Susanne Oxenstierna is Deputy Research Director at FOI. After completing her PhD in Economics at Stockholm University, she has worked for more than twenty years in a wide range of research and technical assistance projects for Russia and other transition economies. Among her recent publications is the co-edited volume *Russian Energy and Security up to 2030* (Routledge 2014).

Evgeniy Plisetskiy is Assistant Teacher in Public Administration and Regional Management at the Faculty of Management and researcher at the Center of Regional Research at HSE in Moscow.

Richard Sakwa is Professor of Russian and European Politics at the University of Kent and Associate Fellow of the Royal Institute of International Affairs, Chatham House. His recent books include *Putin: Russia's Choice* (Routledge 2008) and *The Crisis of Russian Democracy: The Dual State, Factionalism, and the Medvedev Succession* (Cambridge University Press 2011).

Jens Siegert holds a Master's in Political Science. From 1988 to 1999, he worked as a journalist, and from 1993 onward he was based in Russia. In 1999 he became the Director of the Moscow office of the Heinrich-Böll-Stiftung, a position he still holds. He is an expert on Russian domestic and foreign politics with a special focus on civil society issues.

Carolina Vendil Pallin is Deputy Research Director at FOI. She holds a PhD in Political Science from the London School of Economics. Her previous positions include Senior Research Fellow at the Swedish Institute for International Affairs and special advisor for the Swedish Defence Commission. Vendil Pallin is also a member of the Royal Swedish Academy of War Sciences.

Andrei Yakovlev is Director of the Institute for Industrial and Market Studies (IIMS) at the Higher School of Economics in Moscow. He was awarded a PhD in Economics and Statistics at Moscow State University in 1992. Among his recent publications is the co-edited volume *Organization and Development of Russian Business: A Firm-Level Analysis* (Palgrave Macmillan 2009).

Natalia Zubarevich is Professor in the Department of Geography at Moscow State University and Director of the Regional Programme of the Independent Institute for Social Policy in Moscow. She became Doctor of Science at Moscow State University in 2003. She has worked as an expert in the UN Development Program in Russia.

Abstract

What are the challenges for the Russian politicized economic system and what potential does it have to spur growth? Will the dependence on oil and gas prevail? Would strengthening of the institutions underpinning the market economy make a difference? And is there any chance of reform initiatives from below through democratization? The book *The Challenges for Russia's Politicized Economic System* explores different aspects of the close intertwining of politics and economics in the Russian economy. The economic system maintained by the authoritative regime under Vladimir Putin in 2014 entails that large parts of the economy are governed not by the market but by the state. The heritage from the Soviet economy in the form of informal institutions and the industrial infrastructure has become increasingly evident and potent. There are no drivers to modernize the economy and the incentives for entrepreneurs are weak. A dozen international scholars contribute their viewpoints on matters central to the functioning of the economic system. Key conclusions are that rent addiction is a strong powerful and political force, that the eroding constitutional state and deficient institutions hinder attempts to modernization and entrepreneurial activity, and that NGOs have grown stronger under repression. The basis for establishing modern institutions exists among some groups in Russian society. However, the ongoing downturn of the economy and the country's geopolitical aspirations obstruct the development and provide a fertile environment for authoritarian rather than democratic institutions.

Susanne Oxenstierna holds a doctorate in Economics and is Deputy Research Director at the Swedish Defence Research Agency, FOI.

Preface

This book was initiated in the fall of 2013 when it had become evident that, despite weakened growth, economic policy during President Vladimir Putin's third reign would not be geared at modernizing the Russian economy and addressing its long-term systemic problems. In order to increase the understanding of the present interrelations of politics and economics and the internal impediments and drivers to growth in Russia, I invited a group of international scholars to write about the long-term systemic issues of the Russian economy as they saw them. This volume is the result and it is a great pleasure to present new and original work of some of the most well-known specialists on Russian economics and politics on these urgent topics.

The book project included a conference in Stockholm on 20 March 2014, where the contributors presented preliminary versions of their paper to an audience from the Swedish business community, government offices and academia. The four sessions at the conference were chaired by Silvana Malle, Professor Emeritus of Economic Sciences, Verona University; Anders Fogelklou, Professor Emeritus of Law, Uppsala University; Associate Professor Ann-Mari Sätre, Uppsala Centre for Russian and Eurasian Studies (UCRS), Uppsala University; and Professor Michelle Micheletti, Stockholm University. I would like to express my deep gratitude for their genuinely first-class contribution to the conference.

My own work in the project has been supported by the Russia project 'RUFS' at FOI, which is financed by the Swedish Ministry of Defence. The conference was funded by a special grant from *Riksbankens Jubileumsfond* (The Swedish Foundation for Humanities and Social Sciences) which is hereby gratefully acknowledged. I warmly thank Veronica Bard Bringéus, Sweden's Ambassador to Russia, for her engaging opening keynote speech and Heinz Sjögren, Chairman of the Swedish Chamber of Commerce for Russia and CIS, my energetic and most supportive co-organizer, for his indispensable contributions to a successful conference. Sanna Aronsson provided excellent management of all administrative tasks in connection with the event and the law firm Mannheimer Swartling provided the conference venue and support during the conference day which was greatly appreciated.

In addition, particular thanks are due to Michael Bradshaw, Professor of Global Energy at University of Warwick, and Michelle Micheletti, Lars Hierta Professor of Political Science at Stockholm University, who each peer-reviewed a couple of the preliminary papers within their special areas of competence. Finally, I am indebted to Christina Lönnblad who competently edited the English language of the Russian, German, Swedish and Japanese authors.

Stockholm 31 August 2014
Susanne Oxenstierna
Deputy Research Director (PhD Econ.)
Department of Defence Economics
Swedish Defence Research Agency (FOI)
Stockholm
Sweden

Abbreviations and Acronyms

AO	Autonomous Okrug
APEC	Asia-Pacific Economic Cooperation
ASI	Agency for Strategic Initiatives
BEEPS	Business Environment and Enterprise Performance Survey
bn	billion
BRIC	Brazil, Russia, India and China
BRICS	Brazil, Russia, India, China and South Africa
CEFIR	The Centre for Economic and Financial Research
CEPP	Center for Entrepreneurship and Public Policy
CIS	Commonwealth of Independent States
CIT	Corporate Income Tax
CPI	Corruption Perception Index
CPRF	Communist Party of the Russian Federation
CPSU	Communist Party of the Soviet Union
CRIFES	Center for Research on International Financial and Energy Security (US)
CSO	civil society organization
CSR	Centre for Strategic Analysis (RF)
DOLS	dynamic OLS
EBRD	European Bank of Reconstruction and Development
ECA	Eastern Europe and Central Asian countries
EPL	Employment Protection Legislation
EU	The European Union
FE	fixed effects model
FOM	Foundation for Public Opinion in Society
FSB	Federal Security Service
GDI	gross domestic income
GDP	gross domestic product
GEM	Global Entrepreneurship Monitor
Gender-GEDI	Gender Global Entrepreneurship and Development Index
GKO	Gosudarstvennoe Kratkosrochnoe Obyazatyelstvo (T-bills)
GONGO	government organized non-governmental organizations
GPO	General Prosecutor's Office

GRP	gross regional product
HDI	Human Development Index
HSE	National Scientific University – Higher School of Economics (Moscow, RF)
HT	Hausman–Taylor Model
ILO	International Labour Organization
IPO	Initial Public Offering
IS RAN	Institute of Sociology of the Russian Academy of Science
KGI	Committee for Civil Initiatives
KhMAO	Khanty-Mansi Autonomous Okrug
LAO	limited access order
LGBTI	lesbian, gay, bisexual, transgender, intersexual
M&A	merger and acquisition
Mbit/s	megabits per second
MET	high mineral extraction tax
MNL	Multinomial Logit Model
NATO	North Atlantic Treaty Organization
NGO	non-governmental organization
NITs	Scientific Research Centre for Management, Economics and Information Technology
OECD	Organization for Economic Co-operation and Development
OLS	ordinary least squares (a method used in a linear regression model)
OMON	Special forces of the Ministry of Interior RF
OPORA	association for small and medium-sized enterprises in Russia
PES	public employment service
PPP	purchasing power parity
RAIPON	Russian Association of the Indigenous Peoples of the North
RIA	Regulatory Impact Assessment
RIA Rating	Rating Agency of the Rossiya Segodnya International Information Agency
RIC	Russian Investigative Committee
RLMS-HSE	Russian Longitudinal Monitoring Survey – Higher School of Economics
RMS	rent management system
Rosstat	The Russian Federal Statistical Service
RSPP	The Russian Union of Industrialists and Entrepreneurs
RUR	Russian roubles
S&P	Standard & Poor's Rating Services
SNA	system of national accounts
TEA	Total Entrepreneurship Activity
TFP	Total Factor Productivity
TG	trading gains
TPC	temperature per capita

ToT	terms of trade
TsEMI	Central Economics and Mathematics Institute of the Russian Academy of Sciences
UB	unemployment benefits
UI	Swedish Institute for International Affairs
UK	United Kingdom
UMI	upper middle income countries
UNDP	United Nations Development Programme
UNWTO	The United Nations World Tourism Organization
US	United States of America
USD	American dollars (United States Dollar)
VAT	value-added tax
VC	venture capital
VTsIOM	All-Russian Centre for Studying Public Opinion
WGI	Worldwide Governance Indicators
WTO	World Trade Organization
YaNAO	Yamal-Nenets Autonomous Okrug

1 Introduction

Susanne Oxenstierna

What are the challenges for the Russian politicized economic system and what potential does it have to spur growth? Will the dependence on oil and gas prevail? Would strengthening of the institutions underpinning the market economy make a difference? Is there any chance of reform initiatives from below through democratization?

The purpose of this volume is to explore different aspects of the close intertwining of politics and economics in the Russian economy. In the economic system maintained by the authoritative regime under Vladimir Putin in 2014 large parts of the economy are governed not by the market but by the state. Since the mid-2000s, and particularly since the economic crisis in 2009, the tendency in economic policy has been toward more state intervention rather than more market orientation. During this period the heritage from the Soviet economy in the form of informal institutions and the industrial infrastructure has become increasingly evident and potent. There are no drivers to modernize the economy and provide conditions for the creation of new, innovative companies that could spur growth. Instead, oil and gas rents are used to subsidize old loss-making enterprises and regions for political reasons. To the present government maintaining the power balance between different power groups is a more important imperative than economic prosperity.

The book takes as its starting point the rich literature on the political and economic transition in Russia and the situation in Russia after the economic crisis in 2009 to which all of the western and Russian authors in this volume have contributed. The literature is extensive and references are given in individual chapters, but some recent publications that have influenced several chapters should be mentioned here; for example, the handbook on the Russian economy edited by Alexeev and Weber (2013) has served as an inspiration by providing a broad collection of analyses covering systemic topics and an analysis of the main sectors of the Russian economy as well as social and regional issues. Its starting point is the Soviet economic system and phenomena in transitional Russia are analysed drawing on the Soviet heritage as a reference point. Another reference volume is the handbook on economics and political economy of transition edited by Hare and Turley (2013) which is organized according to standard economic topics. This book is devoted to problems that are typical of all transition economies, not only applicable to Russia. It shows that the problems of weak institutions, a poor business climate and the issue of state versus private ownership are common to all these economies to various degrees and remain problem areas in some of them. The monograph on Russia's political economy by Sutela (2012) analyses the Russian economy up to the crisis in 2009 with a stress on developments in energy, the financial sector and welfare. By contrast, this volume goes beyond the situation in 2009 and discusses developments up to 2014. It focuses on four areas in which Russia's economy faces challenges: central issues of the economic system; weak institutions and poor business climate; the implications of the shortage of democracy on the economy; and the inequality of regional development.

By focusing on the systemic, institutional and other principal long-term problems in Russia's economic development, the contributions of this book emphasize the complexity of Russia's political economy – there is no quick fix for this hybrid economic system. Political reforms are needed for the state to transform and provide institutional support and promote modernization.

The context

When the economic reforms started in Russia and other East European countries, nobody actually knew how they would work out and what was going to happen. The desired outcome of the reform process was known, but there was no map for how to go from a command economy to a market economy. Reform governments and economic experts embarked on a huge experiment where the main tools came from standard economic theory. Their recipe included the liberalization of prices and trade, macroeconomic stabilization and privatization.

The former socialist countries that eventually became candidates for accession to the European Union (EU) got a crucial anchor in the reform process and substantial support in the process of creating the institutions supporting a market economy. Russia also received assistance in building new institutions, such as a tax service and a public employment service and in reforming the public administration; however, the country's federal structure, huge geographical area and the possibility of keeping old institutions intact meant that there was only a partial adjustment of the administrative and legal framework of the economy. In addition to formal institutions not fulfilling their role, old informal institutions, in the form of values, beliefs and networks, have remained in the place.

There was also a belief that market reforms would facilitate the development of democracy in the former socialist countries. The countries of Central and Eastern Europe, many of which had a tradition of democracy before becoming Soviet satellites during the Cold War, have been able to develop into democratic market economies within the EU. Russia has taken a different turn, from an evolving democracy under its first president Boris Yeltsin to an authoritarian regime under President Vladimir Putin. The very fact that Putin is now serving a third term as president is an indicator of the anti-democratic tendencies. According to the Russian Constitution, presidents can only serve two successive terms, but Vladimir Putin let his ally Dmitry Medvedev serve one period after his second term, thus creating a short break before his return to the presidency in 2012. Before his re-election, the presidential term was increased from four to six years which means that Putin could stay in power until 2018 or even 2024.

Many people opposed Putin's re-election. As early as December 2011 protests started in Moscow and in the big cities all over the country against the fraud in the Duma elections that had favoured the dominant party Edinaya Rossiya. These increased when Putin announced that he would stand for office again. Nevertheless, drawing on his extensive administrative resources, Putin secured a landslide victory. Only a fraction of the Russian population has liberal values and would like to see its country develop in a democratic direction. The majority prefers a strong leader who will set things right and reinstate Russia as a global great power, a view of the country which corresponds with that of the dominant group in Putin's power circle, the members of the security structures, the *siloviki*. As a result, civil rights have been circumvented, there has been an increase in national security and defence spending in the federal budget, prestige events such as the Olympics in Sochi have boosted nationalistic feelings and Russia's military power has been demonstrated in its attempts to destabilize Ukraine and the annexation of Crimea in 2014.

Putin's economic policies have also had a negative effect. In 2013, the Russian economy grew by 1.3 per cent and forecasts for 2014 are around 0.5–1 per cent growth in the best case, but the World Bank (2014) also predicts a contraction of 1.8 per cent in its high-risk scenario. This is well below the earlier plans of 3–4 per cent. Although progress in 2014 has been affected by the conflict in Ukraine and its consequences, the fundamental causes of the weakening growth are due to the structural problems that have escalated in the Russian economy since the mid-2000s.

Organization of the book

The book is organized in four parts, each containing three chapters. The first part is devoted to basic issues of the economic system. In Chapter 2, 'Putin's rent management system and the future of addiction in Russia' Clifford G. Gaddy and Barry W. Ickes argue that three concepts are central to an understanding of Russia's political economy: resource rents, resource addiction, and the rent management system (RMS). The chapter explains these concepts and how they interact. Gaddy and Ickes discuss the critical importance of resource rents for the economy, and how the presence of rents leads to addiction. They examine the distinctive RMS established by Vladimir Putin and analyse how its likely further evolution will shape the prospects of the economy. The conclusions are that: (1) increasing rent is the only source of significant growth for Russia; (2) rent addiction is a serious problem for the current system and will continue to grow; and (3) for all its flaws, Putin's current RMS is well suited to the likely future possibility of stagnant rents and stronger claims by rent addicts.

In Chapter 3, 'Between light and shadow: informality in the Russian labour market' by Vladimir Gimpelson and Rostislav Kapeliushnikov, another distinctive feature of the Russian economic system is discussed – the prevalence of a substantial informal economy. Gimpelson and Kapeliushnikov find that labour is reallocated from the formal labour market to the informal sector and explore the consequences of this tendency. In their view, informality has become a salient feature of the Russian labour market. In the first decade of this century economic growth in Russia almost doubled the country's GDP, but brought little in terms of additional formal employment. More precisely, the growth was accompanied by a substantial reallocation of labour to the unregulated sector while the level of formal employment was in gradual decline. This raises a set of research and policy-related questions. What is the role of institutions in this productivity-reducing reallocation? Who were the most exposed to informality and its associated outcomes? What are the implications of this expansion of informality for wage inequality, social mobility and earnings opportunities?

Chapter 4, 'State–business relations in Russia after 2011: "New Deal" or imitation of changes?' by Andrei Yakovlev, investigates the changes in the politics of the Russian ruling elite towards ordinary businesses, particularly with regard to measures designed to improve the investment climate in 2011–12. During this period, the Russian government pushed a number of measures, including the creation of the Agency for Strategic Initiatives, the establishment of an ombudsman for entrepreneurs in the Kremlin administration and the elaboration of roadmaps to improve the business regulations. As a result, in 2013, the World Bank noted a significant improvement of Russia's position in its Doing Business Index. However, simultaneously Russia faces a strong capital flight, and entrepreneurs complain about the predatory policy of federal and regional authorities. The chapter considers contradictions in the implementation of the new policy as well as preconditions for a real improvement of the business climate in Russia.

The three chapters in the next part of the book are devoted to the effects of deficient institutions and a weak business climate. Chapter 5, 'Is Russia an "entrepreneurial society"? A comparative perspective' by Ruta Aidis, considers Russia's potential to develop new businesses. The country possesses a large, expanding consumer market and there are abundant opportunities for business start-ups. However, Aidis also points to the fundamental challenges that exist to ensure the viability of business growth and expansion. She uses a comparative perspective to assess Russia's current situation, including results from the 2013 Global Entrepreneurship and Development Index (GEDI), the 2013 Gender-GEDI Index on focused female entrepreneurs and the Startup Ecosystem Report. Aidis identifies a number of key impediments. First and foremost, corruption, combined with the potential for arbitrary prosecution, results in a climate of tremendous uncertainty for Russian businesses. In addition, there is an absence of entrepreneurial education, civil society and financing for all stages of business development. Aidis concludes that in failing to address these fundamental issues, Russia will not reap the benefits of the more recent efforts to encourage entrepreneurial development.

Chapter 6, 'The role of institutions in the Russian economy' by Susanne Oxenstierna, analyses the effects of rent dependence and Putin's rent redistribution system on small and medium-sized enterprises, the new private sector in the Russian economy. The Worldwide Governance Indicators (WGI) are used to analyse the institutions supporting the market economy and the author argues that when a dominant part of the economy is ruled by the management of oil rents to secure the power of the regime, the role of market-oriented institutions becomes limited. The chapter stresses the role of a functioning civil society for the development of institutions and analyses the effects of the present restrictions on voice and civil society for institutional development in Russia. Presently, there seems to be little hope for reform from below of the system.

Chapter 7, 'The impact of oil prices, total factor productivity and institutional weakness on Russia's declining growth' by Masaaki Kuboniwa, presents an analysis of the impact of oil prices, total factor productivity (TFP) and institutional weakness on the declining growth in Russia. He looks first at the background of the Russian economy, estimating the value-added of the oil and gas industry, the terms of trade and trading gains and energy efficiency. Secondly, he presents the impact of oil prices and TFP on declining growth in the light of GDP–oil nexus and production function. Thirdly, he reports the elusive impact of institutional weakness on Russia's growth, employing the World Bank's Governance Indicators and Ease of Doing Business Index.

The third part of the book is devoted to the interdependency of democracy and the economy. In Chapter 8, 'From the dual to the triple state?', Richard Sakwa states that Russia remains locked in an extended moment of transition, giving rise to a dual state and economy and a stalemated political order. Two regulatory regimes in the political and economic sphere coexist, which in shorthand we can label the democratic and the *dirigiste*. Neither system is allowed a free rein and the inherent ordering principles of both are stymied. The long-term balance between the constitutional state and the administrative regime allows the development of a dangerous third arm, the corruption associated with the third state of crony capitalist relations where meta-corruption dissolves into extensive venal corruption.

Chapter 9, 'The basis for institutions among the population in Russia' by Carolina Vendil Pallin, examines the opinions and attitudes of the Russian population to the social and economic development. Pallin argues that a favourable socio-economic development has made a growing section of the Russian population put forward new demands on the country's authorities. These groups still constitute a minority, but an important minority in that they compromise the younger cohort of society and the growing middle class. Catering for these groups or finding ways of not doing so will be one of the main challenges ahead for Russian authorities at the federal, regional and local levels. The chapter analyses socio-economic development in Russian society and opinion polls and attitudes among different sections of the Russian population.

In Chapter 10, 'Russian civil society. Recent developments', Jens Siegert investigates the relationship between Russian civil society organizations (NGOs) and the state. The relationship is both mixed and complex. In some respects, the NGOs are the advanced party of a Russian middle class, developing new, integrative rules of participation, which might help the country on its way to modernization, both socially and economically. Siegert has followed the development of Russian

NGOs from Moscow since the beginning of the century. He finds that so far the NGOs have succeeded in opposing the Kremlin's attempts to suppress them due to their own skill and support from abroad and have emerged stronger than before. The outcome of the post-2012 attempt to suppress NGOs is still uncertain, but Siegert hopes that the NGOs will be successful again.

The final part of the book is devoted to the issue of regional development. In Chapter 11, 'Regional inequality and potential for modernization', Nataliya Zubarevich investigates the inequality between regions in Russia and the redistribution that has occurred between 1998 and 2012. Zubarevich compares per capita gross regional product (GRP), the impact of redistribution of oil rent over the federal budget, social indicators and the Gini coefficient and finds that inequality has been declining in these indicators from the mid-2000s due to different factors. She also examines Russia's internal heterogeneity with the centre–periphery model. The analysis shows that the populations of metropolitan areas, midsize cities, small towns, and rural areas display different degrees of potential for modernization and employ different adaptation strategies in times of economic and political change.

Chapter 12, 'Promoting sustainability in Russia's Arctic: integrating local, regional, federal, and corporate interests' by Robert Orttung, examines which actors are most active in promoting sustainability by examining a case study of the relationship between Moscow and the Yamal-Nenets Autonomous Okrug, Russia's most important region for the production of natural gas. In addition to the state institutions, the analysis considers the role of the corporations involved. Orttung begins by examining the interests and capabilities of the various actors. He then traces the evolution of Yamal-Nenets politics and considers how the region implements social policy. The central conclusion is that those actors with the greatest interest in promoting sustainability have the least influence over policy-making processes.

Finally, Chapter 13 'Russian regional finance: managing resource abundance. A case study of Khanty-Mansi' by Irina N. Ilina, Carol S. Leonard and Evgenii E. Plisetskiy, studies if capacity building has an effect on one oil-abundant region, or if growth is constrained by federal budget policies. The chapter is part of a larger project on governance and growth in Russia's regions that examines the Khanty-Mansi budget strategy for diversification and growth in an oil-abundant region.

Key challenges and conclusions

The general message of the book is that there is little hope for a revival of the Russian economy in the next coming years. All of the chapters identify serious challenges that are not being addressed by the political leadership; on the contrary, in many instances they are reinforced. The military aggression against Ukraine in 2014 further demonstrates that Russia is currently looking backwards instead of forwards. In attempts to reinstate its superpower status it engages in geopolitical and territorial ambitions instead of promoting economic strength and prosperity through technological and social development. Russia currently has the third-highest military expenditure in the world and in recent years defence spending has risen as a share of GDP. Putin supports the subsidized defence industry instead of providing new entrepreneurs with conditions for expansion. Apparently, Russia currently opts for military strength rather than economic power.

The chapters present many interesting conclusions on precise topics. Here I restrict myself to highlight some of the key conclusions regarding the challenges for the Russian politicized economic system that are explored in the volume.

The dual state and the modernization blockage

The notion that Russia is a distinctive type of 'dual state', in which the constitutional state is balanced by the administrative regime, emphasizes the severity of Russia's political and economic crisis. Two regulatory regimes coexist in the political and economic sphere and neither the democratic nor the *dirigiste* orders have free rein. Instead, Russia suffers from a modernization blockage and a political stalemate. Russian politics is characterized by *sublation*, the undercutting of one institution by another, eroding the legitimacy and efficacy of the first. In the framework of the analysis of the dual state, sublation is the mechanism whereby the institutions of the constitutional state lose their autonomy. The long-term balance between the constitutional state and the administrative regime is in danger of allowing the development of a dangerous third arm, the corruption associated with the third state of crony capitalist relations where the sublationary practices of the administrative regime dissolve into systemic corruption.

Rent addiction and rent management is the most powerful economic and political force

Rent addiction and the central role of rent management in balancing the power structure is a central feature of the economic system and an exceptionally powerful economic, social and political force in Russia. To endure, anyone – any leader, any movement, right or left – that attempts to lead Russia will have to deal with the addicts. This means that any other leader would face the same challenges as Putin and his RMS. Whether democrat or autocrat, the issues are the same: accommodate the addicts and watch the economy degenerate progressively more. Moreover, the problem does not stop there. At some point, it may be impossible to satisfy the addicts by diverting flows from other claimants. Rent flows to the addicts themselves will be reduced, which is a trap.

Deficient market institutions deter entrepreneurial activity

The Russian market offers immense opportunities but, at the same time, there are fundamental challenges that still need to be addressed in order to ensure the viability of private business and an entrepreneurial society. These include creating the conditions that foster business growth, improving entrepreneurial education and financing for all stages of business development. Corruption acts as a deterrent for potential business start-ups or business growth. It results in an absence of start-ups and the existence of businesses that do not grow. Russia lacks a civil society that provides stability and assurance to entrepreneurs so that they will be able to reap the benefits of their business activities or, if they fail, so that they have the opportunity to try again. In addition, its role as watch dog is missing and, along with it, the rule of law so that businesses do not have to worry about arbitrary and or politically motivated interference.

Rent-addicted sector blocks market reforms

New small and medium-sized businesses represent the growth potential of the Russian economy. However, they need stronger market-oriented institutions such as the rule of law, a high quality of governance and that corruption is kept at sustainable levels. Moreover, they must be able to access financial resources and profit from a supportive business climate. The old loss-making rent-addicted sector, however, is not interested in changes in that direction and has a strong degree of political leverage to maintain the existing order where personal ties to the political hierarchy rather than competitive business activities can ensure survival.

New modernization or new mobilization?

The Russian elite faces a choice – either to carry out economic modernization 'from above' relying on coercion from the centre, or to rely on the incentives and initiatives of economic agents themselves. The new business – successful medium-sized companies that rose on the tide of the economic boom in the 2000s – can become the driving force of market modernization. However, practical steps to create the necessary competitive environment would limit the power and influence of the *siloviki* group in the Russian elite and could trigger counter-initiatives of 'new mobilization' in the spirit of the Izborsk Club.[1] Thus, it is difficult to foresee a 'new spring' for the entrepreneurial groups in the economy, given the extremely restricted possibilities to voice different opinions, organize collective action around new ideas and hold politicians and other decision makers to account, meaning that there is no effective reform pressure from below. Instead, improvements in the performance of the economy are entirely dependent on reform initiatives from above, and under the present leadership initiatives that could spur growth are not forthcoming. Important but still quite marginal measures such as the introduction of a position of ombudsman for entrepreneurs in the Kremlin, an amnesty for entrepreneurs, and so on, have so far failed to produce any real outcomes in terms of economic growth and an increase in investment – because Russian elites do not share a common vision of the future and different groups in the elite try to realize different modernization scenarios.

The rise of informality

Informality is another salient feature of the Russian economy. The level of informal employment is increasing, standing at present at around 20–30 per cent of total employment. Since much of the adjustment in the Russian labour market comes from the informal sector, the issue of formal job creation is a daunting economic and political challenge. If informality continues to grow, segmentation in the labour market may become more pronounced, with stronger implications in terms of growing poverty and inequality. Meanwhile, modern economic growth is based on the development of human capital, and informality is not a fertile ground for human capital accumulation and its efficient utilization. The much lower productivity in informal jobs equals the underutilization of education and skills. Thus, the growing fraction of the labour force stuck in a low human capital-intensive economy should be of concern to decision makers.

The basis for establishing institutions is growing, but unevenly

As a result of the social and economic development in Russia, a growing section of society, consisting of urban dwellers with higher incomes and education, as well as the younger generation has become inclined to embrace values conducive to the establishment of democratic institutions. Overall, the basis for establishing institutions is growing in Russian society, but unevenly between different groups and regions. However, an external threat or a downturn of the economy could have negative effects, which would delay – or even reverse – the development and provide a fertile environment for the development of authoritarian rather than democratic institutions.

NGOs grow stronger under repression

Over the past quarter-century Russian non-governmental organizations (NGOs) have developed into a stronghold of democratic belief and behaviour within Russian society. Until 2000, the state had largely ignored rather than supported them. Since Vladimir Putin became president, there have been to date three unsuccessful attempts to subordinate the NGOs to the state. As a result, paradoxically, NGOs have become more competent, more professional and better skilled after each attempt. But this outcome gives no guarantee for the future at a time when Russian domestic policy as well as foreign policy are both becoming increasingly anti-democratic and anti-western.

New generations and value change

Russia has seen the emergence of a growing urban middle class with western values and aspirations. However, the voice of this group in political life has waned and instead they engage in different exit strategies, such as sending their children abroad for education and employment and buying property abroad to enable temporary or permanent emigration. The young Russians, however, who have not experienced Soviet times and have grown up in a time with access to information and travel and exposure to both Russian and western culture, represent a different force. Not all of them embrace western values and liberal economic thought, but, in common with most people, they do aspire to achieve a rising living standard and social development. Thus the new generations of Russians will present new opportunities for the development of democracy and a market economy in their country.

Actors with an interest in promoting sustainability have the least influence

In Russia's politicized economy, actors with the greatest interest in promoting sustainability have the least influence over policy-making processes. Local governments and civil society groups generally have the greatest interest in sustainability, but they have little ability to affect policy. The federal government and Russia's major energy corporations have the most power, and they place little emphasis on sustainability. For example, Russia's centralized system makes it possible for the federal government to exercise considerable control over the development of the Arctic. In theory, this oversight could provide for resource development policies that take into account the human needs of the population while minimizing the impact of resource production on the environment. However, the nature of the current government in Moscow places the greatest priority on the development of resources to ensure the ability of the current elites to stay in power. As a result, they have little concern for the environment.

Note

1 The Izborsk Club brings together leading patriotic, anti-liberal Russian analysts with people close to the Kremlin.

References

Alexeev, M. and Weber, S. (eds) (2013) *The Oxford Handbook of the Russian Economy*, Oxford and New York: Oxford University Press.

Hare, P. and Turley, G. (eds) (2013) *Handbook of the Economics and Political Economy of Transition*, Abingdon, UK and New York: Routledge.

Sutela, P. (2012) *The Political Economy of Putin's Russia*, Abingdon, UK and New York: Routledge.

World Bank (2014) *Russia Economic Report. Confidence crisis exposes economic weakness*, World Bank, 31, March. Online. Available: www.worldbank.org/en/country/russia/overview (accessed 24 April 2014).

2 Putin's rent management system and the future of addiction in Russia

Clifford G. Gaddy and Barry W. Ickes

This chapter explores the interaction of three concepts that we believe are central to an understanding of Russia's political economy: resource rents, resource addiction, and the rent management system. Our goal is to explain these concepts, how they interact, and how they form the basis for Russia's political economy and shape its prospects for the future. Our fundamental methodological idea is that the three concepts are basic, and they are interlinked as follows:

1   Russia is a country whose economy is dominated by the rents from its natural resources, mainly oil and gas. Resource rents are defined as the difference between the market value of resources produced and the actual cost of producing them (we elaborate, below). Russia has been dependent on resource rents for centuries, and it is likely to remain dependent for decades to come.
2   Russia, like every rent-dependent country, has a characteristic set of institutions and mechanisms by which those rents are produced, collected, and redistributed throughout the economy. These institutions, together with the mechanisms that enforce them, are the rent management system, or RMS.
3   The combination of Russia's resource abundance and the peculiarities of the non-market, command-administrative economic system that prevailed in the country during the Soviet period made it possible for Russia to develop a physical structure of the economy that was so thoroughly dependent on rents that it deserves the appellation rent addiction.

These three features – rent abundance, a rent management system, and rent addiction – are a 'three-legged stool.' They provide the context for all Russian political economy, in both the Soviet and post-Soviet eras. Almost no major issue – from economic issues such as 'modernization,' 'innovation,' and 'diversification' to the very nature of the political system – can be understood outside this interaction between resource abundance, inherited economic structure, and political economy.

In analysing the future of the system that ties the three elements together, we will argue that: (1) increasing rent is the only source of significant growth for Russia; (2) addiction is a more serious problem than ever and will continue to grow; and (3) for all its flaws, the current rent management system, established by Vladimir Putin, is well suited to the likely future possibility of stagnant rents and stronger claims by addicts. In the following we ask how each of the legs of the 'three-legged stool' might evolve in the future. What will happen to the rent, the addicts, and the rent management system? In each case we begin by briefly defining the concept in question and then proceed to answer the key questions for each. For rent, the question is how much can be expected in the future. For addiction, we want to know how strong the phenomenon is now and how it might be expected to evolve in the years ahead. For the rent management system, the critical issue is how robust and appropriate the current system is to managing rent flows in an environment when the amount of rent and the strength of addiction are as we have established.

Defining rent

We define rent as the revenue received from the sale of a resource minus the cost of producing it.[1] We emphasize that the definition must be applied rigorously, especially as regards how we understand both revenue and production cost. Each of these must be viewed in terms of opportunity cost. Rent is thus the value to the economy of the resource that is utilized. Value is measured by opportunity cost. Hence, the revenue used to calculate rent is not the actual revenue earned from the sale; rather, it is the potential revenue if the resource were sold at market value. This means that any difference between what might be received from the sale of the resource and what is actually received is still part of the rent. Its existence reflects decisions made about distribution of the rent.

In a similar way, production cost is not necessarily the actual cost reported but what the cost would be in a competitive, efficient market economy. Anything above that competitive cost – which we term the natural cost of production – is excess cost. It is by our definition part of the rent that has been allocated.

The purpose of our definition of rents is to draw a sharp distinction between the value of rent that is produced and its *distribution* to various recipients. It is the distribution of rents that is crucial to political economy. It is apparent that some components of the total rent are often hidden from view. We have already noted two components of rent – subsidies and excess costs – that must be included to properly measure total rent. There are other hidden components of rent that are important not for estimating total rent but for analysing how the rent is distributed, 'shared', among various recipients in society. Most notable among these are informal taxes. Informal taxes, informal price subsidies, and excess production costs are like the part of the iceberg that lies beneath the surface: they may turn out to be most important in assessing current and future economic and political developments.

Figure 2.1 is a stylized decomposition of total rent into its most important components. In the figure, the relative sizes of the five components are not intended to reflect precise measurements. It is more important to understand that each of the components is significant. Each represents a share of the total rent, and each has a 'constituency' – vested interests. How the shares are allocated has important

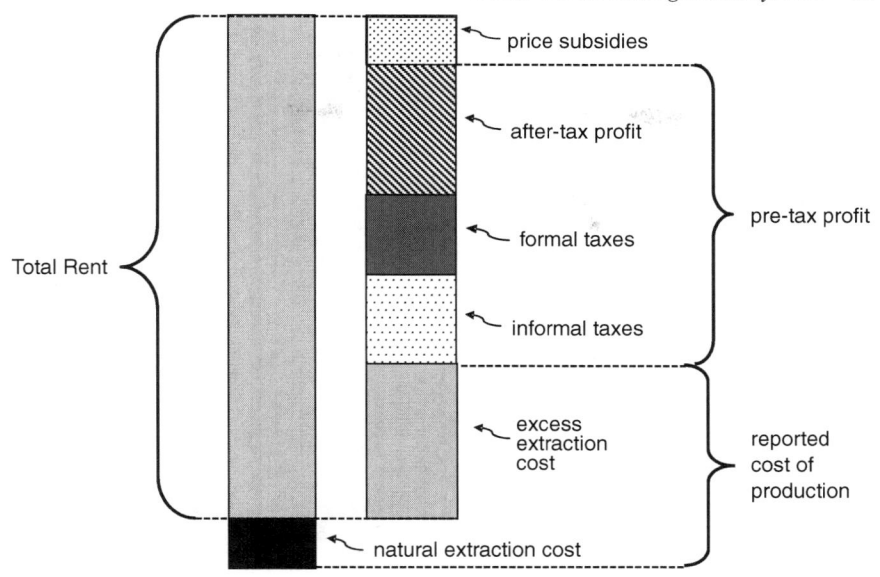

Figure 2.1 The categories of rent.

political consequences. To take one example, one frequently hears statements about the effect that a decline in oil prices would have on the Russian economy, and arguments are usually framed in terms of the effect on revenues to the government budget. But this line of thinking is based on looking at formal taxes alone. In fact, the formal taxes and the formal budget are only a part of the picture. Informal rent-sharing sustains a much broader part of the economy and society. Lower oil prices mean smaller overall rents, and thus less to be shared among all the categories – not just the part represented by formal taxes. We will return to this point in thinking about the future.

How much rent will there be in the future?

Since rent equals the quantity of the resource produced and the per unit price, less the cost of production,[2] we can ask how each of these three variables contributed to the increase in total rent in recent years in Russia. The change in natural extraction cost turns out to have played a very small role. Changes in the quantities of oil and gas produced, and their price, have been far more important. To decompose the extra rent into the price and quantity effects, we performed an exercise whose results are shown in Figure 2.2. Between 1999 and 2013, total rent grew by about USD 4.2 trillion. Of that, 3.2 trillion was due to the increase in the oil and gas prices, and 1.0 trillion to the increase in the quantity of oil and gas produced. That is, over the period higher prices accounted for about 76 per cent of the increase in rent and greater production volumes for about 24 per cent.

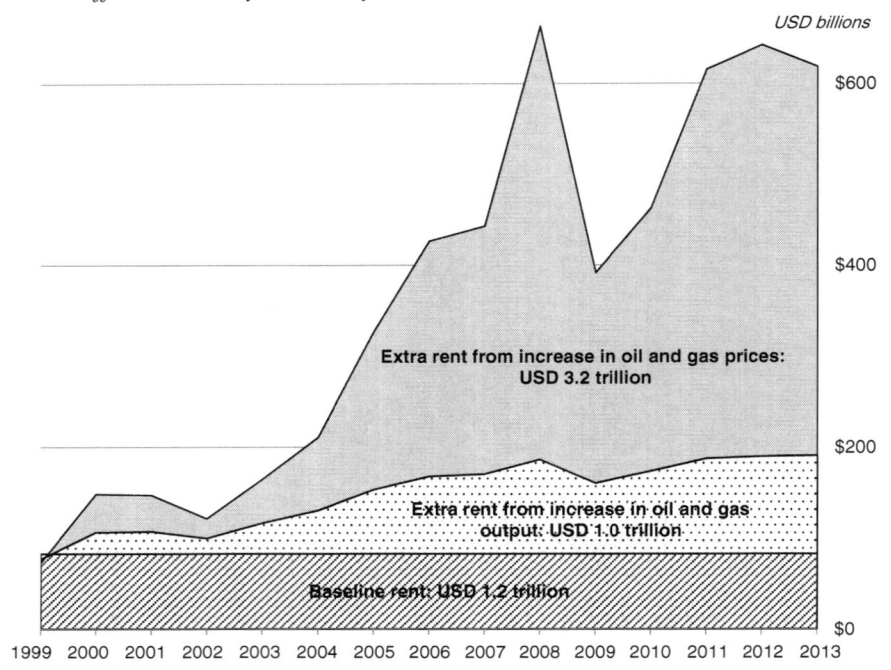

Figure 2.2 Decomposing Russia's rent windfall into price and quantity effects.

Source: Authors' calculations.

Note: 'Baseline rent' is a counterfactual based on assuming constant prices and quantities of oil and gas produced in Russia at levels as of the beginning of the period. The price used here is the average prices of oil and gas for 1997–99 and quantities produced in 1999. (The price of oil in 1999 was around USD 23 per barrel.) The extra rent each year is calculated as the difference between actual rent and baseline rent. The extra rent is apportioned each year into two parts—the part attributable to increased price and the part attributable to increased volume.

This chart on 'extra' rent is valuable in helping to understand how unlikely it is that the rent increase of the 2000s will be repeated. Consider that from 2006 to 2011 Russia's total rent rose by about 50 per cent. Securing that much extra rent between now and 2020 would require that the world oil price rise steadily to over USD 150 a barrel in today's prices by the end of that period. There is no current consensus about where oil prices might be in 2020, with some forecasts of USD 70 per barrel of oil and others predicting USD 160.[3] There is much discussion about how reduced demand in advanced economies and increased supply of oil and gas from unconventional sources will result in lower, rather than higher prices in the future.[4] At the same time, one should not forget how poor our ability to predict oil prices is. Oil prices are highly volatile, and the time series since 1973 looks like a random walk. It is always useful to keep the long historical record of oil prices in mind (Figure 2.3). Moreover, even if the rise in prices was more important for the past rent boom than the increase in production, quantity cannot

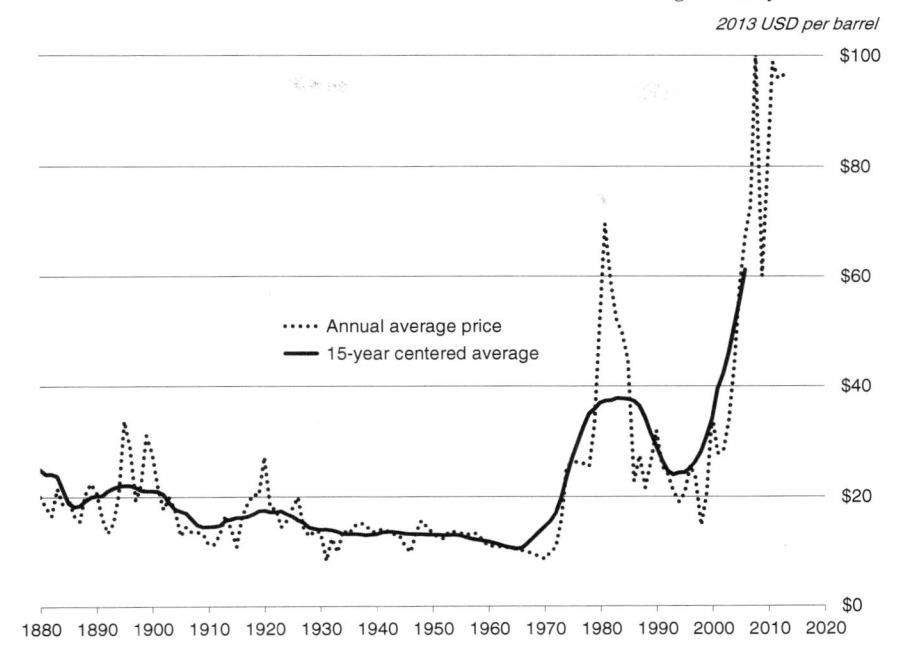

Figure 2.3 World oil prices, 1880–2013.

Source: Authors' calculations using current dollar oil price data from EIA (2014). Adjusted to 2013 prices using US GDP deflator.

be ignored. Maintaining even current rates of production of oil and gas in Russia is a challenge. If production declines, prices will have to increase even more to result in an increase in rent.[5]

Growing without oil and gas?

The rent increase drove GDP growth during the boom years. How fast could Russia be expected to grow *without* a rent boom? The historical record of growth across countries may provide a baseline. The Penn World Table (version 7.1) has data for a large number of countries between 1950 and 2010, including over 3,800 observations of growth in countries with per capita income over USD 5,000. We used these data to determine the average growth rate for a country at Russia's current income level (Table 2.1).

Russia's per capita income today is close to USD 15,000. That suggests it is unlikely to grow faster than 2 per cent a year (line 3 of Table 2.1 shows that the average growth rate of a country in the USD 15,000–20,000 range is 1.9 per cent). But Russia's income is as high as it is thanks to oil. Its institutional structure is closer to that of a USD 10,000 per capita income country, which makes a difference in expected growth prospects. In part, this is good news for Russia. The less

Table 2.1 Historical GDP growth rates in countries with per capita income of USD 5,000 or more 1950–2010

	Per capita income	*Number of years*	*Percent positive growth years (%)*	*Average positive growth rate (%)*	*Average negative growth rate (%)*	*Average overall growth rate (%)*
(1)	5–10,000	1,529	74	5.3	–4.7	2.72
(2)	10–15,000	660	78	5.1	–4.9	2.93
(3)	15–20,000	526	73	4.0	–4.0	1.85
(4)	20–30,000	660	79	3.5	–3.3	2.10
(5)	> 30,000	459	71	3.7	–3.9	1.52
(6)	*Total > 5,000*	*3,834*	*75*	*4.6*	*–4.3*	*2.16*

Source: Penn World Table 7.1.

Note: The table is inspired by Table 1.2 ('Growth rates in good and bad years by per capita income in 2000'), North *et al.* (2009: 5). The data come from Penn World Table 7.1. The GDP growth variable is 'PPP Converted GDP Per Capita (Chain Series), at 2005 constant prices.' Penn World Table 7.1 has data for 190 countries, for a maximum of 61 years (1950–2010). Of the total data set there are 3 834 observations of growth for countries with per capita income of USD 5 000 or greater.

wealthy a country is, the faster it can be expected to grow. Hence, Russia actually has more room for so-called 'catch-up' growth than might appear judged solely on its income level. By this logic, instead of having an expected growth rate of under 2 per cent, Russia's is 2.9 per cent (line 2 of Table 2.1).

On the other hand, these hypothetical growth rates are for countries that are normal. Of course, all countries have their own peculiarities, but by normal we mean that they, unlike Russia, do not have the legacies of spatial and other misallocation from a Soviet past. Russia's vast space and incredible cold, combined with its Soviet past, provide a special set of handicaps. We have referred elsewhere to Russia's legacies as 'Bear Traps' (Gaddy and Ickes 2013a). They are like annual taxes on the level of Russia's wealth. They also impede institutional reforms, and hence they prevent Russia from taking advantage of the extra catch-up growth it should have. How big a penalty do the Bear Traps represent? In previous work, we estimated that Russia's direct location penalty may be as much as 1.5–2.25 per cent of GDP per year (ibid.: 48–9). Indeed, this is only part of the total location penalty – that part due to the cold. There is also a penalty due to distance, or remoteness. Netting out the positive effect of a possible faster catch-up rate (because its oil wealth has reduced Russia's gap to the world leaders more than is warranted by its economic fundamentals) and the negative effect of 'Bear Traps', we could put Russia's likely growth in the range of 0.7–1.4 per cent a year over the coming decade.[6]

There are two fundamental points about this exercise which might seem obvious, but which we feel we need to stress for those who might continue to insist there are clear paths to higher growth for Russia. First, the exercise refutes the notion that so-called institutional reform is the answer. The projected modest growth rates we arrived at are for a Russia that has carried out all these reforms! That is another part of what the notion of a 'normal' Russia implies: it assumes that Russia improves its current below-average institutions, investment climate, and so on to the level of the mean country of its income range. To repeat: in a world with flat oil prices, all the measures typically proposed to improve institutions, reduce corruption, and so on are highly unlikely to raise Russia's annual growth rate to any substantial extent. The implications of the exercise for a second favourite recipe for growth, namely, the diversification of the economy away from oil and gas, should be even more obvious. The countries being analysed to derive an expected growth rate for Russia had no oil at all.

The inescapable conclusion is that it is futile to expect to replace the growth that came from the increase in oil price with some other source. Russia's fate is to be dependent on oil and gas for decades to come. But that is not in itself a bad thing. Russia's problem is not rent dependence. The question is: what is the nature of the dependence and where does it lead? The form of rent dependence that exists in Russia is based on a model that formally and – much more importantly – informally taxes the resource sector in order to support backward, mislocated industries inherited from the Soviet era (a problem now increasingly exacerbated by plans to build new ones equally ill-located). A constructive model of rent dependence is one that embraces the oil and gas industries and makes them the engine of technological development and sustainable growth. It does not tax oil and gas for the sake of supporting inefficient industries. The former model – the one Russia inherited from the Soviet Union – is one that perpetuates the current state of rent addiction; the latter holds the promise of a more globally integrated and interdependent Russia with a chance at leadership positions in important technological areas. We have termed this latter development path the resource track (see the final chapter in Gaddy and Ickes 2013a).

We can frame the question of the longer-term future of Russia's political economy in exactly these terms: Can the country move from addiction to the resource track? If the answer to that question is negative, Russia's future becomes increasingly uncertain. If the system remains trapped by addiction, what happens as the regime tries to manage the addicts when the addictive substance is in shorter supply? There are various scenarios, almost all alarming, about which we speculate in the final section of this chapter.

The rent management system and addiction

Every resource abundant economy has some kind of system to control the flow of rents. From the standpoint of the leaders of the economy, the function of that system is to channel rents to their preferred uses and to prevent their dissipation or diversion. If the management system is weak, then rents will be appropriated by various stakeholders near the source of production. If it is centralized and strong, rents will flow upwards to the leadership.

In the Soviet period, direct dissipation of rents was limited. Rents could not be transformed into consumption on anywhere near the scale on which they were produced. Nor could the rents easily be shifted to private accounts abroad. Rather, those who controlled the flow and wanted to appropriate some for personal gain were limited to semi-legitimate activities. Party leaders and economic planning officials, as well as plant directors, could live better than ordinary citizens on the perquisites of office. But most of the rents were channelled to the production of things that enhanced the leadership's stature and authority, as well as the legitimacy of the Soviet state. This created the phenomenon of addiction through production, which transformed the Soviet economy.

Addiction through production meant investment in enterprises that created goods. It was manifested, above all, by production in heavy industry in giant enterprises – symbols of Soviet accomplishment since the rise of Stalin. The more metal, the more energy, and the more transportation services the plants consumed, the greater the power, prestige, and privilege enjoyed by their directors. The priority users of the equipment produced in such plants were agriculture and defence because they were so well suited to serving the interests of the self-perpetuating elite. And it is no coincidence, therefore, that farming and the military in the Soviet Union were two of the most wasteful sectors in the entire Soviet economy. The goal of the managers was not to produce the most food for a given amount of inputs or to present the most fearsome military for given numbers of men and weapons, but to demand as much equipment and support as many jobs as possible. So, in a way, the real function was to be just that – costly and wasteful.

The production structure that evolved – and this included not just factories, but cities and the USSR's infrastructure of power plants, canals and railways followed the same principle of cost enhancement. The system, therefore, had to be fed with increasing amounts of resources to offset the value destruction. This is the essence of rent addiction. It is important to distinguish addiction, which creates a persistent claim on resources, from wasteful spending, which creates a temporary claim. An addicted enterprise creates a persistent claim on resources. The famous 'bridge to nowhere', from Alaska fame, or the Olympic park in Sochi, on the other hand, are examples of wasteful spending, but they create no permanent claim. If when rents are high they are wasted on the 'bridge to nowhere,' it is easy to cut this off when rents decline. But if the rents are used to create new addicts, then there will be permanent claimants who will demand to be satisfied even as rents dry up.

When the USSR collapsed, the Soviet rent management system collapsed with it. The post-Soviet Russian government, however, had nothing to put in its place. Reformers had a long list of reforms to implement, especially the triad of enterprise privatization, market liberalization, and macroeconomic stabilization. But they did not recognize the crucial role of rent management to the Russian economy. Thus, without a strong management from the top, rent management was decentralized. This bottom-up rent management system that developed in the low-rent years of the 1990s was known as Russia's 'virtual economy' (Gaddy and Ickes 2002). Towards the end of the decade, just before resource rents exploded in the wake of rising global oil prices, it was replaced by a variant created and managed by Vladimir Putin.

Putin's rent management system

Putin's system combines strong state influence with private ownership of enterprises. The particular role of private owners in this system begs an explanation. Most of the companies in Russia's core industrial sectors had been privatized in the 1990s and have remained private. The only significant exception is the oil company, Yukos, which was effectively re-nationalized following the 2003 arrest in of its owner, Mikhail Khodorkovsky, who had challenged Putin's system. The lucrative metals and mining sector is also almost entirely in private hands.

Contrary to conventional wisdom, the Russian leadership under Putin is not hostile to private ownership, even to private ownership of vital sectors of the economy. Putin is aware that private ownership is the only way to make the Russian economy more efficient. The highest priority for the regime with respect to private owners is to ensure that they continue to support the rent distribution system that serves the interests of the regime. For the rent-producing companies, whether state-owned or private, the most important requirement is that they directly support the production and supply chains linking the addicts – the inefficient enterprises inherited from the Soviet economy. Suppliers of material inputs (fuel and energy, metals, components) and services (rail and pipeline) are required to serve the machine-building enterprises. The prices of virtually all these critical inputs are set to transfer value to the rent addicts. Those very same input suppliers are then obliged to purchase the machinery and equipment produced with the implicit subsidies.

Note the method behind the seeming madness. Rather than collecting oil and gas rents exclusively as formal taxes, and then redistributing some of them to addicted enterprises, energy producers provide much of the transfer directly – either in physical form as below market price inputs or in money as excessive payment for orders to the equipment manufacturers, or via intermediate production sectors that serve the oil and gas industry, such as transport infrastructure construction, the electric power sector, or the processing industries. The supply chains can thus be regarded as rent distribution chains. They are mechanisms to disperse rents from resource producers to the addicts who need the rents to survive.

The distribution of rent through production is the most important way rents from natural resources are shared in today's Russian economy. And it is all informal: it is not written into law, and it does not show up on a government budget. Oil and gas rents thus form the currency of power in which corporation owners, the oligarchs, top government officials, and governors of the most important regions are on a nearly equal footing. They are, in effect, rent management division heads in the gigantic enterprise that ought to be known as 'Russia, Inc.' The system combines the virtues of stability, by ensuring that rent is distributed to the regions, cities and plants with the most clout, and efficiency, by assuring that the private owners of rent-generating industries have strong incentives to maximize profits and thereby create more rents. In effect, it preserves the ownership rights of the oligarchs in exchange for their maintenance of the rent distribution system.

How strong is addiction today?

How strong is addiction today? The answer to this question has both an objective and a subjective component. Objectively, it is the number and size of the enterprises that are dependent on rent infusions for their survival, and the degree of their dependence. The subjective element is their political clout – how important are they, for instance, in terms of Putin's political priorities? In other words, strength of addiction is measured not only by quantitative demands for rents but also by the *political power* that lies behind those claims. That power has grown and is reflected in Putin's post-2011 decision to conduct war on the Moscow-based 'creative class' by prioritizing his core constituencies in the heartland of Russia (Gaddy and Ickes 2013a: 96–100). Putin's extraordinary attention to plants like the famous tank and railcar manufacturer, Uralvagonzavod, located in the Urals city of Nizhnyi Tagil, is exemplary. Railway freight cars are the paradigmatic product of the old Soviet-legacy plants in Russia, and it is remarkable how closely output in that industry tracks the ups and downs of the resource rent flow into Russia (Figure 2.4). As plants like Uralvagonzavod persist, they claim more and more physical and labour inputs – and more rent to sustain them.

As Figure 2.5 shows, between 2002 and 2008, 63,000 net new jobs were added in plants producing railroad rolling stock – a 43 per cent increase. Meanwhile,

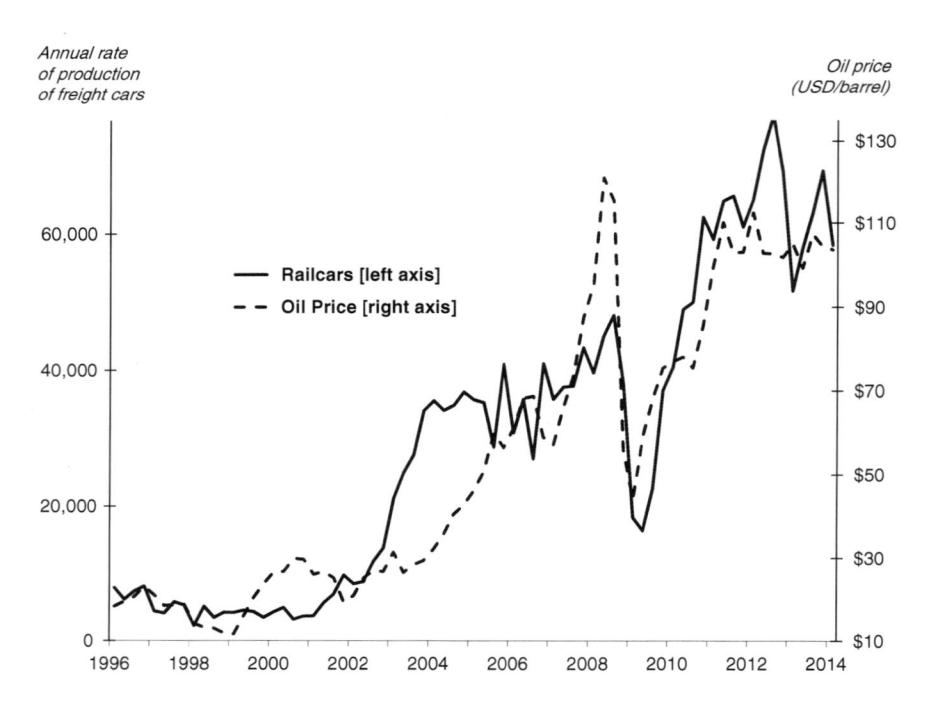

Figure 2.4 The world oil price and Russia's production of rail freight cars, 1996–2014.

Source: Authors' calculations. Data on railcar production from Rosstat. Oil price from IMF (2014).

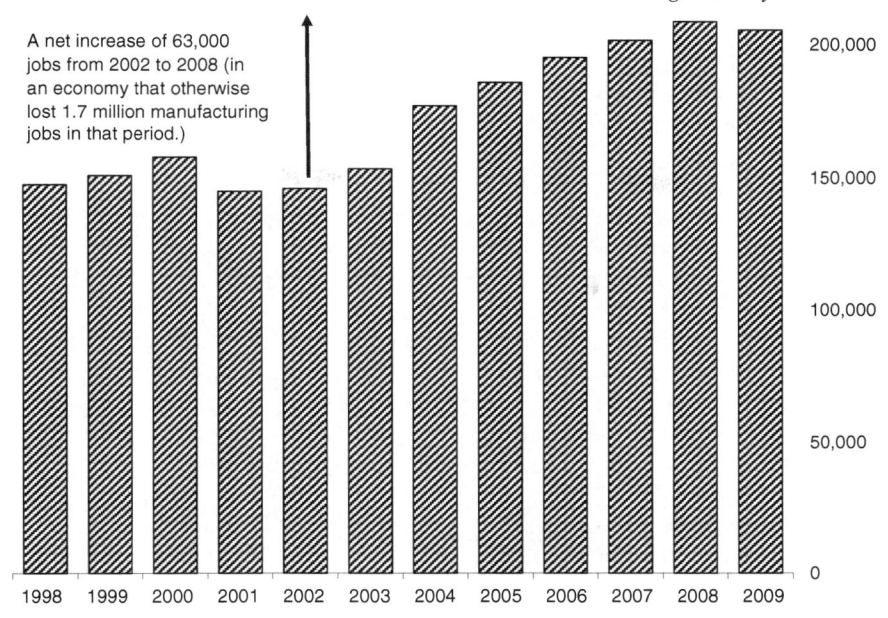

A net increase of 63,000 jobs from 2002 to 2008 (in an economy that otherwise lost 1.7 million manufacturing jobs in that period.)

Figure 2.5 Employment in railroad rolling stock industry, 1998–2009.
Source: Rosstat.

overall manufacturing employment shrank by 15 per cent (1.7 million workers). In the crisis year of 2009, the output of the railroad rolling stock companies dropped 45 per cent, but employment was down by only 1.5 per cent. Overall manufacturing employment dropped over 11 per cent in 2009.

As part of Russia's defence industrial complex, Uralvagonzavod benefits from the single largest effort to support the addicted part of the economy, the massive programme of defence industry modernization launched by Putin. The plan is to channel a total of RUR 23 trillion (around USD 670 billion at 2014 exchange rates) into that sector.

The defence modernization programme, plans to support so-called monotowns, the various Siberian/Far East development programmes – all of this perpetuates the Soviet structural legacy and therefore strengthens addiction. It is not a simple matter to quantify this effect directly. However, the following exercise may offer an indirect approach. Addiction is defined as a dependence on rents to sustain otherwise unviable enterprises. In the Russian economy, viability is critically affected by location. Enterprises located in cold and remote areas are burdened with extra costs. Since cold and distance act, in effect, as a tax on viability, they contribute to the objective component of addiction. Moreover, remoteness in particular enhances the political strength of addicts. When addicts are isolated, their claims on rents have extra strength. Refusing the claims of addicts in remote areas threatens workers who cannot easily move to other companies when the plant is far away from all others. All of this means that by studying shifts in the geographical distribution of economic activity, we can infer something about the dynamics of addiction. Specifically, if the concentration of enterprises in cold and distant locations decreases, then we can conclude that the conditions that promote addiction are weakening (and vice versa).[7]

In earlier work (Gaddy and Ickes 2001; Hill and Gaddy 2003) we created an index called temperature per capita (TPC) to measure the distribution of a country's economic activity in relation to the cold. TPC is simply the population-weighted mean temperature of the country. For example, if the population moves from warmer parts of Russia to colder, eastern regions, TPC falls. This is what happened in the Soviet period as industry was moved from western parts of Russia to the Urals, Siberia, and the Far East.[8] This meant that from the late 1920s to around 1960, Soviet Russia's average 'economic temperature' dropped precipitously. This trend was then interrupted for a decade, but it resumed in 1970–90. Figure 2.6 traces the TPC index in Russia over the entire period of Soviet and post-Soviet history.

What is important for our current discussion about addiction is the trend in the index after the collapse of the Soviet Union. In the decade after 1990, Russia's TPC increased, reflecting a shift of population to warmer areas. But since 2003 the

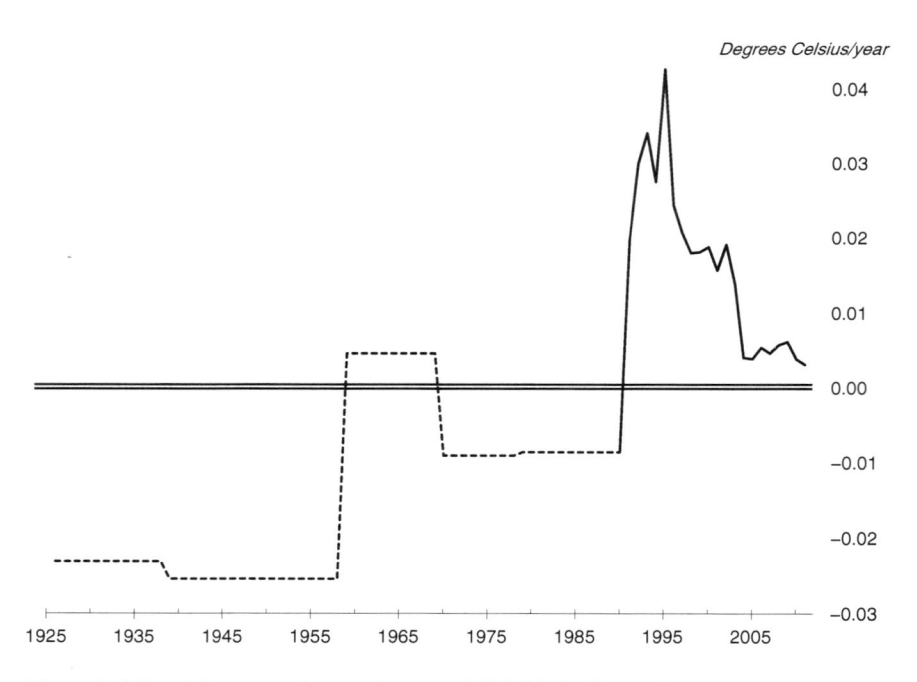

Figure 2.6 Russia's economic warming rate, 1925–2011. Change in 'temperature per capita' (TPC) per year.

Source: Authors' calculations using data on regional temperatures and populations from Rosstat.

'economic warming' of Russia has slowed substantially. Various projections of future population growth by regions suggest the current trend will hold. Figure 2.7 presents the same picture in finer resolution. It measures the year-to-year change in TPC and more clearly illustrates the dramatic difference between the 1990s and the most recent few years.[9]

To state this in terms of addiction, during the 1990s perhaps the most important condition that promotes addiction – namely, geographical location – was weakened. But then in the 2000s that trend was dissipated. In short, contrary to the hopes of some that the legacy of the Soviet physical structure would attenuate over time, the history of the past 15 years shows that this has not been the case.

How can the rent management system cope?

The current system worked exceptionally well during the period of the rent boom. But how well can it cope with shrinking rent and stronger addicts and still achieve its goal of stability and popular legitimacy? Who loses when addicts' claims have to be met but rent overall shrinks? We can take another look at the chart that breaks down the categories of rent, this time identifying who the recipients of the shares are (Figures 2.8 and 2.9).

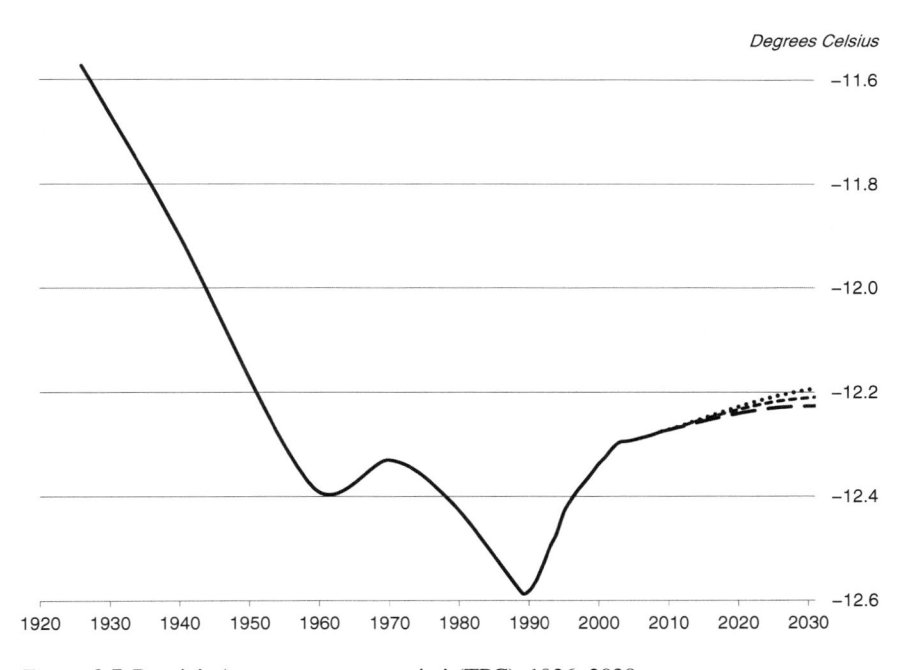

Figure 2.7 Russia's 'temperature per capita' (TPC), 1926–2030.

Source: Authors' calculations using data on regional temperatures and populations from Rosstat.

Categories of Rent Distribution

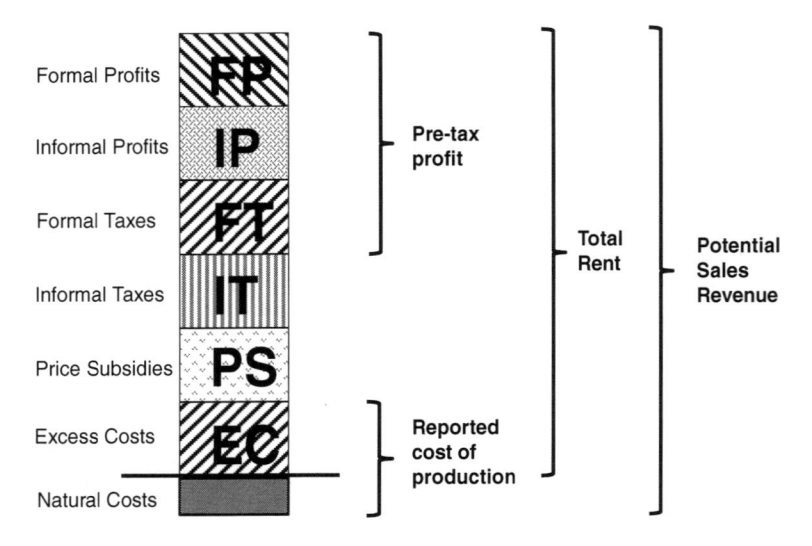

Figure 2.8 Total value and its components.

Categories of Rent Distribution

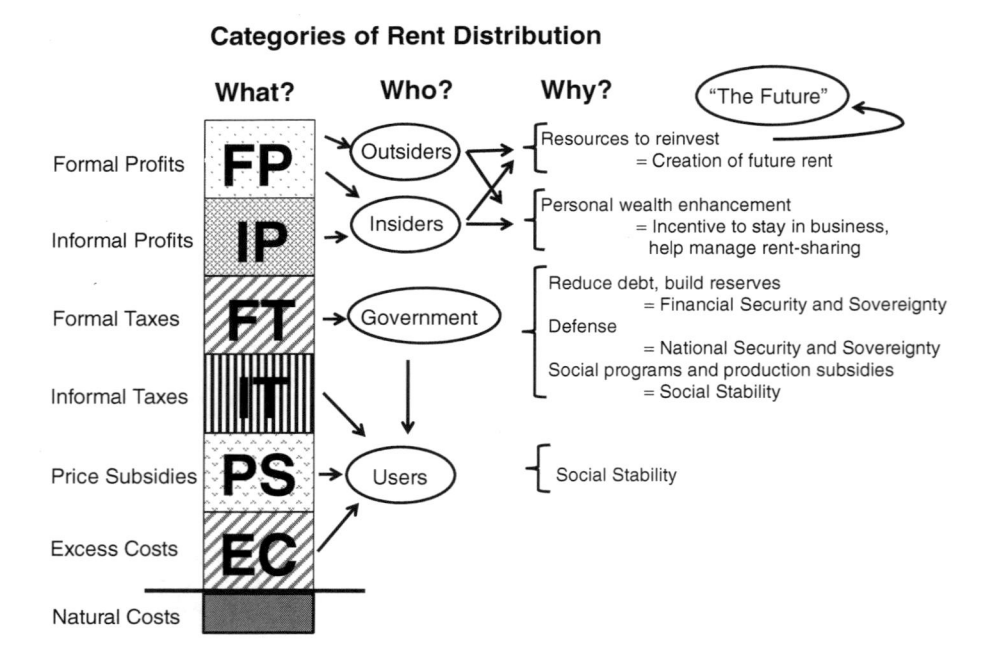

Figure 2.9 Categories of rent distribution.

What are the margins for adjustment when rents shrink? An obvious answer is to end the funding of addicted enterprises. We will explain below why this is not a reasonable outcome. If we exclude this possibility, it follows that some other current recipients of rent flows will have to be denied. There are three ways to do that:

1 Reduce formal and informal profits in favour of higher formal and informal taxes.
2 Cut non-addict budgetary spending such as social, education and health in favour of flows to addicts such as spending on military industry.
3 Reduce investment in future rent production

The problem with each of these choices is that those from whom the rent is being diverted are, by all rational considerations, more valuable users of the rent than the addicts are. Moreover – and this is not evident in the bar chart – there are other measures that can be taken on behalf of the addicts, for instance, greater constraints on factor mobility or stronger protection of rent distribution chains. Such measures benefit the addicts by strengthening their claims on rents.

There will always be a RMS; the question is the particular form it takes. The existence of addiction dictates a set of options for the RMS. That is, given addiction, the primary purpose of the RMS is to deal with the addicts – either keep the addicts supplied with the substance or somehow manage the addiction. Putin's RMS is one particular way of managing the addicts. Russia has had Putin's RMS since 2000. This is a centralized system. One of its key features is that many of the companies that play a critical role in rent distribution are privately owned. But those owners – the so-called oligarchs – are under Putin's control, and their participation in the system is enforced by what is in effect a 'protection racket' run by Putin (Gaddy and Ickes 2011). This component of Putin's system – the method of enforcement of rent distribution – is robust, since the oligarchs are in greater need of Putin's protection now than ever before. Popular sentiment in Russia about the illegitimacy of the oligarchs' property has remained at consistently high (90 per cent or more) levels for years (Table 2.2). The current crisis in Ukraine and the climate of national unity and patriotism make it unthinkable that any oligarch would challenge Putin.

The problem for Putin is not the mechanism by which rent is distributed but rather the difficulty of its successful operation under conditions of flat, perhaps shrinking, rent. It will have to reallocate flows disproportionately, because addicts' claims have priority. As a result of this priority status the flows of rent to addicts are less volatile than to other sectors of the economy. Given his authority, why cannot Putin resolve this difficulty by curtailing the flow of rents to the addicts or by even beginning to eliminate them? The answer is that while this may have been an option for him earlier, Putin is no longer in such a position. Addicts are the source of his political power and legitimacy. He is hostage to them in the same way a lender can end up being hostage to a debtor. It is ironic that he has ended up in this situation as a by-product of the 2011 demonstrations: to counter the 'creative class', Putin turned more to his core constituency

Table 2.2 Attitudes towards the oligarchs

Which of these views on state ownership in industry most closely matches your view? (% of sample)

		Apr-02	Dec-07	Apr-08	Jan-09	Oct-11	Jun-13
1)	All large companies should be state-owned	51	46	41	50	49	45
2)	The country's most important companies should be state-owned; the rest can be held privately	43	46	53	41	42	48
1) + 2)		**94**	**92**	**94**	**91**	**91**	**93**
3)	All large companies should be in private hands	3	2	2	3	2	3
	Difficult to say	4	6	4	6	6	4

Source: *Sberbank Russia Economic Monthly* (2013: 10). Based on an opinion poll by the Levada Center.

based in cities and regions dominated by the addicts, the Uralvagonzavods and the Nizhnyy Tagils. So he reinforced the addiction. Putin's priorities have always been sovereignty and stability. Stability meant deepened addiction. Just as Putin is hostage to the addicts now, the same will be true for any successor. Whether for or against Putin, no successor will be able to rule Russia in even quasi-democratic fashion without accommodating the addicts. Any serious attempt to deny their fix will lead to chaos.

The addicted structure is the most powerful economic, social, and political force in Russia. To endure, anyone – any leader, any movement, right or left – that attempts to lead Russia will have to deal with the addicts. Any other leader will face the same challenges as Putin and his RMS. Whether democrat or autocrat, the issues are the same: accommodate the addicts and watch the economy degenerate progressively more. Moreover, the problem does not stop there. At some point it may be impossible to satisfy the addicts by diverting flows from other claimants. Rent flows to the addicts themselves will be reduced. This is a trap.

Is it possible that time alone will kill off the addicts? The lessons of the past offer little promise. The 1990s showed that passive means will not work. You can deprive addicts of the rent flows, but you cannot kill them. If Putin could not curtail addiction, could some other strong leader cut the addicts off from formal budget support or deny them subsidized energy? It would require enforcing the break-up of the rent distribution chains. To see how that would work, take the counterfactual example of Mikhail Khodorkovsky being successful in his attempt to have Tomskneft cancel contracts with Sibkabel.[10] This would require either a Khodorkovsky running the state, or, at the very least, a federal government that would have intervened and backed Khodorkovsky against the coalition of local government and addicts.

Rather than protect the addicts, our hypothetical alternative leader would, in other words, *enforce* the hardship caused by the demise of the addicts. The government would need to use force against the addicts and their political allies. It seems unlikely that some hypothetical leader will arise who will use authoritarian means to impose hardship on the public to eliminate addiction. Moreover, as time passes the dilemma becomes worse. The longer Russia continues on its current path, the deeper the addiction. This means an increasingly more aggressive shifting of allocations from other users of rents to the addicts.

Scenarios to eliminate addiction

What other scenarios might one imagine in which the addicts were eliminated? How could that happen? There are two forces of relevance to take and hold the power that would be required to eliminate addiction in Russia: (1) the oligarchs and (2) the *siloviki*.[11] Without explaining how either the oligarchs or the *siloviki* could be expected to wrest control from Vladimir Putin, let us merely assume this happens. How might each of them behave, in combination and or against one another?

There are several political scenarios we can examine. Again, assume Putin has vanished from the scene. Then:

(1) The hard-core market economists and oligarchs join together to battle regional governments and the addicted enterprises. Liberals would have full control over the *siloviki* and would be prepared to use them to suppress democracy.[12] For their part, the *siloviki* accept being subordinate instruments ('tools') of the radical market reformers and the oligarchs. Beyond the question of how the oligarchs and liberals might induce the *siloviki* to play this subordinate role, the problem with this scenario is that to offset the burden of closing 'dinosaur' enterprises the government would have to tax the oligarchs. But how can a government of liberals and oligarchs effectively tax the oligarchs? This scenario is a replay of what happened in the mid-1990s.

(2) The *siloviki* – or someone commanding the *siloviki* – begin by eliminating the oligarchs but still pursue a policy to eliminate the addicts. They cut off the addicts from the rent and break up the rent distribution chains. They shut down factories, quell dissent, and forcibly relocate populations. The problem with this scenario is the lack of internal logic. No matter what the *siloviki's* motivation for eliminating the addicts – whether it be to make the economy more efficient and competitive or whether it be to simply appropriate the addicts' rents for themselves – they need to worry about future rent production. But in the absence of the business talents and experience of the oligarchs, the *siloviki* would be incapable of efficiently managing the resource sector, far less so than even the bureaucrats of the Soviet planning system. Moreover, the harsh political climate that would inevitably accompany their repressive measures would almost certainly make it impossible to induce sufficient investment to guarantee the necessary flow of future rents to sustain the economy.

Consider another hypothetical alternative related to this one. Suppose there were a strongman autocrat who was committed to comprehensive reform and therefore wanted to shut down the dinosaurs for reasons of efficiency *and* who had the interests of the population at heart. He would nationalize resource industries and use the rents to compensate the losers, who would be many. Nationalization of resource producers would be necessary to be able to buy off all the losers from a shutdown of the dinosaurs. How might this turn out?

Here, too, there are problems. First, there is the internal logic. The nationalization of privately owned companies would be seen as an anti-market move. While it might be possible for this 'good dictator' to argue that this was a necessary step to implement broader reform and bolster his case by citing the perceived illegitimacy of privatization of the resource industries in the first place, he faces the practical problem of disentangling pure resource companies from ancillary and interconnected businesses in nearly all other sectors. The resource sector is highly integrated with the rest of the economy, in particular the financial sector.

Moreover, the strongman autocrat faces the same problem as the *siloviki* in the previous scenario: if he eliminates the oligarchs who will run the resource companies? Who can produce future rent? But the biggest problem of all that the benevolent autocrat would face is the sheer cost of compensating the losers in the process. This is the problem reformers inside and outside Russia have faced for over two decades. The scale of transfers that would be needed to keep the population content is staggering. It has never been done anywhere in history on this scale.[13]

To get a sense of the magnitudes that would be involved, we construct a back of the envelope calculation. Suppose that the benevolent autocrat will make a transfer equivalent to Russia's average personal income for five years in a lump sum payment to each affected person. The recipient can then use this as income support and to be able to move from isolated regions. In exchange, the benevolent autocrat will cease to supply addicted enterprises, so that rents can be utilized more efficiently for reform. Russia's average per capita income is USD 13,000, so the lump sum transfer would be USD 65,000. How many people would be affected? A very conservative estimate is 25 million people.[14] This gives a figure of USD 1.625 trillion. How large is this figure in the Russian context? Russia's annual rent from oil and gas is about USD 600 billion, so the lump-sum transfers required would be 2.7 years' worth of Russia' s total resource rents from oil and gas!

The size of the transfer wipes out all uses of rent, including formal and informal taxes, for almost three years. This wipes out all government functions and leaves the autocrat with no resources to reform the economy. Why is the amount so large? The current system of coping with the addicts provides just enough resources to keep the 'lights on' in the affected factories and cities (Gaddy and Ickes 2013a). To compensate the employees of affected and associated enterprises sufficiently to maintain their welfare levels is obviously much more expensive, since most will have to move to new regions to find employment when the factories are closed.[15]

(3) To avoid having to clash directly with the population themselves, the *siloviki* allow the market liberals and the oligarchs to do the unpleasant work of eliminating the addicts. That is, they unleash the oligarchs to follow their natural market instincts and act against the addicts. The *siloviki* protect the oligarchs against backlash from the population – but only long enough to eliminate the addicts. They then make the oligarchs the scapegoats, repressing them and the liberals and thereby posing as the 'saviours of the people'. This scenario necessarily requires rather myopic oligarchs.

To the *siloviki*, there must be clear appeal in the second step in this scenario. Nothing would be easier than making the oligarchs the scapegoats. (As we saw above in Table 2.2 on popular attitudes in Russia towards the oligarchs' status.) Getting rid of the oligarchs would thus be an easy step politically. But what then? How do the *siloviki* manage the continued fallout from the hardship? The oligarchs are useful only as long as they exist. Once gone, who gets the blame? Moreover, without the oligarchs the *siloviki* are back in the nationalization scenario. They cannot manage the resource sector efficiently, and they cannot obtain investment for ensuring future rent flows.

The key concept in all these scenarios is that you can only eliminate addiction by *illiberal* means, by force. But the use of force and repression threatens the supply of future rents.

The alternative is to accommodate the addicts. But then we are back to the basic question for today, not the future. How dangerous will it be for Putin begin to reduce rent flows to established claimants? What happens when the addicts themselves begin to see their doses of the drug reduced? How well can Putin and the FSB manage this, preventing a repeat of the strikes by coal miners, and so on? Officially, there seems to be no threat. Officially, there is not a whisper of labour unrest in Russia (Figure 2.10). But somehow, these almost surreal official statistics on strikes, and so on, do not seem comforting. Rather, they suggest a powder-keg waiting for a spark.

And yet, no matter how bad things may get under Putin and his RMS, what is the alternative? We analysed them above. Consider also this hypothesis: the addicts today, in contrast to earlier, *know* that they are addicts. Before, they perhaps really thought they were productive. In the 1990s they may have been susceptible to the argument that with some reform, despite the dislocation and pain, the factories would be successful and competitive. Now they know that is not the case. Their only hope is Putin and his RMS. He and only he is their protector. So no matter what happens, they cannot go against Putin.

This is the paradox of Putin's power. His policies have not weakened the legacies of the Soviet past. The 'Bear Traps' still constrain Russia's future, and addiction remains central. Yet Putin's system of rent management is the only means present to cope with addiction and the production of sufficient rent to keep the economy functioning. This is the legacy of rent abundance and addiction.

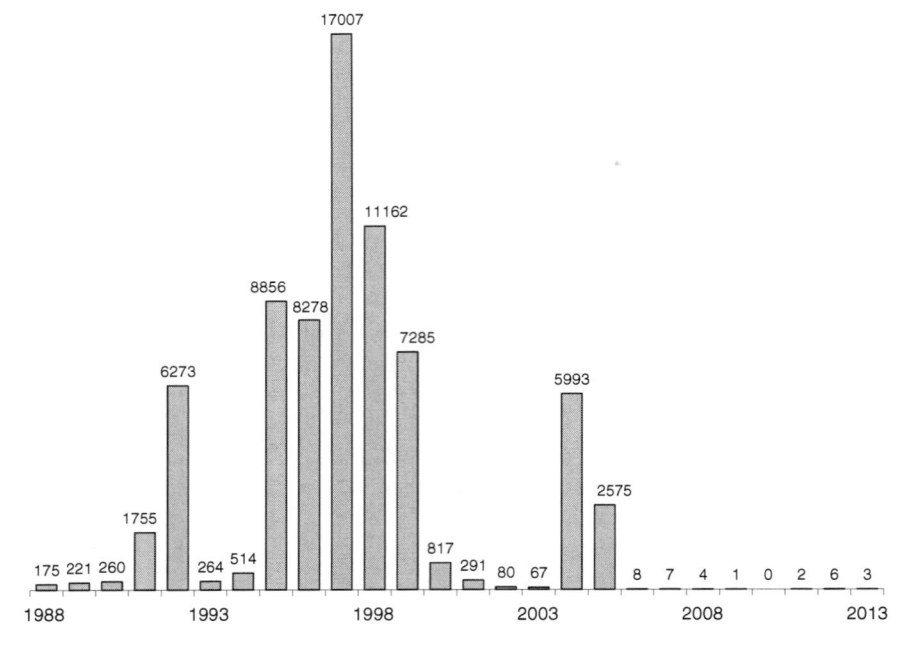

Figure 2.10 Strikes in Russia, 1988–2013.

Source: Rosstat.

Notes

1 We analyze resource rents more fully in Gaddy and Ickes (2005) and discuss the measurement and problems of estimating rents in Gaddy and Ickes (2013b).
2 We stress that these variables must be measured correctly. Therefore, in calculating rent we use world prices to reflect the opportunity cost of oil and gas. With regard to cost it is important to exclude any expenditure in excess of the natural cost of production.
3 The median estimate of forecasters in a Reuters (2013) poll from October 2013 was USD 80 per barrel in real terms in 2020.
4 Note, however, that much of the discussion of increased supplies from unconventional sources ignores the fact this production is dependent on high prices due to high costs of production.
5 The world market for oil is highly integrated so what matters for predicting rents is the world oil price, not what happens in individual markets for Russian oil. Historically, natural gas prices have been tied to oil prices so the volatility in oil prices was transferred to gas prices. Unconventional supplies of gas have led to some decoupling of prices. Moreover, with respect to gas there is the issue of Europe's desire to reduce dependence on Russian gas. Russia, however, has finally signed a long-term contract to deliver gas to China. It seems likely that Russia will be able to find markets for its gas for the foreseeable future.
6 Note that this is the net rate, including both positive and negative growth years. As Table 2.1 shows, growth in the positive growth years is typically about two percentage points higher than the overall average. Popular perceptions of GDP growth rates tend to focus only on the positive rates and forget about the effect of recessionary periods on the long-term average.

7　It is important to recognize that the impact of climate and distance on economic performance is not fixed, and to distinguish the natural, unavoidable costs of geography from policy-induced extra costs. Russia has an abundance of cold, remote locations, but there is no reason that economic activity had to be located in these regions. The problem is that Soviet location policy ignored these costs. Canada and the US also have locations with extremely low temperatures, so a simple comparison should be instructive. Suppose we compare Eastern Siberia and the Russian Far East with Alaska in terms of their relative shares of population and territory for Russia and the United States. If Alaska had been populated according to the Russian model, it would have today not 710,000 residents, but 13 million. Canada's Northwest Territory and Yukon Territory would together have 1.5 million residents instead of the 79,000 they actually have. Conversely, if Eastern Siberia and the Russian Far East had followed the American and Canadian patterns, they would in total have barely one million residents instead of their current 15 million (Gaddy and Ickes 2013a: 51).

8　An initial motivation for this shift was to move industry, especially defense enterprises, further east in anticipation of attacks on the USSR from the west. But in Eurasia, as one moves eastward, temperatures fall. This is discussed further in Gaddy and Ickes (2001) and Hill and Gaddy (2003).

9　Our colleague, Professor Richard E. Ericson of East Carolina University, once remarked that since a rise in the TPC indicates that Russia is overcoming its inherited Soviet spatial handicap, the annual rate of change of Russia's TPC could be considered an 'index of economic rationality'.

10　Panyushkin (2006) tells the story of how in the early 2000s Mikhail Khodorkovsky was summoned to a hearing before the Tomsk provincial legislature. The deputies had expressed concern that Khodorkovsky's local YUKOS subsidiary, Tomskneft, was demonstrating 'lack of support for the local economy'. When Khodorkovsky tried to rebut the charges by citing the huge proportion of regional budget revenues that came from Tomskneft's tax payments, the deputies interrupted to say that he was not getting their point. One of the deputies gave an illustration: Tomskneft had stopped placing orders with the local producer of heavy cables, a major employer in the region. (The deputy in question happened to be the director of that plant.) Why? Khodorkovsky explained that he had made that decision on the basis of simple business principles: the plant's products were of lower quality and more expensive than alternative suppliers. Khodorkovsky confidently asserted that that was the way he would do business in the future as well. That is, he was only willing to purchase from local suppliers if the price did not include excess costs. Khodorkovsky was thus violating one of the basic rules of Putin's RMS. His arrest came not long after this meeting.

11　The term *siloviki* refers to persons working in or with a past in Russia's security structures.

12　This would be an extreme version of Anatoly Chubais's initial plan for Russian economic reform 'By means of a hardline course', *Vek XX i mir* (1990).

13　The only empirical example that might apply is the case of West German transfers to eastern Germany after reunification. Former German Finance Minister Peer Steinbrück (2011) stated: 'Over a period of 20 years, German reunification has cost EURO 2 trillion'. Converted to dollars, that means that West Germany paid an estimated USD 2.76 trillion to bring the 16 million residents of East Germany up to income levels in the west. (And they still remain around 30 per cent lower than in the west.) Admittedly, German living standards are much higher than Russia's. On the other hand, Russia's population is far larger.

14　The best estimate of the excess population in Siberia and the Far East is between 9.6 million and 17.6 million by Mikhailova (2004, cited in Gaddy and Ickes 2013a: 48). The number of addicted enterprises in the Urals region alone far exceeds that of Siberia and the Far East. So 25 million seems very conservative.

15　Needless to say, we are ignoring here the question of what happens when the lump sum payments run out (which, of course, does not necessarily come at the end of five years, as planned).

References

EIA (2014) 'U.S. Crude Oil Wellhead Acquisition Price by First Purchasers (Dollars per Barrel)', U.S. Energy Information Administration. Online. Available: www.eia. gov/dnav/pet/hist/LeafHandler.ashx?n=PET&s=F000000__3&f=A (accessed 14 June 2014).

Gaddy, C.G. and Ickes, B.W. (2001) 'The Cost of the Cold', Working Paper, Pennsylvania State University, May.

Gaddy, C.G. and Ickes, B.W. (2002) *Russia's Virtual Economy*, Washington, DC: Brookings Institution Press.

Gaddy, C.G. and Ickes, B.G. (2005) 'Resource Rents and the Russian Economy', *Eurasian Geography and Economics*, 46(8): 559–83.

Gaddy, C.G. and Ickes B.W. (2011) 'Putin's Protection Racket,' in Korhonen, I. and Solanko, L. (eds) *From Soviet Plans to Russian Reality: Essays in Honor of Pekka Sutela*, Helsinki: WSOYpro Oy, pp. 109–23.

Gaddy, C.G. and Ickes, B.W. (2013a) *Bear Traps on Russia's Road to Modernization*, Abingdon, UK and New York: Routledge.

Gaddy, C.G. and Ickes, B.W. (2013b) 'Russia's Dependence on Resources', in Alexeev, M.V. and Weber, S. (eds), *The Oxford Handbook of the Russian Economy*, Oxford: Oxford University Press, pp. 309–40.

Hill, F. and Gaddy, C.G. (2003) *The Siberian Curse: How Communist Planners Left Russia Out in the Cold*, Washington, DC: Brookings Institution Press.

IMF (2014) Primary Commodity Prices, IMF. Online. Available: www.imf.org/external/np/res/commod/index.aspx (accessed May 2014).

Mikhailova, T. (2004) Essays on Russian Economic Geography: Measuring Spatial Inefficiency. Unpublished PhD Dissertation, The Pennsylvania State University.

North, D.C., Wallis, J.J. and Weingast, B.R. (2009) *Violence and Social Orders: a Conceptual Framework for Interpreting Recorded Human History*, Cambridge: Cambridge University Press.

Panyushkin, V. (2006) *Uznik tishiny*, Moscow: Sekret firmy.

Penn World Table (version 7.1), Groningen Growth and Development Centre. Online. Available: www.rug.nl/research/ggdc/data/penn-world-table (accessed May 2014).

Reuters (2013) 'Oil by 2020 to Fall to $80 in Real Terms – Reuters Poll', 30 October. Online. Available: www.reuters.com/article/2013/10/30/brent-poll-idUSL5N0I-J3ED20131030 (accessed 30 October 2013).

Sberbank Russia Economic Monthly (2013) Report on Opinion Poll by Levada Center on Ownership in Industry, August.

Steinbrück, P. (2011) 'Interview with Former German Finance Minister: "Germans Will Have to Pay"', *Der Spiegel*, 12 September. Online. Available: www.spiegel.de/international/europe/interview-with-former-german-finance-minister-germans-will-have-to-pay-a-785704-3.html (accessed 12 September 2011).

Vek XX i mir (1990) 'Zhestkim kursom', *Vek XX i mir*, 6: 15–19.

3 Between light and shadow
Informality in the Russian labour market

*Vladimir Gimpelson and
Rostislav Kapeliushnikov[1]*

Many transition economies are characterised by widespread and increasing labour market informality (Packard *et al.* 2012). The persistence and proliferation of this phenomenon have multiple causes, including a structural shift towards the small-scale service sector, poor governance and the existence of often unfriendly institutions (the 'grabbing hand' of the state), increasing competition and growing costs for formal businesses and unemployment protection. Many individuals and households are either directly or indirectly affected by the rise in informality and many others appear to be at risk. Though there are a large number of reasons for becoming informal and this has a number of implications, there is one common feature. The informal economic activity unfolds in the shadow of regulations and beyond the reach of state institutions, raising questions about both the quality of these jobs and the quality of the state.

The purpose of this chapter is to summarise our knowledge of informality in the Russian labour market and to embed it into a more general political-economic framework that links it to particular institutional developments. The main question we will consider can be formulated as follows: how did informality in the Russian labour market evolve, and what are its political implications?

Russia presents an interesting case for the study informality since it differs in several important respects from most other informality-ridden countries. First, it is a non-agricultural economy, with the agricultural share of employment currently standing at under 10 per cent and the share of rural population at around 25 per cent. Second, most of the informal employment consists of hired labour, rather than the self-employed, as is often the case in the developing world. Third, the rise in informality can largely be attributed to a protracted transition towards a market economy rather than to the patterns of rural–urban migration that generally accompany underdevelopment. Finally, compared with those in other countries informal workers in Russia possess relatively high levels of education.

The chapter is organized as follows. The first section provides a brief overview of recent labour market trends and describes the institutional framework in Russia. We then use several different data sources to consider the evolution of informal employment and we also investigate the main determinants of informality. The third section looks at the issue of labour market segmentation: is the Russian labour market segmented, with informality forming a special segment?

We address this question by exploring mobility patterns and the consequences of informality on earnings. The chapter then discusses political challenges in relation to informality. The final section concludes with a summary of our findings.

Labour market developments and the institutional setting in Russia

Going informal is often considered as a reaction to the difficulties in getting a formal job when there is weak support for the unemployed. Since access to formal positions for wage and salary workers depends on the tightness in the labour market, in this section we provide a short overview of the major developments at the macro level in the Russian economy over the last decade. Since informality is often related to rigidities in the labour market, we also give a brief description of its particular country-specific institutional properties.

Main labour market developments

Shortly after the financial crisis of 1998, the Russian unemployment rate reached an all-time record high of 14.6 per cent. However, in early 1999, unemployment started to decline rapidly, reflecting the economy's return to a path of growth. Boosted by the strong devaluation of the national currency and supported by the rise in world oil prices, that year the Russian economy entered a period of rapid growth that lasted until 2008. Thereafter unemployment declined gradually, falling to under 6 per cent by the middle of that year.

Meanwhile, the economic recovery was also reflected in other labour market indicators. The employment to population ratio increased by five percentage points, accumulated wage arrears dwindled, the incidence of underemployment was reduced, and the number of annual hours worked increased. Hiring rates remained high and were positively correlated with vacancy rates. The most impressive labour market development, however, was in real wage growth, which, according to Rosstat, stood at between 12 and 15 per cent per annum over the period. As a result, within less than a decade, the performance of the Russian labour market had changed radically for the better. A closer look, however, presents a more complex picture. Protected employment in all types of firms decreased from 52 to about 48 million, or by 7–8 per cent, while there was an increase in the proportion of workers in temporary, casual and informal sector jobs. In other words, the fraction of workers employed in various 'bad' jobs rose continuously, in spite of a robust macroeconomic performance (Gimpelson and Kapeliushnikov 2007; Lehmann *et al*. 2011).

The economic crisis that erupted in 2008–9 caused Russia's GDP to fall by 8 per cent in 2009, but had no immediate measurable consequences in the labour market. There was little actual overnight downsizing in 2008. By 2009, however, the unemployment rate reached 8.3 per cent and other labour market indicators also began to deteriorate: real wage growth turned slightly negative, wage arrears, though quite modest, reappeared, and under-employment rose again.

Nevertheless, this grim period was relatively short-lived and all indicators started to improve soon afterward, signalling that the major threats in the form of unemployment or underemployment as they were seen by the Russian government had been left behind. In 2011–13, the unemployment rate fell further, down to a historical low of 5.5 per cent. This was associated with relatively stable total employment but a continuing gradual reallocation of labour from the formal sector to broadly-defined informal or semiformal jobs. This reallocation can be interpreted as a sign of the trade-off between unemployment and informality, with priority being given to the latter.

Institutional setting

There are many causes for informality. It is often regarded as a direct consequence of excessively rigid labour market institutions. The minimum wage, if set too high, can push low-skilled workers out of formal jobs. Excessively strict employment protection legislation (EPL), collective bargaining pressures, high labour taxes and a high wage premium in the public sector are all likely to suppress labour demand and job creation in the formal sector. As a result, workers can be excluded from formal employment. If, at the same time, unemployment benefits are low and/or difficult to obtain, workers can easily end up in informal jobs, as they provide the only alternative option. Is the Russian labour market excessively rigid, thus raising the likelihood of informality? Not at all. The institutional setting during the transition years did not hinder wage flexibility and accommodated very strong external shocks, though through non-conventional price adjustment (OECD 2012; Gimpelson and Kapeliushnikov 2013). During most of the transition, the minimum wage was fixed at a level that was hardly binding for the majority of firms. Its ratio to the average wage was below 10 per cent during most of the period. Adjustments were irregular, lagged far behind inflation, and had little effect on relative earnings.

The level of unemployment benefits (UB) can also have an impact on the informality (Margolis *et al.* 2012; Vodopivec 2013; Bosch and Esteban-Pretel 2013). If set too high relative to the median or average wage, it pushes up reservation wages, thus causing a reduction in employment. Some of those displaced can go into informality but are more likely to transit into unemployment. If UB are low, the unemployed state is not a viable option for those in need of income. In this case, informal economic activity can play a buffering role as an effective alternative to non-employment. In Russia, the average UB to wage ratio reached a peak of 30 per cent in 1998 but gradually eroded thereafter, ultimately dipping below 8 per cent. This is a very low level by international standards[2] and, given the chronic lack of decent job vacancies at the disposal of the Public Employment Service (PES) can also play an effective role in making informality an alternative option instead of lowering the job search costs for formal job seekers.

EPL is another important pillar. Strict EPL protects insiders from job loss. By doing so, it restricts the outflow from formal jobs but also discourages new job creation. In theory, therefore, it may inhibit labour market mobility, including flows in both directions between formal and informal jobs. Regardless of how we estimate the nominal stringency of Russian EPL, most experts agree that its enforcement is far from perfect. Due to its poor enforcement, the EPL per se is unlikely to be a valid cause for expansion of informal employment. However, given the uneven and incomplete enforcement, firms and workers may choose the optimal degree of informality, trading off its costs and potential benefits.

The taxation of labour is yet another standard candidate for those seeking an explanation of informality expansion in transition countries (Packard *et al.* 2012; Slonimczyk 2012). Creating a tax wedge, it decreases the demand for labour among taxpaying firms. In 2001, the government introduced a tax reform that drastically reduced taxation levels and simplified the process of filing taxes. The pre-reform progressive personal income tax rates were replaced by a single and low flat-rate tax of 13 per cent and there were also changes to payroll taxes. From 2001 onwards, social contributions were unified into a single and smaller social tax with a regressive scale.[3]

As suggested by this short overview, Russian labour market institutions do not appear to represent a significant source of rigidity causing informality. On the contrary, the trade-off between employment and wages was, on every occasion, solved in favour of keeping employment at a stable level, though some institutional decisions might have had an effect. However, there were other factors at work outside the labour market per se that could suppress labour demand and explain the expansion of informal employment. Most important among them were the existence of a notoriously unfriendly business climate and the low enforcement capability of the Russian state. According to the World Bank 'Doing Business Index', Russia is among the lowest-ranked countries (see further Chapters 5 and 6 in this volume). A poor business climate reduces economic activity, discourages new investments, and deters both the entry and growth of formal firms, which reduces labour demand in the formal sector and, thus, makes informality the second-best option for job seekers.

The evolution of informality

The relationship between GDP growth and labour market informality are ambiguous. If economic growth is associated with intensive employment generation in the formal sector, informality can shrink as long as informal workers end up in formal positions. To achieve this positive outcome requires the presence of an institutional environment conducive to massive job creation. However, it is not difficult to think of circumstances in which the rapid economic growth can itself act to speed up informality. Such an outcome is likely, for example, if the growth is largely driven by micro-entrepreneurship and small-scale services that are prone to informality. Another example assumes that the aggregate growth in the country is driven by the formal sector but that its gains stimulate informal economic activity. If a massive injection of incoming petro-dollars is distributed over the population and generates a growing demand for personal services such as home construction, this may easily translate into informality given the generally unfriendly environment for conducting business activity in full accordance with formal rules.

The evolution of informal employment

Labour market informality can be measured in various ways and using different data sources. The estimates usually vary depending on measurement methodology and available data sets, though we expect them to provide a largely coherent picture.

The Russian official statistics applies a version of the productivity-based definition (Hussmans 2004), which links informality to the characteristics of enterprises rather than to particular jobs. Using the standard System of National Accounts (SNA) divisions by institutional sectors, we can say that the Rosstat definition classifies all those who work in entities related to 'the corporate sector' (registered companies) or to 'the government sector' as formally employed, while all those who work in household-related productive units are considered informally employed notwithstanding whether or not they are registered with tax authorities or social protection agencies. Put differently, 'formal workers' according the Rosstat definition are employed by organizations – legal entities – while 'informal workers' are those who work outside such bodies. This definition of informality encompasses all of the self-employed, as well as those wage and salary workers employed by unincorporated micro-businesses or by private individuals outside the formal sector, but it largely overlooks informal workers in formal enterprises.

The first and most straightforward approach to measuring employment in the informal sector is to use the available labour force survey data for the period 1999–2013. The second, 'residual' approach relies on the same definition of informality but measures in a different way, based on regular enterprise statistics. It estimates the difference between total employment and employment in all firms and organizations. The latter component can be obtained from the regularly updated statistical registry which covers all firms officially registered as legal entities. This residual measure (total employment minus employment in all legal entities) encompasses self-employment (both with and without formal registration), workers hired by non-incorporated individual entrepreneurs or households, and family workers, while again also excluding informal workers in formal enterprises. The rationale for considering these groups as working informally (or semi-formally) is that, even if formally registered, they are not covered by standard labour, social security, accounting and tax legislation. These regulations, if even applied at all, are enforced in a simplified and truncated form with multiple exemptions. This residual approach provides a broader but less conventional measure of informality.

According to the first approach, in 2013 informal workers made up about one-fifth of total employment, while the second, 'residual' approach estimate puts the figure at closer to one-third. The gap between the two figures arises from the different methodologies of measurement. The Labour Force Survey (LFS) may not identify all of those who work in small non-incorporated or fully unregistered businesses as informal workers, if such LFS respondents state simply that they are employed by 'a firm'. Having accounted for this omission, we may get a higher LFS measure and a narrower gap. In its turn, the residual approach may misidentify some fully formal workers, thus inflating the estimate. But neither way of measurement fully captures those working in formal firms but without a written contract.

However, the growth rates for both measures are almost identical, as suggested by Figure 3.1. This presents the general trends in informality and economic growth over the period. During this time GDP grew by an impressive 80 per cent over the period 1998–2008. But did it pull workers from informal jobs? As can be seen, the answer is: Quite the opposite! Informality, by either definition, increased at about the same rate and, by the end of the period, it was approximately 60 per cent higher than at the beginning. Meanwhile, there was only a very small change in total employment, while the levels of regulated and protected employment in all types of firms and organizations actually fell. In sum, at this time a large and growing fraction of employment generation happened outside the regulated sector.

The economic crisis of 2008–9 brought a short break in the trend and caused a significant fall (of around 8 per cent) in GDP. This was not immediately reflected in total employment. However, the informal sector in the LFS-based definition

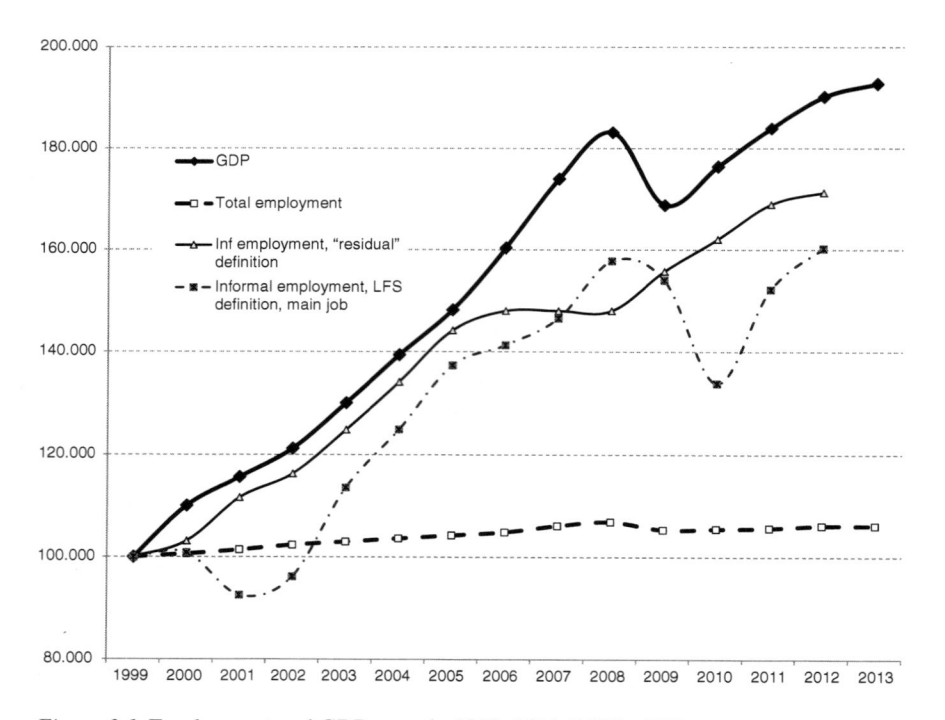

Figure 3.1 Employment and GDP growth, 1999–2011 (1999 = 100).

Source: Authors' estimates based on Rosstat data.

accepted by Rosstat suffered a visible negative shock with a one-year lag. Employment in the residual (outside registered firms) sector was on the rise during the whole period, apparent from some slowdown in 2006–8. Figure 3.1 shows a divergence between the paths followed by the informal employment according to the LFS-based and the residual-based definitions in 2009–10. While the former shrank mostly due to a decrease in the number of dependent wage workers, the latter continued to grow. It is not easy to determine whether this fall in informality was a temporal statistical artefact or actually reflected the real phenomenon. However, in 2011–13, the informal employment (following the LFS-based definition) returned to its pre-crisis peak.

Figure 3.1 presents the hypothesis that during this period, there was a significant reallocation of workers from the regulated formal to the unregulated informal sector. Figure 3.2 illustrates the structure of this reallocation in 2000–12. During this period the formal sector reduced its workforce by almost five million individuals. This contraction was more than compensated for by the expansion of the unregulated sector. In total, the latter gained over 7.5 million workers. Under an extreme assumption that informality was not a possible option, the economy would then have lost over four million jobs rather than gained around three million. The

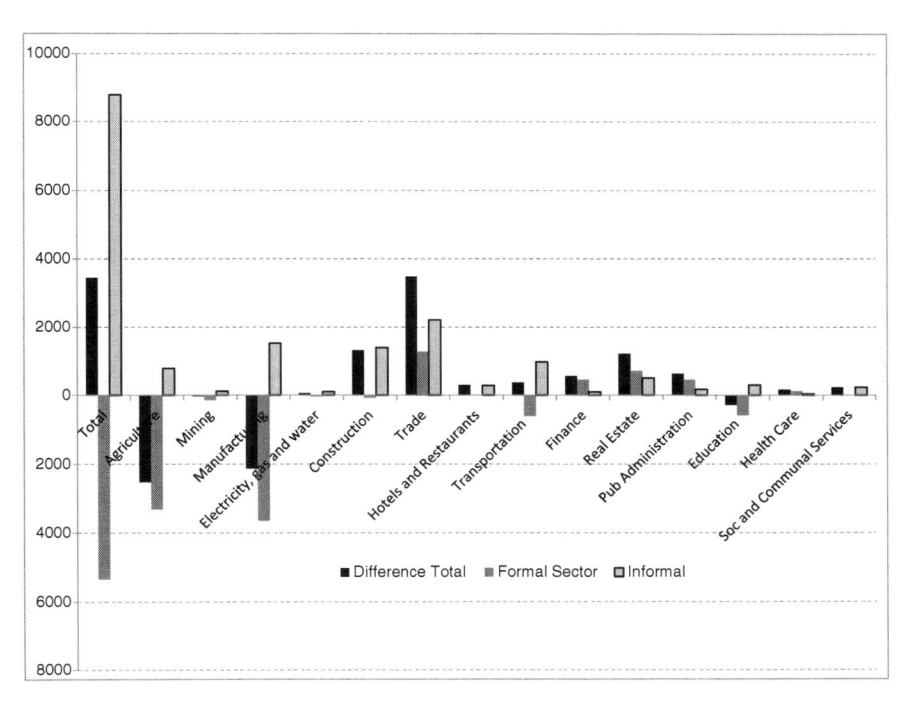

Figure 3.2 Change in total employment, formal and informal employment, 2000–12 (*million persons*).

Source: Authors' estimates based on Rosstat data.

expansion of the unregulated sector occurred mostly in activities such as trade, construction, and transportation. These are industries that are largely populated by micro-businesses and the self-employed.

So far, we have discussed estimates based on official data. As official statistical agencies are usually not very accurate at measuring informality, we may want to check these findings by bringing in alternative data sources that can better serve this purpose. One such a source is the Russian Longitudinal Monitoring Survey (RLMS-HSE) which is a reliable and representative household panel with various informality-related questions.[4] It covers the period 2002–12 using the consistent definition.

Figures 3.3 and 3.4 present the evolution of informal employment according to the RLMS data. The great advantage of this source is that it draws a clear distinction between different forms of informal employment. We can differentiate all employed according to two criteria: formality–informality and self-employed–hired workers. In addition, those involved in irregular informal activities and marginally attached to the labour market but who may occasionally do some paid work constitute the fifth group of workers. As shown by the figures, the expansion of informal employment occurred almost exclusively in wage and salary

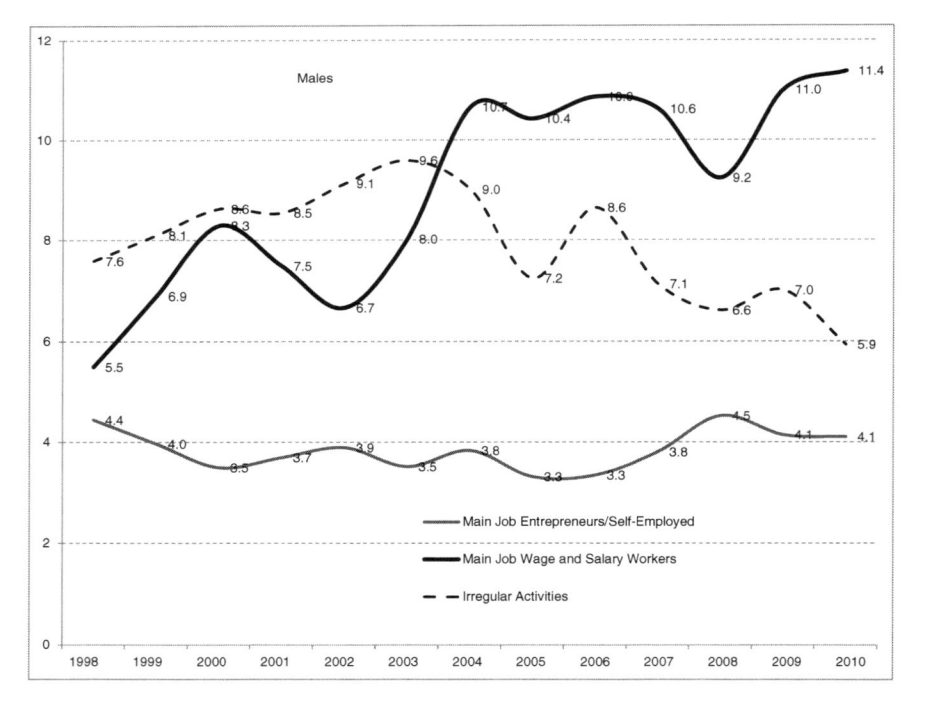

Figure 3.3 Informal employment, self-employment and entrepreneurial activity, men, 1998–2010, RLMS.

Source: RLMS, Gimpelson, Kapeliushnikov and Slonimczyk (2014).

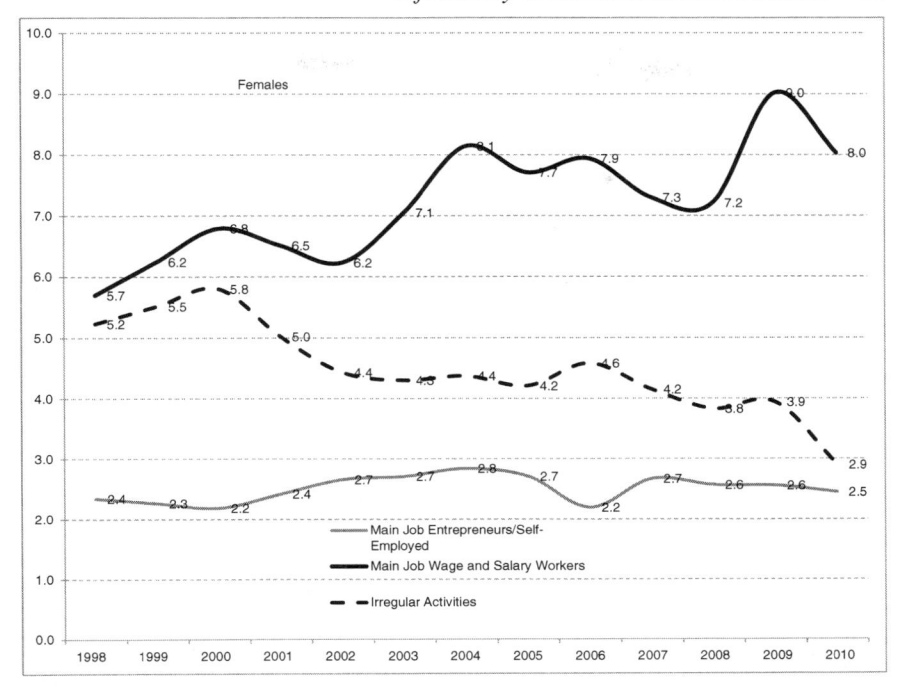

Figure 3.4 Informal employment, self-employment and entrepreneurial activity, women, 1998–2010, RLMS.

Source: RLMS, Gimpelson, Kapeliushnikov and Slonimczyk (2014).

positions. Self-employment fluctuated around its average level, around 4 per cent for males and 2.5 per cent for females, while there was a fall in the proportion of workers performing irregular or casual activities. All of this is in line with the Rosstat data.

In sum, various data sources estimate informal sector employment to be within the range of 20–30 per cent. How does this look in cross-country comparisons? Perry *et al.* (2007) provide approximate relationships between various measures of informality and country per capita GDP. According to them, Russian GDP per capita corresponds to an informality level of 25–30 per cent. As we can see, the actual level is somewhat lower than that which one can follow from these comparisons. Naturally, any cross-country informality comparisons are very approximate and allow only broad conclusions to be drawn. One can safely say that the level of informality in Russia is comparable to that observed in other Eastern European countries and Southern Europe, but is significantly higher than that in the most advanced market economies. However, it would also be fair to say that Russian labour market informality is much more modest than that observed in other BRIC countries and in most other emerging economies. Its current level does not pose any real concern, but its rapid increase may present future challenges. Most of the growth comes through hired employment, rather than self-employment. In this sense, informality is not a form of early micro-entrepreneurship which could potentially be creative and productive.

Informality and productivity

If informal employment is less productive than formal employment, then the reallocation of labour into informality reduces growth and productivity. This also means that an increasing proportion of the total labour force is being used less efficiently than would be the case if formal employment was higher. According to the SNA data, the fraction of Russian GDP produced by the informal sector decreased from about 15 to 7 per cent during the period of 2002–11. Meanwhile, informal employment continues to expand, as we could see, as did the total number of hours worked in the sector. Trying to reconcile these two tendencies, we can say that the formal–informal productivity gap is large and tends to grow further. Unsurprisingly, productivity is much higher in the formal sector than in the informal sector (see Table 3.1).

This gap can be explained in part by the simple fact that household-based subsistence agriculture is inefficient, while at the same time quite popular. Many Russian households are involved in this type of activity, using primitive technologies and little human capital. If this produce is consumed within households and not intended for market sales, then such activity is not considered to be income gaining employment (according to the standard ILO criteria). Then, including agriculture in estimates of formal–informal productivity comparisons is likely to inflate the gap. Exploiting the fact that almost all household-based production is concentrated within the agricultural sector, we can re-estimate the difference including only non-agricultural economic activity. This adjustment produces a smaller gap of 'only' about three times instead of four or five times if agriculture

Table 3.1 Labor productivity 2005–11 (value added per hour; RUR in constant 2008 prices)

	Total economy		Agriculture excluded	
	Formal sector	*Informal sector*	*Formal sector*	*Informal sector*
2005	263	63	272	95
2006	281	67	291	103
2007	301	68	312	108
2008	319	65	330	99
2009	305	69	315	105
2010	316	66	328	103
2011	326	67	337	106

Source: Authors' estimates based on SNA Rosstat data.

is included. However, even in this case, the productivity gap gradually becomes larger over time, rather than smaller.

In any case, it is fair to argue that the observed reallocation of jobs from the formal to the informal sector – the 'de-formalization of employment' – slows down aggregate productivity growth and, therefore, presents an additional challenge to the modernization of the economy.

Who is more exposed to becoming informal?

Even if the informality level is modest on average, it can be quite high for particular demographic groups. As shown by Table 3.2, which is based on RLMS data, informal salaried work and irregular activities are most prevalent among young men and women with low levels of formal schooling. Informal entrepreneurship and self-employment, by contrast, are more common among middle-aged men with technical or university degrees. Informal work is concentrated in service, agricultural and low-skilled occupations. Informal entrepreneurs are usually classified under managerial occupations.

One important issue is whether some age groups are more exposed to informality than others due to a sort of lifecycle (age) effect. New entrants into the labour market are more likely to find jobs in the informal sector. Having accumulated some work experience, they gain formal positions and may finally move back into informality close to or after retirement. This pattern can potentially apply to every cohort. An alternative story is that some cohorts are more vulnerable to informality because they enter the labour market during a period when labour demand in the formal sector is low.

In order to examine this issue in more detail, we estimated a multinomial logit model (MNL) of sector choice with these and other variables as determinants of informal status (Gimpelson *et al.* 2014). This exercise was conducted separately for males and females using the whole data pool for 2000–10. We explored whether the determinants of informality changed over time by estimating the MNL model separately for different subperiods. Among the most remarkable results, we find that the likelihood of informal wage and salary work falls with age. The risk of irregular activities, however, does not differ significantly across age groups. Men with any formal education see the risk of casual work being significantly reduced, but only technical and university degrees seem to have a negative effect on informal wage work. For females, education does not seem to significantly affect any job types besides irregular activities. Finally, the groups in which informality is more prevalent are found in the service, agriculture and fishery activities, and in 'unskilled' occupations.

Summing up, our findings are consistent with the existence of additional search frictions that individuals of young and old age are likely to face. Individuals with low human capital are also more likely to go informal. Finding the first good job appears to be tough and people might churn for some time between informal jobs as a second-best opportunity. The same is true for preretirement and retirement age individuals. In addition, being a student or getting a pension decreases the reservation utility expected from formal employment.

Table 3.2 Incidence of informality, 1998–2010 (%)

		Men					Women				
		Formal Entrep.	*Inf Entrep*	*Formal W & Sal*	*Inf W & Sal*	*All Irreg. Activ*	*Formal Entrep.*	*Inf Entrep*	*Formal W & Sal*	*Inf W & Sal*	*All Irreg. Activ*
Age	16–24	0.1	1.7	63.6	13.7	21.0	0.2	1.3	71.0	14.8	12.8
	25–34	1.5	3.8	73.8	12.0	8.9	0.7	1.8	82.1	9.7	5.7
	35–44	2.3	4.9	74.3	9.2	9.3	1.0	2.7	84.1	7.5	4.7
	45–54	1.6	2.8	78.6	7.9	9.0	1.2	2.7	85.1	5.9	5.1
	55–65	0.9	1.6	84.6	5.5	7.4	0.7	2.2	84.5	6.0	6.7
Education	HS Inc	0.8	2.0	64.2	14.7	18.3	0.6	2.2	70.2	12.5	14.5
	HS	1.0	3.8	70.1	10.6	14.5	0.7	2.4	75.2	11.4	10.2
	Voc	0.6	2.7	76.0	11.3	9.4	0.7	2.7	77.6	11.9	7.1
	Tech	1.8	5.1	78.8	8.5	5.8	1.1	2.8	85.4	6.4	4.3
	Univ	4.0	3.7	83.4	4.6	4.2	1.0	1.6	91.6	3.5	2.3

(*Continued*)

Table 3.2 (Continued)

		Men					Women				
		Formal Entrep.	*Inf Entrep*	*Formal W & Sal*	*Inf W & Sal*	*All Irreg. Activ*	*Formal Entrep.*	*Inf Entrep*	*Formal W & Sal*	*Inf W & Sal*	*All Irreg. Activ*
Occupations	Legislators, Senior Managers, Officials	14.1	16.2	66.3	2.3	1.1	9.7	20.1	67.4	2.6	0.3
	Professionals	1.4	1.4	94.3	1.8	1.1	0.5	0.5	97.4	0.8	0.8
	Technicians & Assoc Prof	1.1	1.9	86.4	7.4	3.2	0.4	0.4	94.2	3.4	1.7
	Clerks	0.6	0.9	89.0	4.7	4.7	0.3	0.0	94.1	3.7	1.9
	Service & Sales Workers	0.9	6.5	67.6	10.1	14.8	1.2	5.6	57.2	25.8	10.2
	Skilled Agric & Fishery Workers	8.5	12.2	53.0	4.9	21.3	2.6	7.9	50.0	10.5	28.9
	Craft & Related Trades	0.5	3.4	71.3	11.6	13.1	0.4	2.6	66.5	8.6	21.9
	Plant & Machine Operators and Assemblers	0.3	2.0	82.8	10.0	4.9	0.1	0.2	94.3	3.2	2.2
	Unskilled Occup	0.0	0.8	63.3	16.2	19.6	0.0	0.1	80.0	8.4	11.4

Source: RLMS, Gimpelson, Kapeliushnikov and Slonimczyk (2014).

Is the labour market segmented or integrated?

This is a key question in the exploration and explanation of informality. One approach sees this sector as a kind of semi-isolated ghetto populated by bad jobs. It assumes that low-educated and low-skilled workers enter the sector involuntarily and have limited exits to better employment and are also overexploited and underpaid there. Much of the literature generated by the ILO follows this research paradigm (Kucera and Ronkolato 2008). Another view sees the labour market as integrated. According to this view, workers choose their preferred sector of employment, voluntarily maximizing their expected utility (Maloney 2004). Therefore, any emerging wage gaps are small, and can be explained by differences in non-wage job amenities. Meanwhile, cross-sector flows provide additional tests on segmentation and, if large, they point out the integrated nature of the labour market. These opposing views suggest ultimately different remedies. Exploring what view of the Russian labour market is more convincing and better supported by the data, we look first at mobility and then at earnings.

Mobility patterns

We explore mobility patterns using two complementary approaches. First, we examine transition matrices linking different labour market states to analyse the intensity and direction of labour market flows. Second, we estimate an MNL model that controls simultaneously for past labour market states and demographic and job characteristics. Jobs in the informal sector are typically considered to be less secure since they are unprotected by regulations. This is well reflected in both the shorter tenures and the higher mobility of informal workers, though that in itself is not sufficient proof for the segmentation hypothesis. They can be mobile in both ways across formality borders. Segmentation means that informal employment becomes an absorbing state with a limited exit. If the pool of informal workers is stagnant with little outflow, then we can expect a segmentation in the labour market. Significant flows but going largely into non-employment could also be considered a valid argument. In contrast, the dynamic interchange between the formal and informal sectors would indicate that the labour market remains integrated without strong internal divisions. The picture becomes more complex if we consider the informal labour market as internally heterogeneous and multi-tiered. In this case, some informal workers are integrated with the formal sector while others are separated in absorbing dead-end jobs. This picture is consistent with the multi-tiered vision of the informal sector suggested by Fields (1990; 2009).

The informality in our data consists of three different substates: informal entrepreneurs, informal salary workers, and casual workers. We estimated conventional transition matrices linking origin and destination states for the period 2003–10. Table 3.3 presents mobility between four aggregated labour market states (formal, informal, unemployed and not in the labour force) and Table 3.4 disaggregates the formal sector into formal salaried employment and formal self-employment,

Table 3.3 Mobility in the Russian labor market (4 states), 2003–10

TRANSITION PROBABILITIES: Pij

	Formal	Informal	Unemployed	Not in labor force	**Pi.**
Formal	**0.891**	0.056	0.018	0.036	0.651
Informal	0.254	**0.563**	0.046	0.138	0.146
Unemployed	0.304	0.221	**0.186**	0.289	0.038
Not in labor force	0.106	0.125	0.057	**0.711**	0.166
P.j	0.646	0.147	0.035	0.172	
	Formal	Informal	Unemployed	Not in labor force	
Average duration	9.1	2.3	1.2	3.5	

Source: RLMS, Gimpelson, Kapeliushnikov and Slonimczyk (2014).

Table 3.4 Mobility in the Russian labor market (7 states), 2003–10

TRANSITION PROBABILITIES: Pij

	FS	IS	SEF	SEI	IA	U	NLF	**Pi.**
Formal salaried	**0.890**	0.034	0.003	0.004	0.015	0.018	0.036	0.640
Informal salaried	0.333	**0.448**	0.009	0.038	0.058	0.037	0.078	0.066
Self-employed formal	0.187	0.038	**0.524**	0.206	0.017	0.004	0.025	0.011
Self-employed informal	0.077	0.090	0.116	**0.621**	0.057	0.007	0.032	0.024
Irregular activity	0.172	0.106	0.003	0.031	**0.358**	0.073	0.258	0.055
Unemployed	0.302	0.090	0.002	0.012	0.119	**0.186**	0.289	0.038
Not in labor force	0.105	0.037	0.001	0.006	0.082	0.057	**0.711**	0.166
P.j	0.634	0.069	0.011	0.025	0.053	0.035	0.172	
	FS	IS	SEF	SEI	IA	U	NLF	
Average duration	9.1	1.8	2.1	2.6	1.6	1.2	3.5	

Source: RLMS, Gimpelson, Kapeliushnikov and Slonimczyk (2014).

Note: Acronyms in columns correspond to the titles in rows.

while the informal sector is broken down into informal salaried employment, informal self-employment and irregular informal activity.

A detailed look at conventional mobility measures calculated and averaged for the whole period of 2003–10 shows that annually about 11 per cent of those in the formal sector left that sector to move to alternative states (the informal sector, unemployment or out of the labour force). Of these, the informal sector was the leading destination, with this outflow constituting about 6 per cent of the initial stock. These values are higher than those reported by Lehmann and Pignatti (2007) for Ukraine, where most of those leaving the formal sector ended up in non-employment. The differences are remarkable considering the multiple institutional and structural similarities between the two countries. If the informal sector is disaggregated, informal wage and salary employment emerge as the destination for 3.4 per cent of those leaving formal salaried employment in the sector of origin.

If we take informal employment as the initial sector, about a quarter of the workers in the stock ended up in formal salaried employment one year later, illustrating high mobility, while 56 per cent remained informal as before. At the same time, informal workers (compared to formal) faced much higher risks of losing employment. However, the probability of a return to employment was also high. Within one year about 30 per cent of the unemployed and 11 per cent of the inactive had secured formal jobs. Migration from non-employment to any informal employment was also very buoyant, especially from unemployment. For individuals moving from unemployment, informal jobs were identified as the destination by 22 per cent of all respondents. These rates were comparable to the outflows from unemployment to formal employment.

The breakdown of informality by substates provides additional evidence that both salaried employment and irregular activities are actively involved in the exchange with other labour market states, while informal self-employment interacts actively with formal self-employment. High rates of exchange between formal and informal employment do not suggest that a strong segmentation of these sectors is a likely outcome. However, informal workers face higher risks of becoming unemployed and especially inactive than do formal workers. Russian informal workers do not form a stagnant pool, and most of those entering the informal sector have good chances of getting out relatively soon.

In other words, the general picture that emerges is a mixed one. On the one hand, counter flows between the formal and informal sectors are of comparable intensity; outflow from the formal sector into informality dominates flows into non-employment; one-third of informally hired workers move into the formal sector within a year; most unemployed and about half of the economically inactive enter the formal sector, avoiding informality as a transient state; any self-employment decreases the risk of unemployment; formal and informal self-employment are involved in an intensive exchange. All of this analysis indicates that rigid barriers separating formal and informal jobs hardly exist.

On the other hand, the fact that employment growth in Russia was driven by the expansion in informality can be interpreted as clear evidence of the difficulties of entering the formal sector. These difficulties can be caused by depressed labour demand in the formal sector, such as a combination of weak job creation by new firms and a slow expansion of employment in existing firms. The disposition of formal workers to move out was low, new vacancies in the formal sector were generated in limited quantities and were not easily accessed by outsiders; states of unemployment, inactivity, informal salaried employment and irregular informal activity are strongly connected by cross-flows, suggesting that informality emerges as a dead-end state. These findings tend to suggest that the labour market is segmented, rather than integrated.

The transition matrices show flows across sectors without conditioning on worker characteristics. The MNL model for sectoral choice controlling for lagged employment statuses suggests that any form of employment decreases the risk of non-employment in the next period. Second, any prior entrepreneurial experience increases the probability of both formal entrepreneurship and informal self-employment. One may speculate that both forms of entrepreneurship are not strictly separated and resemble communicating vessels. However, informal entrepreneurship also increases the relative risk of doing informal salaried work. Third, we find that the only status that significantly increases the relative risks of irregular activities is irregular activities themselves. In general, these workers are marginally attached to the labour force, but such activities appear to constitute an entry point for informal entrepreneurship and, to a lesser extent, informal wage and salaried work. Finally, formal salaried workers are less inclined to any outward transition.

Summing up, our findings are consistent with Fields' idea of a two-tiered structure of the informal labour market (Fields 1990, 2009). On the one hand, informal self-employment seems to be integrated with formal entrepreneurship, and there is some evidence that irregular activities and informal wage and salaried work sometimes lead to entrepreneurial activities. On the other hand, all informal types of employment are self-reproducing and are largely separated from the formal labour markets. The fact that workers who obtain formal salaried positions are less likely to move to any other type of job suggests that they assign a high value to formality and prefer it over the alternatives.

Informal earnings

An alternative way of testing segmentation is to estimate the formal–informal wage gap.[5] If segmentation is associated with persistent earnings differentials, the integrated labour market is unlikely to produce such gaps. How can formal and informal jobs be compared in terms of wages in the Russian case?

Figures 3.5 and 3.6 are based on RLMS data and show the evolution of earnings in each form of employment for men and women, respectively. The decade under consideration was characterized by a continuous increase in living standards in Russia. According to official statistics, in 2010, the average official real wage was 2.7 times higher than in 1998. Informal earnings also increased significantly, though the rate of growth varied across job types. In terms of relative rankings in remuneration, however, there was very little change.

Both male and female entrepreneurs have the highest earnings throughout the period. Unsurprisingly, entrepreneurial income appears to be more volatile relative to other forms of employment. Salaried workers are one step below in the earnings distribution. These figures also suggest that formal status has no strong impact on earnings for wage and salary workers. Finally, individuals performing only casual or irregular activities are at the bottom of the earnings distribution.

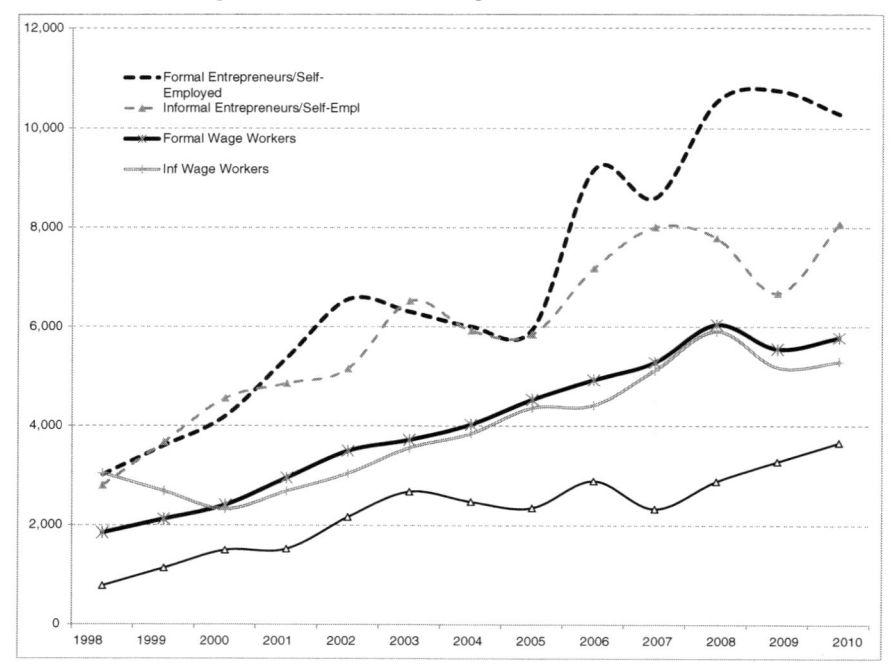

Figure 3.5 Real monthly earnings in formal and informal employment, men,
1998–2010, RLMS.

Source: RLMS, Gimpelson, Kapeliushnikov and Slonimczyk (2014).

One important factor affecting the distribution of earnings is the wide variations in average monthly hours worked across different employment types. Two
points are worth emphasizing here. First, one reason for higher earnings is simply
that entrepreneurs work a larger number of hours per month. In particular, formal
entrepreneurs work 20 per cent more hours than formal employees during the
same reference period. Second, workers performing irregular activities have very
low hours. On average, individuals in this category work only around 20 hours
per week. A simple calculation of an implicit hourly wage puts irregular activities
above those of wage and salary workers. As a result, workers performing irregular activities have median wages comparable to those of entrepreneurs. Average
earnings differentials across job types can reflect the non-random selection of
skills and other productive characteristics into certain types of jobs. We estimated
earnings regressions, controlling for some of the factors that might affect earnings
and be correlated with job type. The specification we used allowed for the effect of
hours to vary across employment types; it also included the set of standard control
variables and added year dummies. In order to partially remedy the potential bias
of the pooled OLS estimator, we estimated the panel fixed effect (FE) model and
the Hausman–Taylor (HT)-type random effects models.

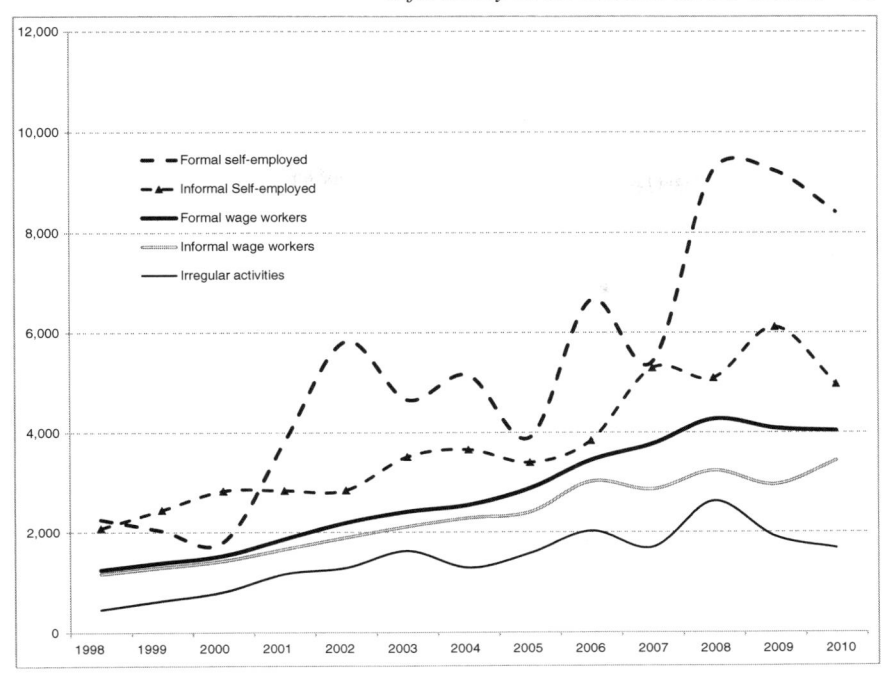

Figure 3.6 Real monthly earnings in formal and informal employment, women, 1998–2010, RLMS.

Source: RLMS, Gimpelson, Kapeliushnikov and Slonimczyk (2014).

Formal entrepreneurs appear to earn on average 36 per cent (males) and 56 per cent (females) higher earnings than formal wage workers, if other factors are kept constant. Informal entrepreneurship brings the same wage premium for males and only a slightly lower premium for women. Informal salary workers only face a small penalty relative to formal salaried workers. Finally, workers in casual and irregular activities are not, on average. paid less than formal salaried workers. This seems surprising, but it reflects the effect of short hours supplied by a worker in this type of employment.

The pooled OLS results suggest that formal entrepreneurs earn a relative premium. The alternative FE and HT models are more 'sceptical' in this regard, denying that this group of income earners enjoy a potential advantage relative to others. The entrepreneurial premium emerges as much smaller in size and statistically insignificant.

If demand for working time is strongly constrained by employment type and workers would be happy to supply more hours than they do, it would still be possible to find a positive and significant effect of formal and informal entrepreneurship relative to any salaried work. This is also the case in relation to the short duration of irregular activities.

Summing up the evidence on earnings across job types, it seems safe to assert that any self-employment brings a statistically significant wage premium compared to observationally similar formal wage workers, while informal salary workers are not significantly penalized given the number of working hours they supply. Male workers involved in an informal irregular activity can even win in relative terms, while female workers emerge as losers in these comparisons. These results are significantly driven by variations in the hours actually worked across job types. As an additional test, this exercise does not provide any strong support for the segmentation hypothesis but detects some signs of it. Given the clear trend to an expansion of informality, the risk of stronger segmentation in the medium-term future can hardly be dismissed.

Informality as a systemic institutional failure

The informality issue cannot be confined by or reduced to partial labour market imperfections. Its persistence raises a number of questions concerning more general relationships between citizens and the state. Still, a modest incidence of the Russian informality and weak symptoms of labour market segmentation should not serve to pacify since the rate of increase in informality against the background of economic growth seems to be troubling, and signalling mounting dysfunctions. As pointed out by Saavedra and Tommasi (2007: 280), 'dimensions and measures of informality are indeed a reflection of broader systemic failures'. Inferior productivity in informal jobs is one of the salient indicators.

Russian informality has a number of features which are characteristic of such failures. Among the most emblematic are the following, though this list is far from complete:

1   Interaction between shrinking labour demand in the formal sector and low unemployment benefit replacement ratios;
2   Distrust in the state and state institutions;
3   Incomplete and selective enforcement of formal regulations;
4   The erosion of the tax base, which potentially leads to underproduction of public goods;
5   Exclusion from access to social protection and various public services;
6   Blurred borderlines between formal and informal activities.

It is easy to see that all of them are strongly interconnected and manifest different dimensions of the same complex phenomenon. 'In other words, several aspects of informality are ultimately a reflection of the way individuals interact with the state and with each other – that is, of the degree of 'formalization' and inclusiveness of each country's *social contract*' (Saavedra and Tommasi 2007: 280). These interactions are shaped by various state-related incentives and constraints that are mutually reinforcing. If individuals do not trust the ability of the state to provide high-quality public goods including judicial and social protection to all fellow citizens, then the incentives to pay taxes are seriously undermined.

The erosion of the tax base leads to further underproduction of public goods, including the enforcement of regulations. Weaker institutional enforcement-related capacity kills the incentives to follow formal rules. In such a situation we are likely to enter a vicious circle that is hard to exit. Informality becomes a deep-rooted social norm that can enforce and reproduce itself and expand into the larger population.

Multiple equilibria and dynamics of social norms

Individual participation in informal transactions (including informal employment) is shaped by incentives and costs, on the one hand, and by social norms, on the other. Social norms can work as additional incentives or contributions to total costs. These norms themselves reflect the long-term evolution of informality and specify a particular path of dependence. If few firms or individuals work informally, because such work is considered illegitimate and is widely condemned, dominant social norms deter the expansion of informality at the given level of enforcement technology. It can be called a good equilibrium. However, if, for any reason, the numbers of informal workers or informal firms in the economy tend to grow, the costs of being informal may decrease and the incentives for it may, on the contrary, increase. This change does not affect solely social norms (how the society sees these violators and whether it is ready to condemn and punish) but also the institutional capacity of the state. The costs of monitoring increase, the likelihood of detection falls, and ultimately the enforcement technology is likely to weaken. Over time, this changes the ratio between formal and informal workers. After reaching a tipping point, this ratio moves towards predominantly informal relationships, which corresponds to a new (bad) equilibrium.

We can impose this simple framework on the Russian informality dynamics that were discussed earlier. The growing rate of informality is an outcome of two macro factors. The first relates to the demand for informal labour, the second constrains workers' choices on the labour market if they leave a job. As we could see, the demand constrained by an unfriendly business climate and inefficient regulations has been in permanent decline. Workers exiting the (formal) sector face limited (and shrinking) employment opportunities in the formal sector, while the replacement ratio of unemployment benefits affecting unemployment as an alternative option remains extremely low. In this context, informal employment emerges as the second-best income-generating option.

The path of dependence in the evolution of the Russian informality has multiple roots and a variety of reasons. However, the Russian state has played a significant role in launching the process in the recent transitional years. Though the macro-economic shocks were extremely strong, the formal safety net that could support the Russian population in coping with hardships remained weak and piecemeal, and it was not even considered to be an urgent policy priority. This sent a clear signal to everybody that survival should rely on available informal and personal resources. A widespread allocation of small land plots and a reduction in the official working hours conducted by the state at that time increased such resources that people might have at their disposal and use as productive assets in their informal activities (Gimpelson and Kapeliushnikov 2007).

Trust

Trust is another important ingredient in the complex web of social interactions. Lower trust in the state and state institutions undermines expectations of public goods. In other words, the lack of confidence undermines the social contract connecting citizens and the state, thereby leading to even higher informality through the creation of positive feedback loops. Ultimately, by opting to be informal, an individual seeks to exit the state-controlled space; she wants to avoid the regulations imposed by the government as well as the associated responsibility.

Aghion *et al.* (2010) present a model explaining the co-evolution of distrust and regulations. They argue that government regulation is strongly and negatively correlated with trust. Distrust in society, including general distrust and distrust of economic agents in the state, leads to heavier government regulation. Economic agents themselves are not able to coordinate efficiently, but corrupt and inefficient state bureaucrats generate even more distrust through their activity. Informality can also be a part of this multivariate equation. On the one hand, informality emerges as a reaction to distrust in the state that major economic agents express. On the other hand, it pushes the state to regulate (government officials often consider informality as a symptom of incomplete regulations that should be expanded) even more, and therefore leads to further regulative failures. We end up with even more regulation, but less trust and more informality. In this triangle, informality is an important element and may emerge as a positive one, since it functions as an adjustment buffer when regulation critically fails.

Of course, important caveats should apply to these arguments. A conventional interpretation of the social contract assumes that individuals and the state exchange tax contributions for the provision of public goods completely voluntarily and consciously. In the Russian context, this condition should be modified. Regardless of their employment status, all individuals are eligible by law for basic pension and free health care. This universal coverage is usually combined with a low level (in terms of quantity and quality) of this provision. At the same time, these goods are financed by oil and gas rent revenues, rather than tax receipts. This has several major implications: access to basic public goods is not conditional upon formal employment and personal contributions, individuals (taxpayers) are alienated from the state and government bureaucrats are not accountable to taxpayers. All these properties are positively correlated with informality.

Incomplete enforcement and blurred borderlines between formality and informality

The division of the Russian labour market into two distinct sectors is too simplified. In fact, formality and informality are intimately intertwined states and form a stretched continuum, rather than providing a black–white dichotomy. Though the formal sector is largely governed by formal regulations, it is also heavily contaminated by informality. Meanwhile, the informal sector is not 100 per cent ignorant of the acting legislation. Gimpelson and Kapeliushnikov (2014: 169) present estimates of compliance with labour legislation, according to which Russian formal workers estimate the level of compliance at 88 per cent, and informal workers at 59 per cent. Formal workers believe that, on average, 8.4 chapters (of a total of 10) of the Labour Code are fully enforced, while informal workers give 5.1 as the estimate. The difference is significant, but so also is the role of informality in the formal sector. These figures are simple averages, while the actual distributions of informal relationships in formal and informal jobs are more complex and largely overlaid.

Poor law compliance in Russia is clearly not a new phenomenon and has a long tradition in the country's history. The well-known saying 'the stringency of Russian laws is offset by their non-observance' is attributed to the Russian satirist Mikhail Saltykov-Shchedrin (1826–89). He was not just a great writer but also a vice-governor of one of the provinces and was, therefore, well informed to comment on the subject. Non-observance of laws and rules is one of the key elements of the flexibility that allows the Russian labour market to adjust to shocks today and, therefore, to perform relatively well. Given the current trend to over-regulation followed by the Russian government in all major spheres of life, such non-observance becomes a challenge and simultaneously a well-embedded property. In the early 2000s, the Russian authorities announced far-reaching plans to bring 'more law and order' into all areas of economic life, including the labour market. In the context of these measures, for example, the non-payment of wages on time became a serious crime punishable by imprisonment. This helped curb the wage arrears epidemic but brought little adherence to the law in other areas. On the contrary, firms began to seek 'refuge' in less regulated and not so well-monitored areas.

Conclusions

The expansion of labour market informality poses several political challenges, which are all intrinsically intertwined. Though labour market informality in Russia is increasing, it has not yet become a problem of the scale facing many Latin American countries. However, this can hardly be a valid argument for ignoring it completely. Many Latin American countries have been trying to reduce informality, while Russia seems to be moving in the opposite direction. The rate at which informality is expanding says more about the problem than the current 20–30 per cent of total employment being accounted for by informal workers. If informality tends to crowd out formality, it can be concluded that job creation in the formal sector faces tough constraints and barriers. As it appears, much of the adjustment in the Russian labour market comes from the informal sector, which is able to expand and react quickly, while the formal sector appears to be overregulated and semi-frozen. This makes the issue of job creation in formal and informal sectors both an economic and a political challenge. It is economic since it affects growth and productivity, and it is political since it relates to the whole set of institutional conditions within which firms are functioning.

The second challenge concerns the 'quality' of informality. Our study suggests that wage opportunities in the Russian informal sector are by and large comparable to those in the formal sector. This – together with the fact of large cross-sectional flows – paints a picture of a rather integrated, not a strongly segmented, labour market. A better account of the non-wage characteristics of jobs would probably add benefits and gains to the formal sector in its competition with the informal sector, though this would hardly change the main conclusion. However, this relatively benevolent picture is not a given forever. If informality continues to expand, then segmentation may become more emphasized, with stronger implications in terms of growing poverty and inequality. These implications are obviously not politically and socially neutral.

The third challenge relates to human capital. Modern economic growth is based on human capital, while informality is not a fertile ground for its accumulation and efficient utilization. Much lower productivity in informal jobs represents the underutilization of education and skills. If workers entering informal jobs are already well equipped with human capital, they face a high risk that much of that will be in little demand. If they enter their working life earlier, with few skills, they are unlikely to acquire many more skills later on. Whatever the reason, it is likely in future that an increasing proportion of the labour force is stuck in a low human capital-intensive economy.

Finally, the fourth challenge deals with the endogenous interaction of informality and regulations, which goes both ways. Since most regulations are introduced and enforced by the state, this challenge is undoubtedly political. Informality emerges as a direct reaction to regulatory failures when regulations are excessive, while the state has only low capacity to enforce them. In such situations, politicians are often prone to introduce still more regulations, thereby contributing to further de-formalization. The vicious circle turns into a reality, while the chances for breaking it become slimmer.

Notes

1 Support from the Basic Research Program of the National Research University Higher School of Economics is gratefully acknowledged. The authors thank Fabian Slonimczyk.
2 The unemployment benefit replacement ratio in the EU-15 is close to 50 per cent and in the Central and Eastern European countries, it is around 25 per cent (Lehmann and Muravev 2011).
3 In 2010, the rates for social contributions were raised again.
4 More on RLMS see www.hse.ru/en/rlms/.
5 The discussion on earnings is based on Gimpelson *et al.* (2014).

References

Aghion, P., Algann, Y., Cahuc, P. and Shleifer, A. (2010) 'Regulation and Distrust', *Quarterly Journal of Economics*, 125(3): 1015–49.

Bosch, M. and Esteban-Pretel, J. (2013) 'The Labor Market Effects of Introducing Unemployment Benefits in an Economy with High Informality', *IDB Working Paper Series*, 402.

Fields, G. (1990) 'Labour Market Modelling and the Urban Informal Sector', in Turnham, D., Salome, B. and Schwartz, A. (eds), *The Informal Sector Revisited*, Paris: OECD, pp. 49–69.

Fields, G. (2009) 'Segmented Labour Markets Models in Developing Countries', in Ross, D. and Kinkaid, H. (eds), *The Oxford Handbook of Philosophy of Economics*, Oxford: Oxford University Press, pp. 476–507.

Gimpelson, V. and Kapeliushnikov, R. (eds) (2007) *Non-standard Employment in the Russian Economy*, Moscow: HSE Publishing House.

Gimpelson, V. and Kapeliushnikov, R. (2013) 'Labour Market Adjustment: Is Russia Different?', in Alexeev, M. and Weber, S. (eds), *Oxford Handbook of the Russian Economy*, Oxford: Oxford University Press, pp. 693–724.

Gimpelson, V. and Kapeliushnikov, R. (eds) (2014) *In the Shadow of Regulation: Informality in the Russian Labour Market*, Moscow: HSE Publishing House.

Gimpelson, V., Kapeliushnikov, R. and Slonimczyk, F. (2014) 'Between Light and Shadow: Cross-sectoral Mobility', in Gimpelson, V. and Kapeliushnikov, R. (eds), *In the Shadow of Regulation: Informality in the Russian Labour Market*, Moscow: HSE Publishing House, pp. 290–332.

Hussmanns, R. (2004) 'Measuring the Informal Economy: From Employment in the Informal Sector to Informal Employment', *Bureau of Statistics Working Paper*, 53, Geneva: International Labour Office.

Kucera, D. and Ronkolato, L. (2008) 'Informal Employment: Two Contested Policy Issues', *International Labour Review*, 147: 321–48.

Lehmann, H. and Muravev, A. (2011) 'Labor Markets and Labor Market Institutions in Transition Economies', *IZA Discussion Paper*, 5905, August, Bonn: IZA.

Lehmann, H. and Pignatti, N. (2007) 'Informal Employment Relationships and Labour Market Segmentation in Transition Economies: Evidence from Ukraine', *IZA Discussion Paper*, 3269, Bonn: IZA.

Lehmann, H., Razzolini, T. and Zaiceva, A. (2011) 'Job Separations and Informality in the Russian Labour Market', *IZA Discussion Paper*, 6230, Bonn: IZA.

Maloney, W.F. (2004) 'Informality Revisited', *World Development*, 32: 1159–78.

Margolis D., Navarro, L. and Robalino, D. (2012) 'Unemployment Insurance, Job Search and Informal Employment', *IZA Discussion Paper No. 6660*, Bonn: IZA.

OECD (2012) *Labour Market and Social Policy Review of the Russian Federation*, Paris: OECD.

Packard, T., Koettl, J. and Montenegro, C. (2012) *In From the Shadow: Integrating Europe's Informal Labor*, Washington, DC: The World Bank.

Perry, G., Maloney, W., Arias, O., Fajnzylber, P., Mason, A. and Saavedra-Chanduvi, J. (2007) *Informality: Exit and Exclusion*, Washington, DC: The World Bank.

Saavedra, J. and Tommasi, M. (2007) 'Informality, the State and the Social Contract in Latin America: a Preliminary Exploration', *International Labour Review*, 146: 279–309.

Slonimczyk, F. (2012) 'The Effect of Taxation on Informal Employment: Evidence from the Russian Flat Tax Reform', in Lehmann, H. and Tatsiramos, K. (eds), *Informal Employment in Emerging and Transition Economies: Research in Labor Economics*, 34: 55–99.

Vodopivec, M. (2013) 'Introducing Unemployment Insurance to Developing Countries', *IZA Journal of Labour Policy*, 2(1). Online. Available: www.izajolp.com/content/2/1/1 (accessed 31 August 2014).

4 State–business relations in Russia after 2011

'New Deal' or imitation of changes?

Andrei Yakovlev[1]

After the 2008–9 crisis, the Russian government began to pay much more attention to the improvement of the country's investment climate. Since then a wide range of important practical steps have been taken in this sphere, including the introduction of a regulatory impact assessment in 2010 and the establishment of the Agency for Strategic Initiatives in 2011. In February 2012, Vladimir Putin announced the '100 steps programme', whose aim is to move Russia's ranking up from 120th to 20th in the Doing Business rating compiled by the World Bank and also to establish a post of Presidential commissioner for the rights of entrepreneurs. That announcement was followed by the development of road maps to simplify getting access to electricity and obtaining construction permits, the change of customs regulations, and the promotion of exports. In September 2012, a special presidential decree was passed concerning governors' activity evaluations regarding the business climate in their regions.

Can these changes be regarded as a 'New Deal' in the government's policy with respect to business, akin to President Franklin Roosevelt's introduction of the New Deal following the Great Depression of 1929–33 in the United States? Or is it rather an imitation of changes designed to weaken the possible protest sentiments among entrepreneurs after mass-scale opposition rallies against the malpractices of the parliamentary elections in 2011? In this chapter, we will find answers to these questions relying on the model of limited access orders developed in the latest works of Nobel Prize Winner Douglass North[2] and his co-authors.

In the first section, I characterize the main features of this new theoretical model and map out the general logic of its possible application to the Russian transition economy. I then use the terminology of this model to show the evolution of state–business relations in Russia before the 2008–9 crisis. The chapter then considers the consequences of the global financial crisis, its impact on the distribution of rent flows, and changes in the policy towards business. I then analyse the views of opponents of these policy changes and show the reasons for internal contradictions of the economic policy, causing a slowdown in economic growth and a cut in investment. The main conclusions are formulated at the end of the chapter.

Concept of 'limited access orders' and its applications for Russia

The fact that business conditions in Russia are unfavourable has been discussed for a long time (Puffer *et al.* 1998; Hellman *et al.* 2003; Kuznetsov and Kuznetsova 2003; Yasin *et al.* 2006; Golikova *et al.* 2007). However, the Russian authorities have recently begun to make visible efforts to change the investment climate. What caused the turnaround toward business, and why had it not happened earlier? To answer that question, it would be useful to consider the situation in Russia from the point of view of a new concept formulated in the latest works of Douglass North and his co-authors (North *et al.* 2007; North *et al.* 2009; North *et al.* 2013). In these works they argue that, in general, any active individual faces two options – he can either try to earn his bread through some kind of productive activities, or he can make an attempt to take away something his neighbour has earned. The second option has destructive implications because the net gain of a winner in an armed conflict is always smaller than the total losses of the losers. In addition, violence curbs opportunities for development because the threat of a compulsory waiver of earned incomes lowers the incentives for productive activity. Thus the limitation of the risks for violence is optimal from the social welfare point of view, but it can act against the interests of individuals with a violent potential. According to North and his co-authors, the resolution to this problem is related to the emergence of *organizations*, which defend their members against external violence and, at the same time, impose sanctions on those members who break the established rules of internal cooperation.

Historically, the first organization of this type was a clan (kin, tribe) headed by a military leader. However, the appearance of clan-type or tribal communities did not resolve the problem of violence; rather, it shifted it to another level, where clashes and conflicts occurred not between individuals but between clans. And here appeared the need for the emergence of the state as a *mechanism to limit and control violence*. North and his co-authors define the social system that emerges at this stage as a 'natural state' or 'limited access order' (LAO). In its initial phases, a natural state is a system of personal agreements between 'specialists in violence' who head individual clans and form the elite of a future state. For a leader of an individual clan, the non-use of force is reasonable, if he and his crowd regularly get sufficient compensation or receive a rent. For this very reason, barriers to access to economic activity, which generate rents for influential social groups, become an essential condition for the existence of a natural state. Equally essential is the limitation of access to political activities, which makes it possible to support rent-making rules of the game.

However, such a social system proves fragile because it is based on personal privileges for 'specialists in violence', and any change in the balance of power between them becomes an occasion for a revision of a formerly achieved agreement on the 'non-use of force'. In this context, North and co-authors emphasize that, contrary to the standard belief shared by many scholars, the monopoly of the state for legitimate violence in the historical context is an exception rather than a rule. In the contemporary world, this exception exists only in the most developed countries where the consensus of elites in the framework of democratic institutions provides conditions for the exercise of centralized political control over military forces and law enforcement agencies. North and his co-authors define these societies as 'open access orders' and stress that the transition from limited access to open access is a key element of social progress and a key challenge for human history. The very first step of this transition is related to a shift from personal privileges to a system of impersonal rights, which are guaranteed, in the first place, to the elite, and only later, to wider groups of citizens. In this context, 'the rule of law for the elite' is the precondition for social stability and economic development. In addition, two further preconditions are important for the shift to the open access order: the rise of economic and political organizations that are independent of the state, as well as of their direct founders. North *et al.* (2009: 23) define them as 'perpetually living organizations', and formations of mechanisms for collective political control of the application of violence by the elites.

A sharp reduction in rent gives grounds for the revision of agreements and changes in the ruling coalition. When there is a decline in the levels of rents, elites either start a 'war against all' again or attempt to reach a new agreement. The latter outcome is more probable if the ruling coalition is comprised of a wide variety of social groups, which are capable of solving the problems faced by society. Thus, social and economic development may be considered to be the process of the gradual extension of access to economic opportunities and political activity, as the involvement of new participants results in greater stability. The stability of the rules is especially important in the context of shock impact – when a country faces economic crises, or social or political shocks. This theoretical approach was selected for analysis because, in my opinion, it explains the realities of the social and economic development in countries such as Russia much better than mainstream economic theory. According to the standard approach, the main problem of emerging economies is their insufficient efficiency caused by a lack of competition and barriers to new market entrants. At the same time, the lack of market competition is explained by a lack of competition in the political sphere. Proceeding from this logic, the recommendations of international financial institutions concerning reforms in the early 1990s included privatization, liberalization, and democratization. All of these measures did actually increase the access to economic and political activity for new players and created favourable conditions for raising economic efficiency.

However, the removal of barriers also diluted rent sources, which had formed the basis for the existence of the ruling coalition, and thereby presented the groups that possessed the potential to use violence with an incentive to use such force. For this reason, in many developing countries, liberal and democratic reforms were accompanied by crime waves, serious social conflicts, and even civil wars. In the economic sphere, this violence assumed different forms – from racketeering businesses, the illegal capture of attractive assets and assassinations of competitors to the deliberate ruin of those firms whose owners were not loyal toward the 'ruling coalition'. Such violent pressure on business has destructive implications for economic development as it destroys all incentives for investment.

This violence can be stopped and, consequently, motivations be created for productive entrepreneurship, to use the term coined by Baumol (1990), only if an agreement is reached between the key elite groups on new mechanisms for generating rent and its distribution among the participants of the 'ruling coalition'. Bureaucracy, including the police and the army, controlling the means of state coercion, and business investing (or not investing) capital in national economic development represent key elite groups in 'limited access orders' Hence, I will hereinafter try to understand the way in which the format of relationships between bureaucratic and business elites was changing in Russia, and how sustainable and productive the present round of negotiations between them will be. In this analysis I use a schematic description of the main stages of evolution of the state–business relations, presented in Table 4.1.

Table 4.1 shows the composition of the ruling coalition for each period, its main sources of rent that support it, and the wider groups constituting its social basis. A separate column is devoted to factors predetermining the movement from 'state capture' in the 1990s to the dialogue of the early 2000s, the subsequent change of the model for 'business capture' with the active participation of members of the law enforcement agencies (*siloviki*) in the mid-2000s, and the resumption of dialogue after the crisis of 2008–9.

Evolution of state–business relations before the 2008–9 crisis

It has been well established in the literature that the size and stability of rent flows are the essentials of the Russian economy and determine the relationship between society, the development of institutions, and economic dynamics (Åslund 1996; Boone and Rodionov 2002; Åslund 2004; Gurvich 2010). In the 1990s, the main sources of rents were privatization, an enormous difference in the prices for the same goods on the domestic and world markets, and domestic and international borrowing (Table 4.1). The key players were the federal and regional bureaucracies and oligarchic businesses. However, all of the sources of rent were largely temporary. By the second half of the 1990s, the most attractive assets had been privatized, the difference between domestic prices and world market prices for consumer goods and raw materials had begun to disappear, and the Russian debt burden had reached a critical level. Meanwhile, the lack of agreements among elites regarding a mutual consideration of interests and the non-observance of uniform rules led to chaos and entailed widespread non-payments and a permanent redistribution of property. Such a 'virtual economy' could not last long and it collapsed in August 1998.

The default on short-term state treasury bills ('GKO') and the sharp devaluation of the rouble did not only become an economic shock, but also led to serious political changes when, for the first time since 1991, the government included representatives of the Communist Party.[3] As a result, the 1998 crisis became something of a 'cold shower' for the new Russian elite. The largest losses from the crisis were inflicted on the middle class. Nevertheless, representatives of the elite understood that in the event of another social cataclysm, they could lose both their

Table 4.1 Main periods in the evolution of state–business relations in post-Soviet Russia

Period	Composition of ruling coalition*	Main sources of rent (formal and informal)	Social base of regime	Causes of break in elite pact
1992–8	**Big business, federal bureaucracy, regional bureaucracy** + criminal groups	Super profits from export and import due to gambling on the difference between domestic and international prices; privatization proceeds; super profits on the government bonds market (similar to financial pyramids at that time); technical assistance and loans from international financial organizations	Small business mostly in trade and services – due to price liberalization and the absence of any enforcement of regulation	Exhaustion of the sources of rent of the 'transitional period' (as they were all temporary), aggravated by the 1997 'Asian' crisis ➔ deep monetary and financial crisis in August 1998
1999–2003	**Federal bureaucracy & big business** + siloviki	Growth in profits of business and tax revenues based on the increase of import barriers and the reduction of exporters' costs as a consequence of a dramatic devaluation of the rouble, and on the strengthening of the law enforcement system	Economically active population and business in the real sector of the economy – owing to wage increases and the opportunity to work for the growing domestic market	Commenced growth in world prices of energy sources and struggle for the control over natural rent between the federal bureaucracy and big business ➔ the YUKOS case symbolizing political defeat of big business
2004–8	**Siloviki & federal bureaucracy** + big business + state owned enterprises	Growing budget earnings from oil export + informal expropriation of part of the proceeds of successful small and medium businesses by siloviki	Managers and employees of enterprises and organizations subsidized or financed by the state (hospitals, universities, schools, the agro-industrial complex, the defence sector) + pensioners	The 2008–9 crisis accompanied by a sharp increase in the social budget spending and the decrease in the amount of rent available for distribution ➔ prevalence of short-term interests within the elite striving to 'have all rents just now'
2009–…	**Siloviki, federal bureaucracy** + state owned firms + big business	Continued (albeit no longer growing) budget proceeds from oil export – against the backdrop of drastically increased social and defence expenditures and deceleration in economic growth	Military personnel and law enforcement officers, workers of the public sector and state-owned enterprises, pensioners	Upset balance, where the amount of rent in the long-term is insufficient to finance the liabilities of the ruling coalition

Note: *Bold depicts the elite group dominant in the ruling coalition.

status and their assets. The awareness of that threat motivated different groups of elite to negotiate the new agreement, which created the conditions for economic development – including a very radical tax reform, at that time characterized by US newspapers as a 'tax revolution' (*Wall Street Journal* 2002).

The period of 1999–2003 is interesting because during this time the state attempted to create new organizations for the collective representation of business interests, and it adhered to the rationale of North's concept. In particular, the Russian Union of Industrialists and Entrepreneurs (RSPP), the largest and most influential business association, which had been established by Arkady Volsky in 1990, was reformed. Initially, RSPP united directors of large state-owned and privatized enterprises, but mostly it did not include representatives of new private companies. As stressed by Hanson and Teague (2005), in the 1990s, RSPP was in opposition to the government. In 2000, the RSPP management structure was reorganized and the Bureau of RSPP Board was set up, which was comprised of owners of all the largest private and state-owned companies. From the summer of 2000 onwards, meetings of Russian President Vladimir Putin with the Bureau of RSPP Board were held two times a year, where the problems facing business and governmental initiatives in economic policy were discussed. Although no formal decisions were made at such meetings, they were objectively extremely important for the coordination of plans on both sides – the state and big business. These meetings undoubtedly facilitated the development of a more adequate economic policy and reduced uncertainty and risks facing businesses.[4]

Along with the reform of RSPP in 2000–1, two new all-Russian business associations were established: *OPORA* of Russia represented the interests of small business, and *Delovaya Rossiya* (Business Russia) represented the interests of medium-sized business. These associations' activities led to reforms aimed at the reduction of administrative barriers to small business – including the simplification of registration and licensing procedures and the reduction of the number of supervisory bodies' inspections. In addition to the previously mentioned tax reform,[5] alterations were conducted in the customs regulation system, such as the unification and reduction of customs tariffs. On the whole, all those measures resulted in a noticeable legalization of Russian business and a significant growth in the tax payments to the federal budget. The restoration of the capacity of the law enforcement system led to a suppression of criminal activity and crime bosses were squeezed out of business and politics. Thus, in Russia in the early 2000s, there was a trend toward the maintenance of a dialogue between the state and business, which created preconditions for economic development and a forming of the 'rule of law for the elite' along the lines of North's concept of 'limited access order'. However, since the mid-2000s, those tendencies have been explicitly reversed. What caused that turnaround?

In spite of all the positive changes of the early 2000s, certain grey zones still remained in the relations between state and business. One of these concerned property relations. The meeting of oligarchs with Vladimir Putin in June 2000 resulted in an informal agreement between big business and the state according to which big business would not interfere in politics and the government would not revise the privatization results (Hanson and Teague 2005). However, that arrangement remained on a strictly informal basis. Moreover, oligarchs understood property guarantees as the right to obtain full income from properties, while the representatives of the top bureaucratic elite interpreted them differently. That ambiguity became the ground for a revision of the arrangements when social differentiation began to increase, and the rise in the global market's oil prices entailed the occurrence of a new significant rent source.

It should be noted that rapid economic growth nearly always intensifies levels of social differentiation. That process was also observed in Russia in the early 2000s when the gaps between rich and poor regions, different sectors, and social groups began to increase. The federal bureaucratic elite perceived that tendency as dangerous, because the maintenance of social stability was one of the fundamentals of the existing political regime. As a result, the state needed additional resources to decrease social differentiation. Therefore, by introducing a new mineral resources extraction tax, the state tried to redistribute oil export earnings in its favour. Big business resisted the tax because such policy was perceived as an encroachment on its profits. The business resistance (most evident on the part of the largest Russian oil company, Yukos) became apparent in stonewalling, through 'friendly' State Duma deputies, a number of bills initiated by the government and in financial support to opposition parties, including CPRF and Yabloko.

Nevertheless, the power balance between the state and business had already changed by that time (Hanson 2005; Sakwa 2009). The top members of the bureaucratic elite brought about the de facto nationalization of Yukos and sent its former owners to prison by relying on members of the security services and law enforcement agencies (*siloviki*) as part of building a power vertical. Criminal cases initiated against the owners of Yukos were obviously a selective application of the law, considering that almost all large companies used similar schemes of tax optimization at this time. Nevertheless, as demonstrated by the results of the 2003–4 parliamentary and presidential elections, the public broadly supported the state actions against Yukos (Yakovlev 2006). In my opinion, this support derived from the widespread feeling in society that the results of the privatization process were unjust, a sentiment that had been ignored by big business.

This conflict led to the collapse of the relatively equal dialogue between the state and business that took place at the beginning of the 2000s. In 2003–4, this model was replaced by the undoubted dominance of the state. Big business became a junior partner, subordinate to the state, and the top federal bureaucracy and *siloviki* became the key players. During this period, the 'state people' believed that they knew everything and had no need of any outside advice. Evidence of this supreme confidence appeared after the resignation of Prime Minister Mikhail Kasyanov's government when the state adopted an active industrial policy (involving creating the Investment Fund, and establishing special economic zones and state corporations) and forced big business to secure state approval for all international agreements.

Many liberal experts did not like this state-dominated model of capitalism (see Ledeneva 2012). Nevertheless, it is necessary to admit that much of what the government did coincided with the interests and expectations of a significant number of market players. For example, the restoration of a unified economic space, which resulted from bringing the regional governors in line, was profitable for most ordinary businesses. The same profitability was observed concerning the relations between the government and large business. While it is possible to support a variety of opinions regarding what was done to Yukos, most players did not like the era of 1996–8, when economic policy was subordinated to the interests of a few large business groups which had supported Boris Yeltsin in his election campaign in 1995–6. Therefore, most business people perceived the new dominating role of the state as the 'lesser evil'.

One significant factor in support of this policy was that at the beginning of and in the middle of the 2000s, the state primarily did what it had previously promised to the public. While one could disagree with the methods used to remove the oligarchs from participating in politics or with forcing the regions into the 'power vertical' system, the state set specific goals and subsequently implemented them. As a result, people began to feel a degree of trust regarding the consistency and predictability in policy, which led to the formation of positive expectations for long-term social and political stability and encouraged active foreign investments in Russia in 2006–7. Those representatives of the middle class who were unhappy with the situation within the country had the opportunity to leave Russia, due to the high demand for specialists in other countries. This migration allowed the country to let off steam. Thus, the distribution of rent between different social groups helped to keep the stability of Russian 'limited access order' and provided few incentives for resistance.

The 2008–9 crisis and its consequences

The 2008–9 crisis demonstrated that the 'power vertical' created in Russia in 2000s is inefficient. Even before the crisis, this system had only worked when signals from the top level met the interests and expectations of the people at lower levels of the bureaucratic hierarchy. At the same time, a serious built-in defect of that model was the asymmetry in passing information signals, which is typical for large hierarchical systems: the lower-level bureaucrats readily reported their success, but were in no hurry to inform the higher authority about problems or failures in their areas of responsibility. During the crisis, it became clear that the authorities knew far from everything about what was happening and only had limited capability to take action.

In particular up to the late autumn of 2008, the government leaders appearing on the central TV channels were telling the audience that Russia's problems with the stock market and the banking sector were only the fallout from the bankruptcy of leading American financial institutions. As early as the summer of 2008, however, large firms in the metallurgy and chemical industry sectors came across a sharp drop in demand and prices on global markets, and in August–September, they started to put workers on forced leave. And the government only initiated a full-scale anti-crisis programme in December 2008. This late response led to an increase in uncertainty and a reduced confidence in the politics of the government. Therefore, many company owners preferred to put their businesses on hold and wait until the government clarified its economic policy. As a result, in 2009, the Russian economy lost 8 per cent of its GDP, a figure that was out of line with contemporary economic indicators. In contrast to the Eastern European countries and Mexico at this time, Russia had no significant external debt, was not facing a large budget deficit, and was not suffering from high inflation. What did cause the downturn, however, were the contradictory signals from the government which resulted in negative expectations regarding government policy.

The destruction of expectations happened not only among market agents but also on the side of the state machinery itself. During the years of economic boom of the mid-2000s, representatives of the bureaucracy and the *siloviki* initially gained informal control over the cash flows of many entities in both the public and the private sectors. Before the crisis, these representatives had expected to draw dividends from that control for many years which, to a certain extent, decreased the current corruption load on business. However, under sharply increased levels of uncertainty, these people determined that it was more prudent to extract the maximum revenue as quickly as possible, leading to increased corruption and the exertion of violent pressure on businesses (Firestone 2010; Zhalinsky and Radchenko 2011a, 2011b; Gans-Morse 2012). These changes provoked businesses to respond with an intense capital outflow from the country.

Finally, the crisis also induced a change of mood in society. Well-educated middle-class professionals, who did not accept life under the 'managed democracy' and who could earlier have considered the possibility of emigration, now observed that because of the global crisis, there had been a decline in demand for their services in developed countries. This meant that they and their children would have to continue to live in Russia. Therefore, it is possible to view the massive protests against electoral fraud at the end of 2011 as a result of the crisis: the protests represented an outburst of accumulated social tension, which in earlier periods would have resulted in emigration.

However, despite all sceptical points listed above, the crisis did have some positive consequences. The theses about modernizing the economy announced by President Medvedev in 2008 and the series of reforms conducted in 2004–8 (including the reform of public procurement in 2005–6, the decision to force public employees to declare their income, and others) demonstrate that the authorities did understand the need for change. However, before 2008, in the absence of significant pressure from outside or below (from non-elite layers of society), the ruling coalition was not ready to change the rules of the game or impose limits on the elite.

The 2008–9 crisis and the resulting changes in the world market led to an increased pressure on Russian authorities. Initially, that pressure came from outside – due to a reduction of the natural rent available for distribution and the intense capital flight to countries with more favourable investment climates. However, the pressure later began to strengthen from the inside – due to the change in expectations, a split among elites and the change of the public mood. As a result, the authorities began to adopt significant policy changes in reaction to domestic and international pressure in the post-crisis period. As early as 2010–11 the government tried to seek feedback from the business community – with the focus on medium-sized businesses, driven by the hope of integrating them into the social base of the regime. Contrary to the widely held opinion, this group of Russian firms is not small. According to a special project initiated by the *Expert* magazine, by 2006 there were approximately 13,000 companies with an annual revenue of between USD 10 and 400 million and the total sales of these firms were about 80 per cent of those of the large enterprises (Vinkov *et al.* 2008; Yudanov 2010). Moreover, the medium-sized enterprises have the greatest growth potential, a fact that has motivated the new focus of governmental policy (Yakovlev *et al.* 2010; Kuznetsov *et al.* 2011). At the same time, because they lacked sufficient political connections, this group of firms became an object for violent pressure from bureaucracy and law enforcement structures. Before the crisis, the side effects of the bad business climate had been compensated for by high profitability, but when high margins no longer existed, business barriers remained in place.

The first signs of this change in policy toward the interests of medium-sized business were important amendments to the Criminal Code and Criminal Procedure Code adopted by the State Duma in 2009 and being implemented in 2010. These amendments restricted the pre-trial arrests and other applications of criminal sanctions on entrepreneurs (Firestone 2011). In May 2010, following the best practices of European countries, the Russian government introduced the Regulatory Impact Assessment (RIA). This is the procedure that stipulates that drafts for federal laws, decrees of the Russian President, and resolutions of the Russian Federal Government should be analysed for exposure of provisions, which: (a) introduce excessive administrative limitations for entrepreneurs; and (b) make entrepreneurs and budgets at all levels of the fiscal system of the Russian Federation involved in groundless expenditures. The key elements of the RIA procedure are public hearings, with the spokesmen of leading organizations representing interests of the business community.

Initially, the RIA procedures functioned solely on the federal level and were applied to legislative acts concerning the organization and implementation of public control, the setting of technical and quality standards, and the introduction of production safety requirements. According to the Ministry of Economic Development of the Russian Federation, more than 1,700 legislative acts were evaluated in 2010–12. In 2012, a decision was made to introduce the RIA at the regional level, beginning in 2013, and also to extend the RIA to amendments to tax and custom regulation.

The next step in the elaboration of the 'new policy' of the government can be connected to two big analytical projects that were advanced in 2010. The first was the 'Doing Business in Russia' project commissioned by the Ministry of Economic Development to the World Bank, with the idea of comparing conditions for starting businesses, registering property, obtaining construction permits, and getting access to electricity in 30 regions (see also Chapters 5 and 6). The second was the Russian BEEPS survey of 4,300 firms in 37 regions (including 30 covered by the 'Doing Business in Russia' project). Taken together, these two projects demonstrated significant differences in business climate conditions between the Russian regions and identified a number of arguments for changes in the incentives system for regional governments.

As stressed above, the 2008–9 crisis revealed the absence of feedback mechanisms in Russia's public administration. The recognition of this fact led to the search for new means of state–business interaction. One of these was the Agency for Strategic Initiatives (ASI) established by the Russian government as an autonomous non-commercial organization in the summer of 2011. Putin is the chairman of the ASI supervisory board. The officially declared goal of ASI is the 'creation of prospects for self-realization of young ambitious leaders who are able to lead Russia to the front line in the world'. The Agency's mission includes the promotion of projects and initiatives advanced by fast-growing medium-sized businesses and social sector leaders, growth in the number of new leaders emerging in medium-sized businesses and in the social sector, and a general improvement of the overall business climate. To achieve these goals, substantial funds were provided to the ASI, and the Agency was able to recruit onto its staff (which amounted to about 150 employees) a number of qualified experts with business experience. To monitor the effectiveness of its projects, ASI invited well-known consulting firms, including the Boston Consulting Group.

The further tasks of the ASI were defined in Putin's February 2012 campaign statement and subsequent decrees on economic policy, which aimed, among other things, to improve Russia's position on the World Bank's Doing Business ranking from 120th to 20th place, and to change the way the governors and federal agencies are evaluated. The practical result of ASI's work was the development of roadmaps for reducing barriers in getting construction permits, changing customs regulations, stimulating exports, and introducing new standards for regional governments' activity to provide an attractive investment climate. In the summer and autumn of 2012, these 'road maps' were approved by the government and became obligatory for government offices. The ASI, in collaboration with 11 regions, has realized a pilot project 'Standard of business climate improvement at the regional level', based on the analysis of best practices shown by regional governments in their investors' relations. In September 2012, a presidential decree included indicators of this standard in a system of gubernatorial activities evaluation.

Another important innovation in the field of state–business relations was the establishment of the post of Presidential Commissioner for Entrepreneurs' Rights and the appointment of Boris Titov to this position in June 2012 (*Financial Times* 2012). According to the federal law adopted by the State Duma in April 2013, positions of commissioners for entrepreneurs' rights were introduced in all regions of the Russian Federation. As an 'ombudsman for entrepreneurs', in 2012–13 Titov pushed a number of initiatives, including the re-examination of criminal cases against entrepreneurs and a proposal about broad amnesty for entrepreneurs who faced criminal prosecution in the 2000s. Both ASI and the office of the ombudsman for the entrepreneurs are working in close cooperation with leading business associations. Their activities help to identify effective officials inside the present public administration, to establish horizontal links between them, and to dissem-inate best practices. However, the ultimate effects of the activities of ASI and the ombudsman for entrepreneurs will depend on the will and ability of the Krem-lin to appoint and promote top-level officials according to their efforts to invite investments and create incentives for economic growth, rather than by the criteria of their political loyalty and personal commitment.

Who is against the 'New Deal' with business and who supports it?

I cannot say that all these measures pushed by ASI or Boris Titov and supported by the Ministry of Economic Development and the Ministry of Finance have resulted in a real change in the business climate in Russia. Moreover, ASI experts believe that regional governments and federal agencies have quickly learned how to respond to the orders from above without there being any changes in the real practice of interaction with business. However, the events of early 2013 indicated that the absence of any effects in the new policy of relations with business is not due solely to covert resistance at the middle and lower levels of the bureaucratic hierarchy. There are influential groups in the Russian elite who, in principle, deny any need to meet the interests of business and, on the contrary, insist on a tough-ening of regulations and firmer control and supervision. These groups are rep-resented, first of all, by the *siloviki* – including the Investigative Committee, the Office of Prosecutor General, the Federal Security Service, the Federal Customs Service, the Federal Tax Service, the Accounting Chamber of Russia, and a num-ber of other agencies. By tradition, the top managers of a number of state-owned companies and state corporations, including the president of the Rosneft Com-pany, Igor Sechin, and the president of the Russian Railways, Vladimir Yakunin, are also associated with the group of *siloviki*.

In the post-crisis period, the general consolidation of the positions of this group of the Russian elite occurred for a number of reasons. First, the crisis aggravated the issue of corruption. Having faced a visible toughening of the budget constraints in 2009 and the subsequent years, the Kremlin and the Federal Government made an attempt to curb the losses from corruption, which had expanded under the period of state capitalism in the mid-2000s. However, the fight against corrup-tion was conducted by strictly administrative methods – by relying on the stricter formal control of spending of public funds and public procurement procedures. Despite numerous criminal cases, this policy failed to bring about a decline in the level of actual corruption – because under the superfluous and controversial sys-tem of administrative regulations established in the 2000s, practically any Russian public official who made decisions on the allocation of funds could be accused of violating some regulations. Nevertheless, the anti-corruption campaign resulted in a substantial rise in the influence of security and law enforcement agencies.

Second, the crisis of 2008–9 and the related uncertainty of economic poli-cies led to substantial capital outflows from Russia. The government responded directly with an attempt to carry out a stronger persecution of entrepreneurs for tax evasion and the use of offshore accounts. Another argument in favour of tougher administrative regulation and control was a number of accidents related to the blatant violations of safety requirements by entrepreneurs, which had caused many deaths. These additional pretexts for investigations became an additional way of exerting 'power pressure' on business. In a certain sense, it gave rise to reciprocal collective actions on the side of the business community, which started to lobby for liberal amendments to the Criminal Code and the Code of Criminal Procedure, changes in the practice of law enforcement, and the introduction of regulatory impact assessment procedures.

Third, political protests in 2011–12 played a substantial role in consolidating the positions of the *siloviki*. In particular, immediately after the mass protests against electoral fraud in December 2011, the government announced a large-scale expansion of financing the army, the Ministry of the Interior, and securities services. In addition, criminal cases were opened against the most active representatives of the political opposition. In 2012, a law 'On Foreign Agents' (Federalnyi Zakon 2012) was enacted in an attempt to impose substantial limitations on the activities of non-governmental organizations (NGOs), and in the spring of 2013, the Public Prosecutor's Office launched a campaign to reveal the 'foreign agents' (see Chapter 10). Finally, the Investigative Committee instituted legal proceedings against the experts who had conducted an independent assessment of the second criminal case against the owners of Yukos Co. on behalf of the Human Rights Council, under the president of the Russian Federation. In May 2013, these activities of the Investigative Committee forced one of Russia's leading economists, Sergei Guriev, to emigrate (*New York Times* 2013).

Such shifts in political life were accompanied by the development of an ideological grounding for the 'mobilization scenario'. In this context, the activities of the 'Izborsk Club', which was established in September 2012, deserve some attention. The economists Mikhail Delyagin and Sergey Glazyev and the political journalists Alexander Prokhanov and Mikhail Kalashnikov became key experts of this new think-tank. The main propositions of the Club's manifesto, prepared in October 2012 and published in January 2013, include an accelerated development of the defence industry, the positioning of the public sector as the 'core' of the national economy, and a requirement to renew and cleanse the national elite (Izborsk Club 2013). The experts of the Izborsk Club believe that all these measures are predetermined by the increased intensity of the geopolitical struggle for control over resources. This struggle will lead to regional wars, larger wars in Eurasia or Africa, armed interventions into many countries, especially those with large unexplored resources (minerals, water, land) and a new world war cannot be ruled out. The experts of the Izborsk Club name Peter the Great and Josef Stalin as the main heroes of Russian history, and regard Stalin's industrialization as the model for the 'project of mobilization' today.

Since its very earliest activities, the Russian mass media has regarded the Izborsk Club as a think-tank close to the Kremlin (Kommersant 2013a). It is worth mentioning that public statements made by the vice-premier Dmitry Rogozin have echoed many of the arguments of the Izborsk Club (Rossiiskaya Gazeta 2013).

Statements of a number of experts from the All-Russian National Front made after the Front's convention in June 2013 are also close to the ideas of the Club (Kommersant 2013b). However, it would be wrong to conclude that Russia's top political elite made its choice in favour of an anti-market 'mobilization scenario'. Pro-business policies do continue to be promoted. In particular, regardless of the *siloviki*'s resistance, Vladimir Putin finally supported the project of amnesty for entrepreneurs, which had been advocated by Boris Titov. In June 2012, Alexander Galushka from Delovaya Rossiya ('Business Russia') became one of three co-chairmen of the All-Russian National Front and in September 2013, he was appointed Minister of Far East Development. In May 2014, Putin announced the rating elaborated by ASI with the support of the Boston Consulting Group and leading business associations that rank the investment environment for Russian regions (*Financial Times* 2014).

Therefore, rather, we can say that at present the Russian elite is standing at a crossroads. On the one hand, Russia is in acute need of modernization in order to compete successfully with other developed and developing economies. Modernization and improvements in the efficiency of resource deployment are the very means for giving new incentives for economic growth, which the ruling elite needs in order to maintain social stability and prevent political protests. The 'new business' – successful medium-sized companies that grew up on the tide of the economic boom in the 2000s – can become the driving force of this modernization. These companies have strong teams of managers; they know the Russian market and have sufficient financial resources. However, in order to realize their potential, these companies need a competitive environment and the protection of property rights. This implies, first, that the unlawful actions of law enforcement bodies must be limited, and the independence of the court system must be guaranteed. In terms of North and co-authors, such measures would mean 'rule of law for the elite' and the expansion of access to business opportunities for new economic agents.

However, practical steps in this direction clash with the stance of the ruling elite, which is fearful of political protests (with the ongoing concern that something on the lines of an 'Arab Spring' could emerge in Russia). This fear constitutes the foundation of the increasing influence of the *siloviki*, which began to exercise dominance not only over business, but over the entire bureaucratic machine, state corporations, and large-scale public sector organizations. This fear is the 'culture medium' for projects of 'new mobilization' in the spirit of the Izborsk Club. And although hardly anyone in the Russian elite in practice believes seriously that such scenarios can guarantee a steady economic development, the very fact that they are voiced in public, along with unlawful activities of law enforcement bodies, produces very strong negative signals to business and the bureaucratic elite.

These signals, essentially, cancel out all effects of attempts to improve the business climate. In particular, I believe, political reasons alone suffice to explain the sharp deceleration of economic growth and the increase in capital flight from Russia since the beginning of 2013. Moreover, these signals rouse negative expectations not only in the business environment, but also in the state machinery (including at its highest levels). The consolidation of law enforcement bodies in the absence of a positive programme, which could take into account the interests of the main elite groups, is understood as nothing more than an attempt of the ruling elite to hold on to its power as long as possible – until an inevitable collapse of this regime and a reiteration of the chaos of the early 1990s.

In other words, the Russian elite is facing a choice – either to carry out economic modernization 'from above', relying on coercion from the centre, or to rely on the incentives and initiatives of economic agents themselves. It is not the first time in Russian history that this choice has been faced: let us remember the late 1920s and the period from the 1950s to the 1960s. However, the present phase has a number of distinct features.

First, the composition of social groups that can be losers in a turn to the 'mobilization scenario' is much wider. They are not only owners and managers of big and medium-sized business, but also people from other elitist groups – including the federal and regional bureaucracy, managers of state corporations, and public sector organizations. Second, in the last twenty years, all of these actors have acquired new and very important skills and knowledge – having had experience of living in a market environment (however imperfect it is), in an atmosphere of open information. Consequently, any attempt to 'strengthen the reins of power' can meet much more resistance in the elite. And strictly because people in the elite have acquired new knowledge and experience, there are more opportunities to find compromises in settlements, which can ensure the balance of political and economic interests and prevent a reiteration of the year 1991.

In Russia, the choice of development scenarios will depend on how much the present ruling elite will be able to look beyond its narrow interests and enter into a dialogue with other elite groups, including not only business but also regional elites and public sector entities. In turn, the readiness of the top elite to conduct this dialogue will largely depend on whether the above mentioned wide social groups will be able to reach an agreement about collective action and work out a new unifying and pragmatic agenda.

Conclusion

In this chapter, we examined the evolution of state–business relations in Russia in recent years from the point of view of the 'limited access orders' concept developed by North and his co-authors. In our analysis, we described the practical steps taken by the Russian government to improve the investment climate in 2010–13 and tried to find an answer to the question of whether this turnaround was a manifestation of the 'New Deal' in economic policy or, on the contrary, the imitation of changes devised to cool off the voices of protest in the business community.

In my opinion, the government's actions are not a mere imitation of changes. The ruling elite needs sustainable economic growth, since the related increase in the incomes of the population constitutes an important factor of social support of the 'limited access order' that currently prevails in Russia. The rapid pace of economic growth before the 2008–9 crisis was a result of increasing oil prices on the world market. The crisis put a stop to the growth of Russia's budget revenues from the export of primary commodities. Attempts taken by the government in the second half of the 2000s to stimulate economic development by public investments did not produce the desired results. Moreover, in order to maintain social stability at the time of the crisis, the government has undertaken a radical increase in social spending, which has restricted the opportunities for further economic growth.

In other words, the events of the 2008–9 crisis have once again shown that sustainable economic growth, which was necessary to maintain the stability of 'limited access orders', was possible only on the basis of private investments. However, a considerable improvement in the business climate was necessary to resume the inflow of private investments. The acknowledgement of this fact became the basis for the resumption of the dialogue between the state and business – initially with Delovaya Rossiya, which represented the interests of successful medium-sized business. According to the concept of North *et al.*, this dialogue and subsequent measures aimed at reducing the costs of doing business could be interpreted as an attempt to extend the composition of the 'ruling coalition' and provide broader access to economic activity for medium-sized businesses.

However, those measures did not produce the desired results, as the steps to accommodate medium-sized business meant an actual limitation of informal sources of rent for *siloviki* who, following the Yukos affair, became the leading group in the 'ruling coalition'. Moreover, the positions of *siloviki* became even stronger following mass-scale protests against the disputed parliamentary elections in December 2011. As a result, the government was trying to take steps in favour of successful medium-sized business without infringing on the interests of the law enforcement bureaucracy, which led to the pursuit of an internally contradictory policy course and insufficient trust from the business.

Therefore, measures to improve the investment climate cannot yet be characterized as a 'New Deal' in state–business relations. This is because different elite groups on the side of the state are still pursuing different interests and, on the whole, the senior political elite lacks a coherent 'vision of the future' and a relevant strategy for Russia's development. The existence of such a strategy supported by the main groups within the elite is a precondition for confidence in economic policy and the resumption of investment and economic growth. The participation of a successful medium-sized business in the development of such a strategy could contribute to a strengthening the stability of 'limited access order' in Russia, but to date it is unclear whether the present participants in the 'ruling coalition' are ready to take such steps.

Notes

1 This chapter is based on the results of the projects conducted by HSE Institute for Industrial and Market Studies as part of the HSE Program of Basic Research in 2013–2014. The author is grateful to Vladimir Gimpelson, Evsei Gurvich, Juuso Kaaresvirta, Silvana Malle, Yakov Pappe, Thomas Remington and Tseren Tserenov for their comments and suggestions. The assistance by Meagan Neil is gratefully acknowledged.
2 Douglass North was awarded the Sveriges Riksbank Prize in Economic Sciences in Memory of Alfred Nobel in 1993.

3 Thus, Yuri Maslyukov became the first vice-premier in charge of economic policy and all economic agencies in the government of Yevgeny Primakov. Before this appointment, he was a notable CPRF figure, the former Chairman of the USSR Gosplan and a member of the Politburo of the CPSU Central Committee. Another member of the CPRF fraction in State Duma Gennady Khodyrev became the Minister for antimonopoly policy.
4 The Yukos affair in 2003 ended this practice of regular high-level consultations between the government and big businesses.
5 With the simplification of the taxation system, the introduction of a flat income tax rate, and regressive rates of the unified social tax.

References

Åslund, A. (1996) 'Reform vs. "Rent-seeking" in Russia's Economic Transformation', *Transition*, 26 January, pp. 12–16.

Åslund, A. (2004) 'Russian Economic Transformation Under Putin', *Eurasian Geography and Economics*, 45(6): 397–420.

Baumol, W.J. (1990) 'Entrepreneurship: Productive, Unproductive, and Destructive', *Journal of Political Economy*, 98(5): 893–921.

Boone, P. and Rodionov, D. (2002) *Rent Seeking in Russia and the CIS*, Moscow: Brunswick, UBS Warburg.

Federalnyi Zakon (2012) Federalnyi Zakon Rossiiskoi Federatsii ot 20 iyulya 2012, No.121-FZ 'O vnesenii izmemenij v otdelnye zakonodatelnye akty Rossijskoi Federatsii v chasti regulirovaniya deyatelnosti nekommercheskikh organizatsij, vypolnyayushchikh funktsii inostrannogo agenta'. Online. Available: www.rg.ru/2012/07/23/nko-dok.html (accessed 4 July 2014).

Financial Times (2012) 'Putin Seeks to Reassure Foreign Investors', 21 June. Online. Available: www.ft.com/intl/cms/s/0/84ae0acc-bba7-11e1-9436-00144feabdc0.html-#axzz2UvfVrlfg (accessed 31 May 2013).

Financial Times (2014) 'Putin Backs Moves to Improve Russia's Investent Climate', 26 May 2014. Online. Available: www.ft.com/intl/cms/s/0/9b7592ac-e738-11e3-aa93-00144feabdc0.html?ftcamp=published_links%2Frss%2Fworld%2Ffeed%2F%2Fproduct#axzz33CpD7LNB (accessed 4 July 2014).

Firestone, T. (2010) 'Armed Injustice: Abuse of the Law and Complex Crime in Post-Soviet Russia', *Denver Journal of International Law and Policy*, 38(4): 555–80.

Firestone, T. (2011) 'Business, Corruption and Pretrial Detention in Russia', *International Law News*, 40(2): 7–9.

Gans-Morse, J. (2012) 'Threats to Property Rights in Russia: From Private Coercion to State Aggression', *Post-Soviet Affairs*, 28(3): 263–95.

Golikova, V., Gonchar, K., Kuznetsov, B. and Yakovlev, A. (2007) 'Russian Industry at the Crossroads: What Prevents Our Companies from Getting Competitive? (HSE policy paper)'. *Voprosy Ekonomiki*, 3: 4–34.

Gurvich, E. (2010) 'Oil and Gas Rent in the Russian Economy', *Voprosy Ekonomiki*, 11: 4–24.

Hanson, P. (2005) 'Observations on the Costs of the Yukos Affair to Russia', *Eurasian Geography and Economics*, 46(7): 481–94.

Hanson, P. and Teague, E. (2005) 'Big Business and the State in Russia', *Europe–Asia Studies*, 57(5): 657–80.

Hellman, J.S., Geraint, J. and Kaufmann, D. (2003) 'Seize the State, Seize the Day: State Capture and Influence in Transition Economies', *Journal of Comparative Economics*, 31(4): 751–73.

Izborsk Club (2013) 'Major Breakthrough Strategy', 30 January. Online. Available: www. dynacon.ru/content/articles/1039/ (accessed 4 July 2014).

Kommersant (2013a) 'Sovetskiy Soyuz vozvrashchayut izgotovitelyu', 11 January. Online. Available: www.kommersant.ru/doc/2102396 (accessed 4 July 2014).

Kommersant (2013b) 'Kremlyu nuzhna novaya "Evropa"', 11 June. Online. Available: www.kommersant.ru/doc/2209932 (accessed 4 July 2014).

Kuznetsov, A. and Kuznetsova, O. (2003) 'Institutions, Business and the State in Russia', *Europe–Asia Studies*, 55(6): 907–22.

Kuznetsov, B., Dolgopyatova, T., Golikova, V., Gonchar, K., Yakovlev, A. and Yasin, Y. (2011) 'Russian Manufacturing Revisited: Industrial Enterprises at the Start of the Crisis', *Post-Soviet Affairs*, 27(4): 366–86.

Ledeneva, A. (2012) 'Cronies, Economic Crime and Capitalism in Putin's *sistema*', *International Affairs*, 88(1): 149–57.

New York Times (2013) 'Economist Who Fled Russia Cites Peril in Politically Charged Inquiry', 31 May. Online. Available: www.nytimes.com/2013/06/01/world/europe/economist-sergei-guriev-doesnt-plan-return-to-russia-soon.html?_r=0 (accessed 4 July 2014).

North, D., Wallis, J.J., Webb, S. and Weingast, B.R. (2007) 'Limited Access Orders in the Developing World: a New Approach to the Problems of Development', *World Bank Policy Research Working Paper No. 4359*, September.

North, D., Wallis, J.J. and Weingast, B.R. (2009) *Violence and Social Orders: a Conceptual Framework for Interpreting Recorded Human History*, New York: Cambridge University Press.

North, D., Wallis, J.J., Webb S. and Weingast B.R. (eds) (2013) *In The Shadow of Violence: the Problem of Development in Limited Access Societies*, New York: Cambridge University Press.

Puffer, S.M., McCarthy, D.J. and Zhuplev, A.V. (1998) 'Doing Business in Russia: Lessons from Early Entrants', *Thunderbird International Business Review*, 40(5): 461–84.

Rossiiskaya Gazeta (2013) 'Nezvezdnye voiny', 4 July. Online. Available: www.rg.ru/2013/07/04/voyna.html (accessed 4 July 2014).

Sakwa, R. (2009) *The Quality of Freedom: Khodorkovsky, Putin, and the Yukos Affair*, Oxford: Oxford University Press.

Vinkov, A., Gurova, T., Polunin, Y. and Yudanov, A. (2008) 'To Make the Midsize Business', *Expert*, 10(599): 32–83.

Wall Street Journal (2002) 'The Putin Curve', 26 November. Online. Available: http://online.wsj.com/news/articles/SB1038271514450758308 (accessed 4 July 2014).

Yakovlev, A. (2006) 'The Evolution of Business–State Interaction in Russia: From State Capture to Business Capture', *Europe–Asia Studies*, 58(7): 1033–56.

Yakovlev, A., Simachev, Y. and Danilov, Y. (2010) 'The Russian Corporation: Patterns of Behaviour During the Crisis', *Post-Communist Economies*, 22(2): 129–40.

Yasin, E., Grigoriev, L., Kuznetsov, O., Danilov, Y. and Kosygina, A. (2006) 'Investment Climate in Russia', *Obchshestvo i Economika*, 5: 3–56.

Yudanov, A.Y. (2010) 'The Conquerors of the "Blue Oceans" ("gazelles" *in Russian*)', *Sovremennaya Konkurentsia*, 2.

Zhalinsky, A. and Radchenko, V. (2011a) 'Criminal Laws: Big Imitation of Reform', *Vedomosti*, 23 June, 113: A4.

Zhalinsky, A. and Radchenko, V. (2011b) 'Criminal Laws: Business Expatriation Policy', *Vedomosti*, 24 June, 114: A4.

5 Is Russia an entrepreneurial society? A comparative perspective

Ruta Aidis

Over the past decade, Russia has imprisoned nearly three million entrepreneurs (Kesby 2012). Currently, 7 per cent of Russia's prison population are incarcerated for business-related activities (Boyde 2013).[1] Though we do not know why all these entrepreneurs went to prison anecdotal evidence indicates that at one of end of the spectrum, entrepreneurs are thrown into jail for minor transgressions where perhaps a warning would have been a better approach. At the other end of the spectrum, there are politically motivated, high-profile cases such as that of Mikhael Khodorkovsky, arrested in 2003 and released in 2013. These types of arrests create a situation of uncertainty where political action may take place against entrepreneurs at any given time.

Nonetheless, this rather sobering statistic seems to have little effect on a continuous stream of entrepreneurial start-ups but, as this chapter will argue, it does impede business growth and expansion which results in a stunted business environment. According to the data collected by the Global Entrepreneurship Monitor (GEM),[2] 6 per cent of the Russian population is engaged in business start-up activities and 35 per cent of these start-ups are necessity driven. To put this into an international context, in the US, 13 per cent of the population is engaged in business start-up activities and 21 per cent are necessity driven, whereas in Sweden, 8 per cent of the population is engaged in business start-ups and 10 per cent are necessity driven. Clearly, Russia has comparatively lower start-up rates and a higher percentage of necessity-driven entrepreneurs. One future challenge for Russia is to attract the best and the brightest opportunity-driven individuals to become entrepreneurs.

Entrepreneurial societies have many benefits. Through business development and growth, entrepreneurship is a job creator and can provide employment for a broad group of individuals, but especially for skilled labour. Since entrepreneurial innovation is unpredictable it promotes diversity – the winning idea, product or service can come from any part of the population. Entrepreneurship can also lead to democratization since it is based on ability and talent and promotes social organization. It also leads to increases in productivity. However, the exercise of creative talents in society can be disruptive and challenging to the status quo. Fostering an entrepreneurial society is an additional challenge of Russia given its rigid political and economic system which has favoured oligarchical development to the detriment of innovative activity through entrepreneurship.

This chapter is structured as follows: the first section discusses the formation of the entrepreneurial society while the second section presents some of the current initiatives for entrepreneurship development in Russia. The chapter then provides a comparative analysis of entrepreneurship development in Russia using the results of the 2013 Global Entrepreneurship and Development Index (GEDI) as well as the 2013 Gender-GEDI results which focus specifically on female entrepreneurs. In addition, I analyse the conditions and characteristics for start-ups in Moscow using the *Startup Ecosystem Report*. Following this, I present the specific strategies adopted by Russian entrepreneurs and then discuss the four main challenges to business growth and development. This chapter ends with a concluding section.

The formation of an entrepreneurial society

Entrepreneurship is a very broad term that is used to define an equally broad range of activities. For the purposes of this chapter, we define entrepreneurship as: (1) the ability of individuals to perceive and create new economic opportunities through innovative activity; (2) to introduce their new ideas to the market (facing uncertainty and risk); (3) as a result to establish a viable business that contributes to national economic growth and personal livelihood (adapted from Thurik and Wennekers 1999). The entrepreneurial society is made up of individuals acting within the constraints and opportunities provided by the context, which is made up of both formal and informal institutions. In many advanced market economies, it is possible largely to 'ignore' the impact of institutions where, for the most part, market institutions are present and functioning. However, there is a growing recognition in the literature of the importance of the institutional environment for entrepreneurship. In 1993, Douglass North received the Prize in Economic Sciences in Memory of Alfred Nobel[3] for his contributions to understanding how economic and political institutions change over time. He stressed that economic, political and social factors must be taken into account if we are to understand the development of those institutions that have played a role for economic growth and how these institutions have been affected by ideological and non-economic factors.

The work of North[4] has been illuminating in its identification of different institutional influences on economic development. Institutions are defined as any form of constraint that human beings devise to shape human interaction. North makes a clear distinction between formal and informal institutions. Put simply, formal institutions are the visible 'rules of the game' such as constitutional law, which can be altered quickly to adapt to changing economic circumstances. Moreover, formal rules are generally enforced by governments. In contrast, informal institutions are the invisible 'rules of the game' made up of norms, values, acceptable behaviours and codes of conduct. Informal rules tend not to be legally enforced. Change to informal rules occurs more indirectly and usually as a result of accidents, learning, natural selection and, most of all, the passage of time (North 1990: 88). Informal rules most often evolve to complement formal rules. North has also identified the often conflictual role between formal and informal institutions in both the historical perspective and in transition economies. Within North's framework, organizations such as firms – existing or potential ones – will adapt their activities and strategies due to the opportunities and limitations in the formal and informal institutions. Institutional development can be intentionally affected by organizational players such as entrepreneurs (North 2005).

Interestingly, institutions can be maintained over long periods of time, even if they are inefficient (DiMaggio and Powell 1983; North 1990). There are several reasons for inefficient institutional outcomes. First of all, even when they clash with new formal rules, informal rules have a tenacious ability to survive because they have become embedded in habitual behaviour (that is, culture) and informal institutions provide a sense of stability. Second, informal institutions may change more slowly due to the influence of path dependence. Though the past cannot be used to neatly predict the future, pre-existing incentive structures in the environment can illuminate the direction in which institutions affect further economic development. This occurs because institutional change is usually incremental and is seldom discontinuous (North 1990: 10). As a result, unproductive paths may persist and, in that sense, history matters. Thirdly, lock-in can occur as a result of a symbiotic relationship between existing institutions and organizations that have evolved as a consequence of the incentive structure provided to those institutions. Even when there are changes in the formal rules, organizations which benefitted from the outdated informal rules and which would lose their benefits if they adopted new informal practices complementary to formal rule changes will continue to participate in detrimental informal rule practices in order to retain their position of power. Fourthly, when formal and informal institutions clash, as in the case where formal rules are changed but informal rules have not changed, noncompliant behaviours proliferate and this can result in the formation of underground economies (Feige 1997: 22). North's emphasis on the influence of formal and informal rules and institutions on economic outcomes is relevant for emerging economies such as Russia (Aidis and Estrin 2013).

If the institutional framework rewards piracy then 'piratical' organizations will come into existence; and if the institutional framework rewards productive activities then organizations and firms will come into existence to engage in productive activities (Baumol 1990). In the case of Russia, the oligarch model of wealth creation and industry domination has created a culture where rules do not apply to the well-connected and powerful but are applied indiscriminately to those who do not enjoy this special status.

A considerable literature argues that weak institutions, notably the quality of the commercial code, the strength of legal enforcement, administrative barriers, extra-legal payments and the absence of market-supporting institutions, represent a significant barrier to entrepreneurship (McMillan and Woodruff 1999, 2002; Djankov *et al.* 2004; Aidis *et al.* 2008). In a study comparing new firms in Poland, Slovakia, Romania, Russia and Ukraine, Johnson *et al.* (2000) establish that insecure property rights, in addition to weaknesses of macroeconomic stability and adequate financing, inhibit the development of the private sector.

Important institutional influences on entrepreneurship include social norms and values (informal institutions). They determine access to critical resources such as education and access to markets. In addition, formal institutions create the legal framework and business regulations and they also affect the rule of law. But well-functioning institutions, no matter how strong, cannot substitute for individual drive and aspirations for entrepreneurship. Therefore the two basic components of the entrepreneurial environment are (i) individual entrepreneurial motivations, activities and characteristics and (ii) informal and formal institutions.

As shown in Chapter 2 of this volume, Russia's resource-driven economy and its overreliance on oil exports is an impediment to the development of an entrepreneurial society – resource-driven economies in general have little incentive to embrace 'disruptive' activities. Rather they tend to go hand in hand with a ruling elite, monopolistic behaviour and the unequal distribution of access to resources – in other words, they tend to be resource-rich but innovation-poor.

Improvements for SME development in Russia

Since coming to power in 2000, President Putin has focused on growing the state-owned conglomerates, giving them tax breaks and encouraging them to expand. Entire industries, including banking and transportation, have become dominated by state-controlled companies, which at present account for at least 50 per cent of the Russian economy (Vasileva 2013). The development of small and medium-sized firms (SME) was not prioritized, was often criminalized and was not seen as an important contributor to Russia's economic development. However, during President Medvedev's rule (2008–11), several new initiatives were created to address the problems in the Russian business environment. In order to address the lack of funding, in 2007 the Russian government established the venture capital company Rusano, whose mission was to invest in niche companies operating in the nanotechnology domain. So far it has invested USD 6.3 billion in more than 100 firms within and outside Russia. In 2011, the Agency for Strategic Initiatives (ASI) was created specifically to improve the conditions for entrepreneurship, facilitating dialogue between business and government and promoting business-friendly reforms. A year later, in 2012, the government appointed Boris Titov as an ombudsman to safeguard the rights of entrepreneurs. The creation of industrial parks has been one of the most effective business development initiatives in Russia. According to Ernst and Young's Entrepreneurship Barometer, 32 per cent of entrepreneurs surveyed in Russia currently use or have used business incubators, compared to the G20 average of 21 per cent (Ernst and Young 2013). This is a positive sign that new initiatives are taking root in supporting and helping new business development. Moreover, in 2013 the Russian government allocated USD 200 million government-backed financing to invest in internet start-ups (ibid.). Russia has also made some improvements to business regulations as measured by the World Bank's Ease of Doing Business Index. In the 2013 Index, Russia climbed 19 places to be ranked

92nd out of 189 countries and is now the leader for BRIC[5] countries (see also Chapter 6, Table 6.2 in this volume).

Russia has been active in raising its international profile for entrepreneurship. In March 2014, it hosted the 3rd annual Global Entrepreneurship Congress in Moscow. The Global Entrepreneurship Congress is an interdisciplinary gathering from around the world where entrepreneurs, investors, researchers, thought leaders and policymakers work together to help bring ideas to life, drive economic growth and expand the development of entrepreneurship. Improving regulations and access to funding as well as building incubators and innovation parks are important, but do not address the most fundamental and detrimental issues affecting Russian businesses. In a survey of 6,000 businessmen conducted by OPORA[6] in 2012, 42 per cent of the respondents reported 'severe difficulties' in starting a new company. Corruption is often cited as the underlying cause: 27 per cent added that frequent inspections by regulators led to bribes being paid (Vasileva 2013). In addition, as mentioned earlier, the threat of criminal prosecution is another continuing problem for Russia's businesses. The combination of corruption and the potential for prosecution creates tremendous uncertainty in Russia's business environment.

Comparative GEDI analysis of Russia

The Global Entrepreneurship and Development Index (GEDI) is a diagnostic tool used to distil the complex relationship between individuals, institutions and entrepreneurship into clear and implementable results (Acs *et al.* 2013). Countries are ranked according to their identified strengths and those areas where improvements are required. Pairs of institutional and individual variables form pillars that are further divided into three main subindices. Tables 5.1, 5.2, and 5.3 provide comparative insights into Russia's strengths and areas that are in need of improvement.

Russia ranks in 69th place out of 118 countries in the GEDI 2013 index, with an overall score of 0.23. Table 5.1 shows the three top strengths and the three top areas for improvement for Russia and also the other three BRIC countries. Russia's main strengths include the fact that many of its start-up business owners are college educated and that its population is generally well educated. A critical feature of a start-up with high growth potential is the entrepreneur's level of education (Bates 1990). It is widely held that entrepreneurs with higher education degrees are more capable and willing to start and manage high-growth businesses. Russia also boasts a large domestic market. The main areas for improvement for Russia are the low levels of informal investors,[7] the low levels of exporting start-ups and the high levels of corruption. Informal investors are an important source of financing since they provide an alternative and often more flexible financing for businesses than do banks or other formal institutions. The low number of exporting start-ups is unsurprising given the size of Russia's domestic market. Yet moving into foreign markets is a critical step for growth-oriented businesses and offers important scope for innovation. When we compare the three main strengths and areas for improvement in Russia with the other BRIC countries, there are

Table 5.1 The BRIC countries compared using the GEDI 2013 results

Country	Rank	Strengths	Areas to improve
Russia	69	• High level of college-educated business owners • Highly educated population • Large domestic market size	• Few informal investors* • Low levels of exporting start-ups • High levels of corruption
Brazil	72	• Large domestic market size • Entrepreneurship is considered a good career choice with high social status • Risk acceptance by the general population	• Few informal investors* • Low levels of exporting start-ups • Low level of start-ups introducing new products or services
China	59	• Large percentage of the population say they know an entrepreneur • Most markets are not dominated by only a few firms • Risk acceptance by the general population	• Low percentage of start-ups active in the technology sector • Low levels of exporting start-ups • Few start-ups are active in markets where there are few competitors selling the same product
India	89	• Large percentage of the population say they know an entrepreneur • Entrepreneurship is considered a good career choice with high social status • Most markets are not dominated by only a few firms	• Few informal investors* • Few growth oriented start-ups • Low percentage of start-ups active in the technology sector

Source: Data compiled from Acs *et al.* (2013).

Note: *An *informal investor* refers to a person who invests his or her own money in a start-up company. In return this individual receives convertible debt or ownership equity in the company.

two primary issues. On the one hand, it is encouraging to see that access to tertiary education for the general population, and for business owners in particular, is much higher in Russia than in the other BRIC countries. On the other hand, the high levels of corruption are also a uniquely Russian problem. In terms of strengths, Brazil also boasts of the large size of its domestic market as one of its top three strengths. Two of the three areas in need of improvement are also similar for a number of the BRIC countries: Russia, Brazil and India have few informal investors, and Russia, Brazil and China have low levels of exporting start-ups.

In Table 5.2, Russia's top-scoring and worst-scoring three variables are compared with those of Sweden (ranked in 2nd place) and the USA (ranked 1st). It may be noted that Russia and the USA shared the same two strengths: a highly educated population and a large domestic market. However, it is revealing that while Sweden and the USA count the presence of a good business climate as one of their top three strengths, this measure is not as high scoring for Russia. Even more striking is that while Sweden includes a low level of corruption as one of

Table 5.2 Russia, Sweden and the USA compared using the GEDI 2013 results

Country	Rank	Strengths	Areas to improve
Russia	69	• High level of college-educated business owners • Highly educated population • Large domestic market size	• Few informal investors • Low levels of exporting start-ups • High levels of corruption
Sweden	2	• Good business climate – low business risk • High level of new technology absorption by companies • Low levels of corruption	• Few growth oriented start-ups • Few start-ups using new technology • Few informal investors
USA	1	• Good business climate – low business risk • Large domestic market size • Highly educated population	• Small percentage of the population say they know an entrepreneur • Few start-ups using new technology • Small percentage of the population recognize good conditions for starting a business

Source: Data compiled from Acs *et al.* (2013).

its top strengths, for Russia a high level of corruption is one of its main areas in need of improvement. The results of this analysis indicates that while a number of areas in the business environment need to be strengthened, in Russia's case, it is important that other SME-focused initiatives do not take precedence over addressing corruption, the most insidious and detrimental factor that underlies the functioning of an entrepreneurial society.

The Gender-GEDI

The Gender-GEDI is an adapted version of the GEDI index that includes a number of additional gendered indicators to measure 'high potential' female entrepreneurship development. The Gender-GEDI was launched in 2013 and included 17 countries (Table 5.3). Russia was ranked in 10th place, the USA was ranked in 1st place and Uganda was ranked in 17th place. In Table 5.4 we compare the pillar scores for the BRIC which were all included in the Gender-GEDI Index. In terms of final rankings for the BRIC countries, China ranked in 8th place, Russia in 10th place, Brazil in 14th place and India in 16th place.

In order to gain some insights into Russia's specific strengths and areas for improvement, we compared Russia's six main strengths and three main weaknesses to those of the other BRIC countries. We limit our analysis here to gendered issues, though the factors affecting the general business environment discussed in the GEDI analysis above must also be taken into consideration in the case of female entrepreneurs (see Table 5.4). Three of Russia's strengths are unique when compared to the BRIC countries. These include the fact that a high percentage of

Table 5.3 The 2013 Gender-GEDI rankings

Rank	Country	Overall score	Rank	Country	Overall score
1	USA	76	10	Russia	40
2	Australia	70	11	Turkey	40
3	Germany	63	12	Japan	39
4	France	56	13	Morocco	38
5	Mexico	55	14	Brazil	36
6	UK	51	15	Egypt	34
7	South Africa	43	16	India	32
8	China	41	17	Uganda	32
9	Malaysia	40			

Source: Aidis *et al.* (2013).

female start-ups are growth oriented (32 per cent); there is a relatively high percentages of female start-ups in the tech sector (5 per cent); and a large percentage of female business owners are highly educated (87 per cent). Russia and Brazil both have reasonably good levels of female managers (37 per cent and 36 per cent respectively) and all BRIC countries are characterized by moderately good access to childcare.[8] Russia's female start-up activity ratio is 6:10, i.e. 6 female start-ups to every 10 male start-ups, which is at a moderate level. Both and China have higher female start-up activity ratios at 9:10 and 8:10, respectively. India has a lower female start-up activity ratio than other BRIC countries with only five female start-ups for every ten male start-ups. In terms of areas to improve, all four countries have low levels of exporting businesses (the lowest being for Brazil at 6 per cent while Russia has 13 per cent exporting female start-ups). Low levels of female internet use also characterize all of the BRIC countries, with India having the lowest percentage of 6 per cent of internet users being female and the figure for Russia being substantially higher, at 32 per cent. Russia and India both chart a low level of SME support and training. This indicator considers if training is available over a wide geographical area, is accessible to women as well as men, and is affordable for the majority of intended beneficiaries. It also evaluates if the length of training takes into account women's time burdens, and if it is culturally appropriate.[9]

Through this analysis, we find that in Russia, well-educated female entrepreneurs are tending to start businesses that are growth-oriented and a proportion of which are in the tech sector. Compared to other BRIC countries, Russia is at a good starting point. In order to increase the pool of high potential female entrepreneurs, however, Russia will need to focus on improving access to SME training and support programmes, providing broader access to the internet as well as introducing initiatives to facilitate exporting by female entrepreneurs. However, as was already raised in the GEDI analysis above, fundamental barriers to business development such as corruption must be addressed.

Table 5.4 The BRIC countries compared using the 2013 Gender-GEDI results

Country	Rank	Strengths	Areas to improve
Russia	10	• High growth-oriented start-ups (32%) • Moderate female managers (37%) • Moderate/Low-tech sector start-ups (5%) • Highly educated business owners (87%) • Moderate female start-up activity ratio (6.4 for 10 men) • Moderate childcare 3/5	• Low exporting business 13% • Low female internet use 32% • Low SME support & training 2/5
Brazil	14	• High female start-up activity (9.4 to 10) • Moderate female managers (36%) • Moderate SME support 3/5 • Moderate childcare 3/5	• Low tech sector start-ups 0% • Low highly educated business owner 12% • Low growth oriented start-up 7% • Low exporting start-ups 6% • Low female internet use 36%
China	8	• High female start-up ratio 8:10 • Moderate childcare 3/5 • Moderate SME training 3/5	• Low tech sector start-ups 0% • Low highly educated business owner 19% • Low growth oriented start-up 7% • Low exporting start-ups 15% • Low female internet use 35% • Low female managers 17%
India	16	• Moderate access to childcare 3/5	• Low tech sector start-ups 0% • Low highly educated business owner 11% • Low growth oriented start-up 6% • Low exporting start-ups 14% • Very low female internet use 6% • Low female managers 14% • Low SME support 2/5 • Low female start-up activity ratio 5:10

Source: Data compiled from Aidis *et al.* (2013).

Moscow as a start-up hub

To gain a comparative perspective as to the specific characteristics of Moscow as a high-tech start-up hub, we use research conducted by the Startup Genome. In 2012, Moscow was identified as one of the top 20 global cities for start-ups. Using seven separate indices ranging from funding, performance and talent to support, mindset and trendsetter, Moscow is ranked 14th out of 20 cities (Table 5.5). Silicon Valley is ranked in 1st place followed by Tel Aviv (2nd), Los Angeles (3rd) and Seattle (4th), while Melbourne, Bangalore and Santiago are ranked in 18th,

Table 5.5 Start-up Ecosystem rankings for top 20 global start-up hubs

Start-up hub city	Ranking	Start-up output index	Funding index	Company performance index	Talent index	Support index	Mindset index	Trendsetter index	Differentiation from SV index
Silicon Valley	1	1	1	1	1	1	1	1	1
TelAviv	2	2	1	12	8	5	9	17	18
Los Angeles	3	4	6	2	3	13	11	4	11
Seattle	4	19	7	6	2	4	6	11	14
New York City	5	3	4	8	12	9	8	7	8
Boston	6	10	1	7	8	7	7	5	20
London	7	7	5	10	9	2	3	14	17
Toronto	8	6	9	3	10	3	15	12	5
Vancouver	9	13	12	9	4	14	2	9	19
Chicago	10	8	15	5	14	7	13	18	9
Paris	11	14	13	4	17	6	12	15	6
Sydney	12	5	14	16	6	12	16	1	3
Sao Paulo	13	9	10	15	19	11	5	16	4
Moscow	**14**	**16**	**19**	**18**	**11**	**10**	**14**	**8**	**22**
Berlin	15	15	11	13	13	20	18	5	10
Waterloo	16	11	18	14	16	17	17	10	13
Singapore	17	18	8	19	8	16	20	19	12
Melbourne	18	12	17	20	8	10	19	3	18
Bangalore	19	17	16	17	18	15	10	20	10
Santiago	20	20	20	11	20	19	4	13	7

Source: Startup Genome (2012).

19th and 20th place respectively. Interestingly despite is moderate overall ranking, Moscow is ranked 2nd in terms of the 'Differentiation to Silicon Valley' Index.

Moscow's high rank indicates that its start-up entrepreneurs are very similar to those found in Silicon Valley in terms of demographics and their types of start-up companies. Also similar to Silicon Valley, new businesses in Moscow tend to quickly adopt and integrate new technologies, management processes and business models. There are also some notable differences, however: In Moscow, more entrepreneurs tend to be highly educated than is the case in Silicon Valley (69 per cent have a Master's degree in Moscow compared with just 37 per cent in Silicon Valley). Moscow receives relatively low scores in the areas of funding, company performance and start-up output. Moscow is ranked 19th out of 20 countries for funding (finishing ahead of only Santiago). In terms of numbers, Moscow start-ups receive, on average, 80 per cent less funding than Silicon Valley start-ups. The funding gap is most prevalent in the early stage of funding yet later stage funding is also in short supply. In terms of company performance, Moscow's start-ups tend to stay small and do not expand. In terms of numbers of start-ups, there are 89 per cent fewer start-ups in Moscow than in Silicon Valley.

Specific strategies for start-up success in Russia

There are other characteristics specific to the entrepreneurial culture in Russia that are considered in further detail below. It is not uncommon for young Russian entrepreneurs to start three or more companies at the same time (Naumov 2013). This seems to occur in response to Russia's market volatility as well as being a response to the uncertainties of potential political action. This strategy can have its drawbacks, however. Russian entrepreneurs need to divide their efforts, energy and finances over several companies while in the USA, most founders dedicate 100 per cent of their time and energy to a single start-up.

Given Russia large domestic consumer markets, many of Russia's most successful tech start-ups have been based on adapting established western internet models to fit the domestic market. Examples of these types of firms include Darberry (similar to Groupon) and Yandex (a search engine similar to Google). This strategy provides tremendous opportunities in the short term, but to secure sustained long-term growth, Russian start-ups will need to adopt a 'born global'[10] strategy and build globally viable companies. This is also visible in Russia's relatively low level of start-up companies that export their goods or services: 10 per cent in 2012, compared with 21 per cent in Easterm Europe and Central Asian countries (ECA) or 20 per cent for Upper Middle Income (UMI) countries (World Bank 2012). However, highly successful high-tech companies, such as the email/ website company Mail.ru, have entered the global arena to finance additional expansion and growth through its successful Intial Public Offering (IPO) on the London Stock Exchange in 2010.

Elena Masolova is just one example of the new generation of successful Russian high-tech serial entrepreneurs. In the early 2000s she had founded Pixonic, a game developer and publisher for worldwide social networks. She is Pixonic's

CEO with 46 employees, 40 games and 20 million users (Risner 2012). Masolova also created Darberry which, after only six months of operation, was acquired by Groupon for an estimated USD 50 million. Masolova has also been involved in making plans to improve Russia's business environment. For example, she founded AddVenture, a seed investment fund and is also a partner at Ruvento, an accelerator and venture fund. In 2013, Masolova founded Eduson.tv – a new online business learning service for which she received USD 1 million in seed financing. Yet the rather young and emerging nature of Russia's entrepreneurship culture also results in a lack of mentors, advice and support for entrepreneurs. A survey of entrepreneurs revealed that 61 per cent identified the need for mentors (Ernst and Young 2013).

Challenges for business growth and development

There are a number of challenges for business growth and development in Russia. The most important are corruption, financing, education and civil society. In this section I discuss each of these four challenges as it manifests in the Russian environment.

Corruption

Corruption was endemic in Russian society during the Soviet period and, in contrast to its Baltic neighbours, corruption continues to impact Russian society on a large scale. According to Transparency International's Corruption Perceptions Index, in 2013, Russia was ranked 127 our of 175 countries (similar to Iran and Kazahkstan) . This indicated a small improvement from 2012 when Russia was ranked 133 out of 176 countries (see also Chapter 6).

Corruption can be particularly detrimental for business development and growth. As Aidis and Adachi (2007: 393) noted: 'It is very difficult, if not impossible to engage in legal business practices without also engaging in illegal business practices such as bribing and corruption'. Take, for example, the case of Yoanna Gouchtchina, a successful mobile tech entrepreneur who founded ZeeRabbit (similar to AddWords – an app that sends targetted advertisements to users). Gouchtchina wanted to expand into the pharmaceuticals industry but she soon fell foul of the pervasive culture of bribery in that sector (Anderson 2014). She was adamant that she would not engage in such practices and as a result, after months of preparation, she exited without even having had the chance to start.

Table 5.6 presents some of the key corruption indicators, as compiled by the World Bank's Enterprise Surveys. According to the World Bank's Graft Index, 16.1 per cent of Russian firms responded that they had been asked or expected to pay bribes, compared with only 7.5 per cent for firms in UMI countries (World Bank 2012). However, when firms are broken down according to size classes, 23.4 per cent of medium-sized enterprises (20–99 employees) in Russia were asked or expected to pay bribes. In fact, in terms of the five additional measures of corruption including tax inspectors, government contracts, construction permits, import

Table 5.6 World Enterprise Survey corruption indicators, 2012

Corruption indicators	Russian Federation	Small Firms	Medium Firms	Large Firms	EEA	UMI
Incidence of Graft Index	16.1	12.5	23.4	9.1	13.3	7.5
Percentage of firms expected to give gifts in meetings with tax inspectors	7.3	4.1	8.0	15.2	12.5	7.5
Percentage of firms expected to give gifts to secure a government contracts	20.7	18.1	25.8	12.1	17.6	15.9
Percentage of firms expected to give gifts to get a construction permit	26.8	20.6	29.4	33.8	23.2	14.1
Percentage of firms expected to give gifts to get an import license	27.5	8.9	47.1	7.7	14.4	8.7
Percentage of firms expected to give gifts to get an operating license	12.6	8.0	20.9	6.2	12.6	7.0

Source: World Bank (2012).

Key: Small Firms (1–9 employees); Medium-sized Firms (20–99 employees); Large Firms (100 + employees)EEA = Eastern Europe and Central Asia countries; UMI = Upper Middle-Income countries

Note: The Graft index represents the share of all interactions between firms and public officials in which a bribe was expected.

licenses and operating licenses, Russia's percentages for corruption exceed those in ECA countries, UMI, countries, as well as those in Higher Income countries.

In Russia, the enforcement of laws occurs in a selective and arbitrary manner and there is no consistency or stability from the regulatory environment on which firms can rely.[11] This creates an environment where functioning under the radar is often the preferred strategy. Table 5.7 shows some key metrics for the regulatory environment. On average, Russian firms spend more days obtaining basic licenses and permits than is the case in either Eastern Europe and Asia (EEA) or UMI countries.

Education

Russia has historically invested heavily in education and it continues to produce a highly education population. Around 88 per cent of the adult population have attained at least an upper secondary education and 54 per cent have a tertiary qualification, making the proportion of the Russian population with a tertiary-level qualification one of the highest in the world. Only three countries have a higher tertiary attainment rate among 25–34-year-olds than that found in the Russian Federation (55 per cent) (OECD 2012). Concerns about future skill levels in

Table 5.7 World Enterprise Survey: regulations, taxes and business licensing indicators, 2012

Regulations, taxes and business licensing indicators	Russian Federation	Small firms	Medium-sized firms	Large firms	EEA	UMI
Days to obtain import license	47.1	27.6	54.6	49.2	16.7	23.3
Days to obtain construction-related permit	129.6	125.8	131.1	134.4	80.2	83.3
Days to obtain operating license	56.3	46.2	56.8	71.9	26.0	40.9

Source: World Bank (2012).

Key: Excerpt from larger table; EEA = Eastern Europe and Central Asia countries; UMI = Upper Middle Income countries.

Russia are focused more at the secondary level, where the country's participation rate is below the G20 average. Despite large increases in national income invested in education in recent years, expenditure on education represents 5.5 per cent of GDP, a much lower value than the OECD country average (6.3 per cent) (ibid.). Kirill Varlamov, a software developer, expresses a different opinion regarding the business education: 'Education is probably the weakest area of the Russian entrepreneurship ecosystem. We need more programs and higher quality. In particular, we badly need world-class training at MBA level' (Ernst and Young 2013: 5).

Similarly, entrepreneurship has yet to be embedded fully in Russian culture. Fewer than 50 per cent of local respondents agreed that their culture is supportive of entrepreneurship or that it is encouraged as a career choice (ibid.). Russia's entrepreneurship culture is still comparatively young and the broader population has no adequate understanding of the fundamental cycle of entrepreneurship from start-up and growth to IPO and exit or the fact that high business failure rates often characterize thriving business ecosystems. According to the survey of Flash Eurobarometer (2012), in Russia only 48 per cent of the respondents agree that their school education helped them to develop a sense of initiative and a sort of entrepreneurial attitude.

Without this basic knowledge, entrepreneurs have a harder time accessing the resources they need, whether they be employees, clients or investors. In addition, skills shortages are a real bottleneck for some businesses who have difficulty in recruiting people with the right marketing, sales and strategic skills. In order to build a knowledge-based economy, Russia needs to integrate more business elements into its education system (Ernst and Young 2013). As Varlamov further notes: 'We need more people graduating from higher-quality programs and also better business schools' (ibid.)

Financing

In most countries, entrepreneurs complain about the lack of financing. But research in Russia shows that large gaps in financing exist which may be lead to fewer start-ups and less growth potential. In a recent survey, 59 per cent of local entrepreneurs surveyed say that it is difficult to access funding in Russia (Ernst and Young 2013). As is shown in Table 5.8, Russia does exhibit higher levels of Merger and Acquisition (M&A) funding relative to other G20 countries,[12] but this seems to be an exception since venture capital (VC) and IPOs are very limited. Moreover, Russian entrepreneurs are faced with two problems: not only is it difficult to access equity capital, but Russia's banking system is not a viable option for providing initial start-up or growth capital through debt financing.

Civil society

The final and perhaps most fundamental challenge facing Russia's business environment is the development of civil society and the fostering of a culture of 'giving back'. Table 5.9 provides a comparative view of Russia's rankings for the

Table 5.8 Access to funding: Russia and G20 compared

Access to funding	Russia	G20 average	Average for time period
IPO amount invested (% of GDP)	0.01	0.22	2009–11
Domestic credit to private sector (% of GDP)	44.5	99.0	2008–10
Venture capital availability (scale: 1 = impossible to 7 = very easy)	2.3	3.0	2009–11
M&A deal value (% of GDP)	5.0	3.4	2010–12

Source: Ernst & Young Entrepreneurship Barometer 2013 – Russia. (Original sources: The World Bank, Dealogic, IMF, World Economic Forum.)

Table 5.9 Worldwide Governance Indicators for Russia, 1998–2012

Governance indicator	1998	2004	2012
Voice and Accountability	24.13	30.29	19.91
Political Stability	14.90	7.69	20.85
Governance Effectiveness	21.95	43.90	40.67
Regulatory Quality	30.39	50.00	38.76
Rule of Law	18.18	19.14	23.70
Control of Corruption	17.56	25.37	16.27

Source: World Bank (2013).

Key: *Voice and Accountability*: measures political, civil and human rights; *Political Stability* measures the likelihood of violent treats to, or changes in, government including terrorism; *Government Effectiveness* measures the competence of the bureaucracy and the quality of public service delivery; *Regulatory Quality* measures the incidence of market-unfriendly policies; *Rule of Law* measures the quality ofcontract enforcement, the police, and the courts, as well as the likelihood of crime and violence; *Control of Corruption* measures the exercise of public power for private gain, including both petty and grand corruption and state capture.Yearly scores shown in percentile ranks (0–100).

Worldwide Governance Indicators in the 1998–2004–2012 time period. Russia's scores for four out of six indicators has declined since 2004 in the critical areas of Voice and Accountability, Government Effectiveness, Regulatory Quality and Control of Corruption. This is of great concern for Russia's future as an entrepreneurial society. Without the fundamental assurance of a stable, reliable and functioning governance structure, entrepreneurial activities will be prevented from reaching their full potential. Even though Russia's score has been increasing for two measures, Political Stability and Rule of Law, their overall percentile rank, at 20.85 and 23.70 respectively, is still at comparatively low levels.

Another aspect of civil society that needs to be developed in Russia is philanthropy and the concept of 'giving back' to society. At present, this is still in its infancy, but there are some positive signs of development. The female entrepreneur Elena Masolova, referred to earlier, has become active in improving the start-up environment in Russia through founding AddVenture, a seed investment fund. She is also a partner at Ruvento, an accelerator and venture fund. When entrepreneurs are successful, it is important that they also use their wealth for greater social good. The Giving Pledge is a voluntary campaign that invites the world's wealthiest individuals and families to commit to giving more than half of their wealth to philanthropy or charitable causes either during their lifetime or in their will. It was initiated by Bill Gates and Warren Buffett in 2010 and at the time of writing has more than 60 participating billionaires. In 2013, Vladimir Potanin became the first Russian to sign the Giving Pledge.

Conclusions

Russia possesses a large and expanding consumer market and in the short and medium term there will be abundant opportunities for Russian start-ups. The low starting point of Russia's business environment also provides plenty of room for improvements through the copying of western business models and adapting them to the Russian market which will remain a large and profitable market. The institutional environment has also been improving for entrepreneurs through government initiatives such as the ASI, VC funding through Rusano and funding targeting high-tech start-ups. The various attempts to fill the large funding gaps by the government signals a positive shift in public policy. In addition, the appointment of an ombudsman to safeguard entrepreneur rights indicates that there are further attempts to support an entrepreneurship culture. The fact that Moscow is identified as one of the world's top 20 start-up hubs is also a very positive sign. It indicates that many conditions in Russia are right for developing an entrepreneurial society.

However, some fundamental challenges still need to be addressed in order to ensure the viability of private business and an entrepreneurial society. These include creating conditions that foster business growth, and improving the standard of entrepreneurial education and financing for all stages of business development. Corruption and civil society impact entrepreneurial society in the most profound and fundamental ways. Corruption acts as a deterrent for potential business start-ups or business growth. It results in an absence of start-ups and also the proliferation of businesses that do not grow. Civil society provides the stability and assurance to entrepreneurs that they will be able to reap the benefits of their business activities or, if they fail, that they will have the opportunity to try again. Ideally, it ensures the rule of law so that businesses do not have to worry about arbitrary and or politically motivated interference. Russia does not ensure these yet.

The new generation of young, bright and enthusiastic entrepreneurs in Moscow provides hope for the development of a productive entrepreneurial society in Russia. If they succeed, they will be the mentors, angel investors and entrepreneurial advocates for future generations. The presence of individual entrepreneurial drive is clear and by reducing and removing corruption and regulatory interference from the equation, more start-ups will follow. To see them grow and flourish, however, Russia must be committed to taking further steps to improve its business environment.

Notes

1 In 2013, an amnesty for thousands for Russian businessmen convicted of economic crimes was announced but in reality affected only 12,000 while thousands more remain behind bars (Boyde 2013).
2 The Global Entrepreneurship Monitor (2013) uses what it calls 'Total Entrepreneurship Activity' (TEA) to measure business start-up activities. TEA is the percentage of 18–64 population who are either a nascent entrepreneur or owner-manager of a new business (no more than 42 months old).
3 Sweden's Central Bank's Prize in Economic Sciences in Memory of Alfred Nobel, established in 1968.
4 See, for instance, North (1990, 1994, 1997).
5 Brazil, Russia, India and China.
6 OPORA ROSSII is a civil organization for small and medium-sized enterprises in Russia. It organizes about 450,000 entrepreneurs.
7 An informal investor refers to a person who invests his or her own money in a start-up company. In return, this individual receives convertible debt or ownership equity in the company.
8 In terms of availability, affordability and quality. This indicator also includes the role of the extended family in providing childcare.
9 These data are from 2010 and is originally from the Women's Economic Opportunity Report by the Economist Intelligence Unit. It is used in the 2013 Gender-GEDI Index.
10 In contrast to a firm that is initially focused on the domestic market and then expands its operations internationally, a born-global firm is a venture launched to exploit a global niche from the first day of its operations (Kudina et al. 2008).
11 The high-profile case of Mikhail Khodorkovsky, founder of Yukos, is an example of this. Though he was charged with tax evasion, the political motivations for his arrest and imprisonment were obvious.
12 G20 countries: Argentina, Australia, Brazil, Canada, China, France, Germany, India, Indonesia, Italy, Japan, Korean Republic, Mexico, Russia, Saudi Arabia, South Africa, Turkey, United Kingdom, United States.

References

Acs, Z., Szerb, L. and Autio, E. (2013) *The Global Entrepreneurship and Development Index (GEDI)*, Cheltenham: Edward Elgar.

Aidis, R., Acs, Z., Weeks, J., Szerb, L. and Lloyd, A. (2013) The Gender-Global Entrepreneurship and Development Index, Executive Report. Online. Available: http://dell.to/1pP12KR (accessed 6 May 2014).

Aidis, R. and Estrin S. (2013) 'Institutions, Incentives and Entrepreneurship', in Acs, Z., Szerb, L. and Autio, E. (eds), *The Global Entrepreneurship and Development Index (GEDI)*, Cheltenham: Edward Elgar, pp. 18–25.

Aidis, R., Estrin, S. and Mickiewicz, T. (2008) 'Institutions and Entrepreneurship Development in Russia: a Comparative Perspective', *Journal of Business Venturing*, 23: 656–72.

Aidis, R. and Adachi, Y. (2007) 'Russia: Firm Entry and Survival Barriers', *Economic Systems*, 31: 391–411.

Anderson, R. (2014) 'Female Russian Mobile Tech Entrepreneur Adapts to Succeed'. Online. Available: http://thewaywomenwork.com/2014/02/female-russian-mobile-tech-entrepreneur-adapts-succeed/ (accessed 6 May 2014).

Bates, T. (1990) 'Entrepreneur Human Capital Inputs and Small Business Longevity', *The Review of Economics and Statistics*, 72(4): 551–9.

Baumol, W. (1990) 'Entrepreneurship: Productive, Unproductive and Destructive', *The Journal of Political Economy*, 98(5): 893–921.

Boyde, E. (2013) 'Opportunities Multiply for Russia's Entrepreneurs', *Financial Times*, 17 November.

DiMaggio, P. and Powell, W. (1983) 'The Iron Cage Revisited: Institutional Isomorphism and Collective Rationality in Organizational Fields', *American Sociological Review*, 47: 147–60.

Djankov, S., Miguel, E., Qian, Y., Roland, G. and Zhuravskaya, E. (2004) Who are Russia's Entrepreneurs?, Mimeo, World Bank.

Economist Intelligence Unit (2010) 'Women's Economic Opportunity Report'. Online. Available: http://graphics.eiu.com/upload/WEO_June_2010_final.xls (accessed 6 May 2014).

Ernst and Young (2013) 'The G20 Entrepreneurship Barometer 2013 – Russia Profile'. Online. Available: www.ey.com/RU/en/Services/Strategic-Growth-Markets/EY-G20-country-report-2013-Russia (accessed 6 May 2014).

Feige, E. (1997) 'Underground Activity and Institutional Change: Productive, Protective and Predatory Behavior in Transition Economies', in Tilly, C., Nelson, J. and Walker, L. (eds), *Transforming Communist Political Economies*, Washington, DC: National Academy Press, pp. 21–34.

Flash Eurobarometer (2012) 'Entrepreneurship in the EU and Beyond', *Flash Eurobarometer*. Online. Available: http://ec.europa.eu/public_opinion/flash/fl_354_en.pdf (accessed 6 May 2014).

Global Entrepreneurship Monitor (GEM) (2013) Data. Online. Available: www.gemconsortium.org.

Johnson, S., McMillan, J. and Woodruff, C. (2000) 'Entrepreneurs and the Ordering of Institutional Reform', *Economics of Transition*, 1: 1–36.

Kesby, R. (2012) 'Why Russia Locks Up So Many Entrepreneurs', *BBC News Magazine*, 4 July.

Kudina, A., Yip, G.S. and Barkema, H.G. (2008) 'Born Global', *Business Strategy Review*, 19(4): 38–44.

McMillan, J. and Woodruff, C. (1999), 'Interfirm Relationships and Informal Credit in Vietnam', *Quarterly Journal of Economics,* 114(4): 1285–320.

Naumov, M. (2013) 'Why Young Russians Live and Breathe Entrepreneurship', *Forbes*, 13 March.

North, D. (1990) *Institutions, Institutional Change and Economic Performance*, Cambridge: Cambridge University Press.

North, D. (1994) 'Economic Performance Over Time', *American Economic Review*, 84: 359–68.

North, D. (1997) 'The Contribution of the New Institutional Economics to an Understanding of the Transitional Problem', Wider Annual Lectures, United Nations University World Institute for Development Economics Research, Helsinki.

North, D. (2005) *Understanding the Process of Economic Change*, Princeton: Princeton University Press.

OECD (2012) 'Country Note: Education at a Glance, OECD Indicators 2012, Russian Federation'. Online. Available: www.oecd.org/education/EAG2012%20-%20Country%20 note%20-%20Russian%20Federation.pdf (accessed 6 May 2014).

Risner, E. (2012) 'Young Russian Female Entrepreneur Takes on Tech', *The Way Women Work*, 20 July. Online. Available: http://thewaywomenwork.com/2012/07/young-russian-female-entrepreneur-takes-on-tech/ (accessed 6 May 2014).

Startup Genome (2012) Startup Ecosytem Report Part 1. Online. Available: www.start-upgenome.co/ (accessed 6 May 2014).

Transparency International (2013) *Corruption Perceptions Index 2013*. Online. Available: http://cpi.transparency.org/cpi2013/results/ (accessed 6 May 2014).

Thurik, R. and Wennekers, S. (1999) 'Linking Entrepreneurship and Economic Growth', *Small Business Economics*, 13: 27–55.

Vasileva, Y. (2013) 'Russia's Small Businesses Squeezed, Eye Exit', AP. Online. Available: https://news.yahoo.com/russias-small-businesses-squeezed-eye-exit-065520118--finance.html (accessed 6 May 2014).

World Bank (2012) 'Enterprise Survey: Russian Federation Country Profile 2012'. Online. Available: www.enterprisesurveys.org/~/media/FPDKM/EnterpriseSurveys/Documents/Profiles/English/Russia-2012 (accessed 6 May 2014).

World Bank (2013) *Worldwide Governance Indicators 1996–2012*. Online. Available: http://data.worldbank.org/data-catalog/worldwide-governance-indicators (accessed 6 May 2014).

6 The role of institutions in the Russian economy

Susanne Oxenstierna

Following a strong recovery in 2010 after the 2008–9 economic crisis, the Russian economy has shown signs of declining growth in 2012–13. Growth in 2012 was 3.4 per cent, and in 2013, 1.3 per cent, which is well below the expectations in earlier official strategies and forecasts. Part of the explanation for this decline lies in the stagnation of global demand for Russian commodities and it is quite clear that the Russian growth model, which is largely based on the growth of foreign demand for Russian hydrocarbons, is now exhausted. Future growth requires that productivity increases through structural change, investment, organizational modernization and technical innovation. The confidence crisis following the Ukrainian crisis in early 2014 has added to the systemic problems and makes the prospects for the Russian economy even more uncertain, as is manifested in capital flight and a weak propensity to invest. Growth forecasts for 2014–15 vary between a decline in GDP to growth of just 1–2 per cent (World Bank 2014a).

Is the present politicized economic system able to meet the challenges and restore growth? Can it facilitate a more efficient allocation of resources among sectors, less resource waste, innovation, productivity increases and stronger competition? Are stronger institutions part of the remedy? Following the shift away from a command economy in the 1990s and the consolidation of the market reforms at the beginning of the 2000s, the Russian economy has experienced re-nationalizations and increasing political interference. As a result, in early 2014, the Russian economic system is a hybrid of, on the one hand, the old Soviet heritage and state intervention and, on the other, a market economy, with private ownership, modern and sound budgetary rules, and accession to the World Trade Organization (WTO). In addition, this economic model is characterised by an increasing shadow economy and widespread corruption. Liberal economists in Russia argue for a renewed market reform for Russia to allow it to compete in the global environment, overcome capacity constraints and support innovation. They have also started to emphasize the need for real democracy to enable modernization (Åslund 2012: 382).

The purpose of this chapter is to analyse the systemic characteristics of economic development in Russia after 2009 and to assess the potential of the economic system under Vladimir Putin to resolve the impediments to future growth, in particular by improvements in the economic institutions. As a starting point, the chapter uses a development of the model of Gaddy and Ickes (2010; see also Chapter 2) on 'rent addiction' and the 'rent management system' to create a framework for the discussion of how different parts of the economy may be affected by market-oriented institutions. Hence, the emphasis of the analysis does not lie on rent addiction in itself but on its effects on the parts of the economy still under market forces, 'the new private sector', which has been added to the model. The nature of institutions important for economic growth is investigated using the *Worldwide Governance Indicators* (WGI 2014). These institutions are relatively weak in Russia because of the shortage of democracy. The chapter discusses the implications of the 'democracy shortage' on economic development, particularly through the restrictions on civil society and generally weak channels of 'voice' for citizens and organizations.

The chapter is organized as follows: The first section presents a simplified model of the economic system and analyses the implications of rent addiction and rent management for the rest of the economy. The second section discusses the quality and development of economic institutions and other business indicators in Russia. The third section explores the role of civil society for economic growth and the final, fourth, section draws the conclusions.

The economic system under Vladimir Putin

In 2002, the European Union (EU) proclaimed that Russia was a market economy (EU Commission 2007: 5) and ended most technical assistance in the economic field. However, despite the dramatic change of the economic system at the beginning of the transition, throughout its transformation towards market and democracy, Russia has retained aspects of the old Soviet economy. When prices and trade were liberalized in 1992, a new private sector began to emerge, driven by new entrepreneurs. Trade was the activity in which many of these gained their initial capital. The result of this change is that at present over 20 per cent of Russian GDP comes from small and medium-sized enterprises (SMEs), which account for around 22 per cent of total employment (OPORA 2010). Some of these new private companies have even grown into big corporations. Yet this is still a very low share of GDP for SMEs since in most developed economies, a share of over 50 per cent would be expected. However, in Russia, the informal sector plays a large role in the economy and, since 2012, several policy measures, such as the increase in social taxes, have led many SMEs to de-register and continue their activity informally. The role of the small-scale sector may therefore be larger than is suggested by official statistics (see a further discussion on the informal sector in Chapter 3 and on SMEs and entrepreneurship in Russia in Chapter 5).

However, parallel to this market-oriented development, large Soviet-type companies, sometimes privatized but mostly state-owned or state-controlled, have survived in the defence sector and other parts of machine building and traditional heavy industry. These companies have adopted a variety of survival strategies to cope with the transition. As described by Gaddy and Ickes (2002), in the 1990s, barter chains and a 'virtual economy' emerged that kept these companies alive.

The labour market was another area where adjustments took their particular Soviet course. Prior to the start of the economic reforms in 1991, labour market experts were convinced that market reform would lead to a considerable displacement of workers and high unemployment in Russia. At the time, predictions of unemployment rates of around 25 per cent were common (Gimpelson and Kapelyushnikov 2013: 693–4). However, this did not happen in Russia. Instead, the main part of the labour market adjustment took place through wage flexibility. Wages fell dramatically while employment fell only marginally and unemployment rose slowly.[1] The phenomenon of 'wage arrears' is another specific characteristic of Russia's labour market. It means that labour is not laid off, but instead that wages are not paid and, in the best cases, workers are paid in kind. This has kept the rate of open unemployment low, but wage arrears are an alien form of adjustment compared to what usually occurs in a western capitalist market economy, where labour market adjustment takes the form of unemployment and the reallocation of workers to more productive sectors. During the 2009 crisis, wage arrears increased and real wages decreased, while unemployment even declined, which shows that a large part of the economy is not competitive (Oxenstierna 2009: 20–1).

In the 2000s, there was a surge in oil prices and growth picked up. This implied an improvement in the fiscal situation and Russia entered a period of high growth during which it was possible to subsidise inefficient companies with low productivity.[2] However, in 2009, this inefficiency became very costly and more problematic due to the economic crisis and the fact that financial and real resources had become scarce. At first, it seemed that the Russian government intended to address these problems with then President Dmitry Medvedev's modernization programme, but since Vladimir Putin resumed the presidency in 2012, the 'Soviet-type sector' has regained government support both morally and financially, and instead of energy, IT and pharmaceuticals, quoted by Medvedev as core industries for the modernization, the defence industry is seen as a driver in the attempt to increase growth and innovation (Oxenstierna 2009, 2012; Putin 2012). However, assessments of the Russian defence industry show that it is both obsolete and inefficient. In its report to the Duma Defence Commission in 2012 the Russian Audit Chamber noted that 30 per cent of the defence industry companies were loss-making and that only 20 per cent of the companies were deemed to be in such a shape that they could be modernized. According to the Audit Chamber, the remaining 50 per cent of the industry are in such a state that any restructuring would be meaningless. Instead, it would be better to build new companies and replace them (Oxenstierna 2013: 114).

Soft budget constraints and soft credit prevail and obviously conserve the old industrial structure. Why is the subsidized sector maintained and why is it so difficult to modernize it? There are several reasons for this. First of all, it is evident that during his election campaign, Putin made promises to regions dominated by such companies to continue to support them. In Russia, there are still so-called monotowns, cities or even regions that are dependent on one single company. It is estimated that there are around 400 of these, of which half are big energy and exporting companies, and half belong to sectors that are problematic (Oxenstierna

2011: 8). These companies fulfil a social role and it is difficult to close them because there are no other employers in the city or region. The relative geographical isolation of many defence companies has contributed further to immobilizing the workforce, for which there are few alternative job openings (Oxenstierna and Westerlund 2013: 15–17).

The rent-dependent economy

The more general explanation for the continuing existence of loss-making firms in the economy is that they are an important part of Putin's power and control system and also part of what Clifford Gaddy and Barry Ickes characterize as 'rent addiction' in Russian society.[3] The concept of 'rents' refers to the profits earned from owning or controlling an asset, usually natural resources. In the Russian case, these are generated primarily by the extraction and exports of commodities such as oil and gas. Rents are redistributed by the regime and Gaddy and Ickes also introduce the concept of a 'rent management system (RMS)', which means that rents are distributed to where they are needed to balance the power elites. In the model advanced by Gaddy and Ickes, the use of rents to subsidize loss-making companies creates 'addicts' that demand more and more rents and, since many people are employed in these enterprises and they represent important political support for the regime, this makes it impossible to get out of the vicious circle. Rent addiction creates a distorted allocation of resources, inefficiency and excessive costs of production that are borne by all actors.

The rent management system is a heritage from the Soviet era when, for ideological reasons, extra money such as oil rents in periods of high oil prices could not be spent on private capital or consumption goods by the power elites. Opening a factory and spending the money on productive assets was possible, however. In addition, the advantage of productive assets, in comparison with financial assets or consumption, is that they can be used to extract more rents over a long period of time since they employ workers and have a need for investment. The system of rent management is an important part of Putin's power vertical and one rationale behind the inefficiency that prevails in the Russian economy. Rents may be collected by the state in the form of taxes. They may also be collected and redistributed in the form of the excessive costs for inputs and services, such as high prices for railway transport, or high-cost construction which is typical for companies in the rent-dependent sector (see Figure 2.1 in Chapter 2). The indirect costs of lack of infrastructure and other societal services also affect the economy and create extra costs for all economic actors.

In this study, the emphasis of the analysis does not lie on rent addiction in itself but on its effects on other parts of the economy. In addition to the 'rent-creating sector' and the 'addicts', here named the 'rent-dependent sector', a third sector, called the 'new private sector', has been added to the model. The 'new private sector' represents the SMEs, the parts of the economy that are not directly involved in the rent management system but operate on the market. This is the part of the economy that is most affected by prevailing market institutions. Figure 6.1

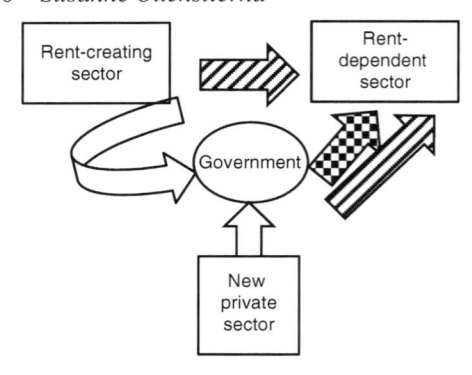

Figure 6.1 Schematic model of a rent-dependent economy.

Notes: Transparent/white arrows – tax payments. Checked arrow – subsidies. Striped/shaded arrows – extra payments to rent-dependent sector due to high monopoly prices and high costs.

Source: The author.

depicts a simplified model of a rent-dependent economy consisting of four sectors: the government, the rent creating sector, the rent-dependent sector, and the new private sector. The rent creating sector earns rents by selling commodities, in Russia predominantly oil and gas. It pays taxes to the government [transparent/white arrow] and rents are redistributed by the government to the rent-dependent sector in the form of subsidies, transfers and state orders [checked arrow]. However, the state also redistributes rents when it procures goods and services from the rent-dependent sector or invests in this sector by paying a high price due to inefficiency and excessive costs in the rent-dependent sector [striped arrow]. The rent creation sector also has rents directly extracted by the rent-dependent sector when it buys goods, invests or lend money directly to rent-dependent companies [striped arrow].

The new private sector, consisting mainly of SMEs, operates in a market framework and pays taxes [transparent/white arrow]. It is also indirectly affected by the rent management system through high cost levels, the lack of infrastructure, and other aspects, but it is not a formal part of the rent management system. This is a reason why the conditions for SMEs have been highly neglected and many times worsened under the present regime.

Types of boundaries and control

Rent addiction and rent management imply that large parts of the economy are controlled by political forces rather than by market forces (Figure 6.2). The rent creating sector is dependent on external markets and the rules prevailing there, which means, for instance, that stronger competition rules on export markets will affect the behaviour of rent creating companies abroad and have an impact on their costs and revenues. The influence of external markets is depicted by the oval with

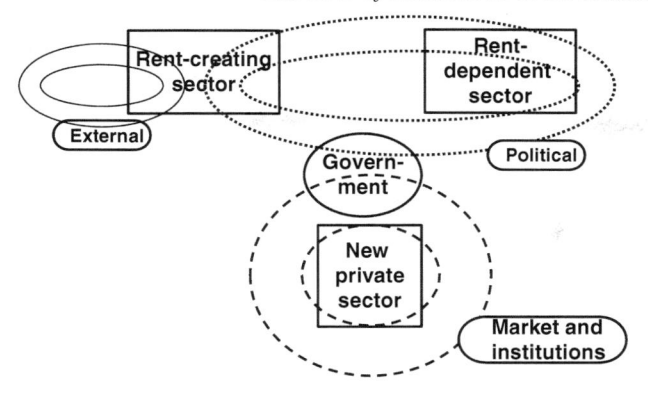

Figure 6.2 Types of boundaries and control in a rent-dependent economy.

Notes: Oval with whole line – 'controlled by external markets'. Oval with dotted line – 'control by Putin and the rent management system'. Circle with dashed line – boundaries set by market and institutions.

Source: The author.

the whole line labelled 'external'. However, the oil and gas companies are under political control at home and need to follow political directives on the domestic scene. The rent-dependent sector is entirely under political control. The exercised political control is depicted in Figure 6.2 by the oval with a dotted line labelled 'political'. The new private sector is the only sector that can truly be influenced by market forces, economic policy and market oriented institutions such as rule of law and competition. The control of markets and institutions is illustrated by the circle with a dashed line.

When a substantial part of the economy is controlled by a political rather than an economic rationale raising productivity and efficiency in the economy becomes difficult since it is not the goal of the system. It follows that the role of market institutions in the economy is limited and their effect severely constrained.

Are stronger institutions a remedy?

Institutions are a set of basic principles essential for the economic system to work that are upheld by structures in the economy (Ericson 2013: 59).[4] For instance, competition is protected by laws that are followed up by state agencies such as an anti-monopoly or a consumer protection agency. Similarly, free trade, which is considered vital for growth and development, is reflected in a country's trade policy, protected by multilateral agreements and upheld by international organizations such as the WTO. It is evident that the institutions supporting a market economy differ from those found in the Soviet command economy. However, it deserves to be noted that even though the formal institutions collapsed quite quickly in the 1990s, the informal institutions of the Soviet system have mostly remained intact throughout the transition, and this has disturbed the modelling of the new market-oriented institutions in Russia. It follows that the institutional environment for transitional Russia has largely been formed by Soviet attitudes rather than by the formal western models on which market institutions are based (ibid.).

The politicized economic model introduced under Putin has further aggravated the difficulty in developing a fully market-oriented institutional framework. As was presented above and can be seen in Figure 6.1, the economic model has three sectors, where it is the 'new private sector' that would primarily profit from better market institutions. This sector could grow if the business climate, entry and competition improved and governance became more business-friendly. The rent-dependent sector, however, would not gain from increased market orientation. It defies competition and is better off with the informal rules that give it preferential treatment on a non-market basis. The rent creation sector with its dual framework – the external market on the one hand and the politicized rent distribution on the other – could gain from a better market allocation on the domestic market; however, since this sector also suffers from efficiency problems, stronger competition from private companies may not be readily accepted.

Taking the temperature of Russia's institutions

Russia's deficient institutions are reflected in the *Worldwide Governance Indicators* (WGI 2014). The WGI project constructs aggregate indicators of six broad dimensions of governance. The six aggregate indicators are based on 31 underlying data sources reporting the perceptions of governance of a large number of survey respondents and expert assessments worldwide:

- Political stability and absence of violence/terrorism;
- Voice and accountability;
- Government effectiveness;
- Regulatory quality;
- Rule of law;
- Control of corruption.

The aggregated estimate of governance lies in the range between –2.5, very weak, and +2.5, very strong. I will not comment here on the indicator 'Political Stability and Absence of Violence and Terrorism'. However, the last four indicators reflect the quality of vital market-supporting institutions, and the indicator 'Voice and Accountability' reflects the degree of democracy and the possibility of making politicians responsible.

Figure 6.3 describes regulatory quality and government efficiency. As can be seen, both of these indicators improved dramatically at the beginning of the 2000s. This was under Putin's first presidency and the time of the 'Gref plan' which, to a large extent, consolidated the reforms of the 1990s. Both these indicators deteriorated, however, in the mid-2000s during Putin's second term and have since stabilized at around –0.4.

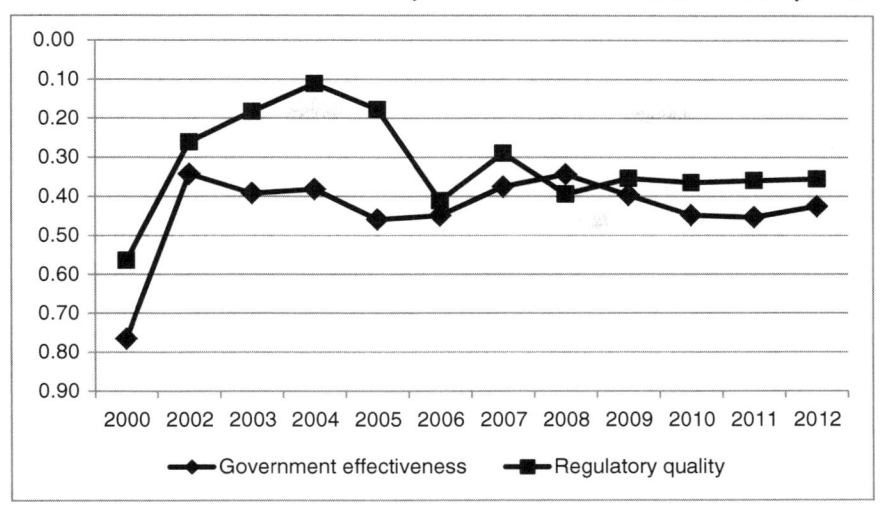

Figure 6.3 Government effectiveness and regulatory quality, Russia, 2000–12.

Source: WGI (2014).

Note: The estimate lies between –2.5, very weak, and +2.5, very strong.

Figure 6.4 depicts the development of rule of law and control of corruption. On both of these indicators, Russia scores much worse than it does for both government effectiveness and regulatory quality. Rule of law improved from a low of –1.2 at the beginning of the 2000s to about –0.9, where it remained until 2008, when it improved again slightly to over –0.8. Control of corruption, however, has deteriorated since the improvement in 2002–3 and is now below its value at the beginning of the 2000s.

Corruption is usually defined as the misuse of public office for private gain. It comes in many varieties – from the extortion of bribes and kickbacks from businessmen and citizens to the embezzlement of budget funds (Treisman 2013: 209). The worsening of the control of corruption WGI indicator is accompanied by an inferior rank in the Corruption Perception Index (CPI) of Transparency International (TI). As shown by Table 6.1, in 2013, Russia's rank in the TI CPI was 127th of the 177 countries surveyed with a score of 28. TI considers that a CPI under 50, on a scale from 0 (highly corrupt) to 100 (highly clean), indicates a serious problem with corruption. This rank is considerably worse than it was in 2001, when it stood at 79, although, at that time, Russia's score was worse, at 23. This reflects the fact that a country's ranking is dependent on which other countries are included in the survey and how they score. In 2013, several countries have the same score and rank as Russia: Azerbaijan, Gambia, Lebanon, Madagascar, Mali, Nicaragua and Pakistan. The only countries in the former Soviet space that have a worse CPI than Russia are Kazakhstan, which ranks 140th (with a score of 26), Ukraine, which ranks 144th (with a score of 25) and the Central Asian Republics.

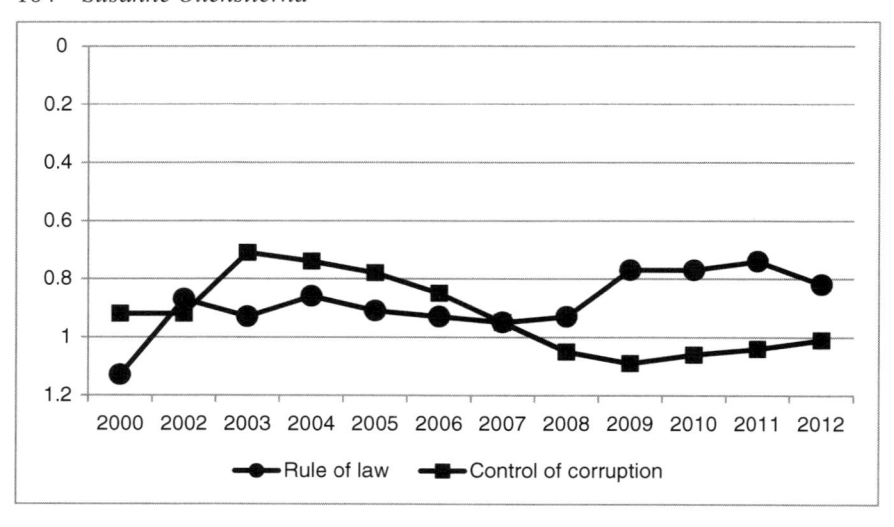

Figure 6.4 Rule of law and control of corruption, Russia, 2000–12.

Source: WGI (2014).

Note: The estimate lies between –2.5, very weak, and +2.5, very strong.

Table 6.1 Russia's Corruption Perception Index and rank

	2001	2002	2003	2004	2005	2006	2007	2008	2009	20010	2011	2012	2013
CPI score	23	27	27	28	24	25	23	21	22	21	24	28	28
Rank	79	71	86	90	126	121	143	147	146	154	143	133	127

Source: Transparency International (2014).

That citizens have voice, that is, the opportunity to voice their opinions and influence their situation, and that politicians can be made accountable are essential ingredients in any democracy. In Putin's Russia, the voice and accountability indicator has seen a steady decline since Putin first came into power in 2000, when the estimate stood at –0.4. By 2012, however, it was down at –1.0 (Figure 6.5). I would argue that the low voice and accountability indicator largely explains the low score in other WGI indicators such as 'rule of law' and 'control of corruption'. The declining trend in the voice and accountability indicator summarizes the increasing democracy shortage in Russia and implies that citizens have very limited opportunities to influence policies in their country.

The analysis of Russia's institutions using the WGI shows that the institutional framework is weak and has deteriorated in recent years. The fact that such a large part of the economy is governed by political goals and the leadership's need to balance power, rather than by economic logic, makes it difficult to anticipate

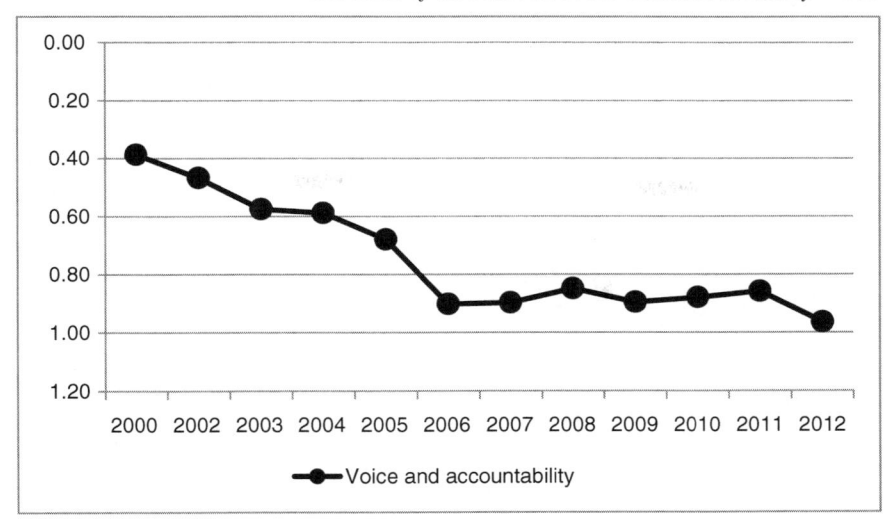

Figure 6.5 Voice and accountability, Russia, 2000–12.

Source: WGI (2014).

Note: The estimates lies between –2.5, very weak, and +2.5, very strong.

improvements in the institutional framework. Better institutions would benefit the 'new private sector' that would get better opportunities to expand under a stronger rule of law and less corruption. However, in the case of the rent-dependent sector, which relies on its political contacts, stronger institutions would be a disadvantage (see Figures 6.1–6.2).

The business climate

In his initial economic decree, Putin (2012) called for an improvement of the rating of Russia in the World Bank Doing Business Index from 120th place in 2011 to 50th in 2015 and 20th in 2018. Thus, it is pertinent to ask: How do Russian businesses experience the business climate? In recent years, various surveys have been conducted to investigate this question. The European Bank of Reconstruction and Development (EBRD) and the World Bank periodically poll executives of firms in transition countries in the Business Environment and Enterprise Performance Survey (BEEPS) which has existed since 1999 (Treisman 2013: 210). The 2012 BEEPS[5] for Russia nationally and for 37 regions shows that most enterprises in Russia identify corruption, the lack of access to finance and the absence of skills in the workforce as the main constraints on doing business. Medium-sized enterprises cite workforce skills as their main constraint ahead of access to finance. Large enterprises primarily suffer from lack of properly skilled workers followed by corruption. Innovative companies have more problems with the business environment as a whole than an average enterprise (BEEPS 2012). In some regions, deficient infrastructure – transport, electricity, and telecommunications – is a first-hand binding constraint. However, tax administration, business licensing, and customs and trade regulations do not seem to be perceived as constraints (ibid.). The latter point at measures intended to ease the starting business procedure and tax payments over the years have had some effect.

The World Bank's 'Ease of Doing Business Index' is used widely to compare the business climate in different countries and it provides a ranking of the relative attractiveness of the business environment. This is the index to which Putin chose to relate his business climate targets. Judging from this index, the business climate in Russia is not very attractive. In 2013, an improvement to the 92rd rank (from 120th in 2011) was registered (out of a total of 189 countries). The index has ten different aspects that are listed in Table 6.2 and the separate rank is indicated after each indicator. As seen in Table 6.2, only in enforcing contracts and resolving insolvency is Russia among the top 50 economies, the rank sought by 2015 according to Putin's plan. Russia is flanked by Croatia (89), Albania (90), Barbados (91), Serbia (93), Jamaica (94) and the Maldives (95). China is ranked 96th (World Bank 2014b).

If Russia is compared to the group of 26 countries in Eastern Europe and the former Soviet space, it has a total rank of 21, outperforming only Serbia, Ukraine, Bosnia and Herzegovina, Tajikistan and Uzbekistan. Russia's partners in the Customs Union, Belarus, with a global rank of 63, and Kazakhstan with 50, do much better, with rankings of 11 and 8, respectively, among the former socialist countries. Moreover, in this entourage, Russia scores best on enforcing

Table 6.2 Russia in World Bank 'Ease of Doing Business Index', 2013

	Rank among all 189 countries	Rank among 26 EE & CA countries*
Ease of Doing Business Rank	**92**	**21**
Starting a business	88	22
Dealing with construction permits	178	22
Getting electricity	117	14
Registering property	17	7
Getting credit	109	22
Protecting investors	115	21
Paying taxes	56	9
Trading across borders	157	21
Enforcing contracts	10	1
Resolving insolvency	55	8

Source: World Bank (2014b).

Note: *EE – Eastern Europe; CA – Central Asia.

contracts (followed by Belarus as second), registering property and paying taxes (see Table 6.2).

Thus, despite years of measures and legislation aimed at making the business climate more appealing, Russia still finds itself near the bottom of the East European and CIS league and sits somewhere in the middle of the 189 countries ranked in the index. The reason is that such a large part of the economy is part of the rent management system and that the large companies and strong economic players in Russia are not particularly interested in changing the situation. Making it easier for new companies to enter the market and thereby getting competitors is not in their interest. Rich companies can manage the high cost environment and loss-making companies rely on their political contacts and their lobbying strength.

The shortage of democracy and civil society

The weak rule of law and voice and accountability in the Russian economy reflects the fact that the separation of powers between the legislative, executive and judicial branches of state power, defined in the Russian Constitution from 1993, is not actually manifested in Russian society. The executive branch, primarily represented by the president, is involved in all branches of power and there is no independent judiciary. Developments with regard to diminishing citizens' rights and basic freedoms follow from this breach of the constitution. Putin showed a positive attitude towards civil society in his political programme in 1999, but when in power he tried to bring independent NGOs under state control. The Civic Assembly initiated in November 2001 was an attempt to establish platforms of communications between the state and NGOs but it failed (Siegert 2011: 538–9). A complete breakdown in the dialogue between the state and civil society came with the arrest of Mikhail Khodorkovsky, who had used the Open Russia Foundation to finance NGO projects and the 'Orange Revolution' in Ukraine. From the Kremlin's point of view, NGOs supported by western donors played an important part in the events in Ukraine (ibid.). During Putin's second term control over civil society increased.

The restrictions on the freedom of speech and assembly in Russia, imposed since 2012, the lack of independent media and the crackdown on civil society organizations imply that there is very limited room for Russian citizens to voice their opinions and influence the direction of social and economic development.[6] Instead, development in Russia is again unilaterally managed from above and politicians are not accountable to their electorate in any efficient way. Under the present leadership, economic development will be restricted by the continuation of the subsidizing of unprofitable rent-addicted industry and the redistribution of oil rents. The main goal of Putin is to remain in power and secure his position, and the rent distribution system is needed to regulate the power balance between different groups. This is quite a different goal compared to stimulating growth and supporting innovative new companies.

The importance of 'voice' and civil society

The concept of 'voice' in the economic literature comes from the theory first advanced in *Exit, Voice and Loyalty* (Hirschman 1970). Hirschman takes standard economic theory as his starting point and attempts to explain behaviour that is not predicted by standard economic models. Market actors express 'voice' when they try to influence the quality of goods and services instead of just choosing another provider. 'Exit' is the predicted behaviour of an economic agent that is dissatisfied with a good or a service, at least in a competitive environment where there are alternatives.[7]

Translated into a political setting, 'voice' is how citizens try to influence the political elites and get their main concerns onto the political agenda. In democracies, there is a mutual interest in effective channels of voice since power elites and political parties want to stay in power and adjusting to citizens' demands may increase their chances of doing so. Citizens may also choose 'exit' by voting for somebody else. When that is not possible, however, and the space for voice is restricted, exit may take the form of emigration or 'internal emigration' which means that citizens withdraw from political life and do not participate in social activities that require an interface with power structures. They vote with their feet. Internal emigration was a common behaviour in the communist states of the past where political opposition was repressed. Hence, civil society strengthens 'voice' in a society by giving support, structure and sustainability to certain ideas and movements. It strengthens 'voice' and makes individuals refrain from 'exit' by offering organized channels of expression and protest and a party for negotiation with power. For that reason, a strong civil society is seen as an important ingredient of democracy.

What functions could civil society perform and why is it so important also for the economy that people participate in it? Civil society is often associated with its *advocacy* role since it can identify problems that are not addressed by the political elite and bring them to public attention, thereby creating public opinion, awareness and change. In many countries, NGOs have taken on a 'watchdog' function: they monitor consumers' rights, freedom of speech, ecological matters or anti-corruption schemes and generally act as bodies that hold the politicians accountable. These issues are represented both by local civil society organizations and by international NGOs such as Greenpeace, Amnesty and Transparency International.

Economists often refer to civil society when investigating the development of *social capital* (see Glaeser *et al.* 2002). Participation in civil society organizations gives individuals the opportunity to develop as they meet and work with people outside their own group, class or work environment, which strengthens *social cohesion*. Large parts of civil society are engaged in expressive functions, such as book clubs and different networks, which play an important role in forming and diversifying social capital. Furthermore, in many countries, civil society is an important *economic actor* in itself, generating employment and value added. As reported by Ghaus-Pasha (2004: 4–5), a survey of 36 countries by Johns Hopkins University shows that the civil society sector spent on average 5.4 per cent of GDP and employed an equivalent of 4.4 per cent of the economically active population in the period in the surveyed countries 1995–2000. According to another report by Johns Hopkins University (2013), the employment share is as high as 7.4 per cent in the 13 countries examined. The contribution to GDP was 4.5 per cent (ibid.).

Finally, some civil society organizations complement or replace the state in certain functions and *regulations*. In many countries, trade unions and employers' organizations are fully responsible for wage negotiations within a framework set by the state. Another example of the state delegating regulatory functions is the occurrence of certain professional associations that certify their members' right to operate in their profession through conferring a certain title – such as lawyers or auditors – so-called 'self-regulation'.

In Russia, all of these functions of civil society are still in their embryonic state. Due to the present restrictions on the freedom of speech and assembly, organized civil society will not develop. Because real citizen participation is not encouraged, the economy forgoes many initiatives from the population that could improve quality of life and standards of living. When civil society is weak, society has to rely solely on reforms from above and when the regime is neither democratic nor market-oriented, modernization and democratization are far-fetched.

Conclusions

Market institutions play only a limited role in the Russian economy and improving the prospects for growth with 'western' economic policy or improving the institutional framework will be difficult and have a limited effect. Only some parts of the economy profit from market reforms and stronger institutions. The old rent-dependent sector has a high degree of political support. It follows that more substantial political reforms are needed to solve the structural impediments and efficiency problems of the Russian economy. Society needs to become more democratic and more transparent.

The present politicized economic system does not facilitate a more efficient allocation of resources between sectors, less resource waste, productivity increases or stronger competition by enabling the 'entry' of new actors into different areas. Thus, economic growth cannot be restored to previous levels within the present economic system. The World Bank (2014a) expects at best 1.1–1.3 per cent growth in 2014–15 and, in a more pessimistic scenario, a contraction by 1.8 per cent in 2014. The confidence crisis caused by the Ukrainian events in early 2014, causing capital flight and uncertainty regarding to what extent Russia will respect its commitments, has contributed to this picture.

The reforms in the 1990s, and their subsequent consolidation in laws and regulations in the early 2000s, managed to break the hegemony of the Soviet command economy and introduced a private sector and strong market elements into the Russian economy. However, the changes never completely overcame the old Soviet heritage that is embedded in both the infrastructure and the industrial structure. Many Soviet-type enterprises survived, and with them formal and informal behaviour. Even though formal institutions were abolished, informal institutions and networks remained, which has systematically undercut the development of new market-oriented institutions and their supporting social capital.

The remedy to attain stronger growth is to allow the growth of the new private sector, mainly consisting of SMEs. This requires stronger market-oriented institutions. Growing innovative companies need to be able to rely on the primacy of basic institutions such as rule of law, a high quality of governance and that corruption is kept at a reasonable level. They must also be able to access financial resources and profit from a supportive business climate. The old loss-making sector, however, is not interested in changes in that direction and has a strong political leverage to maintain the existing order where personal ties to the political hierarchy rather than competitive business activities can ensure survival. For change to happen, the rent dependence and rent management system needs to be deconstructed, which is not in the interest of the present regime. Redistribution of rents is a vital tool for maintaining political stability. It may be expected, therefore, that political management of the economy and state intervention will continue, with economic stagnation as a result.

The restricted possibilities to voice different opinions, to organize collective action around new ideas and to hold politicians and other decision makers responsible mean that there is no effective reform pressure from below. Instead, improvements in the performance of the economy are entirely dependent on reform initiatives from above, and initiatives that could spur growth are not forthcoming under the present leadership. As a matter of fact, the Russian campaign to destabilize Ukraine may be seen as a way of diverting attention from an already stagnating living standard. The uncertainty it has caused regarding Russia's economy has hurt the confidence in the Russian state as a business partner, however, and made the prospects for growth even gloomier.

The democracy shortage in Russia is thus closely interlinked with the efficiency challenges of the economy. The preferences of the population are not reflected in the direction of economic development since economic policy does not rest on a democratic foundation. Indicators reflecting the institutions 'voice and accountability' have followed a downward trend since Putin's first presidency. Today, Russian society is polarized on many political and economic issues, but civil society is weak and restricted and cannot fulfil its function either as watchdog or as a channel of ideas and entrepreneurship. Without political reform and a market-oriented democratic government, it is difficult to see how the performance of the economy could improve.

Notes

1 High wage flexibility and low sensitivity of employment to fluctuations in output has been a trademark of the Russian labour market in the 2000s as well. GDP doubled between 1998 and 2008, but total employment grew by only 7–8 per cent over this ten-year period (Gimpelson and Kapelyushnikov 2013: 695). Real wages, however, grew by 10–20 per cent annually and cumulatively tripled over this period (ibid.: 701).

2 As an example of low productivity, on SIPRI's lists of the world's 100 largest defence industry companies between 2007 and 2010, the few Russian companies included have between twice and four times as many employees as western companies with comparable sales revenues (Oxenstierna and Westerlund 2013: 17–18).
3 See Chapter 2 in this volume and Gaddy and Ickes (2010, 2013a, 2013b).
4 See also Chapter 4 by Andrei Yakovlev and Chapter 5 by Ruta Aidis on Douglass North's pioneering work on institutions.
5 The survey comprises more than 4,200 randomly selected enterprises.
6 A comprehensive account of the development of Russian civil society in recent years is found in Chapter 10 by Jens Siegert.
7 Hirschman also introduces the concept of 'loyalty' as a bridge between exit and voice. If the individual has a loyalty bond with the organization or company that he/she is dissatisfied with, there is a greater chance that he/she will try to use voice to improve the situation before taking the exit option.

References

Åslund, A. (2012) 'Sergey Glazyev and the Revival of Soviet Economics', *Post-Soviet Affairs*, 29(5): 388–403.

BEEPS (2012) *The Business Environment and Enterprise Performance Survey. The Russian Regions: Results*, EBRD. Online. Available: http://ebrd-beeps.com/wp-content/uploads/2013/09/beeps2012fc_rus.pdf (accessed 6 February 2014).

Ericson, R. (2013) 'Command Economy and its Legacy', in Alexeev, M. and Weber, S., *The Oxford Handbook of the Russian Economy*, Oxford and New York: Oxford University Press, pp. 51–85.

EU Commission (2007) *The European Union and Russia: Close Neighbours, Global Players, Strategic Partners*. Online. Available: http://eeas.europa.eu/russia/docs/russia_brochure07_en.pdf (accessed 20 February 2014).

Gaddy, C.G. and Ickes, B.W. (2002) *Russia's Virtual Economy*, Washington, DC: Brookings Institution Press.

Gaddy, C.G. and Ickes, B.W. (2010) 'Russia after the Global Financial Crisis', *Eurasian Geography and Economics*, 51(3): 281–311.

Gaddy, C.G. and Ickes, B.W. (2013a) 'Russia's Dependence on Resources', in Alexeev, M. and Weber, S., *The Oxford Handbook of the Russian Economy*, Oxford and New York: Oxford University Press, pp. 309–40.

Gaddy, C.G. and Ickes, B.W. (2013b) *Bear Traps on Russia's Road to Modernization*, Abingdon and New York: Routledge.

Ghaus-Pasha, A. (2004) 'Role of Civil Society Organisations in Governance', paper presented at the *6th Global Forum on Reinventing Government Towards Participatory and Transparent Government*, May 2006, Seoul, Republic of Korea. Online. Available: http://unpan1.un.org/intradoc/groups/public/documents/un/unpan019594.pdf (accessed 25 June 2014).

Gimpelson, V. and Kapelyushnikov, R. (2013) 'Labor Market Adjustment: is Russia Different?', in Alexeev, M. and Weber, S., *The Oxford Handbook of the Russian Economy*, Oxford and New York: Oxford University Press, pp. 693–724.

Glaeser, E.L., Labson, D. and Sacerdote, B. (2002) 'An Economic Approach to Social Capital', *Economic Journal*, 112: F437–58.

Hirschman, A.O. (1970) *Exit, Voice and Loyalty*, Cambridge, MA and London, UK: Harvard University Press.

Johns Hopkins University (2013) *The Global Civil Volunteering*. Online. Available: http://ccss.jhu.edu/wp-content/uploads/downloads/2013/04/JHU_Global-Civil-Society-Volunteering_FINAL_3.2013.pdf (accessed 25 June 2014).

OPORA (2010) *Competing for the Future Today: the New Innovation Policy for Russia*, Moscow: OPORA Russia.

Oxenstierna, S. (2009) *The Russian Economy 2009: Steep Decline Despite Crisis management*, FOI-R-2853-SE, Stockholm, December.

Oxenstierna, S. (2011) *Rysk ekonomi och försvarsekonomi 2010: Ökande försvarsutgifter och ambitiösa beväpningsmål*, FOI Memo 3500, February.

Oxenstierna, S. (2012) 'Rysslands ekonomiska modernisering', *Nordisk Östforum*, 26(1): 7–30.

Oxenstierna, S. (2013) 'Defence Spending', in Hedenskog, J. and Vendil Pallin, C. (eds), *Russian Military Capability in a Ten-Year Perspective – 2013*, FOI-R-37–34, Stockholm, December, pp. 103–20.

Oxenstierna, S. and Westerlund, F. (2013) 'Arms Procurement and the Russian Defense Industry', *Journal of Slavic Military Studies*, 26: 1–24.

Putin, V. (2012) 'Podpisan Ukaz o dolgosrochnoi gosudarstvennoi ekonomicheskoi politike', 596, 7 May. Online. Available: http://kremlin.ru/news/15232 (accessed 28 May 2013).

Siegert, J. (2011) 'The Evolution of Civic Activeness', in Lipman, M. and Petrov, N. (eds), *Russia in 2020: Scenarios for the Future*, Washington, DC: Carnegie Endowment for International Peace.

Transparency International (2014) *Corruption Perception Index*. Online. Available: http://cpi.transparency.org/cpi2013/results/ (accessed 24 June 2014).

Treisman, D. (2013) 'Corruption in the Post-communist Transition', in Hare, P. and Turley, G. (eds), *Handbook of the Economics and Political Economy of Transition*, Abingdon and New York: Routledge, pp. 209–16.

WGI (2014) *Worldwide Governance Indicators*. Online. Available: www.govindicators.org (accessed 23 June 2014).

World Bank (2014a) *Russia Economic Report: Confidence Crisis Exposes Economic Weakness*, World Bank, 31 March. Online. Available: www.worldbank.org/en/country/russia/overview (accessed 24 April 2014).

World Bank (2014b) *Doing Business – Economy Ranking*. Online. Available: www.doingbusiness.org/rankings (accessed February 2014).

7 The impact of oil prices, total factor productivity and institutional weakness on Russia's declining growth

Masaaki Kuboniwa

The chapter presents an analysis of the impact of oil prices, total factor productivity (TFP) and institutional weakness on the present growth retardation in Russia. First, I discuss Russia's dependence on oil and natural gas and provide an estimate of the value-added of the oil and gas industry generated by revenues from domestic production and exports of oil and gas. Russia's oil windfalls are captured using the concepts of terms of trade and trading gains (terms of trade adjustment). The GDP–oil nexus is also explained through energy efficiency or intensity. Next, the impact of oil prices and TFP on growth is analysed using the estimation of regressions for the GDP–oil nexus and production function. There then follows an investigation of the relationship between TFP and growth in the present Russian economy. Finally, the elusive impact of institutional weakness on Russia's growth is considered, using the World Bank's Governance Indicators (WGI) and the Ease of Doing Business index.

Value-added of the oil and gas sector in Russia's GDP

Based on Russian official statistics, the average share of value-added of oil and gas (crude oil, oil products and natural gas) in overall GDP for 2005–13 was only 10 per cent. If this were true, it cannot be claimed that Russia relies heavily on oil and gas. As shown by Kuboniwa *et al.* (2005), the official picture is a result of its specific methodology where all revenues from exports of oil and gas are included in the trade and transportation sectors and the net taxes on exports. In order to capture the correct picture of the role played by the oil and gas industry in the Russian economy, it is necessary to rearrange revenues from exports of oil and gas and export taxes on these as part of the value-added of the oil and gas sector.

The export revenues from the oil and gas industry are measured by calculating the differences between exports in foreign trade prices and domestic producer prices. Exports of oil and gas in foreign trade prices are taken from foreign trade data in USD (available on the websites of Rosstat and the Bank of Russia). Exports of oil and gas in producer prices are calculated from the official data on export quantities (ton or cubic meter) and quarterly or monthly producer prices. Export taxes on oil and gas are paid by the export revenues. Data on export taxes are available from a website of the Russian Ministry of Finance or the database of the federal laws of Russia. I regard all revenues from exports of oil and gas as part of the value-added of that sector at basic prices. Although export taxes can be considered to belong to a category of taxes on products or indirect taxes, I here consider taxes on oil and gas exports as corporate income taxes according to the usual practice in most oil exporting countries, for example Norway.

Figure 7.1 shows the result of our estimates for 2005–13. Figure 7.2 summarizes the average picture for the period. The average share of the estimated value-added of the oil and gas industry in overall GDP is 20 per cent – that is, twice the official figure of 10.2 per cent. The average gross revenue from oil and gas exports amounts to about 10 per cent of GDP, of which 6.8 per cent are paid to the federal government as export taxes and 3.1 per cent remain in the companies. It should be emphasized that export taxes are much larger than companies' net revenues from exports. The share of total value-added of the oil and gas industry reached its peak of 22 per cent in 2005, fell to 17.5 per cent in 2009 due to the reverse oil shock coupled with the Lehman shock, and increased to 20 per cent in 2013.

The estimates of the share of total value-added of the oil and gas industry for 2005–6 are slightly smaller than the results of 24–5 per cent recorded in Ustinova (2010) and Kuboniwa (2012) based on input–output tables because the latter includes additional domestic activities of the oil and gas industry and taxes on oil and gas other than export taxes. Due to the lack of disaggregated input–output

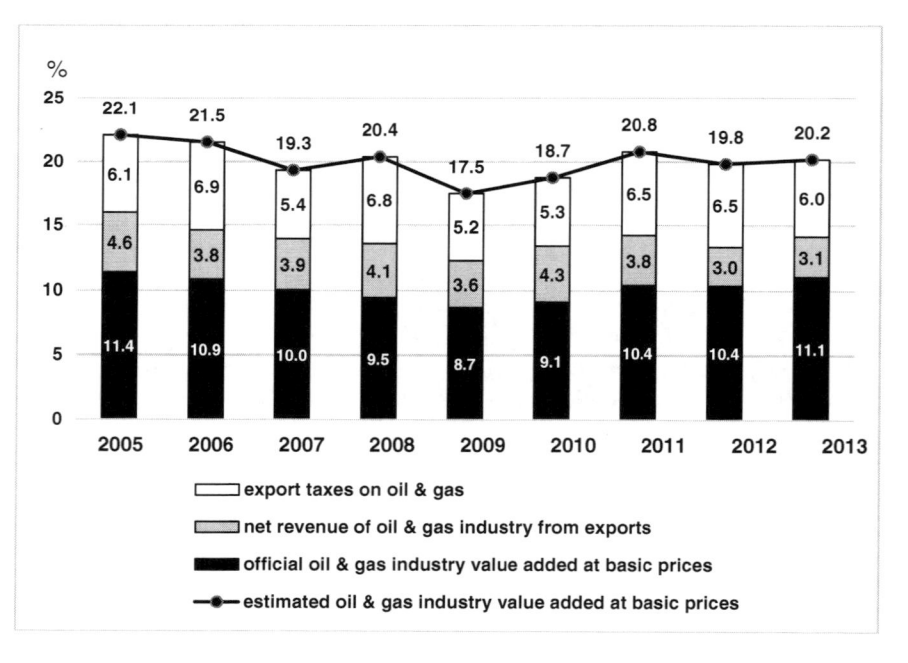

Figure 7.1 Share of value-added of the oil and gas industry in overall GDP (%).

Source: Author's calculations from Rosstat website and Ministry of Finance website.

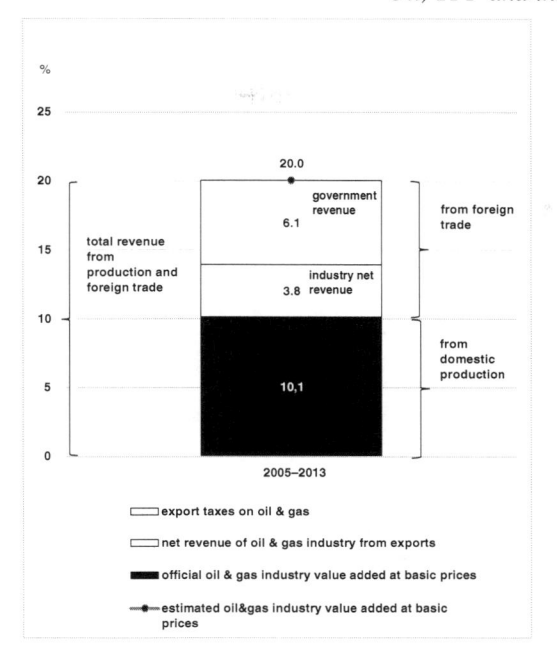

Figure 7.2 Average share of value-added of the oil and gas industry in overall GDP (%).

Source: Figure 7.1.

tables from 2007 onward, our simple method may also be appropriate. It should
also be noted that our estimate only considers the formal activities of the oil and
gas industry. However, our methodology is rather robust because it can always
be reproduced from systematically written evidence. The results may also provide evidence for part of the resource rents suggested by Gaddy and Ickes (2010,
2013).

Terms of trade and trading gains

Windfalls arising from rapidly rising oil prices for Russia can be captured by trading gains due to improvements in terms of trade. The concept of 'trading gains/
losses' is explained in United Nations *et al.* (2008) *System of National Accounts*
(SNA) This concept is called 'terms of trade adjustment' in the World Bank's
WDI. According to the SNA 2008 (United Nations *et al.*, 2008, section 15.188),
the real gross domestic income (GDI) measures the purchasing power of a country's total income generated by its domestic production. The terms of trade (ToT)
is defined as the ratio of the export price P^e to the import price P^m that is to
say, P^e/P^m Here, $P^e = E_n/E_r$ and $P^m = M_n/M_r$ where E_n and M_n are exports and
imports in current prices, respectively, and E_r and M_r are exports and imports in

constant prices, respectively. Due to improvements in the ToT caused by the rise in export prices relative to import prices, the purchasing power of the country in international markets increases in relation to real GDP. The trading gains (TG) or terms of trade adjustment from the changes in the ToT can be formulated as nominal net exports deflated by the import price index *minus* the conventional real net exports:

$$TG = \left(E_n - M_n\right)/P^m - \left(E_r - M_r\right) \tag{7.1}$$

It follows from equation (7.1) that

$$TG = E_n / P^m - E_r = E_r \left(P^e / P^m - 1\right) \tag{7.2}$$

It follows from (7.2) that $TG >=< 0$ if $ToT = P^e/P^m >=< 1$. If the terms of trade or P^e/P^m improve (worsen), the trading gains should increase (decrease). At the base period $P^e = P^m = 1$ and, hence, TG must be zero.

The real GDI is defined as the real GDP plus the real trading gains:

$$\text{real GDI} = \text{real GDP} + \text{real TG} \tag{7.3}$$

In general, if imports and exports are large relative to GDP and if there is a marked change in ToT resulting from a large increase in export prices relative to import prices or a decrease in import prices relative to export prices, the magnitude of potential trading gains or losses would be large. Indeed, as will be shown, this is true for the Russian economy. It can be noted that trading gains can also be spent on additional purchases of imports and domestically produced goods. Although, in the literature, real GDI is often discussed as an alternative welfare concept in place of, or in addition to, real GDP, Kuboniwa (2012, 2014) focuses on the impact of changes in terms of trade or trading gains (losses) on real GDP.

Figure 7.3 shows annual data on movements of ToT along with Urals oil prices for 1990–2013 in Russia. As can be seen, the ToT has a strong positive relationship with oil prices. In 2000–8, rising oil prices caused substantial improvements in ToT. Huge improvements in ToT with rapidly rising oil prices imply that import prices did not show any large increases in response to oil shocks. In contrast to the 1970s, the 2000s did not witness sufficiently parallel changes in import prices with oil prices.

Figure 7.4 demonstrates that improvements in the ToT brought about trading gains or terms of trade adjustments. The trading gain in 2000 constant prices amounted to USD 155 billion in 2008 (36 per cent of GDP). In 2009 this fell to USD 46 billion (12 per cent of GDP). It then showed a continuous recovery, amounting to USD 162 billion (37 per cent of GDP) in 2012 and USD 174 billion (39 per cent of GDP) in 2013. Kuboniwa (2012) clarified the strong positive impact of oil prices on GDP through the channel of terms of trade or trading gains.

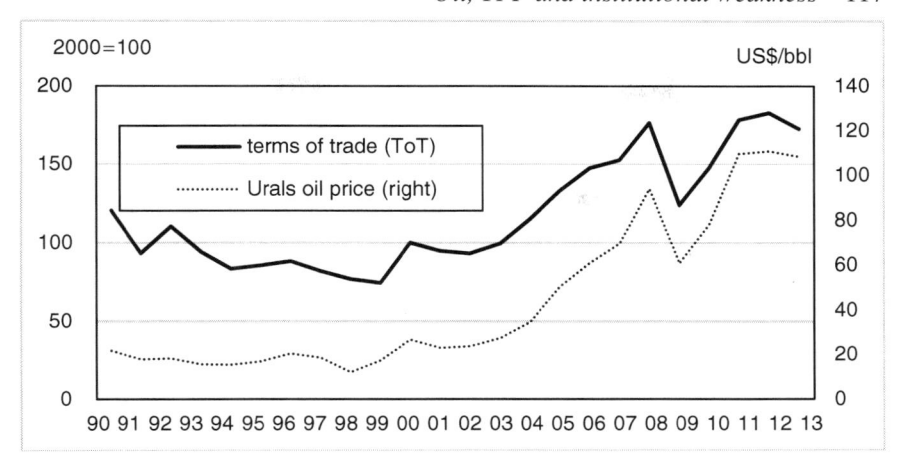

Figure 7.3 Oil prices and terms of trade.

Source: WDI, Bloomberg-Thomson Reuters and author's estimates.

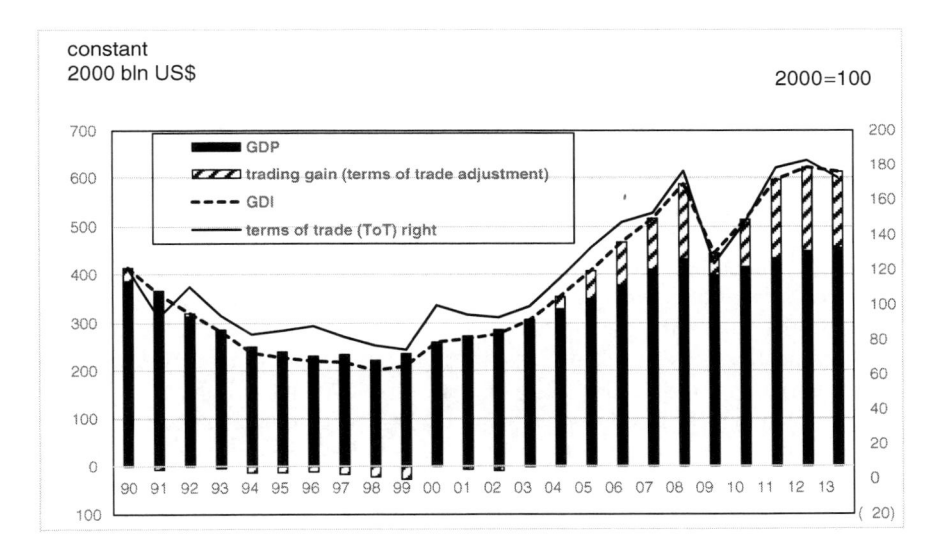

Figure 7.4 Trading gains (terms of trade adjustment) at constant USD 2,000.

Source: Author's estimation based on WDI (accessed 15 August 2014).

In addition, Kuboniwa (2014) demonstrates the impact of increases in oil prices on GDP through another channel, namely improved energy efficiency in Russia.

Figure 7.5 shows movements in energy consumption, including oil and gas consumption, electricity consumption and total primary energy consumption along with real GDP for 1990–2013. In the 2000s there were energy-saving efforts in

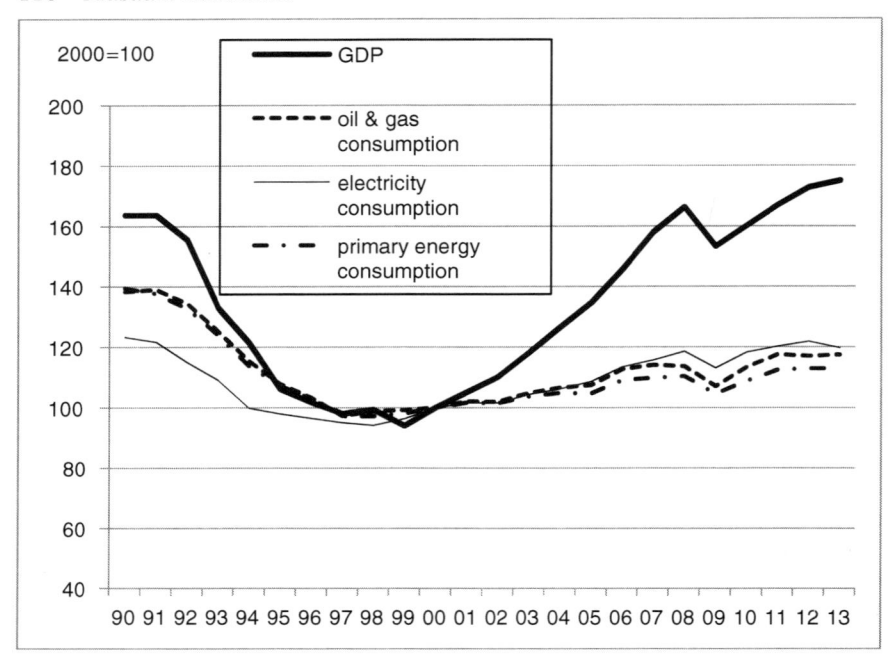

Figure 7.5 Increase in energy efficiency (decreases in energy intensity).
Source: BP (2014) and Rosstat website.

Russia, although the absolute level of energy consumption is still very high, also in comparison with other emerging economies and developed countries. Unlike in the Soviet Union, the present Russia was forced to save energy in response to rising domestic prices for oil and gas resulting from increases in their international prices, even though domestic prices for crude oil and gas are still much lower than their international prices. Improvements in the energy efficiency or the energy intensity of a country have a direct impact on its further modernization or total factor productivity (TFP).

Present situation of the impact of oil prices and TFP

Figure 7.6 shows the seasonally adjusted quarterly real GDP of Russia, with quarterly nominal Urals oil prices for 1995Q1–2014Q2.[1] As shown by this figure, Russia faced a 5.2 per cent contraction of GDP in 1998 during the Russian financial crisis, with falling oil prices. Russia recovered quickly from its recession and showed steady growth, with rising oil prices for 2000–7. During this period, Russia grew at an annual average rate of 6.7 per cent. In 2009, due to the world financial crisis coupled with the collapse of the oil bubble, Russia showed

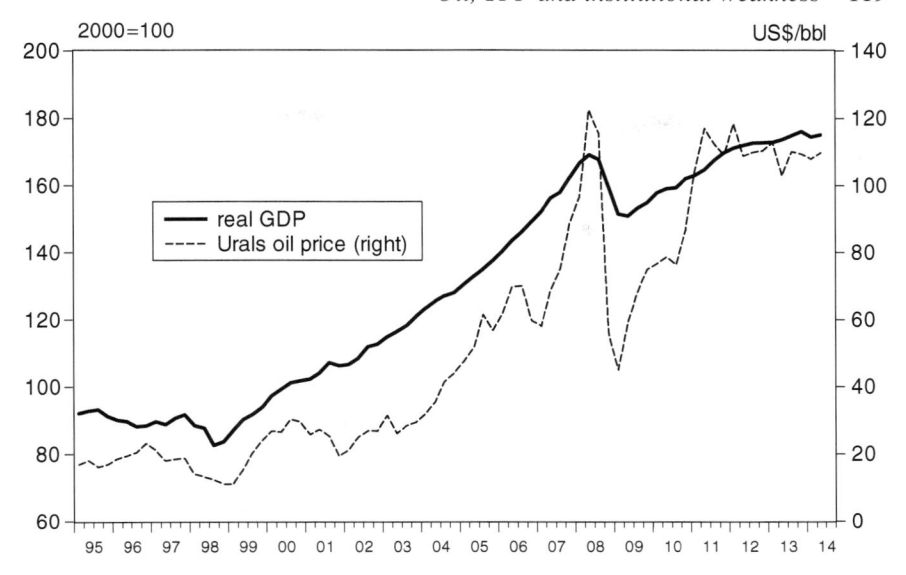

Figure 7.6 GDP growth and oil prices.

Source: Rosstat website and Bloomberg-Thomson Reuters.

a large decline in its GDP – −7.8 per cent. Russia witnessed a rather strong recovery immediately after the world financial crisis in 2008–9. However, it has now begun to show a decline in growth with a growth rate of 1.3 per cent in 2013.

Using DOLS (dynamic OLS) for the sample 1995Q3–2014Q2,

$$gdp = 0.181oil + 0.0056t \text{ (annualized trend rate of 2.3\%). Adj. } R^2 = 0.972, \quad (7.4)$$
$$\quad [4.803] \qquad [4.453]$$

where $gdp = \log(\text{real GDP})$, $oil = \log(\text{oil price})$, t = a linear time trend and [.] denotes t-statistic. Equation 7.4 shows the long-run relationship between changes in real GDP and nominal Urals oil prices, that is to say, $\{gdp, oil\}$. Oil prices for Russia are Urals oil prices. The correlation coefficient between the logarithms of Brent and Urals oil prices is 0.999.

It follows from equation 7.4 that a 10 per cent increase in oil prices leads to approximately a 1.8 per cent increase in the growth of Russia's GDP. The underlying annualized growth trend of about 2.3 per cent corresponds approximately to the TFP growth, which reflects Russia's modernization processes. Equation 7.4 thus shows the long-run relationship between growth in total factor productivity, oil prices and GDP. Both oil prices and TFP contributed to economic growth in the 2000s (Kuboniwa 2012, 2014).

When using DOLS for sample (adjusted) 2008Q2–2013Q2, the equation is

$$gdp = 0.110oil + 0.0037t \text{ (annualized trend rate of 1.5\%), Adj.R}^2 = 0.985. \quad (7.5)$$
$$[8.610] \qquad [9.160]$$

Equation 7.5 implies that a 10 per cent increase in oil prices leads to only a 1 per cent increase in GDP growth. The underlying annualized growth trend of about 1.5 per cent is much less than 2.3 per cent. Both elasticity with respect to oil prices and TFP fell markedly during this period. Considering that the oil price decreased by 2.2 per cent in 2013, equation 7.5 offers a quite good approximation of the growth result in 2013 (0.11 * −2.2 per cent + 1.5 per cent = 1.3 per cent).

Consider a Cobb–Douglas production function with a steady technical progress: $Y = A\exp(\lambda t)K^a L^{1-a}$, where Y = real GDP, K = capital stock adjusted for utilization based on the REB (Russian Economic Barometer), L = actual employment, λ = TFP, a = capital distribution ratio, and A = a constant. I estimate the linear regression: $y = ak + \lambda t + \log A$, where $y = \log(Y/L)$ and $k = \log(K/L)$. Data on fixed capital adjusted for utilization and employment are shown by Figure 7.7. Using a canonical co-integrating regression (CCR) for the sample 1995Q2–2013Q4 based on the data compilation method in Kuboniwa (2011),

$$y = 0.342k + 0.0067t \text{ (annualized trend rate of 2.7\%). Adj. R}^2 = 0.956. \quad (7.6)$$
$$[3.966] \qquad [4.513]$$

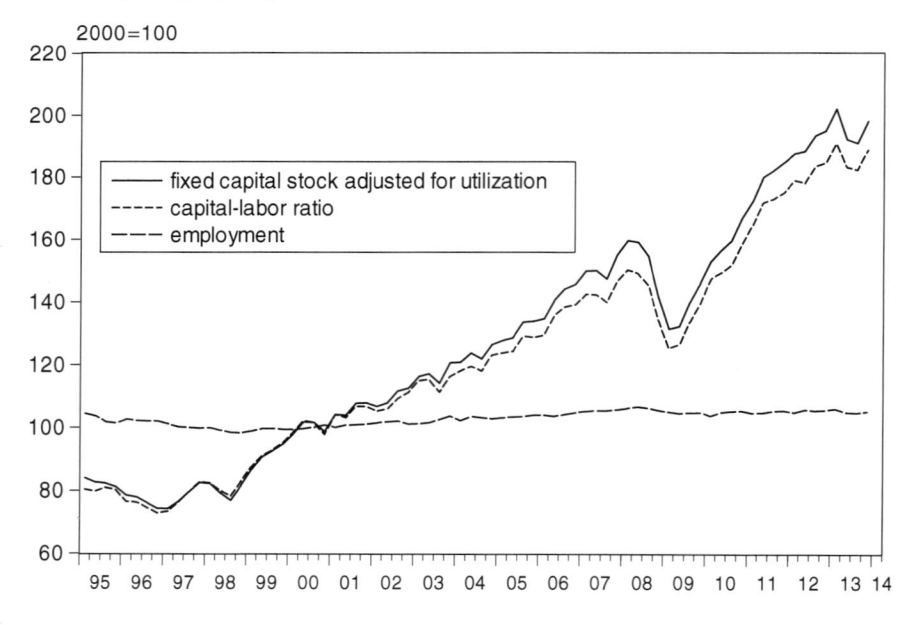

Figure 7.7 Capital stock and employment.

Source: Author's estimation based on data supplied by Rosstat, website of Rosstat and REB.

That is to say, $a = 0.342$ and $\lambda = 0.0067$. This implies that the capital distribution ratio accounts for 34 per cent, which corresponds to a conventional ratio, while the annualized rate of λ (TFP) accounts for 2.7 per cent, which corresponds to a time trend coefficient of equation (7.1a). With the sample 2009Q1–2013Q4, productivity becomes

$$y = 0.194k + 0.0039t \text{ (annualized trend rate of 1.6\%). Adj. } R^2 = 0.979. \quad (7.7)$$
$$[4.716] \quad [4.046]$$

Both the capital distribution ratio and TFP show marked decreases. TFP in equation (7.7) corresponds to that in equation (7.5). This implies that the present growth retardation has been caused by large decreases in the elasticity of the capital-labour ratio and overall TFP.

It is helpful to look at manufacturing output in this context in order to achieve a correct understanding of Russia's dependence on oil. Figure 7.8 presents data on the real monthly manufacturing output of Russia for 1995M01–2014M07 with its Hodrick–Prescott filter trend $(\lambda = 14,400)$.[2] Monthly data on Russia's manufacturing output for 1995–98 are estimated by using the regression based on the official data on manufacturing output for 1999–2014 and the data on industrial output for 1995–2014. International Financial Statistics (IFS) monthly data on Russian industrial output for 1995–

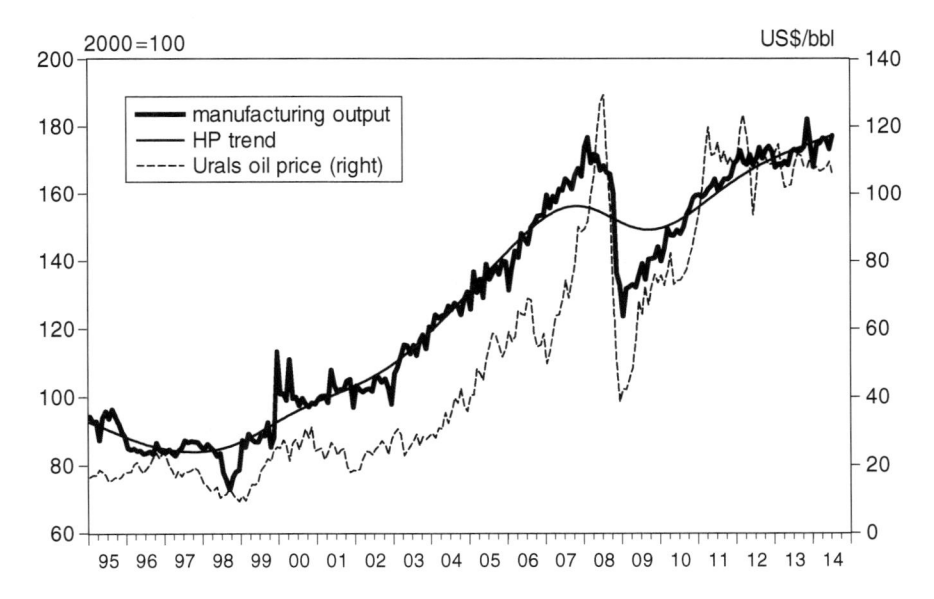

Figure 7.8 Manufacturing output and oil prices.

Source: Based on CEIC database and Bloomberg-Thomson Reuters.

98 are modified by adjusting for the official annual data for 1995–98. Russian manufacturing recovered after the world crisis and reached its pre-crisis peak level in 2013M11.[3]

Using DOLS for sample (adjusted) for 1995M10–2014M06, we get

$$manu = 0.233oil + 0.0014t \text{ (annualized trend rate of 1.7\%). Adj.R}^2 = 0.947, \quad (7.8)$$
$$\quad [7.155] \quad\quad [3.857]$$

where $manu = $ log(real manufacturing output). Equation 7.8 also shows a strongly positive relationship between changes in oil prices and manufacturing output for 1995–2014. It follows from this equation that a 10 per cent increase in oil prices leads to a 2.3 per cent increase in Russia's manufacturing growth. The underlying annualized trend rate of 1.7 per cent reflects TFP in manufacturing. The elasticity of manufacturing with respect to oil prices is larger than that of GDP, whereas the underlying trend of manufacturing is smaller than that of GDP. However, for the sample (adjusted) 2010M01–2014M04

$$manu = 0.241oil + 0.0015t \text{ (annualized trend rate of 1.8\%). Adj.R}^2 = 0.946. \quad (7.9)$$
$$\quad [11.084] \quad\quad [5.873]$$

In contrast to overall GDP growth, both the elasticity and the trend rate for 2010–14 are slightly greater than those for the whole sample. This suggests that recent growth retardation might have been brought about through TFP losses in mining and trade sectors other than manufacturing. However, this should need further investigation. For instance, using equation 7.9, I approximate a manufacturing output growth of 1.3 per cent in 2013 $\left(0.241 * -2.2 \text{ per cent} + 1.8 \text{ per cent} = 1.3 \text{ per cent}\right)$ that is much larger than the actual figure of 0.5 per cent.

The impact of institutional quality

Figure 7.9 shows the net capital inflow/outflow of the private sector. As is well known, a large capital outflow occurred during the world financial crisis, reflecting the institutional weakness of the Russian economy. After some recovery of growth, Russia's capital inflow/outflow has shown a negative trend with rather chaotic movements. The capital outflow of about USD 60 billion in 2013 was largely brought about by Rosneft's absorption of TNK-BP.

One well-known indicator of institutional quality is the Worldwide Governance Indicators (WGI), a research dataset summarizing the views of the quality of governance provided by a large number of enterprises, citizen and expert survey respondents in an economy (Kaufmann *et al.* 2010). Figure 7.10 shows Russia's absolutely low level of worldwide governance (rule of law), which ranks it at 162nd of 212 countries/regions in 2013. The first is placed by an oil/gas-rich country, that is, Norway. India, Brazil and China are 101st,

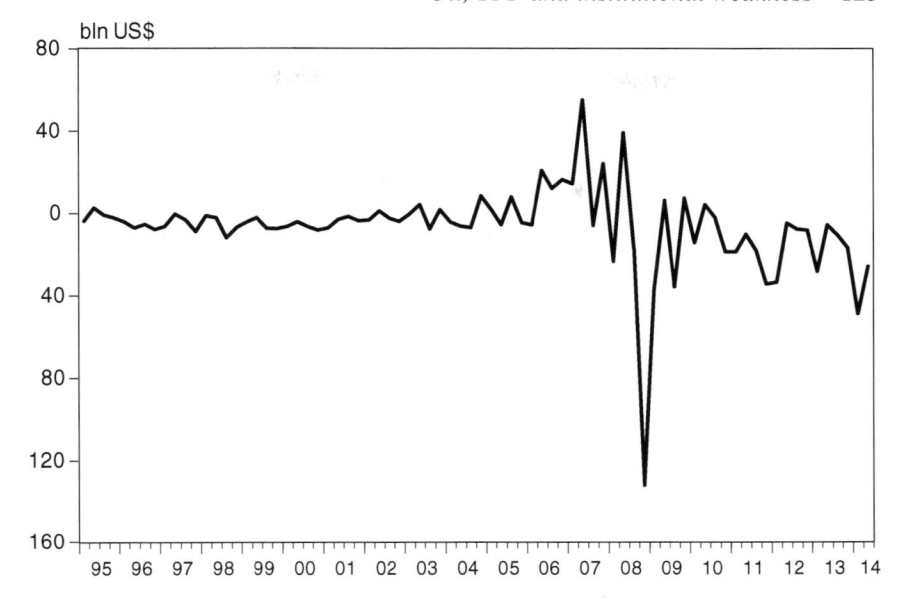

Figure 7.9 Net capital inflow/outflow: private sector (bln USD).

Source: website of Bank of Russia and CEIC database.

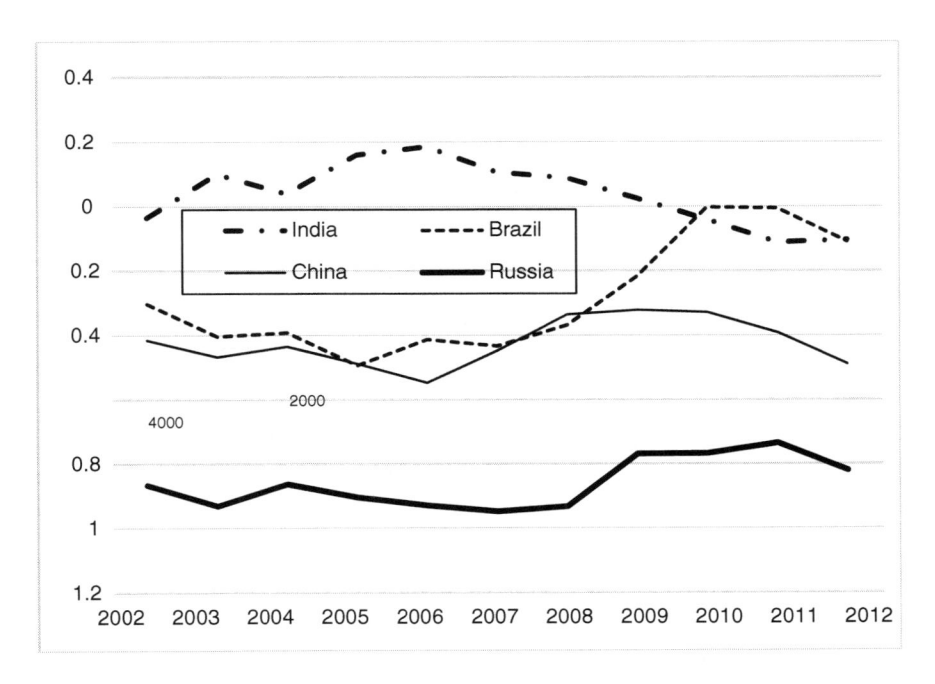

Figure 7.10 Absolute low level of worldwide governance (rule of law) of 212 countries/
regions, 2013.

Source: WGI.

103rd and 130th, respectively. Russia shows an improvement during the world crisis in 2009. Generally, this indicator does not reflect a country's growth performance in a well-defined manner. For a small annual sample 2002–12 of Russia, I have

$$gdp = -1.2\log(\text{WGI} + 2.5) + 0.05t. \ \text{Adj.}R^2 = 0.955. \qquad (7.10)$$
$$[-5.321] \qquad\qquad [10.813]$$

GDP growth has a strongly negative relationship with the WGI that should reflect the quality of the institution.

Another well-known indicator of the quality of a country's investment climate is the 'Ease of Doing Business Index'. A high ranking on this index means that the regulatory environment is more conducive to starting and operating a local firm. This index averages the country's percentile rankings on ten topics, made up of a variety of indicators, giving equal weight to each topic. The latest ranking is benchmarked to June 2013.

Table 7.1 shows this index for Russia and other BRIC countries. The 2013 edition presents new opportunities for foreign companies and investors, bearing in mind that Russia moved up 19 places from 2012 and became the top-ranked BRIC country, emerging ahead of China (96th), Brazil (116th) and India (134th). This change pleased President Vladimir Putin, and many expected a higher growth in 2013. However, the growth results in 2013 and the first half of 2014 were rather disappointing. Russia's moving up was primarily the result of a large improvement in 'getting electricity', which rose from 184th place to 117th place. Following the break-up of the Unified Energy System, there are many players, including the generator, local governments, and private distributors' intermediate, and 'getting electricity' is not a transparent process. The Ease of Doing Business Index is based on interviews with businesses. Additional anecdotic evidence of the problems can be attained in discussions, for instance, Nissan in St Petersburg was forced to pay USD 5 million for getting electricity (author's interview at Nissan in Japan). Anyway, this indicator does not reflect a country's short-run growth and investment opportunities. In general, it is complicated to design a good index of the quality of institutions in relation to the economic growth of a single country. Cross-section or panel data for many countries are needed. Wedeman (2012: 178) found a weakly hump-shaped relationship between the Transparency International Corruption Perceptions Index (CPI) score (inverted) or national corruption and the average growth of many countries for 1992–2008, although he regarded China as an outlier with a much higher growth than other countries with similar levels of corruption. Ahmad *et al.* (2012) also statistically found the existence of a hump-shaped relationship between corruption and long-run economic growth, using the International Country Risk Guide corruption index of 71 countries. In other words, up to a certain development level, the deepening of corruption of a country may increase the level of economic growth. In this context, Russia may

Table 7.1 Comparison of countries in 'Ease of Doing Business Index' as of December 2013

	Russia		China	Brazil	India	Singapore	USA	Norway	Japan
	2013	2012				2013			
Ease of Doing Business Rank	92	112	96	116	134	1	4	9	27
Starting a Business	88	101	158	123	179	3	20	53	120
Dealing with Construction Permits	178	178	185	130	182	3	34	28	91
Getting Electricity	117	184	119	14	111	6	13	17	26
Registering Property	17	46	48	107	92	28	25	10	66
Getting Credit	109	104	73	109	28	3	3	73	28
Protecting Investors	115	117	98	80	34	2	6	22	16
Paying Taxes	56	64	120	159	158	5	64	17	140
Trading Across Borders	157	162	74	124	132	1	22	26	23
Enforcing Contracts	10	11	19	121	186	12	11	4	36
Resolving Insolvency	55	53	78	135	121	4	17	2	1
Average	*90*	*102*	*97*	*110*	*122*	*7*	*22*	*25*	*55*

Source: http://www.doingbusiness.org/rankings.

Notes: Average scores are author's calculations. The number of ranked countries is 189.

still remain at a developing stage with a mutually complementary or dependent relation of institutional deficiency and growth.

In Russia, as is shown by Figure 7.11, even the assembly of foreign-made automobiles is facing a declining growth due to its relatively narrow technological base. To sum up, it is difficult to identify some major breakthrough leading to the subsequent development of the Russian economy.

Concluding remarks

This chapter has analysed Russia's recent economic slowdown from the perspectives of oil prices, TFP and institutional quality. Overall declining growth can be captured by the impact of oil prices and TFP, whereas the estimated TFP decline

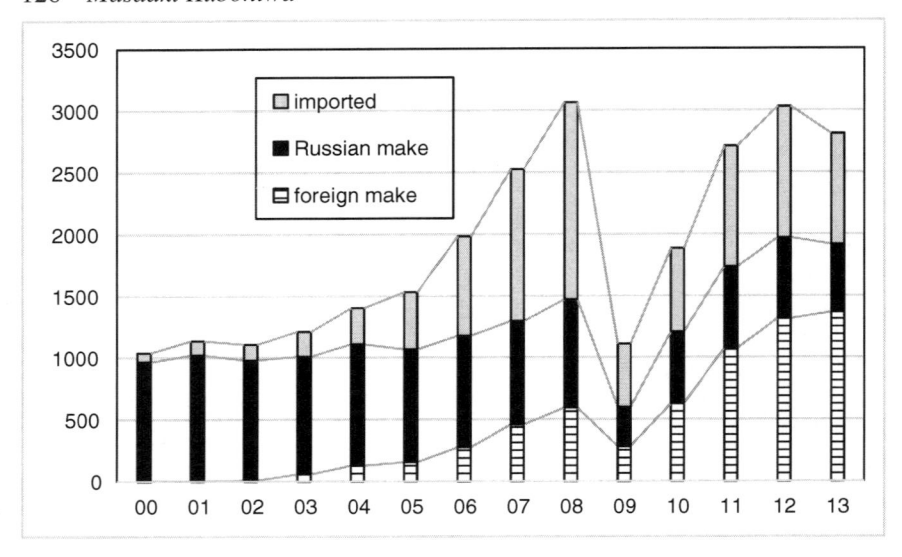

Figure 7.11 Russian car market, 2000–13 (thousand units).

Source: Autostat, CEIC database and author's estimates.

does not satisfactorily explain the growth of output in manufacturing. Indexes of quality of institutions, including WGI and the ranking in the World Bank's ease of doing business, are insufficient to capture the output performance in present-day Russia. It is rather difficult to find some major breakthrough leading to a further diversification development of the Russian economy. Furthermore, recent developments in Russia–Ukraine relations may deepen Russia's declining growth more than had been expected at the beginning of 2014.

Notes

1 Q1, Q2 etc. denote the first quarter of the year, the second quarter, etc.
2 Russian official data are seasonally adjusted by X-13. X-13ARIMA-SEATS is a seasonal adjustment software developed by the United States Census Bureau.
3 M stands for month. M01 is January; M11 is November, etc.

References

Ahmad, E., Ullah, M. and Arfeen, M. (2012) 'Does Corruption Affect Economic Growth?', *Latin American Journal of Economics*, 40: 277–305.
BP (2014) *BP Statistical Review of World Energy 2014*, London: BP.
Gaddy, C. and Ickes, B. (2010) 'Russia After the Global Financial Crisis', *Eurasian Geography and Economics*, 51(3): 281–311.
Gaddy, C. and Ickes, B. (2013) 'Russia's Dependence on Resources', in Alexeev, M. and Shlomo, W. (eds), *The Russian Economy*, Oxford and New York: Oxford University Press, pp. 309–40.

Kaufmann, D., Aart Kraay, A. and Mastruzzi, M. (2010) 'The Worldwide Governance Indicators: Methodology and Analytical Issues', World Bank, *Policy Research Working Paper* 5430.

Kuboniwa, M. (2011) 'Russian Growth Path and TFP Changes in Light of the Estimation of Production Function Using Quarterly Data', *Post-Communist Economies*, 23(3): 311–25.

Kuboniwa, M. (2012) 'Diagnosing the "Russian Disease": Growth and Structure of the Russian Economy', *Comparative Economic Studies*, 54(1): 121–48.

Kuboniwa, M. (2014) 'A Comparative Analysis of the Impact of Oil Prices on Oil-rich Emerging Economies in the Pacific Rim', *Journal of Comparative Economics*, 42(2): 328–39.

Kuboniwa, M., Tabata, S. and Ustinova, N. (2005) 'How Large is the Oil and Gas Sector of Russia? A Research Report', *Eurasian Geography and Economics*, 46(1): 68–76.

United Nations, Commission of the European Communities, IMF, OECD and World Bank (2008) *System of National Accounts 2008* (SNA 2008). Online. Available: http://unstats.un.org/unsd/nationalaccount/sna2008.asp (accessed March 2014).

Ustinova, N. (2010) 'Oil and Gas Sector in Russian Supply and Use Tables', paper presented at the 18th International Input–Output Conference, Sydney, Australia, 20–25 June.

Wedeman, A. (2012) *Double Paradox: Rapid Growth and Rising Corruption in China*, Ithaca and London: Cornell University Press.

8 From the dual to the triple state?

Richard Sakwa

Russian politics is characterised by the dominance of a powerful yet diffuse administrative regime, recognising its subordination to the normative state on the one side and its formal accountability to the institutions of mass representative democracy on the other. However, it is not effectively constrained by either, hence the 'regime' character of the dominant power system. Russia is therefore a distinctive type of 'dual state', in which two regulatory regimes in the political and economic sphere coexist, which in short-hand we can label the democratic and the *dirigiste*, allowing neither free rein and impeding the inherent ordering principles of both. The Russian dual state is unlike the one in Nazi Germany, where the system was based on a degree of predictability, with the prerogative regime operating in certain defined instances. Ernst Fraenkel (1941, reprinted 2006) described how the prerogative state acted as a separate law system of its own, although the formal constitutional state was not dismantled. There were two parallel systems of law, with the 'normative state' operating according to sanctioned principles of rationality and impartial legal norms while the 'prerogative state' exercised power arbitrarily and without constraints, unrestrained by law. In Russia, however, at any given time it cannot be predicted which order will predominate. No full-blown 'prerogative state' has emerged, ruling through emergency decrees and sustained repression. Instead we have an 'administrative regime' as the protagonist of the normative state. There is no prerogative state as such in Russia, constituted through formal but extra-constitutional decrees or laws, but instead there is informal behaviour by an administrative regime that fulfils some of the functions of the prerogative state but that has no independent legal or institutional status of its own.

I have described the workings of this dual state elsewhere (Sakwa 2010, 2011). The question posed in this chapter is whether the arbitrariness of the administrative regime has transformed into something else, dubbed in this chapter the 'triple state'. By the triple state I mean the degeneration of the administrative regime into a primarily self-serving body where personal self-interest trumps the pursuit of rational, although possibly mistaken, public policy goals. The classic dual state of the first two terms of Vladimir Putin's presidency set itself up as a tutelary body standing outside the constitutional order. Its legitimacy derived from the claim that by constituting itself as a separate domain it could challenge the powerful interests, notably the oligarchs and regional bosses, that had benefitted from what Joel Hellman (1998) called the 'partial reform equilibrium'. Special interests could be brought to heel and the interests of the state be defended. In the early years of Putin's leadership this was a defensible, although highly contested, claim.

An activist state, in the form of a distinct administrative regime, emerged that broke the independent power and authority of the early winners (oligarchs and red directors), notably in the Yukos affair (Sakwa 2014). The economy now became systemically politicised, accompanied by elements of predatory state interventionism. This was more than the conventional notion of a weak state environment, but one in which the institutions of the constitutional state (notably impartial adjudication by the courts) were susceptible to interference and distortion by the administrative regime. One part of 'the state' in certain respects was too strong, allowing the administrative regime to shape outcomes; while the other part, the legal and regulatory side, was too weak. A recent study of international partnerships illustrates the bargaining relationship between foreign and domestic partners in a weak institutional environment, nicely bringing out the dynamics of the politicised dualism of Russia's business environment (Henderson and Ferguson 2014).

The chapter will move in four steps. First, I will consider the workings of the dual state. This will be followed by a discussion of the concept of *sublation,* the mechanism whereby the administrative regime subverts, but does not destroy the autonomy of the institutions associated with the constitutional state. In the third part I examine various models of the third state, including a discussion of the 'deep state' idea as applied to Italy and Turkey. The fourth section draws a parallel with Second Empire France, a situation which has remarkable similarities with contemporary Russia, and reinforces the point by further examining the parallels between Putinism and Berlusconi. The conclusion seeks to draw out the broader arguments of the chapter.

The dual state

In modern political theory the constitutional state is an entity that exists separate from any particular ruler, endures beyond the life span of a particular government, and is rooted in the public good. It is regulated by impartial norms of law and managed by a disinterested bureaucracy. In Russia, this Weberian ideal has been subverted by the administrative regime, which draws its legitimacy from claiming to apply the principles of the constitutional state and authority from its representation of the common good, but in practice the polity and the state effectively become the property of the regime, and increasingly of the leader himself. When talking about strengthening the state, the system in fact too often only reinforced the prerogative powers of the regime. In other words, a new form of a patrimonial regime was consolidated.

Instead of consolidating the rule of law, the authority of constitutional institutions such as parliament and the formal procedures of modern governance, regime practices predominate accompanied by the development of a whole range of para-constitutional bodies, such as the seven (later eight, joined by a ninth with the annexation of Crimea in March 2014) federal districts, the State Council and the Civic Chamber. The regime never repudiated the formal framework of the constitution, but the sphere of discretion (which exists in all political systems) has become extraordinarily wide. The tutelary politics of the administrative regime are predicated on its high level of decisionism; the ability to decide in a Schmittian fashion who is a friend or foe; and what is or is not right for the country and its economy. This fosters the practice of legal populism, allowing the regime to avoid direct coercion. The law is used to advance policies that run counter to the spirit of constitutionalism, thus eroding trust in its institutions. The legal system has been subordinated to political authority and in certain cases, such as in the Yukos prosecutions, undermined the consolidation of independent courts and the rule of law in general.

The administrative regime takes the form of a dominant power system, but is balanced by the constitutional state. The administrative regime is careful not to step outside the bounds of the formal letter of the constitution, but it is constantly pressing against the limits of its spirit. The administrative regime is embedded in a range of para-constitutional institutions, each of which undermines the official constitutional body created to fulfil parallel functions. This is accompanied by the development of a range of para-political bodies. For example, instead of allowing United Russia to develop as an autonomous political force of its own, facing up to its own weaknesses, lack of coherent programmatic development, and overwhelmingly bureaucratic character, Putin created the People's Front to offset the failings of his own creature. This was a classical Putinite trope: fearing falling hostage to a body of his own making, he created another. As for the factions, notably the conventional distinction between the *siloviki* and the *civiliki*, it is important to stress that these are not deeply entrenched clans. Their existence does not reflect profound societal cleavages but situational political preferences and the distinctive class structure of a semi-reformed post-communist state. Although the great army of officialdom and the *securocracy* exploit the arbitrariness fostered by the administrative regime, the system is not simply its servant. Russia's developmental stalemate is predominantly of a political character.

Two political systems operate in parallel. On the one hand, there is the system of open public politics, with all of the relevant institutions described in the constitution and conducted with pedantic regulation in formal terms. At this level, parties are formed, elections fought and parliamentary politics conducted. However, at another level a second para-political world exists based on informal groups, factions, and operating within the framework of the inner court of the presidency. As long as Putin remained the indisputable arbiter, this Byzantine level did not openly challenge the leader but sought to influence his decisions. This second level is more than simply 'virtual' politics, the attempt to manipulate public opinion and shape electoral outcomes through the exercise of manipulative techniques, but acts as a substantive alternative sphere of policy contestation. The suffocation of public politics intensifies factional processes within the regime and corruption in society as a whole. Putin cannot control the factional process, but his statecraft lies in the ability to balance the factions and to ensure that none delivers a knock-out blow to its rivals, endangering not only their political status and property, but possibly their physical existence as well. This would allow the dominant group to dominate the executive, and thus effectively capture the presidency. To counter this, Putin plays a whole orchestra of instruments, including bringing in the population through para-constitutional and para-political instruments to maintain the formalism of the constitutional state.

The regime governs by exploiting uncertainty, and this practice has now spread into the operation of other spheres. In such a system there tends to be few permanent winners or losers, hence attempts by those who temporarily find themselves in a winning position to grab as much as they can while the going is good before a new turn drives them into the loser's camp. This has provoked the systemic stalemate in which Russia now finds itself. This is more than the 'hybridity' characteristic of regimes in post-Soviet Eurasia but represents a historical conjuncture of extended developmental stasis. Historical experience suggests that such a blockage is overcome by either revolution or collapse. However, the distinctive features of Russia's dual state may allow an evolutionary transcendence of the stalemate; but it may equally spiral into rampant authoritarianism, corruption and decay.

Sublation

In geology sublation is the process whereby one continental plate forces itself under another, and in politics sublation means the undercutting of one institution by another, gradually eroding its legitimacy and efficacy. In our analysis of the dual state, sublation is the mechanism whereby the institutions of the constitutional state lose their autonomy. As we have seen, the dual state in Russia does not openly proclaim its superiority over normal procedures of law, electoral competitiveness and constitutionality, as would be the case if a state of emergency was openly promulgated, and instead more subtle mechanism operate. Three mechanisms are crucial to understanding how the administrative regime operates.

The first is *para-constitutionalism*, the creation of institutions that are not directly anti-constitutional but which subvert the operation of constitutional institutions. These include the creation of the seven (now nine) federal districts (which undermined federalism), the State Council (undermining the work of the upper chamber, the Federation Council), and the Public Chamber (which acts as a public forum detracting from the State Duma). These are all formally constituted bodies which lack constitutional underpinning but which the regime uses to buttress its authority and legitimacy and a method through which it tries to enhance the manageability of public affairs. As far as Putin was concerned, the public good (as he saw it) took precedence over the tiresome proceduralism of the constitutional state, although punctilious in regard to pedantic legalism. These bodies did provide some short-term benefits, but at the cost of the long-term credibility of the institutions which they shadowed. Their existence subtracted from the efficacy of the constitutionally-mandated bodies, the process of sublation.

Second, *para-politics* is the process whereby entities are created in the public realm to stymie and shape the conduct of free and open pluralistic politics, but which lack the autonomy to act as independent subjects of a competitive political sphere. Following the Orange Revolution in Ukraine in Autumn 2004 the creation of the Nashi youth organisation was an exemplary case, designed to occupy the streets to prevent colour-style popular rallies against the regime (Horvath 2013). In a rather more sophisticated version, the creation of the All-Russian People's Front by Putin on 6 May 2011 was designed to broaden the flagging appeal of the United Russia by co-opting civic associations and to help him win the presidential elections in 2012. Putin stated that 185 Front members would be included on United Russia's 600-strong candidate list for the Duma election, while only 167 of the 315 current deputies would be included (Smirnov 2011). Thus even before the 'coup' of September 2011 Putin was mobilising his political resources to prepare for a possible return to the Kremlin. In the end, the Front subtracted from the regime's own pedestal party, United Russia. Faced by sustained attack in the 2011–12 elections, and irredeemably tarnished by the moniker 'party of thieves and swindlers', the regime looked to an alternative instrument to mobilise the electorate and to associate its supporters. Sublation in this case saw the Front assuming some functions of United Russia.

Third, the existence of *factions* is another example of sublation compromising the public political role of political parties. The Russian policy process is shaped by the clash of competing factions. I avoid using the term 'clan' to describe the phenomenon since this would suggest a permanency and hardness to the groups that is typically lacking (Sakwa 2011: 85–130). Factional constellations are groupings based on broad professional, geographical and ideational alliances that are constantly shifting, but which, although held together by the 'weak force' of mutual self-interest and policy orientations, nevertheless exist and populate both the formal and informal spheres of politics. Important issues of policy are determined not by open parliamentary or party politics, but by shadowy groups based on teams working in the interstices of the political system. For example, in his study of energy policy in the Arctic, Orttung (2011: 9) argues that 'The unstable nature of the Russian political system, which is characterized by clan conflict rather than far-sighted planning, means that the country is unlikely to develop a coherent strategy to develop its Arctic resources'.

The *siloviki* are the archetypal faction, with a clear presence in Russian politics but for that no less hard to pin down. The easiest way is simply to look at those with a security service background, and this does help estimate the scale of their presence, but it says little about the struggles between various subfactions within those with a security background. In 2007 there was a nasty '*siloviki* war' as two subfactions fought for power and access to state resources, one of whom appealed to the allegedly selfless traditional values of the security services (Sakwa 2011: 184–209). The St Petersburg contingent that has dominated Russian politics following the rise of Putin is conventionally split between the security officials, and the liberal economists and lawyers. Surkov, deputy head of the presidential administration until December 2011 with responsibility for managing political life, was associated with a 'democratic statist' orientation, which advanced the notion of sovereign democracy in an attempt to combine the universals of democracy (as they understood the term) and the particular challenges facing Russia. The *siloviki* were temporarily balanced by the *civiliki* in the Medvedev years, comprising only about a quarter of top officials, but with Putin's return to the Kremlin for a third term they soon occupied nearly half of the top posts.

Sublation inhibits not only rational policy making but, above all, contributes to the impasse in constitutional development, and this has been something apparent from the very beginning of Russia's state development. The gulf between the visible part of politics and various subterranean processes became apparent very early on in Boris Yeltsin's rule. The 'democratic' revolution of 1991 was quickly captured by the Yeltsin group, which, despite its reformist achievements pushed through by the economic liberals, soon became transformed into 'the family', with all of its mafia 'deep state' implications. The first incarnation of the *siloviki*, the Alexander Korzhakov, Mikhail Barsukov and Oleg Soskovets group, provoked the first Chechen war in December 1994, but was effectively defeated by the counter-move of the liberals led by Chubais in 1996; however, the same Chubais sponsored Putin's move to Moscow in 1996 and helped smooth the ascent of the 'enlightened securocrats' later in the decade. The degradation of the constitutional state continued as representatives of *vlast* became in certain respects the power of *avtoritety*, the godfathers in the mafia tradition (Sakwa 2014: 68–73).

The factional networks of personal affiliations cut across occupational and professional categories, such as the courts, the executive and the legislature, and even to a degree beyond conventional alignments such as the *siloviki* and the liberals. An example of the latter is the Ozero dacha collective of Putin's closest associates, who all have a country cottage near Putin's not far from St Petersburg (Pribylovsky 2012). The factions engage in sublation by undermining the formal channels of policy aggregation through the informal advancement of programmes and principles. In some spheres their influence is stronger, and, as one would expect, the economy is one of these, and in others weaker, notably foreign policy, where since 2004 the foreign minister, Sergei Lavrov, has effectively dominated the process. The various oligarchs lack a recognisable factional identity of their own, and instead align themselves with political leaders, although as a group they undoubtedly look back to the Yeltsin period, when they were independent political actors. After the Yukos affair, they kept their heads under the parapet and instead fought behind the scenes to advance their interests.

In politics, factional contestation is determinative. In the Medvedev years the factional groupings in the end aligned along a classic bipolar axis. Those in favour of a second term for Medvedev were led by economic liberals such as Arkady Dvorkovich, the former head of the presidential administration Alexander Voloshin, and the first deputy prime minister Igor Shuvalov. Opposing them were the more conservative partisans of Putin's return for a third term, led by the deputy prime ministers Igor Sechin and Sergei Ivanov, and the head of Russian railways, Vladimir Yakunin. There were some fundamental policy disagreements, notably over the pace of privatisation, oil revenue taxation and strategy, regional

policy and state investment in the economy and the management of state enterprises, debates that continued after Putin's re-election. The key element in Putin's
'regime-craft', a skill no less important in the Russian context than statecraft, was
the 'levelling of elites'; ensuring that no group acquires excessive influence. This
requires tactical skills of the highest order, but is in constant tension with the more
strategic vision required to achieve success in statecraft. On his return it appeared
at times that Putin was tired of endless tactical balancing and threw in his lot with
the conservatives, accompanied by the attempt to transcend factional logic by
elevating a more personalistic style of leadership.

Putin's return represented a victory for the Sechin camp, but in the manner typical of Putin's management of factional politics, this victory was diluted. Putin
remained true to his promise to appoint Medvedev prime minister, and thus the
liberal camp retained a powerful institutional base. In addition, Putin appointed
Dmitry Rogozin as deputy prime minister responsible for the military-industrial
complex, and thus an alternative leader of the *siloviki* camp was introduced.
However, Putin was forced to dismiss the minister of defence, Anatoly Serdyu-
kov, when Sergei Ivanov, Rogozin and Alexander Bastrykin, the head of the
Investigative Committee of Russia (*Sledstvennyi komitet Rossii*, SKR) closed
ranks to ensure his dismissal to face corruption and personal misconduct charges.
This was one of the rare occasions on which Putin was forced to give up a trusted
ally against his personal inclinations. Sechin went on to head Rosneft and the oil
sector in general, and feared, on the one hand, the further consolidation of the
power of alternative leaders of the *siloviki* faction, Rogozin and Ivanov (with
whom he does not enjoy close relations); and, on the other hand, the replacement
of the weakened Medvedev by a more active liberal at the head the government,
such as Kudrin or Dvorkovich, who would dismantle the state capitalist features
of the economy. Kudrin acted as a 'strategic reserve' for Putin on his return to
the Kremlin.

The concept of sublation is thus crucial to understanding the policy process in
the Putin years, but it is also important to understand its limits. The creation of the
tutelary administrative regime, governing through various practices of sublation,
means that Russia is not Ukraine, where powerful oligarchs have traditionally
been key players in shaping policy, and indeed political, outcomes (Matuszak
2012). Sublation in Russia is of a distinctive sort, reflecting the shifting balance
between the two wings of the dual state.

Models of the third state

Russia remains locked in an extended moment of transition, giving rise to a dual
state and economy and a stalemated political order. The combination of the two
provided Russia with a degree of short-term managerial capacity, but there remains
a blockage on economic modernisation accompanied by a political stalemate. The
long-term balance between the constitutional state and the administrative regime
is in danger of allowing the development of a dangerous third arm, the corruption
associated with the third state of crony capitalist relations where the sublationary

practices of the administrative regime are in danger of dissolving into systemic corruption. What would such a 'third state' look like? To help our analysis of dualism in Russia, a comparative and conceptual analysis of some other countries will help put our problem in context.

One such model focuses on the concept of the deep state. The administrative regime and the constitutional state are joined by what in Italy is called the 'deep state'. This is a subterranean nexus of bureaucratic power, the security services and various types of criminal organisations. In Russia, this dense network of corrupt relationships is variously called 'the mafiya' or some similar designation. In both Russia and Italy this third state reaches into the very heart of government and is characterised by two types of corruption. The *venal* sort is focused on classic bribe taking and giving, transferred for services that should be free but which take on a pecuniary character in a system in which elements of degradation erode ordinary transactions. The scale of this is unknown, of course, but is reflected in Transparency International's Corruption Perception Index. There is a second form which I call *meta-corruption*, when the autonomy of the political system is eroded and administration is placed at the service of criminal and inappropriate activities, undermining the independence of the courts and the impartial management of social processes. The concept of the 'deep state' is applied in several contexts. In Italy it is used to describe the interaction of state officials, security agencies and organised crime, and was particularly prominent during the period of political stress in the 1970s (McSherry 2005: 43–5). Several incidents from that time still remain unexplained, notably the death of Aldo Moro, prime minister from 1963 to 1968 and then again from 1974 to 1976, who was kidnapped by the Red Brigades on 16 March 1978 and killed after 55 days of captivity precisely at the time when he was reciprocating the Communist Party of Italy's idea of a 'historic compromise' to create a 'national solidarity' government (opposed by the United States). The bombing of Bologna railway station on 2 August 1980 killed 85 people amid persistent rumours of Italian secret service involvement (for a popular account, see Jones 2007).

But it is in Turkey that the idea of a deep state has had the most profound impact, and the most pertinent comparisons with Russia. Following the military coup of 1980, the 1981 constitution reserved a privileged place for the military as the defender of the Kemalist secular, nationalist, militarist and semi-isolationist (in the sense of keeping out of wars, although Turkey joined NATO in 1952) political order. This tutelary element is reminiscent of Putin's representation of the functions of his regime in defending political order by transcending the spirit of the constitution, dubbed a 'domain democracy' (Merkel 2004). In Turkey, the military was empowered to intervene to defend the constitution, and thus, by definition, became supra-constitutional. The relevant clauses were abolished by the government of Recep Tayyip Erdo an in the early 2000s as it pursued its ambition to join the European Union. Hailed as a progressive measure by Turkey's allies, paradoxically the removal of a balance against the Justice and Development Party (AKP) after its crushing electoral victory (winning 52 per cent of the popular vote in the 2012 election) opened the door to majoritarian populism and accelerated

Islamisation. The persecution of the Ergenekon secularist and nationalist 'Kemalist' organisation (allegedly part of the deep state) by then had already led to the imprisonment of some 500 officials and officers, including members of the High Command, while in separate prosecutions the same number of journalists had been detained. The 'Putinisation' of the Turkish regime became a matter of popular discussion following the harsh crackdown on the wave of protest catalysed by plans to redevelop Taksim Square, including the destruction of Gezi Park, from May 2013.

The idea of 'Putinisation' became popular, but the level of repression there far outweighed anything that Putin had done by that stage. Putinism in Russia has tried to avoid direct coercive behaviour, although enormous resources are devoted to maintaining the security apparatus. This brings us to the second type of 'third state', a deeply embedded security state. Russia spends some USD 60 billion a year, about 3 per cent of GDP, on the security services, and roughly the same amount in addition on regular military forces. A core Putinite practice is the allocation of resources to groups who would normally be disadvantaged in a market economy – state employees, pensioners, and, in the case under discussion, the security apparatus. The overblown security apparatus generates interests of its own, with department piled upon section, each of which fights for its own perpetuation, its slice of the budgetary pie, and to advance its vision of the world. More than this, Russia's security state is a core element of the politicised economy, allowing raiding by security officials in cahoots with susceptible judges and corrupt officials (Hanson 2014).

A powerful description of the rise and operation of various security force factions is provided by Felshtinsky and Pribylovsky, including the way that the Korzhakov faction provoked the first Chechen war. Putin was appointed head of the FSB on 25 July 1998 to reform the body and not simply as their emissary in the power system (Felshtinsky and Pribylovsky 2008: 87–92). In other words, even in their sensationalist account a political level remains outside the deep state, which retains decisional autonomy. This is also reflected in the excellent account of the 'new nobility' by Soldatov and Borogan, in which they note that 'Putin opened the door to many dozens of security service agents to move up in the main institutions of the country, perhaps hoping that they would prove a vanguard of stability and order. But once they had tasted the benefits, agents began to struggle amongst themselves for the spoils' (Soldatov and Borogan 2010: 241). There is no unity of purpose in Russia's third state, and instead a mix of venal and meta-corruption erodes the quality of government at all levels.

This has not prevented a great flood of literature describing how 'the secret police control all the centres of the economy, security and social life' – a quotation taken from Francesca Mereu's addition to the genre, *My Friend Putin*, which was published in Italian (2011). The book contains a foreword by the well-known journalist and politician Paolo Guzzanti, who chaired the parliamentary commission into the so-called Mitrokhin case, examining KGB activities in Italy between 2002 and 2006. Guzzanti was a close friend of Berlusconi but broke with him over the latter's continued commitment to Putin, whom he called 'friend Vladimir', from which the book draws its title. Like Masha Gessen's book of the same genre, the basic idea is that Putin was the spearhead of a group of former security officials who took control of Russia, including quite explicitly its economic assets. For Gessen (2012), Putin came to power with a conscious plan to install some sort of dictatorship, and her analysis leaves out any complicating details such as policy conflicts over the economy or external relations, and assumes some sort of perfect state of governability. Mereu (2011) sees Putin more as a figurehead for the group, talking in terms of 'Putin's project'. He came to power as the representative of the 'the family', the Yeltsinite group that being desperate to manage the succession in 1999–2000 to preserve the status quo under a new leader.

According to Mereu, the oligarchs headed by Berezovsky offered Putin a deal whereby he would occupy the presidency while they would continue to rule from behind the throne. Putin allegedly agreed to the deal unreservedly. The bombings of the apartment blocks in September 1999 and the second Chechen war were then organised by the KGB in support of Putin's election. Once in power, the KGB then turned its hand to exploiting vulnerable entrepreneurs, closing down media diversity, killing enemies such as Alexander Litvinenko and Anna Politkovskaya, and it thrived in conditions of high oil prices. A *rentier* class consolidated its power, disposing of the country's wealth to its personal advantage. An appendix argues that Berlusconi adopted and imitated from Putin such features as the personality cult, the stifling of media freedom and attacks on the independence of the judiciary, rather than the other way round. The ensuing merger of power and property with little public oversight and minimal public scrutiny created the new system of 'Putin incorporated' (Kalashnikov 2013).

Putinism thus represents a new international style of governance. In contrast to the Soviet years, there is no need for total media control, and thus websites and newspapers were largely left untouched – at least until the Ukraine crisis of 2013–14 unleashed a wave of repression against potential 'colour revolution' technologies. As is argued by Derk Sauer, the head of Sanoma Independent Media, which own 60 per cent of the Russian magazine market, Putin modelled himself not on Brezhnev but on Berlusconi: 'It's not for nothing that they are such good friends. They understand that if you control the main TV stations and make propaganda there, you'll go far'. This led to the paradoxical outcome that 'there's complete press freedom for the informed but none for the uninformed' (Kuper 2013).

But does this constitute a deep state? Is there some force in Russia that can override elections, the government and administration to impose its will, by force if necessary? In Egypt the deep state was based on a 'power triangle' between the military (above all the army), the security services (the police and security policy under the control of the interior ministry), and the political authorities. The coup of 3 July 2013 showed the power of this deep state, which overthrew the legally elected Muslim Brotherhood president that had taken office in June 2012, Mohamed Morsi, and thereafter ruled as a junta, reinstating Mubarak's secret police, gunning down oppositionists, and reimposing the emergency rule of the Mubarak years. Putin and his associates warn constantly against popular democratic revolutions spinning out of control like this, and with some justice. In the Soviet Union and in Russia the regular military has long resisted becoming politicised, especially after the bitter experiences of 1991 and 1993 when they were drawn into political battles, but the MVD and other security agencies have, in effect, armies of their own who could act as the praetorian guard of the regime.

The dual state model suggests that even in Russia's politicised economy there are opportunities for individuals to exploit the tensions between the two branches of the dual state to achieve justice. Equally, the constitutional state provides the normative framework for a pushback against the abuses of the third state. President Dmitry Medvedev's reform of the militia in 2010 demonstrated concern that the abuses of the third state were beginning to threaten the very notion of governance. Rather than fighting criminality, there was much evidence that militia personnel were themselves engaged heavily in a range of illegal activities, including extortion and various scams, the most notorious of which were the Hermitage Capital affair and the death of Sergei Magnitsky. As a report in *The Economist* (18 March 2010) noted, 'Police violence is not new in Russia, but a recent wave of publicity is. A simple explanation is that police lawlessness has exhausted people's patience and that pent-up anger has finally burst into newspapers, websites and even state television.' Medvedev fired Moscow's police chief and launched a reform of the interior ministry (MVD). Police numbers were slashed by 20 per cent and central control was reasserted over regional police forces. There were new requirements on police conduct during searches and other operations, and all police personnel were re-certified in further efforts to root out corruption and incompetence. The Soviet-style name 'militia' was rebranded with the western-style 'police'. Thousands were fired as part of the re-attestation of all serving officers, but there were also questions over the efficacy of the reforms. Taken in isolation and without a reform of the state, police reform was not able to change the fundamental relationship in which, in the words of *The Economist* report, 'The main function of law-enforcement agencies in Russia is not to protect the public from crime and corruption, but to shield the bureaucracy, including themselves, from the public. To ensure loyalty the system allows police and security services to make money from their licence for violence.' One of the most common was 'raiding businesses for competitors'.

More disturbingly, under Putin traditional antagonisms were overcome and the MVD fell under the influence of the Federal Security Service (FSB), which intervened at all levels of business life, including into the affairs of state agencies and corporation, although the legwork was left to the police. In that context, police reform could only be successful if the abuses of the third state more broadly were addressed. As the lawyer and independent scholar Vladimir Pastukhov (2013; and see also 2012) argues, Putin did not eliminate arbitrariness but gave it 'a more or less organised character'. The securo-judicial apparatus remained a powerful instrument of regime power, but it was as factionalised as the rest of the system. Despite Medvedev's calls for reform, the law enforcement agencies remained a law unto themselves. On 1 January 2011 the Investigative Committee was removed from the jurisdiction of the General Prosecutor's Office (GPO) to become the free-standing Russian Investigative Committee (RIC) answerable directly to the president. The head of the GPO, Yuri Chaika, was furious at this drastic reduction in his power, but this was just one of the interdepartmental conflicts plaguing the Putin system of Byzantine politics. The separation represents yet another case of sublation, weakening the procuracy and creating a counter-weight to its authority. Headed by the pugnacious Mikhail Bastrykin, who became one of the most powerful and independent figures in Putin's power elite, RIC was involved in the prosecution of some high profile individuals, including Sergei Storchak, Magnitsky and latterly, the opposition activist Alexei Navalny. Bastrykin stressed that one of RIC's main tasks was to fight corruption (Yamshanov and Vasenin 2010).

In short, it is an exaggeration to argue that Russia has a 'deep state' as defined above, but the powerful security–economic nexus acts as part of the blockage on modernisation and has now constituted itself as a type of third state, undermining the normative claims of the administrative regime to govern in Russia's best interests. In the context of a dual state a regime has emerged that can trump the stipulations of the constitution, but which remains constrained by the constitutional framework. Its subversions of legality remain illegitimate as defined by the system itself, and there has been no legal invocation of emergency rule. Instead, there is a system of meta-corruption, in which the agents of the state are heavily implicated and which potentially constitutes itself as a third state. The security forces have a special role, but even their illicit political and economic activities are balanced by other features of the complex organism that is the Russian power system. Unable to act as a state within the state, they have operated as a substate within the regime. In other words, the administrative regime is itself in danger of being sublated by the forces that it has unleashed in the third state.

Second Empire Russia

One of the more potent comparisons of contemporary Russia could well be with Second Empire France. We have a Bonapartist situation where social forces are equally balanced (above all between the bureaucracy and nascent political representations of the middle class), allowing the regime to act with autonomy. The Russian government continued the revolution in property and power that had begun in the late Gorbachev years, but at the same time restored elements of the previous regime. Promoted as the ideology of reconciliation, invoking shades of the *trasformismo* of late nineteenth-century Italy, the inconclusive nature of the system takes the form of a dual state, with all of its inherent contradictions and accompanying stalemate that has allowed elements of the third state to flourish. Both contemporary Russia and the France of Louis Napoleon were hybrid in their very essence. Neither are a 'regime type' in the classical sense understood in political science. Instead, both represent what Stepan and Linz (2013: 20) call a 'situation', a condition of impermanence, however long it may last. Thus the Putinite stability is unstable in its very essence. There can be achievements, such as the Sochi Olympics, economic investments and elements of modernisation, but until the regime question is resolved the whole system remains 'provisional', even if it lasts for decades. Like Napoleon III's France, an enormous amount of development can take place, yet the clash between two different orders and types of regulatory regime means that the system is indeed a 'situation'. This applies equally to the political sphere, where in both countries elections gained a plebiscitary character and the political authorities were not held accountable to their outcomes, yet the whole procedure of elections was important for the stability of the system. Thus the comparison between the two countries has important heuristic qualities, and helps shed light on the character of contemporary Russia's politicized economy.

Following the 1848 Revolution and the overthrow of the 'bourgeois' rule of Louis Philippe, Louis Napoleon seized power in a coup in 1849 and ruled until the Franco-Prussian War of 1870, at which point he went into exile in England. In 1850 he declared the creation of the 'Second Empire' and thereafter he ruled as Napoleon III. The subsequent two decades witnessed enormous economic development, with the massive expansion of industry and the railways and the reconstruction of Paris under the guidance of Baron Haussmann. However, fundamental political issues remained unresolved as the ideals of the French Revolution, principally the concept of popular sovereignty, came into contradiction with renewed imperial rule. Like the Putin system, the second empire represented a system in which the potential for evolutionary political development was blocked, yet did not repudiate the revolutions to which they were heir.

Putin's administration claims to stand above the historic divisions of the modern era, and indeed, purposely sought to reconcile the forces that had torn Russia apart in the twentieth century. The democratic process was managed by a force that stood outside democracy, co-opting those elements of political society willing to compromise and marginalising the rest. This is a type of passive revolution, which for Antonio Gramsci entailed 'an abortive or incomplete transformation of society'. This can take a number of forms, including one where an external force provokes change, but this lacks a sufficiently strong domestic constituency and runs into the resistance of entrenched interests. When the forces are equally balanced a stalemate emerges, giving rise to a situation of 'revolution/restoration' (Gramsci 1971: 104–20). We have a Bonapartist situation where class forces (in particular, the entrenched bureaucracy resisting the challenge of an independent bourgeoisie) are equally balanced, allowing the regime to act with autonomy (cf. Cox 1999: 16). The Russian government continued the revolution in property and power begun in the late Gorbachev years, but at the same time restored elements of the previous regime.

Thus the Putinite 'situation' and the politicised economy can be better understood by comparison with mid-nineteenth-century France. The contradictions that brought Louis Bonaparte, the nephew of Napoleon I, to power in the coup on 2 December 1851 were powerfully described by Marx (1968: 97–180), and his eloquent indictment has resonance today for the Putin system: 'Instead of *society* having conquered a new content for itself, it seems that the *state* only returned to its oldest form, to the shamelessly simple domination of the sabre and the cowl' (1968: 99). The 'virtual politics' of the time is sharply characterised:

[A]lliances whose first proviso is separation; struggles whose first law is indecision; wild, inane agitation in the name of tranquillity, most solemn preaching of tranquillity in the name of revolution; passion without truth, truths without passion; heroes without heroic deeds, history without events; development, whose sole driving force seems to be the calendar, wearying with the same tensions and relaxations; antagonisms that periodically seem to work themselves up to a climax only to lose their sharpness and fall away without being able to resolve themselves; pretentiously paraded exertions and philistine terror at the danger of the world coming to an end, and at the same time the pettiest intrigues and court comedies played by the world redeemers... (Marx1968: 116)

Following the coup Marx notes that France appeared to have escaped the despotism of a class (the bourgeoisie) only 'to fall back beneath the despotism of an individual', and in comments that have resonance today argued 'This executive power with its enormous bureaucratic and military organisation, with its ingenious state machinery, embracing wide strata, with a host of officials numbering half a million, besides an army of another half million, this appalling parasitic body, ... enmeshes the body of French society like a net and chokes all its pores' (1968: 170), a description that is astonishingly apt for the workings of the administrative regime. In sum, 'Only under the second Bonaparte does the state seem to have made itself completely independent. As against civil society, the state machine has consolidated its position...' (1968: 171). To overcome the contradiction and to keep the public gaze on himself, Napoleon III needed to 'spring constant surprises, that is to say, under the necessity of executing a *coup d'état en miniature* every day' (1968: 180). This is not unlike the Putinite system, with its surprising turns, sudden demarches, and unpredictable decisionality.

In the Russian case these miniature coups are prevalent at times of succession, precipitated by the regular cycle of elections and constitutional term limits. The heightened decisionism of the administrative regime ultimately becomes a mode of governance, undermining the quality of the decisions at home and tempting voluntaristic actions abroad. As argued in this chapter, duality is a feature of all political systems, but as D'Arcais puts it in his study of 'Berlusconismo': 'All Western governments, more or less, are marked by the gap between the poetry of constitutions and the prose of power as it is exercised. What is decisive, however, is precisely the degree of this "more or less"' (D'Arcais 2011: 139). Italy, in his view, had endured a long-term creeping coup that subverted the independent functioning of institutions and allowed the deep state to flourish. The response here and elsewhere could only be the genuine consolidation of the liberal democratic constitutional state.

Conclusion

Putin came to power in 2000 promising to root politics in the normative power of the constitution, but instead the neopatrimonial order brought all institutions and political processes under the tutelage of the administrative regime. The power system is susceptible to weaknesses of its own, above all fragmentation and elite factionalism. Putin's reconstitution of the state shifted the basis of presidential hegemony away from dependence on oligarchic or other forces. However, the failure to move away from the 'manual control' of political processes prevented a more self-regulating system from emerging, and instead the mechanical approach created a system that showed signs of brittleness and a lack of adaptive resources. Above all, the dualism identified earlier is in danger of degenerating into a triple system in which the merger of power and property jeopardises the viability of the economy as a whole. Venal corruption in an uncontrolled triple state is in danger of metastising into meta-corruption and degeneration of the whole system.

A number of cultures contend for primacy. The traditional tsarist-patrimonial view is in part supplanted by Soviet progressivism, and this in turn is challenged by a westernising project based on markets, democracy and international integration. The internal clash of civilisations and inherent value pluralism entails very different representations, for example, of the role of private enterprise and property rights, and, equally, about Russia's place in the world. The lack of a single natural hegemony allows Putin's eclecticism to triumph. The stalemate thus assumes a cultural and civilisational dimension, as various projects of modernity jostle to dominate but none enjoys that peculiar combination of class, ideology, and institutional resources to enjoy a hegemonic position, and instead a number of partial projects have combined to create an explicitly self-referential social order exposed to attack from all sides. None of its constituent elements has been able to enjoy the fruits of victory, but by the same token none has been definitively defeated. The 'situation' allows a new form of second empire to emerge, in which very similar developmental and great power concerns are prominent.

The Putinite system represents managed modernisation in an era where the collapse of the communist system was accompanied by the exhaustion of original ideas for social renewal in their entirety. Thus Putin devised a synthesis of his own, drawing on parts of the Soviet debris but also devising some original solutions to Russia's distinctive developmental challenges. The terrain in which he operates encompasses not just the ruins of state socialism, but also one in which the great ameliorative projects of modernity, of both the right and the left, had run into the ground, and thus all that was left was the attempt to revive a centrist ideology and pragmatic and incremental political project. These were the elements that thrived before the great ideologies of modernity, notably in Second Empire France. Putin's mix includes state-led developmentalism, traditional statist paternalism, accompanied by a critique of the sovereignty-eroding tropes of globalisation theory. It also contains the potential to degenerate into a self-serving 'third state', where the regime's developmental rhetoric is engulfed by meta-corruption. The self-proclaimed tutelary administrative regime is in danger of succumbing to the temptations of the third state.

In Russia a single regime has perpetuated itself since 1991, with elections a secondary, legitimating, practice. Elections are not determinative of government, but they do send a signal to the regime, and are thus not entirely nugatory. The regime, however, discredits its operative legitimating mechanisms, which becomes evident when there is a divergence between popular attitudes and electoral outcomes. Above all, just as the constitutional state is vulnerable to the depredations of the administrative regime, so the latter's developmental purpose is undermined by the pathologies of the third state. It is only a matter of time before 'the situation' is transcended. This could take the form of intra-systemic reform that allows the constitutional state to strengthen; or it could take the catastrophic form of regime collapse provoked by external conflict, as in France in 1870.

References

Cox, R.W. (1999) 'Civil Society at the Turn of the Millennium: Prospects for an Alternative World Order', *Review of International Studies*, 25(1): 3–18.

D'Arcais, P.D. (2011) 'Anatomy of Berlusconismo', *New Left Review*, 68: 121–40.

Felshtinsky, Y. and Pribylovsky, V. (2008) *The Age of Assassins: The Rise and Rise of Vladimir Putin*, London: Gibson Square.

Fraenkel, E. (1941/2006) *The Dual State: A Contribution to the Theory of Dictatorship*, translated from the German by E.A. Shils, in collaboration with Edith Lowenstein and Klaus Knorr, Clark, NJ: The Lawbook Exchange.

Gessen, M. (2012) *The Man Without a Face: The Unlikely Rise of Vladimir Putin*, New York: Riverhead Books.

Gramsci, A. (1971) 'Notes on Italian History', in *Selections From the Prison Notebooks of Antonio Gramsci*, edited and translated by Quintin Hoare and Geoffrey Nowell Smith, London: Lawrence & Wishart.

Hanson, P. (2014) '*Reiderstvo*: Asset Grabbing in Russia', *Russia and Eurasia*, PP 2014/03, London: Chatham House.

Hellman, J.S. (1998) 'Winners Take All: The Politics of Partial Reform in Postcommunist Transitions', *World Politics*, 50(2): 203–34.

Henderson, J. and Ferguson, A. (2014) *International Partnership in Russia: Conclusions from the Oil and Gas Industry*, Basingstoke: Palgrave Macmillan.

Horvath, R. (2013) *Putin's 'Preventative Counter-Revolution': Post-Soviet Authoritarianism and the Spectre of Velvet Revolution*, London and New York: Routledge.

Jones, T. (2007) *The Dark Heart of Italy*, London: Faber & Faber.

Kalashnikov, M. (2013) *Putin inkorporeited: Kak Putinu obustroit Rossiyu,* Moscow: Algoritm/Eksmo.

Kuper, S. (2013) 'What Putin Learnt from Berlusconi', *Financial Times*, 31 May.

Marx, K. (1968) 'The Eighteenth Brumaire of Louis Bonaparte', in *Marx and Engels: Selected Works in One Volume*, London: Lawrence & Wishart, pp. 97–180.

Matuszak, S. (2012) *The Oligarchic Democracy: The Influence of Business Groups on Ukrainian Politics*, OSW Studies, Warsaw: Centre for Eastern Studies.

McSherry, J.P. (2005) *Predatory States: Operation Condor and Covert War in Latin America*, Boulder: Rowman & Littlefield.

Mereu, F. (2011) *L'amico Putin: L'invenzione della dittatura democratic*, Reggio Emilia: Aliberti Editore.

Merkel, W. (2004) 'Embedded and Defective Democracies', *Democratisation*, 11(5): 33–58.

Orttung, R. (2011) 'Conflict Over Arctic Energy: States, Corporations, Politics', *Russian Analytical Digest*, 100: 7–10, 26 July.

Pastukhov, V. (2012) *Restavratsiya vmesto reformatsii: Dvadtsat let, kotorye potryasli Rossiyu*, Moscow: OGI.

Pastukhov, V. (2013) 'Legenda No. 1917', *Novaya gazeta*, 22 August.

Pribylovsky, V. (2012) *Kooperativ 'Ozero' i drugie proekty Vladimira Putina*, Moscow: Algoritm.

Sakwa, R. (2010) 'The Dual State in Russia', *Post-Soviet Affairs*, 26(3): 185–206.

Sakwa, R. (2011) *The Crisis of Russian Democracy: The Dual State, Factionalism and the Medvedev Succession*, Cambridge: Cambridge University Press.

Sakwa, R. (2014) *Putin Redux: Power and Contradiction in Contemporary Russia*, London and New York: Routledge.

Smirnov, V. (2011) *Front Putina: Protiv kogo?*, Moscow: Algoritm.

Soldatov, A. and Borogan, I. (2010) *The New Nobility: The Restoration of Russia's Security State and the Enduring Legacy of the KGB*, New York: Public Affairs.

Stepan. A. and Linz, J.J. (2013) 'Democratization Theory and the "Arab Spring"', *Journal of Democracy*, 24(2): 15–30.

The Economist (2010) 'Police Brutality in Russia: Cope for Hire', 18 March. Online. Available: www.economist.com/node/15731344/print (accessed 31 August 2014).

Yamshanov, B. and Vasenin, V. (2010) 'Neposredstvennaya zhizn: Predlozheniya ot Bastrykina – sozdat edinyi sledstevnnyi komitet i vvesti otchety o raskhodakh chinovnikov', *Rossiiskaya gazeta*, 7 September.

9 The basis for institutions among the population in Russia

Carolina Vendil Pallin

He will never understand me or my mother, since he has not lived a single day in a Soviet country. I… and my son… and my mother… We all live in different countries, even though all this is Russia. But we are all tied together in a monstrous way. Monstrous! We all feel betrayed.

Svetlana Aleksievich (2013: 284)[1]

The quote above comes from the last part of Svetlana Aleksievich's trilogy of Russian voices and is intriguing even though it mirrors something that should be obvious in a society that has undergone such profound crises and transformations as have taken place in Russia during the past two to three decades. The way deeply held beliefs and behaviour patterns change and coexist in society often receives considerably less attention than, for example, the day-to-day power struggles within the Kremlin, the opinion rating of Vladimir Putin and the possible future of opposition figures such as Aleksei Navalnyi or Mikhail Khodorkovskiy. However, the existence of certain values and norms among the population is imperative for the successful establishment of democratic institutions in society (Inglehart and Welzel 2005: 158; Tikhonova 2011: 12; IS RAN 2013: 7–8).

Among the most important institutions that underpin a democratic society is rule of law, that political leaders are held accountable in free, open and fair elections as well as respect for basic human rights and freedoms such as a free media and the right to form political parties and movements, religious freedom and the right to express one's opinion freely as long as this does not infringe on the rights and freedoms of others. All these democratic institutions can also play an important role in economic reform. For instance, rule of law is a necessary precondition for the right to dispose of one's property or for companies to seek arbitration against corrupt or otherwise incorrect decisions of authorities and the abuse of power of individual officials. Addressing the problem of corruption without instituting a greater degree of rule of law is difficult to imagine in Russia. A free media, transparency and the existence of an opposition that can contest power in elections are equally imperative in order to detect and combat arbitrary decisions and misuse of power.

This chapter aims to establish whether there is a growing demand for democratic institutions in Russian society. This is done by looking at how income and consumption patterns have changed in society, but also at changes in values and norms in society.

Modernization and development of values in society

Socio-economic development tends to set powerful forces in motion. First, this chapter assumes that with increased income and investment in housing and more durable consumption such as a car, a demand for institutions, such as rule of law, that protect property is more likely to emerge. Likewise, as sections of the population get used to consumption that is tied to increased mobility both when it comes to travelling and with regard to using the internet and mobile phones to access and share information, they are more likely to embrace institutions that guarantee the right to use this mobility freely, such as a democratic polity that guarantees, for example, freedom of information, the right to travel and a free media.

Second, there is a growing literature on the connection between socio-economic development and the development of values conducive to democracy. There has been a debate on whether the establishment of institutions can foster democratic values (see, for example, Di Palma 1990) or whether the pre-existence of values beneficial to democracy is necessary for institutions to survive. Ronald Inglehart and Christian Welzel (2005) have argued convincingly that social change is, above all, a process of human development and that what they term as self-expression values, in other words values that place an emphasis on the individual, on human rights and freedoms, make it more likely for democracy to root and develop. Their modernization theory says that in a post-industrial society, where people are no longer concerned with existential security and making ends meet, where socio-economic development has led to an increase in GDP per capita and the economy has become diversified with more and more people working in the service sector, self-expression values are likely to become increasingly widespread. The younger generation is the first to embrace new values as they experience increasing existential security during their formative years (ibid.: 94–114).

There are also cultural differences and one of the experiences that Inglehart and Welzel single out as having had a negative impact on the development of self-expression values is the number of years spent under communism. In addition, the economic hardships for the population in Russia in the 1990s made development go backward rather than forward as a large section of the population found their existential security threatened. As a result, self-expression values did not develop during this period (ibid.: 81–3).

Another factor that works against the development of self-expression values among the Russian population is the tendency for wealth in oil-exporting countries with rent-seeking economies to end up in the hands of the elite rather than being more evenly distributed (ibid.: 160). Even in Russia, however, the economic wealth entailed by increasing incomes from energy exports incomes did trickle down to sections of society other than the very rich. Socio-economic development has taken place and this is especially true for large urban centres where increasing per capita incomes have been coupled with a growing diversification of the economy with large shares of the population working in the service sector. Smaller cities and the countryside have not seen the same development, as will be evidenced below. In other words, at least some of the younger cohorts have experienced better material conditions in their formative years than the above generations. They have got used to better living conditions, to owning a mobile phone and the access to computers and internet.

The overall aim of this chapter is to explore whether there is a growing demand for institutions in Russian society based on how the behaviour and values of the population have evolved. More specifically, the chapter explores the differences between different sections of the population, between different age groups and different strata according to socio-economic development. We would expect that among sections of the population with higher incomes as well as among the younger generation, it should be possible to observe an evolution of self-expression values, that is, values that place more emphasis on individualism. The view of the state and its role should change from one that provides employment security and material support to a state that guarantees the rules of the game, but where citizens are by and large left to their own devices to build their future. At the same time, if socio-economic development has been slow or almost non-existent for certain sections of society, we would expect a much lower rate of self-expression values here and more concern about existential security and material support.

In order to examine the basis for establishing democratic institutions in Russian, this chapter first explores different and often overlapping groups in society that are identified according to socio-economic development and age. Second, some changes in behaviour are analysed such as consumption and investment patterns, investments in real estate and the increasing mobility in Russian society. Belonging to a specific group in society based on income, education, age and where you live as well as consumption patterns and property will provide experiences that, in turn, form a value and norm system. Finally, the overall trends in opinion surveys are examined.

Rather than focusing on politician's ratings in opinion polls, this chapter thus aims to explore deeper patterns of values and behaviour. Specific political preferences can change almost overnight as a result of a political or economic event or even after a single foolish or, for that matter, brilliant political speech by a politician. Norms and values concerning freedom, rule of law and private property as well as other aspects of human rights, on the other hand, are bound to have evolved with time and thus be durable and tied to aggregated individual experiences rather than to single events. Indeed moral, social and political values can be considered as the 'ultimate underpinnings of attitudes' (Feldman 2013: 602; see also Shestopal 2011: 36). The emphasis is on examining how society has changed during the past decade, but this is, when possible, done against the backdrop of behaviour and values in the 1990s.

The chapter builds on secondary sources that include opinion polls, focus group surveys, other sociological research and statistics. The fact that the sources are secondary ones invariably leads to a certain time lag. Even articles published as late as in 2013 in peer-reviewed journals draw on material that will have been collected a couple of years earlier. As far as possible, recent research has been used and whenever the latest data are older than 2010, this is highlighted. However, since changes in values occur over long time periods, finding the latest data is of less importance than tracing long-term trends and finding data that break down values according to which population group the respondents belong.

As stated above, an effort has been made to use material with long timelines or that breaks down research according to different groups in society, since the aim is both to map the current situation and to detect changes that have occurred in Russian society following the fall of the Soviet Union. Since the chapter builds on a variety of research rather than on data from an individual project, it is often difficult to draw comparisons; questions have been stated differently, timelines constructed with various measure points, and so on. The aim is to provide an overall picture of values and changes in behaviour rather than exact measurements and the use of different surveys and statistics has been considered to be a valid approach.

Some of the research used is possibly coloured by political bias. For example, the research carried out by the Centre for Strategic Analysis (*Tsentr strategicheskikh razrabotok*, CSR) headed by Mikhail Dmitriev was closely tied to, and at times even commissioned by Aleksei Kudrin's organization, the Committee for Civil Initiatives (*Komitet grazhdanskikh initsiativ*, KGI). Similarly, the Levada Center[2] is often considered as belonging to the liberal flank, although it does have a reputation for independence and sound methodology. The Russian Federal Statistical Service, Rosstat, on the other hand, is sometimes accused of inflating data. Opinion pollsters such as All-Russian Centre for Studying Public Opinion (VTsIOM) and the Foundation for Public Opinion in Society (FOM) list the Presidential Administration among their most important customers and are considered to be less independent from the authorities than, for example, the Levada Center. The chapter must be read, therefore, with these caveats in mind. The fact that a wide range of data are used should give a broad picture rather than one skewed in one particular political direction. Overall, opinion polls often fail to deliver clear-cut answers and are open to interpretations. The results often appear to be counterintuitive and contradictory because they challenge presuppositions or because the questions were constructed in a specific manner (for discussions on this, see Hale 2011; Levinson 2012, 2013).

Different groups in Russian society

Following the unexpected demonstrations in 2011–12, a great deal of attention was given to the middle class. However, focusing on a young, urban technology-savvy middle class risks missing a number of important societal trends as concerns development. Among those who have contributed to nuancing the picture of Russian society is Aleksei Levinson at the Levada Center, who talks of a 'functional differentiation' that is considerably more than just differences in income distribution. Rather it is a rising 'multitude of role situations, in which individuals find themselves (different occupations, professions, positions inside groups and associations)' (Levinson 2013: 33). The social stratification according to a middle class and a lower class and the periphery of these is one important way of analysing Russian society. However, it is equally important to keep in mind the widening gap between regions and between urban centres and the periphery as well as the considerable differences between age groups and gender.

A Russian middle class? And the rest?

The size of a Russian middle class is a topic that has generated both research and debate. Indeed, the middle class has even been discarded as a myth, a class that does not exist in Russia (Samson and Krasilnikova 2012). Nevertheless, most researchers do acknowledge that it is a usable concept, although they differ in how to define and measure it and, consequently, come up with different sizes and development trends for it. Usually, the middle class is defined using a mix of income bracket, education, self-image and functional specifics (Franke and Vendil Pallin 2013: 30–1; Tikhonova and Mareeva 2009: 75ff.). Using such definitions, the middle class constitutes 20–30 per cent of the Russian population.

However, mapping the values and concerns of other sections of society is of equal importance in attempting to understand human development in Russia. The question of how to divide the rest of the population into classes or social strata is even more open to debate than that of the size of the middle class. In the early 1990s there was a sharp increase in income inequality in Russia. This is indicated by the Gini coefficients for both income inequality and wage inequality (Ovcharova *et al.* 2013: 15–16). When the population is divided into five groups, ranging from the 20 per cent that have the highest income to the 20 per cent with the lowest income, it becomes obvious that the group which is best off receives increasing shares of the total income per year whereas the group with the lowest income is receiving a dwindling share of total incomes in Russian society (Figure 9.1). It is also quite clear that those who constitute the nucleus of the lower class are more likely to remain there. In Tikhonova's (2012) analysis, about 6–8 per cent of the population belong to the underclass and the nucleus of the lower class. Moreover, almost as many are at risk of ending up in the lower class in the next few years. These groups have only elementary education, they are more often employed in temporary jobs and with little or no prospect of saving up money to improve their living conditions. The sense of insecurity is often acute (ibid.).

Differences between regions and centre–periphery

Furthermore, there are substantial differences between regions in Russia. Among the most developed are oil- and gas-rich regions and the federal cities Moscow and St Petersburg whereas certain ethnic republics struggle with serious economic and social problems. This is evident from a survey of the Human Development Index (HDI), which measures incomes, education and longevity (Zubarevich 2011).

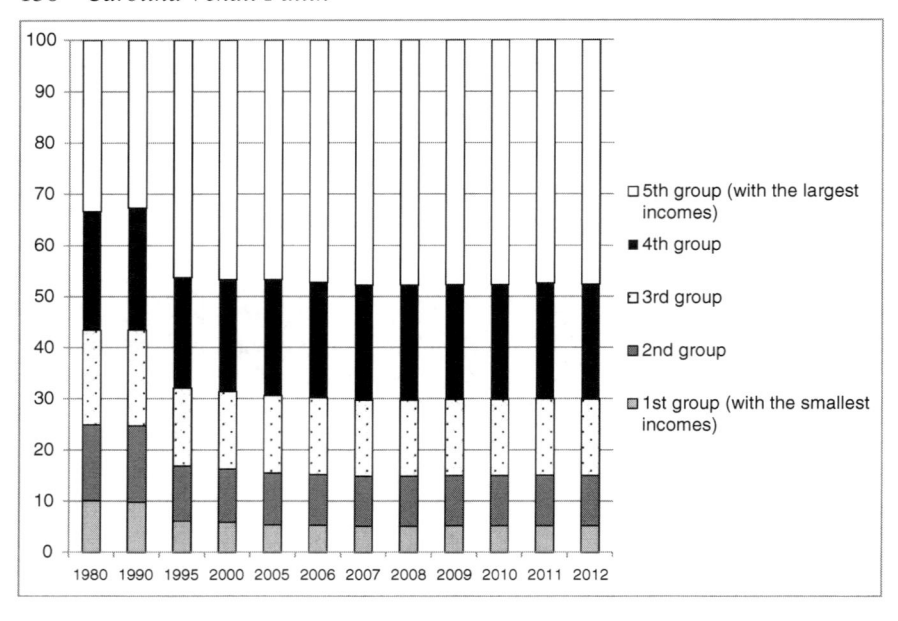

Figure 9.1 Distribution of the total income among five groups of the population, 1980–2012 (%).

Source: Rosstat (2012: 186).

Note: Each groups constitutes 20 per cent of the population. For the years 2005–10, the data from the 2010 population census has been used.

However, it seems that the divide between centre and periphery is of even greater importance. Nataliya Zubarevich (2013) has divided Russia into four Russias. The first Russia consists of cities with a population of over 250,000 citizens and with diversified economies, while industrial cities with a population of 20,000–250,000 constitute the second Russia. The first Russia is likely to protest against poor institutions, but the second Russia is more likely to become involved in socio-economic protests. Indeed, 'the two Russias speak a different language and have difficulty understanding each other' (ibid.). The third Russia consists of villages and small, rural towns. Its population is aging and shrinking and lives mainly off the land, while the fourth Russia consists of the underdeveloped republics in the North Caucasus and Tyva and Altai in southern Siberia. These republics are reliant on transfers from the federal budget and constitute actual or potential trouble spots (see further Chapter 11 in this volume).

Zubarevich's findings are substantiated by other research and federal statistics. Living in a village and/or in a region that is among the least prosperous constitutes one of the most prominent factors connected to poverty. Among the low-income households in Russia, an overwhelming majority (66 per cent) lived in villages and cities that were smaller than 50,000 people (Rosstat 2012: 193). There is a widely held assumption that pensioners are poorer than other groups in the population, but in fact where you live is a more important factor in determining affluence or poverty in Russia (Ovcharova *et al.* 2013: 22–9). The official statistics are substantiated by research on the societal structure in Russia (Tikhonova 2012: 33–7). Indeed, the Russian sociologist Nataliya Tikhonova notes the tendency towards a 'ghettoization of a substantial proportion of "small town" Russia, with the increasing spread there of the type of culture that characterizes an underclass' (ibid.: 42).

Within the first Russia, Moscow stands out as an exceptional case for a number of different reasons. It has the most diversified labour market, the highest level of education among its citizens, the highest influx of a diversified workforce and the lowest level of unemployment as well as the highest level of wages and consumption (even after adjusting for higher costs of living). On the downside, it also has the largest housing problems and a low share of children among its population. Furthermore, Moscow is a federal city and not a municipality.[3] This makes the city more independent since it receives budget revenues without having to depend on transfers from the federal centre (Zubarevich 2012).

The special conditions that apply to the population in Moscow, both the advantages and the disadvantages, are bound to colour the values and moral systems of its inhabitants. Those who are lucky enough to own an apartment or a house in Moscow or in greater Moscow are bound to regard it as a security and capital given the rapid rise in property prices. This will have consequences for how citizens in Moscow view rule of law and the protection of the right to own property.

Moscow's mayor Sergei Sobyanin noted in 2013 that in Moscow 'the level of demand, demands on authorities are considerably higher than in the countryside' (Gabuev and Surnachevaya 2013). This is probably true and is evident also in focus group surveys and opinion polls, where Moscow often stands out. In the 2013 CSR study, respondents in Moscow were more concerned with what they described as a cultural and moral crisis than was the case in the rest of the country. They furthermore expressed discontent with insecurity, the lack of respect for individual rights and freedoms and the state of the social sphere. Overall, the Moscow respondents harboured a higher degree of anxiety (*trevozhnost*) for the future as compared to other cities (CSR 2013: 44–57).

Age groups and gender

The differences in income between age groups are not as large as one would perhaps expect intuitively. As evidenced above, where you live is a more important factor than age in determining your level of income. Often, the similarities between age groups are more striking than the differences. For example, in CSR's research, there is no significant difference in the degree to which the respondents in different groups according to age express anxiety or aggression (CSR 2013: 32–3).

Nevertheless, a number of interesting trends can be observed. In a study carried out by VTsIOM, it was clear that, for example, people aged 24–33 with a middle to higher education were more likely to believe that the internet provided the opportunity to influence the authorities (Nechaev and Brodovskaya 2013: 10). A majority of Russians think that they cannot significantly influence their circumstances themselves but are dependent on the state and the economic situation of the country as a whole. Overall, there is a strong belief that changes must be initiated and controlled from above, but there is a notable difference between age groups. Those under thirty are more likely to assert that their own circumstances depend on their activity rather than on the state whereas the eldest take the opposite view (see Table 9.2). That those over sixty depend on the state is hardly surprising, but the fact that younger people are more looking to their own abilities than the cohort of the population that is in its most productive age, with higher incomes than the under-thirties is noteworthy. This is, furthermore, well in line with earlier research that focuses on attitudes among the younger generation, such as the study carried out in Yaroslav in 1993–2004 by Hahn and Logvinenko (2008) and research on the confidence in achieving one's dreams presented by Gorshkov and Tikhonova (2013: 10–11).

When it comes to differences between genders, there is an overrepresentation by women among the group in society that constitutes a 'low-resource group'. Moreover, the ratio of women who are raising young children is substantially higher (about two-thirds) in what Tikhonova (2012: 39) calls the 'zone of formation of the lower class' compared to about a third in the middle class, and 'about 60 per cent are raising children in incomplete families (common law marriage, divorce, single mothers, etc.)'. This will, in turn, most probably have consequences for their outlook on life.

Consumption patterns, housing and mobility

The Russian middle class is the section of society that is more likely to own property(including a house or an apartment), use the internet regularly, own mobile phones and travel abroad (Dmitriev and Misikhina 2012: 66–7). This is connected to its incomes but also to its relative high level of education and its own sense of identity. At the same time, it is clear that consumption across the whole population has increased. When it comes to capital goods, a protracted period of economic growth has resulted in figures of 170 television sets per 100 households in 2011 and 122 refrigerators and freezers per 100 households; the numbers in 2000 were 124 and 113, respectively (Rosstat 2012: 201). Even taking into account the considerable income differences, many households appear to have been able to increase consumption at least on the margin.

Consumption and investment patterns

Overall, in the 2000s there has been an increase in the consumption of goods other than foodstuffs and services (Ovcharova *et al.* 2013: 30–1). The middle class has the highest level of consumption and its consumption pattern differs from that of other groups since it devotes a considerable share of its resources to vacation and culture events (Dmitriev and Misikhina 2012: 60). Furthermore, it tends to own more capital goods, not least foreign cars (ibid.: 60–4). When considering overall statistics, it is obvious that consumption patterns have changed for the population as a whole over the past decade. Food and clothing no longer constitute more than half of consumption (Rosstat Online). This feature is most pronounced among the share of households that dispose of the highest incomes, where approximately a third of consumption is spent on food and clothes. This group of households spends considerably more on transport and leisure than other households (Rosstat 2012: 198).

Housing

The middle class has better living conditions overall, but especially when it comes to the Russian eternal 'housing question' (*zhilishchnyi vopros* or *kvartirnyi vopros*). A considerable proportion of the middle class owns housing and capital goods which leads to new demands on what the state should be able to deliver in terms of property protection, fighting corruption and building institutions that eradicate fortune seekers and embezzlers in the sphere of, for example, private health care (Dmitriev and Misikhina 2012: 59–78). The middle class is in favour of private ownership in the housing sector, and this appears to be the case even for those who have not benefitted from the privatization programme. Although it has been suggested that when tenancy rights were strengthened in the Soviet era, tenants came to see themselves as de facto owners of their apartments, legal ownership is crucial 'to a sense of autonomy, security and satisfaction' (Attwood 2012: 925).

For the middle class an important aspect of owning an apartment or a house is the fact that it regards this as part of its savings towards its pension. For most people belonging to the middle class, it is reasonable to expect to receive that their pension payments will amount to only around 10–20 per cent of their income during their working lives (Dmitriev and Misikhina 2012: 70–1). The current pension system has in fact been created in order to achieve a balance between state income and expenditure than to diminish the difference in incomes at different stages in life. In conditions of high inflation and crises in the fund market, it therefore makes more sense for the middle class to invest in its own health or in real estate (Ovcharova *et al.* 2013: 12).

In the 'nucleus' of the lower class, around 40 per cent are renting only a room or a bed in a dormitory rather than having their own separate flat or house. This is especially noteworthy considering that a majority lives in small villages, where the shortage of housing should be less pressing than in large urban centres (Tikhonova 2012: 40). Connected to the question of privatization of housing is that of the cost of utilities. These have risen sharply in some municipalities, but this is also something that sparks protests, particularly among an elder generation 'who spent much of their adult lives under the Soviet regime, since they have come to see cheap housing as a civil right' (Attwood 2012: 908).

Transport

Over the past couple of decades, the use of public transport has fallen from its highest point, measured in terms of billions of kilometres travelled by passengers (passenger-kilometres), when it reached 791 billion (in 1990) to a figure of just 502 billion in 2011 (Rosstat 2012: 486; Popov 2012: 154). Following the pattern in western countries, meanwhile, car ownership increased significantly even during the economic crisis in the 1990s. And it did so in spite of the substantial and increasing costs involved (such as service and running costs, car insurance and taxes) and the risks for traffic accidents – four times higher than in leading countries in Western Europe (Popov 2012: 156). Even the traffic jams and the access to a developed infrastructure for communal travel in Moscow do not appear to have dampened the wish to own a car, considering that there have consistently been more cars per capita in Moscow compared to Russia as a whole (Rosstat 2012: 203).

Car ownership is, furthermore, connected to a sense of freedom. Consequently, any infringements on this liberty or abuse of privilege by the elite (such as the undue use of priority lanes, parking that obstructs traffic or frequent disruptions of traffic for VIP motorcades) spark protests on the internet in the form of blogs and YouTube-clips, but also develop into real life protests (Lonkila 2011; Franke and Vendil Pallin 2012: 45).

Travelling abroad

Travelling abroad is another way in which Russians are becoming more mobile and one important aspect of this is 'the growth of transnational flows that in turn form a culture of individual long-distance travel' (Popov 2012: 152). 'Over the last few decades considerable numbers of Russian citizens have become acquainted with the role of the "international tourist"' (ibid.). In 2011, just under 30 million Russians travelled to the 'Far Abroad', that is, to countries that are not members of the Commonwealth of Independent States (CIS). The most important tourist destinations during this period were Turkey, China and Egypt (Rosstat 2012: 304).[4] In an international comparison, Russian tourists became the fifth-largest spending group – behind those from China, Germany, the USA and the UK (UNWTO 2013: 13). Rosstat does not divide the travellers into groups according to income bracket, but it is safe to assume that travelling to the West for tourism is something that is out of reach for most people that do not belong to the middle class or the rich. The fact that those who are well off value the right to travel abroad as a human right is furthermore an indication of this (Levada Center 2014b).

Internet and mobile phones

There has been a rapid increase in both internet penetration and mobile phones in Russia. In 2013, 46 per cent of the population aged above 18 stated that they used the internet daily while 57 per cent used it at least once a month. Internet use is the highest among young people and within the middle class. The next generation ('kids online') use the internet already and live with it (Oates 2013: 79–80). The younger share of the population and especially those belonging to the urban middle class are mobile both when in terms of travelling and with regard to searching

Table 9.1 Internet penetration in different cities and localities in summer 2013 (%)

City/locality	Internet penetration (%)	Share of Internet users in Russia (%)
Moscow	74	11
Saint Petersburg	69	4
City of 1 million or more	62	11
City of 500,000–1,000,000	61	8
City of 100,000–500,000	64	19
City of less than 100,000	56	27
Village	44	20

Source: FOM (2013).

for information outside the state-controlled sphere (Franke and Vendil Pallin 2013: 32–3). They are furthermore the group in society that immediately feels the consequences of attempts to limit these freedoms.

Moscow and other big cities have higher levels of internet penetration than other regions in Russia (see Table 9.1). There are two factors that may have influenced this situation: the infrastructure for using the internet is more developed there and the costs are considerably smaller measured in RUR per Mbit/s (NITs Ekonomika 2011: 13; Yandex 2012).

Values and attitudes among the Russian population

The ratings of Vladimir Putin stopped falling in 2012, but there had been a slow, but steady change in values among the population. According to a report based on opinion polls, focus group surveys and psychological research, the think-tank CSR (2013: 9–10), a new equilibrium had become established by 2012–13, where Putin and United Russia were viewed favourably by just above 40 per cent. In their view, the lower threshold for Putin's ratings was decided by the 'charisma of a strong leader' and patriotism, whereas the ceiling for his popularity was determined by the 'loss of hope' and the fear of strong power authorities (ibid.: 26–7). These changes were bound to have political consequences even in a political system such as that of Russia which appears to be cemented in conservatism (Gorshkov 2013: 3).

Liberalism vs conservatism

According to Lilia Ovcharova (2012), the middle class is dominated by people who are younger and better educated and who live in large urban centres. However, whereas it became dominated by business people during the 1990s, it has turned increasingly conservative as it has come to be dominated by civil servants and the employees of state companies. Caution should be exercised when trying to distinguish between conservative and liberalist approaches in Russian society and should always be made bearing in mind its historic experiences. Thus, in asking questions about how respondents perceived democracy, a Russian research team distinguished between liberal-individualists, those with an authoritarian-communitarian inclination, and people with mixed ideological preferences. The liberal understanding of democracy was distinguished by an emphasis on freedom of thought and free elections as well as 'personal and economic freedom'. Further important components were that the state answers to society, and that there is equality before the law and equal opportunities. In the authoritarian-communitarian understanding of democracy, the emphasis is based on features like power, submission, discipline, the need for order, appeals to the law and moral norms. The power relationship was described in terms of the authorities, the state, people, the people or simple people (Shestopal 2011: 38–9).

The individual vs the collective

Perhaps even more interestingly, in today's Russia collectivism appears increasingly to be giving way to individualism. Whereas collectivism implies an identity that emphasizes the importance of belonging to a group and 'sacrifice of individual goals for the common good is highly valued', individualism goes hand in hand with autonomy and is linked to high levels of self-expression values (Inglehart and Welzel 2005: 136; see also Sakwa 2009: 1–29).

To capture the potential for modernization in shifting values and norms in Russian society, Tikhonova (2011) notes how individualism is gradually growing at the expense of collectivism by asking respondents to choose between pairs of statements (Table 9.2). What is striking is the degree to which the younger generation is prone to give individualist answers rather than relying on the collective.

The question is, of course, whether this is explained primarily by age variations rather than changing values that are first embraced and entrenched among the young. In other words, will the young become more collectivist as they enter the higher age brackets? However, an opinion poll from Levada suggests that these developments are part of an ongoing trend of changing values in society towards individualism. When it comes to the relationship between the state and the citizens, the trend is clear: the view that the state should take care of its citizens is giving way to the opinion that the role of the state should rather be confined to establishing 'the rules of the game' (Figure 9.2).

Rule of law and corruption

Another interesting and related change is the increased emphasis overall in society on the need for rule of law. For example, Tikhonova (2011: 22) concludes that there is an increasing readiness to embrace the law as the main social regulator. The middle class is more worried about corruption and crime than about material

Table 9.2 Value orientations in different age groups (%)

Values in alternative pairs	18–30	31–40	41–50	51–60	60 and older
I am convinced that I can take care of myself and my family and therefore I do not need material support from the state.	53	45	42	33	12
Without material support from the state I and my family would find it difficult to survive.	47	55	58	67	88
My circumstances now and in the future will depend first and foremost on my [actions].	59	54	50	35	20
Little depend on my [actions], the economic situation in the country is important.	41	46	50	65	80
Changes in Russian society must be conducted from 'above' and the authorities must be in control of how they are carried out.	58	65	65	66	71
Changes must be carried out from 'below' and depend on people who take initiative and the healthy forces within society itself rather than on authorities.	42	35	35	34	29
The affairs of the country depend on simple citizens.	23	21	19	20	17
The affairs of the country do not depend on simple citizens at all, but only on managers (rukovoditeli) and politicians.	77	79	81	80	83

Source: Tikhonova (2011: 24–5).

problems such as making ends meet at the end of the month – although it does express concern about issues such as healthcare and future pensions. At the same time, the middle class is more likely to think about emigration and send its children to school abroad. It thus has the possibility to opt out of trying to transform society. 'Strategies of "vote" give way to strategies of "exit"' (Samson and Krasilnikova 2012: 21).

Human rights and freedom

Closely related to questions of rule of law is the issue of human rights. The view of freedom is changing with it being increasingly interpreted as 'freedom to protect one's interests within the framework prescribed by the law' rather than 'freedom from' the actions of others (Tikhonova 2011: 23; see also Sakwa 2009: 5–11). A Levada Center (2014b) poll on Russian attitudes to human rights confirms an overall trend towards a greater emphasis on human rights among the population. Among the noteworthy differences between different income groups are that those that are designated as poor appear less anxious about human rights issues such as freedom of speech and the right to travel abroad. Instead, this group

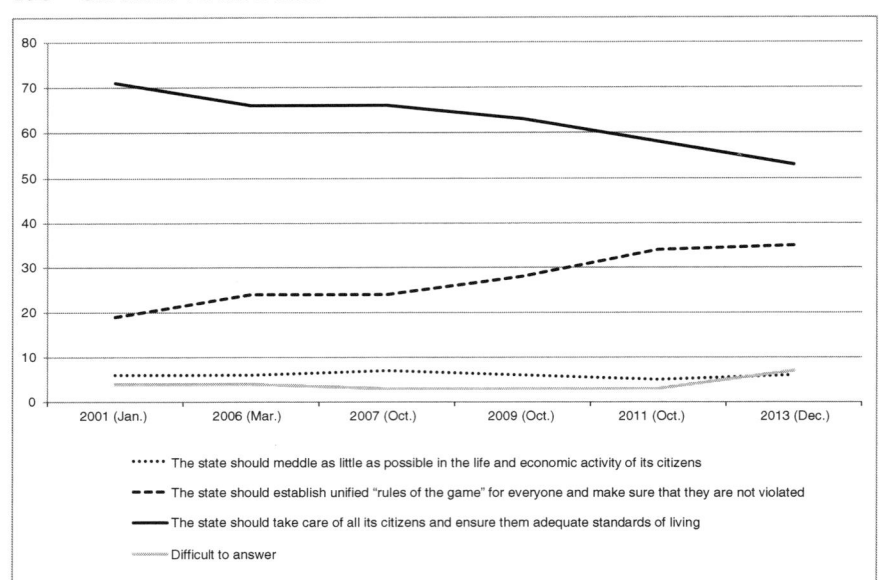

Figure 9.2 In your opinion, what should be the relationship between the state and its citizens? (%).

Source: Levada Centre (2014a: 47).

is most concerned about the right to receive free education, healthcare and their security in old age and in case of illness. The right to work is, moreover, a high priority, whereas the right to information as well as freedom of speech and confession are rated considerably lower (Table 9.3).

Overall, those with a better economy also rate the right to life and free education very highly. However, the group designated as 'rich' stands out in that it rates the inviolability of private life and home as higher than the right to life. Concurrently, it is also concerned with freedom of speech and the right to elect political representatives (Table 9.3). It is interesting to note that these latter values are among the rights that have increased the most in rating since 1994, according to the yearly polls by the Levada Center (2014b). Furthermore, when the interests of the state are pitched against the rights of the individual, a majority feels that the individual should have at least the right to fight for its right against the state (ibid.).

Another interesting aspect is the gap between the moral and value system that Russians stated they preferred in their country, on the one hand, and the one that they perceived to exist in a study published in 2013, on the other. The desired moral and value system includes 'the family and home', 'law' and 'human rights, but respondents did not consider these to be the prevailing principles in Russia today. The difference was especially striking when it came to law and human rights (Figure 9.3).

Table 9.3 Russians on their rights according to consumer status (%)

	Total	Poor	Medium income	Well off	Rich
The right to life	69	66	70	72	58
The right to free education, healthcare and care in old age and during illness	65	81	66	55	55
The right to a well-paid occupation according to one's education/training	53	62	52	47	50
Inviolability of private life, home	52	56	50	53	60
Freedom of speech	39	34	40	38	51
The right to a subsistence minimum guaranteed by the state	37	43	38	32	33
The right to own property	37	31	38	38	34
The right to information	27	19	29	25	23
Freedom of confession	27	16	27	31	25
The right to elect representatives to institutions of power	21	20	22	18	36
The right to travel to another country and return	20	10	21	24	27
Difficult to answer	4	1	4	5	11

Source: Levada Center (2014b).

Note: The poll was conducted 20–24 December 2013 and is based on 1 603 people above 18 years old. *Poor* – needs to save in order to buy food and clothing; *medium income* – money enough for food and clothing, but need to save to buy more expensive things (television or refridgirator); *well-off* – can buy certain expensive things (television or refridgirator), but needs to save in order to buy a car; *rich* – can buy a car.

Fear and anxiety

The present-day Russian population has a number of fears and anxieties. Tikhonova (2012: 40) identifies a 'nucleus of the lower class' that lives with a more or less constant 'sense of unfairness regarding what is happening, and, at the same time, a feeling of hopelessness'. She also notes that 56 per cent in this group fear for themselves or their loved ones and that many live in poor housing conditions. Moreover, many find themselves in long-term unemployment or are working odd-jobs and as many as 90 per cent believe that they will be unemployed in the coming year (ibid.: 42). In other words, this group still lives under conditions where it has to fight for its existential security. The middle class, as mentioned above, is more likely to worry about crime and corruption.

There is, furthermore, a continuing fear of repression in society. In a 2013 focus group study that involved a psychological test, respondents reacted very negatively to pictures of the special forces OMON of the Ministry of Interior Affairs (MVD). They were perceived as 'a force directed against the people' (CSR 2013: 17). Overall among the population, the fear of repression had once more increased in 2013 with a majority constantly or from time to time fearing its return (Table 9.4).

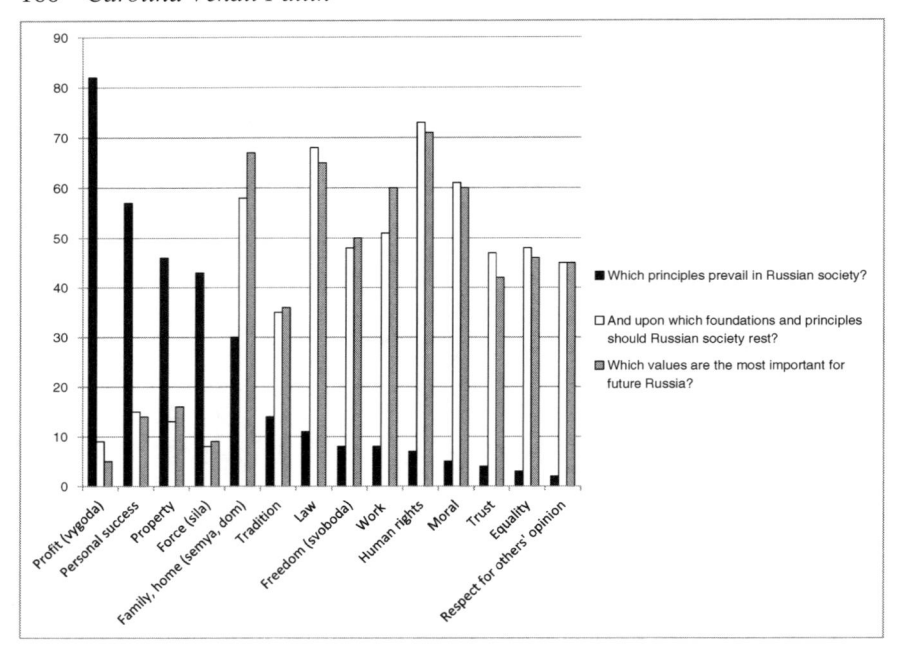

Figure 9.3 Values in Russian society – actual, desired and those important for the future Russia (% *of answers*).

Source: IS RAN (2013: 15).

Table 9.4 Are you afraid of a return of mass repression? (%)

	1994	1999	2003	2008	2013
Not afraid at all/rather not scared	26	34	51	47	38
Sometimes yes, sometimes no	16	14	21	17	23
Constantly afraid/afraid	37	28	19	17	30
Difficult to answer	20	23	10	19	10
Number of respondents	*3,000*	*2,000*	*2,000*	*1,500*	*1,600*

Source: Levada Center (2014a:18).

Conclusion

The most frequent answers to a question about what unites modern Russia apart from history, culture, language and territory were 'common hardships' (*obshchie bedy*) at 38 per cent and 'dissatisfaction with the authorities' (*nedovolstvo vlastyu*) at 36 per cent. Only after this came 'friendly relations' (35 per cent), religion (29 per cent), the state or pride in one's country (IS RAN 2013: 37–8).[5] The aim of the question was to try to identify what are the components of the identity of a Russian citizen. The result brings us back to the quote by Aleksievich at the beginning of the chapter. A multitude of values and behaviour patterns exist side by side in Russia today. The country is united by history, culture, language and territory, but it would be naïve to believe that this unity automatically leads to a unity of opinion and interests among the population.

Indeed, there are substantial differences between income groups and between generations. As is evidenced above, socio-economic development has resulted in a situation where it is of importance to examine not only the aggregated changes in income, consumption and values but also those that have taken place within different groups in society. The different groups have radically different concerns and therefore also different values. There is a well-off group in society that owns property and is increasingly mobile and there is also a considerable difference in outlook between different age cohorts. Urban dwellers with higher incomes and the younger generation are more inclined to embrace self-expression values conducive to the establishment of democratic institutions.

This suggests that the basis for developing institutions is growing in Russian society, albeit unevenly between different groups and regions. However, Inglehart and Welzel (2005: 93) emphasize that their predictions are 'probabilistic not deterministic'. Russia's cultural tradition, as well as its historic experiences, will continue to colour its development path. The fact that the Russian population has been quick to acquire tendencies of increased authoritarianism as expressed in an increasing fear of mass repression is probably linked to its historic experiences during communist rule. The future values in Russian society will, moreover, be influenced by external events and crises. The conflict with Ukraine, and by continuation with the West, has the potential to result in a situation where the population is again more concerned about threats to their survival. A severe downturn in Russia's economy could also have negative effects, which delay or even reverse the development of values of self-expression, thereby providing a fertile environment for authoritarian rather than democratic institutions.

Nevertheless, there is every reason to expect that in a longer-term perspective, socio-economic development will change the value systems in Russia. The overall trend during the past ten years and also comparing with the data from the 1990s is one where there is a greater emphasis on self-expression values such as individualism, human rights and freedoms and rule of law and this is especially true among those who have experienced a higher degree of socio-economic development and among the younger cohorts. The perceived gap between the moral and value system that Russian respondents desire and that which they perceive to exist is striking and suggests that there is a growing demand for institutions that guarantee values such as law and human rights. The view that the state should establish the rules of the game rather than provide social guarantees is also winning ground among the younger section of the population and the urban middle class. This trend constitutes a challenge for the Russian political leadership to reform Russian society and the political system in order to accommodate and mediate between different groups' expectations, demands and aspirations.

Notes

1 Author's translation.
2 The Levada Center is a Russian non-governmental organization that conducts socio-logical research and opinion polls. The center is named after the Russian sociologist Yuri Levada (1930–2006).
3 St Petersburg is also a federal city and is the second most affluent city, but it lags considerably behind Moscow in spite of this. Since the annexation of Crimea, Sevastopol has joined this group of federal subjects. This city has even less in common with Moscow.
4 Finland was also among the top destinations, but not exclusively for tourism, but rather for trips with 'private purpose' *(chastnaya tsel)*.
5 The respondents were allowed to choose several answers to each question.

References

Aleksievich, S. (2013) *Vremya sekond khend*, Moscow: Vremya.
Attwood, L. (2012) 'Privatisation of Housing in Post-Soviet Russia: a New Understanding of Home?', *Europe–Asia Studies*, 64(5): 903–28.
CSR (2013) *Novoe elektoralnoe ravnovesie: srednesrochnyi trend ili 'vremennoe satishe'?*, Moscow: Centre for Strategic Research.
Di Palma, G. (1990) *To Craft Democracies: an Essay on Democratic Transitions*, Berkeley: University of California Press.
Dmitriev, M.E. and Misikhina, S.G. (2012) 'Potreblenie i spros na instituty v protsesse stanovleniya rossiiskogo srednego klassa, *SPERO*, 16: 59–78.
Feldman, S. (2013) 'Political ideology', in Huddy, L., Sears, D. and Levy, J. (eds), *The Oxford Handbook of Political Psychology*, 2nd edn, New York: Oxford University Press, pp. 591–626.
FOM (2013) 'Internet v Rossii', *Analiticheskiy byulleten*, 43. Online. Available: http://fom.ru/SMI-i-internet/11288 (accessed 19 February 2014).
Franke, U. and Vendil Pallin, C. (2013) *Russian Politics and the Internet in 2012*, FOI-R-3590-SE, Stockholm, December.
Gabuev, A. and Surnachevaya, Y. (2013) 'Vsya eta politizatsiya nichego khoroshego ne dast', *Kommersant Vlast*, 41: 8–16.
Gorshkov, M. (2013) 'The Mass Consciousness in Russia', *Sociological Research*, 52(2): 3–61.
Gorshkov, M. and Tikhonova, N. (2013) 'Mechty rossiyan i realnost demoskopii', *Polis*, 5: 7–26.
Hahn, J.W. and Logvinenko, I. (2008) 'Generational Differences in Russian Attitudes Towards Democracy and the Economy', *Europe–Asia Studies*, 60(8): 1345–69.
Hale, H.E. (2011) 'The Myth of Mass Russian Support for Autocracy: the Public Opinion Foundations of a Hybrid Regime', *Europe–Asia Studies*, 63(8): 1357–75.
Inglehart, R. and Welzel, C. (2005) *Modernization, Cultural Change, and Democracy: The Human Development Sequence*, New York: Cambridge University Press.
IS RAN (2013) *Differentsiatsiya grazhdanskikh i politicheskikh praktik v Rossii: institut-sionalnaya perspektiva*, Moscow: IS RAN.
Levada Center (2014a) *Obshestvennoe mnenie – 2013: Ezhegodnik*, Moscow: Levada Center.
Levada Center (2014b) 'Rossiyane o svoikh pravakh', 27 January. Online. Available: www.levada.ru/27-01-2014/rossiyane-o-svoikh-pravakh (accessed January 2014).

Levinson, A. (2012) 'Chuvstva i nadezhdy storonnikov Putina', *Vedomosti*, 30 October. Online. Available: www.vedomosti.ru/opinion/news/5525131/chuvstva_storonnikov_putina#ixzz2AIZTJOTv (accessed 27 April 2014).

Levinson, A. (2013) 'Rossiiskoe obshchestvo do i posle 2012 goda', *Vestnik obshchestvennogo mneniya*, 1: 20–35.

Lonkila, M. (2011) 'Driving at Democracy in Russia: Protest Activities of St Petersburg Car Drivers' Associations', *Europe–Asia Studies*, 63(2): 291–309.

Nechaev, V. and Brodovskaya, Y. (2013) 'Politicheskie funktsii interneta v vospriyatii rossiyan', *Monitoring obshchestvennogo mneniya*, 3: 8–21.

NITs Ekonomika (2011) 'Otraslevoi doklad "Internet v Rossii: Sostoianie, tendentsii i perspektivy razvitiya"'. Online. Available: www.fapmc.ru/magnoliaPublic/rospechat/activities/reports/2012/item6.html?print=true (accessed 16 August 2012).

Oates, S. (2013) *Revolution Stalled: the Political Limits of the Internet in the Post-Soviet Sphere*, New York: Oxford University Press.

Ovcharova, L. (2012) 'Russia's Middle Class: at the Centre or on the Periphery of Russian Politics?', in Fischer, S. (ed.), *Russia – Insights from a Changing Country*, EU ISS Report, 11: 28–35.

Ovcharova, L.N., Pishnyak, A.I., Popova, D.O. and Shepeleva, E.V. (2013) 'Izmeneniya v dokhodakh i potreblenii rossiiskikh domashnikh khozyaistv: ot bednosti k srednemu klassu', *SPERO*, 18: 7–36.

Popov, V. (2012) 'The Culture of New Mobility in Russia: Networks and Flows Formation', *Mobilities*, 7(1): 151–69.

Rosstat (2012) *Rossiiskii statisticheskii ezhegodnik*, Moscow: Federal Statistical Service.

Rosstat *Federal State Statistical Service*. Online. Available: www.gks.ru.

Sakwa, R. (2009) *The Quality of Freedom: Khodorkovsky, Putin, and the Yukos Affair*, Oxford: Oxford University Press.

Samson, I. and Krasilnikova, M. (2012) 'The Middle Class in Russia: an Emerging Reality or an Old Myth?', *Sociological Research*, 51(5): 3–25.

Shestopal, E. (2011) 'Predstavleniya, obrazy i tsennosti demokratii v rossiiskom obshchestve', *Politiya*, 62(3): 34–47.

Tikhonova, N.E. (2011) 'Dinamika normativno-tsennostnykh sistem rossiyan i perspektivy modernazatsionnogo proekta', *Vestnik Instituta Sotsiologii*, 3: 11–27.

Tikhonova, N.E. (2012) 'The Lower Class in the Social Structure of Russian Society', *Sociological Research*, 51(5): 26–44.

Tikhonova, N.E. and Mareeva, S.V. (2009) *Srednii klass: Teoriya i realnost*, Moscow: Alfa-M.

UNWTO (2013) *UNWTO Tourism Highlights – 2013 Edition*, New York: UNWTO.

Yandex (2012) *Razvitie interneta v regionakh Rossii – vesna 2012*. Online. Available: http://download.yandex.ru/company/ya_regions_report_spring_2012.pdf (accessed 20 September 2012).

Zubarevich, N.V. (2011) 'Modernization and the Russian Space', in *National Human Development Report for the Russian Federation 2011: Modernization and Human Development*, Moscow: UNDP, pp. 126–40.

Zubarevich, N.V. (2012) 'Moskva na fone drugikh krupneishchikh gorodov Rossii: chto pakazyvaet statistika', *SPERO*, 17: 57–68.

Zubarevich, N.V. (2013) 'Four Russias: Human Potential and Social Differentiation of Russian Regions and Cities', in Lipman, M. and Petrov, N. (eds), *Russia 2025: Scenarios for the Russian Future*, Basingstoke: Palgrave Macmillan, pp. 67–85.

10 Russia's emerging civil society

Jens Siegert

Ever tried. Ever failed. No matter.
Try again. Fail again. Fail better.
Samuel Beckett

What is civil society? This question is not as banal as it might appear. Most authors and agents use the term 'civil society' as a sort of acting subject. But that is, in my opinion, an incorrect perception. 'Civil society' is not an acting subject. What can be identified as subjects are civil society organizations which I will refer to below as non-governmental organizations (NGOs). Civil society is rather a normative concept for judging whether a society behaves in a more or less civil way.

The purpose of this chapter is to examine the development of Russia's civil society and its NGOs, which are autonomous organizations independent from the state. NGOs are subjects acting in the collective, the social and often even political sphere of a society. It is possible to describe them, ask them about their views and analyse how they act. Quite often they are registered in accordance with governmental regulations. Sometimes they ally themselves with each other. In other cases, they compete against each other or they challenge the actions of the government. It is not uncommon for NGOs not to adopt any legal status, but to exist only as informal associations of citizens.

The term *civil society* refers to a social partnership between individuals and families on the one hand, and the state on the other. The term refers to people who have voluntarily formed an association to together carry out a socially useful activity or philanthropic work. This definition of civil society excludes organizations carrying out an economic activity with the purpose of drawing profits. It also places no importance on the institutional forms of these organizations. They do not need to have an official legal status and they can operate without having the approval of the state. The underlying principle of civil society is that it has to be voluntary, autonomous from the public authorities and its composition is always in the process of change, which is what gives it such diversity.

The outline of the chapter is as follows: In the first section, I discuss the general basis of civil society. The second section describes the emergence of NGOs in Russia since the break-up of the Soviet Union. In the third section, a comparison is made of the conditions during Soviet times and Putin's relationship with civil society in his first and second terms of office. The fourth section discusses the interim period with President Medvedev. The fifth section analyses the situation of the Russian civil society before and after Putin's return to power in 2012. In the sixth section, I raise some special issues that are relevant for understanding the relationship between the state and civil society in modern Russia. The seventh section analyses the NGOs during the protests in 2011–12. Section eight presents the conclusions of the study.

The research presented in this chapter is based on my more than 20 years of work as a resident collaborator of the German Heinrich Böll Foundation, a foreign NGO based in Moscow. In this capacity, I worked together with many Russian NGOs, engaged in different thematic fields such as human rights protection, ecology, gender issues, migration and refugees, consumer protection, freedom of expression and freedom of speech, the protection of rights of those liable to military service, urban development and many others. In describing the development of Russian civil society, I mainly resort to this personal and professional experience.

Civil society – theory and reality

Civil society actors and NGOs are an essential part of the political system because they notice and identify problems in society earlier than the state authorities, if the latter even become aware of this at all. Somewhat simplified, one can divide civil society actors into three main groups (Habermas 1971: 46):

- NGOs operating in the space between the state and society, that is, playing an intermediary role.
- Groups involved in building up social capital; this includes self-help groups, veterans' associations, cultural groups, sports clubs, and so on, as well as Christian bodies and other religious groups, which represent a specific case by virtue of their particular relations with the state authorities.
- Non-governmental charitable organizations, such as cooperatives and church organizations providing social assistance. This category also includes the Red Cross.

In theory, all of these organizations are parts of civil society, but such a broad definition is impractical for the purposes of making a more detailed analysis of relations between the state and civil society. Therefore, in this chapter I concentrate on the first group – that is, organizations that perform an intermediary function between state authorities and society, which are usually referred to as NGOs.

The areas in which NGOs work can be called the focus of civil society activity The involvement of the general public in NGOs' activities – their desire and need to act in the public good – makes it possible to say that NGOs are the bearers of a new political culture. In cases where the public recognizes that NGOs' activities are genuinely useful for society, this can give rise to new legitimate forms of social and political interaction. Civil society organizations also help establish trust between public agents. Trust is an ephemeral factor that reduces the transaction costs and facilitates the diversity of public structures and relations in society (Luhmann 2000). In today's increasingly complex societies, trust is becoming increasingly important. Today, neither the state authorities nor public groups, and even more so individuals, can foresee all consequences and ensuing risks that their actions might have. Therefore, to be able to act in the public sphere, they all need to trust their own and others' professional assessments. Trust is therefore the 'lubricant' for public progress, above all economic progress. Without this lubricant, the wheels turn more slowly, action is less effective, and there is a constant threat of breakdown.

This is why in modern societies, whether in the private or the public sphere, coercion or the framework providing for them is being increasingly replaced by trust and right as the prime resources for managing and resolving conflicts. However, going against this trend, Russian society is dominated by an atmosphere of complete distrust on all sides. This distrust is primarily directed against the state authorities, including the legal system, and economic agents, but it also extends to public organizations. Paradoxically, this mistrustful attitude is often linked to the altruistic principles that underlie social and political efforts.

Russian civil society emerges

One of the main differences between the political systems of today's Russia and that of the former Soviet Union is the constitutional right of freedom of association of the former. That right applies not only to political parties, but also to civil society organizations, of which there are already several hundred thousand in the country. Another important differentiating characteristic between the Soviet Union and Putin's Russia was, until 2012, the widespread freedom of its people to define their lives as they wished. The freedom to think what you want and to say what you think, to travel where you want to go, return when you like, to live with whom you wish, to love whom you wish, to work where you wish, all within the framework of given social and economic possibilities, was naturally part of the *social contract* between Putin and the population of the 2000s. According to the social contract, Putin determines politics and controls the most important economic resources. But he also cares for the growing prosperity of as many people as possible, does not interfere in the private lives of his citizens, and does not bother about what they think and believe. Since Putin's return to the Kremlin in 2012, however, these liberties have been threatened.

To understand the developments of Russian civil society, one must take a closer look at how Russia's NGOs have evolved since the end of the Soviet Union. Even before the end of the Soviet Union, in the last years of perestroika, civil activists played a role in mediating between the state and society. A certain alliance was linking part of the old Soviet political elites and the new democrats took shape in the very early independent Russia. That alliance was not very stable, however, and it finally broke up in connection with the constitutional crisis in 1993, which led to a small but bloody civil war in the autumn of that year, the first Chechen

War and the circumstances surrounding the presidential elections in 1996. As a result of those three events, the temporary – and unequal – partners NGOs and the state went different ways. The gap between ethical imperatives and political compromises should not be too large in NGO activities. One reason for this is that for NGOs, this gap must certainly be significantly narrower in NGO activities than in the sphere of politics. The influence of NGOs is based not on holding high offices but instead mainly on achieving a good reputation in society and trust among the citizenry. Many civil activists were either unable – or did not want – to subordinate their behaviour and activities to the political power struggle.

Putin's first and second terms: managing the NGOs and controlling civil society

Following Vladimir Putin's first election to the presidency in 2000, the Kremlin immediately began to subjugate all parts of the Russian political sphere. Previously, actions in those spheres had not been independent in the proper sense of the word but they were, at least, controlled by different centres of power. Civil society actors also became the object of the Kremlin campaign.

The more prominent among the NGOs responded by establishing regional and supraregional coalitions. During the first part of Putin's first term, the Kremlin recognized some of the leaders of these NGOs as negotiation partners. The Civil Forum, the creation of which the Kremlin called for in the autumn of 2001, represents the first serious attempt to integrate independent NGOs into the system of what at a very early stage began to be called the *managed democracy*. That attempt proved largely unsuccessful and a peace, of a sort, prevailed between the Kremlin and a group of independent NGOs until the autumn of 2003. Two political events occurred at the end of that relatively peaceful period: the arrest of Mikhail Khodorkovsky and the Orange Revolution in Ukraine.

In the eyes of the Kremlin, NGOs supported by Western donors played a decisive role in the regime change in Ukraine in the winter of 2004–5. That view, combined with the fear that something similar could happen in Russia, led the Russian authorities to set up a Public Chamber, fully under their own control, and to adopt a new law on NGOs in early 2006. That law replaced all prior regulations on civil society organizations and tightened the controls over them. Perhaps even more importantly, it sent a signal to society and governmental authorities at all levels: NGOs are suspected of being a potential threat to state security.

The state attempted to use the Public Chamber to legitimize 'officially elected' representatives of civil society as a whole and, at the same time, to de-legitimize the independent NGOs that were not members of the Public Chamber. But the de-legitimizing part of this move did not succeed. Although most civil society organizations did not enjoy the support of a broader public, the NGOs exhibited an impressive resilience and remained steadfast. The tightening of state controls over the sphere of politics, particularly over the party system, compelled the Russian NGOs into the role of surrogate political parties. In some cases, they were forced to play a double role – a role, although a weakening one, that they continue to play today – acting both as a political opposition and as a channel of communication between the political elite and society. The difficulty for the Russian elite was how to strike a balance between providing the economic freedom required for effective development while preventing this freedom from spreading into aspects of political and public life. In the end, the state agents chose the 'hands-on management' method as their means of establishing control over civil society.

This situation has created a type of NGO in Russia that is practically unknown in developed democracies – organizations acting as mediators between the state authorities and parts of the general public. Some of these communication channels have been given institutional form – for example, the Presidential Commission on Human Rights, which was set up in 2002 with Ella Pamfilova as chairwoman. In 2004, the Commission was reorganized as the Presidential Council for Developing Institutions of the Civil Society and of Human Rights. Up until the end of Putin's second presidency, the council members included a number of people from influential opposition NGOs.

The outcome of these first ten years of Vladimir Putin's rule was contradictory for many Russian NGOs. In the first term after his election, NGOs experienced growing pressure from state authorities to integrate in a new established corporate political system. The state focused its attacks on them in the sphere of administrative regulations, such as tax laws, questions of registering as legal bodies or their reporting duties to state authorities. As a result, NGOs transformed themselves into organizations, thus working in a more professional way.

The interim period: Medvedev's modernization rhetoric

In February 2009, then President Dmitri Medvedev showed some liberal signs. Among other matters, he approved a renewed list of members for Pamfilova's Presidential Council, half of whom were now people known for their uncompromising criticism of the Kremlin. With the help of the council, some of the provisions in the 2006 law on NGOs that had particularly been hampering the work of small NGOs and those in the regions were amended, and some efforts were made to reduce the red tape, thus making it hard to establish new NGOs. Pamfilova stepped down as the council's chairwoman in the summer of 2010, criticizing the fact that the state continued to limit the possibilities for NGOs to work independently. The circumstances surrounding the appointment of her successor, Mikhail Fedotov, did, however, show that the Kremlin still wanted to maintain contacts with opposition-minded NGOs.

Recent surveys show that civil society activity is not regarded particularly highly in today's Russia (Levada Center 2011). But, at the same time, an as yet diffuse sense of discontent is growing in society as people become sick of the slow pace of reform, corruption, bureaucratic arbitrariness and the Kremlin's monopoly on power. The economic crisis has made problems linked to the political system more visible, and President Medvedev responded by proposing a renewed version of modernization rhetoric, reminiscent of that heard during Putin's first term.

Not later than December 2007, after the parliamentary elections, the last more or less independent political parties lost their final hope of re-entering parliament. In this situation, the opposition had three broad options:

- They might have joined one of the parties of the so-named systemic opposition, at that time the Communist Party, the so-named Liberal Democrats of Vladimir Zhirinovsky or the Just Russia Party. However, the Kremlin sometimes did not give its permission.
- They could go on and become marginal political actors under the threat of being criminalized.
- They could join existing NGOs or found a new one themselves, join some 'higher school' or university as a lecturer or become journalists at one of the not so many remaining newspapers or radio stations, which had been able to preserve at least some independence.

The return of Putin and the winter of protest

The situation changed fundamentally in the autumn of 2011, with two decisions by Vladimir Putin playing a decisive role in the developments. First, he declared his intention to once more run for the presidency in March 2012. Second, on 5 December 2011, policemen in Moscow and St Petersburg arrested several hundred people who were protesting against the falsification of the parliamentary elections the previous day. The announcement of Putin's almost certain return to the Kremlin acted as something of a trigger for what happened afterwards. However, one must be aware that nearly all agents and observers of the Russian political development, Putin's advisers as well as the majority of oppositional politicians, experts and journalists, at that given time agreed that Putin did have the power to make such a decision without being aware of serious political drawbacks.

Surprisingly, the political establishment and its opponents did not bear in mind the relevance and importance of elections. Almost nobody thought that election fraud could be a possible trigger for political protest in Russia. This is particularly astonishing since, within the last decade, elections have been playing an important and decisive role in changing several (semi-)authoritarian regimes like in Georgia, Ukraine, Tunisia and Egypt. In reality, history seldom works like a time continuum, but makes smaller or bigger leaps forward. In such times, people become particularly aware of sudden changes in society – and, in particular, societies that have become immobile. Such ossified political systems lose their ability, or their will, or often both, to react appropriately to societal, political and economic challenges. Something similar was occurring in Russia in the protests of winter 2011–12. Without doubt, Russian society changed and progressed more quickly under the surface than what we could see. Another determinant of the events could be characterized as 'Putin's modernization dilemma'. It consists of two parts:

First, the economic modernization of the country was a principal aim of Putin's policy from the beginning. Moreover, it was perceived by the Kremlin as an inevitable precondition to enable Russia to achieve the status of a super-power. This importance attributed to economics is what explains the temporary alliance between market-liberal economists and certain groups from the state security structures, mostly the so-called *gosudarstvenniki* (people who always put the interest of the state first), which also includes the *siloviki* (people from within state security structures). However, at a very early state in Putin's rule, economic modernization had to play second fiddle to the interests of staying in power. The economic crisis, which began at the same time, in 2008, when the interim president Dmitry Medvedev came into office, showed clearly that a comprehensive economic modernization would be unsuccessful unless the polit-ical system were opened up at least a little. Even before the protests in Decem-ber 2011, a large proportion of active, well-educated and mobile young people had lost their faith in Putin. Yet it is these very people who are most likely to carry out the crucial necessary modernization. At the same time, these very peo-ple are also most likely those who might reinforce a more civil development of Russian society.

Second, in his foreign policy, Putin encountered a similar problem. Over these years the country's foreign policy acquired an increasing anti-western momentum. At the same time, notwithstanding Russia's membership in the BRICS,[1] a club of countries with emerging economies, there will be no sustainable modernization in Russia without good (or at least not bad) economic as well as political relations with the West. In the end, the West is still the leading force in the world regard-ing modern technologies and institutions. Moreover, Russia is in urgent need of foreign investment and incoming know-how. Furthermore, an open confrontation with the West, especially a military one, would be very expensive and would be considered to slow down the process of modernization.

However, this was only true until the spring of 2014. At the beginning of his third term as president in 2012, Putin yet seemed to be undecided about how to find a way out of this dilemma.

Different parts of Russian society continue to drift apart. How far this process has already advanced is shown by the formula of *The Four Russias*, proposed by Natalia Zubarevich (2012) (see also Chapter 11 this volume). I would suggest adding another complementary aspect, a sociocultural division of Russian soci-ety into a modern–postmodern Russia and a patriarchal and religious pre-modern Russia with memories of the Soviet myths. Lev Gudkov (2012: 10), a sociologist and head of the Moscow-based Levada Center, even makes a threefold distinction between a pre-modern, a modern and an anti-modern Russia. This division is not a new one; it can be traced back in Russian history at least to the beginning of the nineteenth century. In 2011, however, there was an intensification of the 'cultural confrontation'. On the one hand, Putin's state is, step by step, more openly sup-porting those forces in society that adhere to a patriarchal worldview. On the other hand, it makes increasing use of the obscurant, anti-western flank of the political spectrum, to counter the ongoing erosion of its power. From 2013 onwards, Putin launched a re-ideologization of state politics, relying more and more on this worl-dview. This will be discussed in more detail below.

In all this discussion one should not forget the significant sections of society who are losers in the modernization processes – or who at least consider themselves to be on the losing side. These people constitute a natural foundation of support for Putin. For them, he might no longer be the admired leader, who is guiding the country from a glorious past into a bright future, as he was in his first and second term as president. Yet he remains a kind of last resort against the upcoming modernity with all its impositions. On the other side of Russian society, the modern-postmodern one, we can see a growing demand for certain rules and effective state institutions that leads to a resolute rejection of Putin's rule. From their point of view, the protest against Putin has a sociocultural character. It is directed against a traditional model of relations between the state and society, which is not only becoming less and less effective, but which modernized Russian people perceive as an illegitimate restriction of their freedom.

Key issues in the evolution of civil society

A society without politics

One thing had been quite obvious for many years: participation in any debate concerning institutionalized power was politics. Accordingly, in the Soviet Union, politics did not exist outside the Communist Party or, more accurately, no politics was permitted outside the party. Anyone who dared to try would be punished harshly and vanish, first into labour camps and later often into enforced exile. All of this changed with perestroika. Politicians began to emerge, initially from under the maternal wings of Gorbachev's Communist Party and gradually increasing in independence. The brief flowering which followed lasted roughly until the early autumn of 1993 when Yeltsin ordered shots to be fired at the parliament building. During that interlude, politics was indeed rather free and democratic. In terms of political history, Russia was suddenly very modern.

The realms of political politics (*politicheskaya politika*) – that is, the struggle for political power that is organized primarily, although not exclusively, through political parties – on the one hand, and civic politics (*grazhdanskaya politika*) on the other, parted ways after 1993. This slight confusion of terms, which essentially continues to this day, was not meaningless. The widening of the notion of the political, which in the West was closely linked to the emergence of the civic initiative movement during and after 1968, and the related process of dismantling hierarchies, particularly in terms of the power relations between state and society, as well as the individual, man and woman, did not really begin in Russia or Eastern Europe until after the collapse of the Soviet Union. German philosopher Jürgen Habermas (1971) coined the term *structural transformation of the political sphere* to describe this widening legitimacy of political involvement outside the structures provided for and controlled by the state when it took place in the West.

In the West, the transformation of the political sphere resulted in a considerable expansion of the notion of politics, as expressed in the once-popular dictum that 'the private is political' (Roth and Rucht 2008). Issues, such as domestic violence, that had previously been regarded as private affairs suddenly became political. As a result, it gradually became legitimate, as opposed to legal, which had been the case before, to stand up for one's rights without the direct use of political parties and state institutions. This newly developed sphere, where one engaged in politics without becoming a politician, was initially named 'new social movements' before being later labelled 'civil society'. Most Soviet dissidents and later Russian political and civil actors, like, indeed, many of their western precursors, were, of course, unaware of, let alone familiar with, these fancy notions, even though the dissidents in communist Poland, the Soviet Union or Hungary had made a significant contribution to their development. They simply grasped the freedom because they demanded, quite rightly, the right to determine the fate of their societies, and their own fates in particular.

The innocence of the *perestroika* period ended suddenly in 1993, when fire was opened on the parliament building in Moscow and later with the 1994 Chechen War, followed by Yeltsin's rigged election of 1996 and the bankrupting of the oligarchic state in 1998 during Yeltsin's second term in office. In the minds of most people, politics once more became separated from the involvement in public affairs. Politics were regarded as dirty, corrupt, dangerous and morally suspect, and involvement in public affairs as beneficial and endowed with a certain dignity, albeit that it was viewed with some suspicion by those used to being deprived of their dignity, while at the same time being increasingly marginal. 'I'm/we're not involved in politics' was the new mantra of the civil activists, aimed at winning the support of the population as well as at signalling to the powers that be that they represented no threat to their power.

This relationship was subsequently formalized by Vladimir Putin's introduction of 'managed' and later 'sovereign' democracy. He quickly transformed himself into 'Russia's only politician', with a clear line being drawn between politics and involvement in public affairs. Politics was exclusively a matter for the Kremlin. Whoever did not accept this was either marginalized or eliminated. At the same time, involvement in public affairs that did not follow explicitly political goals was co-opted by the state. A human rights NGO registered with the Ministry of Justice was allowed to deal with human rights issues; an environmental NGO with the environment; and a sociological research institute could carry out opinion polls. To put it briefly, experts were allowed to speak about their areas of expertise.

Many NGOs were thus constrained by means of various special advisory bodies, panels, committees and commissions reporting to the president, the government, the 'X ministry' and the 'Y governor', the police or the mayor while, at the same time, gaining some, albeit limited influence in decision-making as well as a degree of protection against state repression, or so most of them would believe. Similar corporate structures were set up for non-state research institutions, think-tanks and lobby groups. What appeared to be a permanent arrangement was, however, disrupted in the winter of 2011–12 by the resurgence of mass protests and, thus, the return of a politics that was outside the Kremlin's control.

A different middle class

In the year after the winter of the protests 2011–12, many observers wondered whether the genie was now out of the bottle and whether the Kremlin would attempt to squeeze it back in using ploys and threats. Two years later opinions still vary. Some think that Putin has taken back the control. Others see the current peace as the calm before the next storm. I would tend towards the latter viewpoint, though it is hard to predict. The most important question is therefore not whether there will be unrest in the country in some foreseeable future, but rather how and where, who will be the bringers of possible changes and how they imagine their future world.

It was the protests of the winter of 2011–12 which, at least in part, turned politics back into a public affair in Russia. There were, of course, protests against Vladimir Putin and his government before this period. But they all had their limits, from the pensioner protests against the so-called overhaul of state benefits at the beginning of 2005, to the Strategy-31 protests against restrictions on freedom of assembly since 2009 (article 31 of the Russian Constitution establishes the freedom of assembly). None of these had a direct impact on the political system and its legitimation mechanisms. However, the winter of 2011–12 was different, leading to considerable shifts.

This analysis has focused on that part of the protest against Putin which was fuelled by the idea of a liberal, market-oriented state, which observes the rule of law. This was the emancipatory protest of an emerging urban, well-educated and economically fairly prosperous middle class, which is demanding more democratic involvement, more freedom and a more open society – both inwards and outwards. But the protest also has another side, a dark side, which is most visibly reflected in consistently fiery xenophobic protests. The supporters of these protests are mainly people living in relatively precarious situations which, although primarily of a particular social nature, are also significantly characterized by the experience and fear of decline – by experiences and fears that touch individuals and small groups, but also by a collective fear which applies to the country as a whole.

President Putin continues to respond experimentally to the presently very marked regional, sectorial and social differentiations in society. Managed democracy was one such experiment which worked quite well for a time. It built upon the notion of a 'united Russia' which incorporated all of the people in the country as far as possible. By contrast, since Putin's return to the Kremlin in the spring of 2012, there has been talk of an 'overwhelming majority' which is represented by Putin's politics, whereby, logically, minorities are excluded. As with all politics, a populist ruler such as Putin needs a social basis upon which he can depend. This social basis must thus agree with him on the essentials. Or such agreement must be generated and preserved without any unjustifiably great effort, such as by means of propaganda. And this agreement, of course, also needs to be supported by material interests. The majority, which lends its consent, must gain from the order imposed from above.

Across the developed world, the middle classes function as a stabilizing force with regard to political authority. Yet the middle class in Russia which, according to its number and significance, could stabilize the country, leaves much to be desired. The number of people who can be counted among the Russian middle class has been at around 20 per cent since the beginning of the twenty-first century and has barely changed. The size of the Russian middle class is a very much debated issue. I am using the term middle class in this text, according to the Russian economist Alexander Auzan (2012), predominantly determined from a pattern of sociocultural behaviour and not one measured solely by income only. The World Bank (2014) stated, in its *Russian Economic Report 31*, that the size of the Russian middle class grew from 30 per cent of the population in 2001 to 60 per cent in 2010 and linked this principally to economic factors. A research report of the Institute of Sociology of the Russian Academy of Science, released in the spring of 2014, finds the lower proportion of 42 per cent in 2014 (Tikhonova 2014).

There is actually a difference between Moscow as well as, with a few reservations, St Petersburg and some other million-plus cities, and what can be roughly described as the 'rest of the country'. This difference is also manifested in the sociocultural characteristics of each inhabitant who can be counted as members of a middle class according to their living conditions and their income. In Moscow, St Petersburg and a clutch of other million-plus cities, people often have a higher level of education and in the last 10 to 15 years, their lifestyles have caught up to rival those of the inhabitants of Western European cities. They are relatively mobile, tend mostly towards more or less liberal views, often work in industries removed from the state and in their private lives also keep themselves removed from the state, as far as this is possible.

In the 'rest of the country', such people are much more difficult to find. There, the middle class, defined in economic terms, consists mainly of civil servants. I want to try to paint a small portrait of this group in the next few paragraphs. This portrait is based primarily on my observations, reading and conversations. I am unaware of any comprehensive studies which concern this part of the population. The following may be considered, therefore, as a hypothesis.

The 'provincial' middle class largely consists of relatively young people. They are often in the process of climbing the regional career ladder. These include small businessmen, managers in medium-sized or large companies, but first and foremost they are officials of all stripes: in the police force, the state prosecutor's office, the regional and town administrations and subdivisions of federal authorities. Socioculturally, most representatives of this class continue to live a very Soviet lifestyle, albeit with a few striking differences. If asked, almost all these people would consider themselves patriots. As such, they tend towards harsh, often violent solutions to political questions. The problems in North Caucasus, for example, are not understood as a result of state politics heavily reliant on the army, police and secret services; rather, in contrast, they are perceived as a sign that the Russian central state is too soft against 'the Caucasians'. Everyday racism and everyday xenophobia are widespread. In these circles, Vladimir Putin is not just a political, but also a moral leader. Many also feel close to Putin because he rose through the state from ordinary circumstances, something that corresponds to their own life experiences. Putin's enemies are also the enemies of this middle class, with liberal political views having a hard time in this environment. Broadly speaking, two groups can be distinguished. The older generation leans towards a kind of humanized Stalinism, and supports the idea of a strong leader who is broadly benevolent, but who can be tough when necessary. The younger group has a pointedly more nationalistic political preference. There is also a leadership cult here, but with a strong ethnic Russian element.

Mission of NGOs in a society with deep authoritarian roots

At the end of the first decade of the twenty-first century, without possessing political authority and declaring themselves as non-political, most NGOs in Russia gained a status of groups supporting the state on the one hand, but claimed a certain moral superiority on the other hand. By and by, this status might have been converted into political influence and, if things went well, have led to the appearance of new, more democratic norms and practices and even transformed into new sustainable institutions. Authoritarian states tend to react towards such non-political movements only if they become too public, too political, and too active. The Russian state did so in 2005–6 as a reaction to the Orange Revolution in Ukraine. It adopted a new law on NGOs to tighten the control and limit their political impact.

By and large, a state has three means at its disposal to limit the influence of civil society actors: economic welfare, the participation of its citizens and the exercise of force. The less of the two former that is at hand, the more authoritarian tendencies tend to dominate state actions. The participation of citizens in deciding what is good for their country has systematically been limited since Putin came into power in 2000 with his social contract. The economic development of Russia since 2008–9 is not very optimistic. In the short and medium term, the state must count on fewer material resources being available. It has been Putin's repeated reaction to tighten the screws and limit the participation rights of the Russian citizens and NGOs have been the main target of authoritarian measures every time. This approach worked out well in his first two terms as president and it helped keep him in power after the protests in the winter of 2011–12.

The tightening of control by those in power in authoritarian regimes in crisis situations has proven quite effective. But such an approach does not solve the underlying problems and, therefore, its positive effects from the point of view of the government will dwindle away sooner or later. In our case, the above-mentioned Putin's dilemma indicates that the tightening of control reduces the state's ability to address the problems, as emphasized by many experts. In other words: Putin pays for the tightening control over society through the weakening of institutions. NGOs, on the other hand, demand better institutions. This explains why NGOs in Russia have repeatedly become a target of the state's repressions in times of crisis in the first case.

NGOs and the protest winter of 2011–12

Within the last 25 years, more than 200,000 NGOs have emerged, in almost all sectors of Russian society (Siegert 2011). Many NGOs had covered a long distance from rather inexperienced activists in the 1990s, than gone through a phase of rapid development and professionalization, which often occurred as an answer to the attempts of the state to make them part of the corporate system of the managed democracy, in order to end up in the role of a surrogate opposition in the second presidential term of Vladimir Putin. At the same time, many NGOs acted as communication channels between the Kremlin and a big part of society. This was also in the Kremlin's interest because the people there were in need of making decisions, but could not be certain that their controlled media drew an appropriate picture of what was happening in the country. At the same time, quite a number of citizens, working in NGOs, experienced that mutual trust often makes things much easier to deal with than playing the zero-sum game.

In practice, the state and independent NGOs cooperated constantly on many different issues, even on an institutional basis. During President Medvedev's term (2008–12) organized political competition did almost not exist and different kinds of NGOs developed three different patterns of behaviour towards the country's leadership. A first group openly and without any limitation cooperated with the state. Among these NGOs, one can find many so-called government organized non-governmental organizations (GONGOs). A second group consisted of those NGOs which were convinced that limited cooperation with the state, even an authoritarian state, is necessary, because they have to solve practical problems which would, in many cases, not be possible without cooperation. A third group comprised NGOs which preferred to cooperate with the state only on a very limited number of practical questions. Most NGOs in this group were in close relations with the so-named non-systemic opposition. It goes without saying that it is not always possible to demarcate the borders between these three groups very clearly. One and the same NGO could both cooperate with the state and simultaneously criticize it harshly. But those have been exceptions.

Each of these three groups has had its favoured institutional information and cooperation channel with the state: The first acted through the Kremlin-controlled Public Chamber, set up in 2006; representatives of the second group have, in many cases, been members of the Presidential Council for the Development of Civil Society and Human Rights; the third group preferred to act through the expert council at the office of the Commissioner for Human Rights of the Russian Federation, chaired by Vladimir Lukin until the spring of 2014 and since then by Ella Pamfilova.

The re-opening of the public political field in the autumn of 2011 not only shattered this pattern of behaviour on the part of the Russian NGOs, which had been hitherto rather stable for quite a long period of time, but it forced them to reconsider their public and political role. The most important experience they gained at the very beginning of the protest was that the unexpected return of public politics did not lead to increased influence of the NGOs. Some of the functions that NGOs conducted turned out to be redundant. The surrogate opposition was, within days, replaced by a real one. At the same time, as organizations the NGOs did not play a leading role in the newly established protest movement on the streets. The NGO leaders mostly retained their influence, but more often as individuals rather than as representatives of their organizations.

Nevertheless, the organizational, infrastructural and knowledge resources of many NGOs played a certain, but not decisive role in strengthening the protest movement. However, this did not safeguard the NGOs against becoming a main target for the attempts of the state to counter and push back the opposition. One of the reasons for state pressure on NGOs has been that the Kremlin probably overestimated the role of the NGOs and the foreign funding of their activities and underestimated the profound changes that the Russian society was undergoing in the Putin years.

The rollback after the winter of protest 2011–12

After a short fight or flight response, the Kremlin decided to punch back hard in the spring of 2012. Ever since this time, the Kremlin has been trying to take over, fence in and limit politics and its protagonists. This is basically the main purpose of all pieces of new legislation that were quickly cooked up, mainly in 2013: the liberalized law on parties, the re-criminalizing of the law on slander, the tightened law on treason, and the laws imposing restrictions on the Internet.

As far as NGOs are concerned, the most significant of these new laws is the so-called foreign agent's bill. This piece of legislation imposes a new definition of politics, one that is, ironically, not more limiting but rather more comprehensive. Everything is now politics and, as a result, the state prosecutors have found politics in everything: sociology is now politics; environmental initiatives are politics; legal scholars and practicing lawyers exerting influence on the practice of law and the dispensation of justice is politics; providing advice to the local government is politics; monitoring legal violations by the state is politics. And to 'conduct political activity' is forbidden, if an NGO gets foreign funding and does not register as someone 'functioning as a foreign agent'.

By the spring of 2014, about 1,000 NGOs have been controlled by prosecutor's offices, the Ministry of Justice, the tax authorities and several other government bodies. About 60 NGOs got an administrative decision from the prosecutor's office. More than 20 of these NGOs have been ordered to register as a 'foreign agent', because, from the point of view of the prosecutor's office, they have been violating the law and virtually all have been acting as 'foreign agents'. The other NGOs got a 'warning' that they might violate the law and where asked to register as a 'foreign agent' in advance of 'conducting political activities' (ClosedSociety. org 2014). Almost all of the NGOs complained against these decisions. Many of them succeeded in challenging the decision in court. Some NGOs, mostly those dealing with LGBTI (lesbian, gay, bisexual, transgender, and intersexual) issues and observing elections, dissolved themselves, because their leaders were under threat of being criminalized under the 'foreign agent's bill' and they assumed that they would not be able to protect themselves in court. No NGO actually registered itself as a 'foreign agent'. As the Memorial Society had stated as early as September 2012, two months before the law came into effect, they believed that the law was 'unethical and unlawful' (Memorial 2012). In May 2014, the Ministry of Justice got the right to include NGOs in the register of 'foreign agents' without their content. Five organizations, among them two branches of the election monitoring NGO *Golos*, were instantly labelled 'foreign agents'. All five of these NGOs had been ordered to register as 'foreign agents' by court decisions, but did not comply.

What has made the relationship between Putin and civil society such a complex one? In fact, it is hardly surprising. Nearly all the powers that be in the second half of the twentieth century and the early twenty-first century have struggled with self-organized groups. Since Putin came into power, there have been three waves of protests. One main task of the campaigns against NGOs, at least up to the spring of 2014, was to discredit them in the eyes of the population. This proved to be quite effective. Furthermore, the NGOs have been very busy defending themselves since the new law came into effect. A large amount of resources had to be raised to organize and conduct this defence. So far, Russia's NGOs have emerged, from each round of confrontation with Putin, stronger, more skilful and with an enhanced reputation. Over the past 25 years, a considerable section of Russian society has developed a profound sense of its own civic dignity that simply will not allow it to subject itself to the kind of self-humiliation and eating of humble pie required of the NGOs under the foreign agent's law. And to this, Russia's authorities under Putin have certainly made a significant – albeit reluctant and involuntary – contribution.

Re-ideologization – from the United Russia to an overwhelming majority

The most important differentiating characteristic between the Soviet Union and Putin's Russia until 2012–13 was the widespread freedom of its people to define their lives as they wished. This freedom was a part of the social contract of the 2000s. On the whole, Putin kept his promise, probably because it is only in this combination that both strands of his power base could hold together: on the one side the so-called *gosudarstvenniki*, and on the other a free-market liberal elite. Their free-market liberal economic policy is to increase Russia's prosperity, to make it great again and, not unimportantly, through their economic successes, to secure Putin's sovereignty and thereby his power. This all worked very well until the economic crisis of 2008–9. Up to this time the majority of people in Russia were certainly satisfied with the overall result. During the economic crisis, however, confidence in a rosy future for the country took a hit. The discourse on modernization under the interim president Medvedev restored a little hope and fresh air. But, once Medvedev declared in September 2011 that he would step down and Putin came back in the spring of 2012, this air quickly ran out. The switch from an ideologically neutral or, better yet, only selectively and instrumentally ideological state, to one which calls for following the ideology and, at the very least, restraint in its dissent, showed itself at first in a change of concept. Instead of being president of a 'united Russia', from early 2012 Putin claimed to be representing only the politics of an 'overwhelming majority' (Chechel 2013).

The outline of this form of politics was sketched quickly. It can, conveniently, be seen in the repressive measures taken against the protesting opposition, especially against NGOs. Ever since that time the political classes have been conducting themselves, as has been conveyed to western societies, like right-wing conservatives, religious zealots, closer to or already past the limits of obscurantism. The most prominent examples are the anti-homosexuality laws, the so-called 'Dima Yakovlev law' which forbids the adoption of Russian children by US citizens, the law to 'protect religious feelings' and the increasingly hysterical public discussion of apparent falsifications of history, in particular involving World War II. Taken together, these events come together as a kind of antithesis to the 'western' maligned, reviled democratic modernity, an antithesis of the *open society* that has prevailed in the West since the middle of the twentieth century. And with time, this crude mixture of a sense of threat and resentment towards the foreign and the human, neo-religious bigotry and a geopolitical worldview intensified into a kind of ideology – not yet a very consistent one, but thoroughly usable. Internally, it is employed against the opposition and externally against the West.

Vladimir Putin gave credence to these ideological substrata in detail for the first time in September 2013 in a half-hour speech before the Valdai Club (2013), an annual meeting of politicians, experts and journalists working on Russia. A quick summary of the report is as follows: the West, and in particular Europe, which here means the EU, has strayed from its Christian occidental path and deteriorated into a hotbed of decadence, sin and weakness. A textbook example of this is the claim of the 'rise of gays' everywhere, which is believed to have led directly 'to discrimination against supporters of traditional sexual relationships'. A new, but essentially old mission for Russia has arisen from this: saving the Christian West, even though it does not deserve it. There is not much fundamentally new in any of this. It was the preoccupation of the Soviet Union, to not be the West, to be the anti-West or the better West.

Outlook

In the winter of 2011–12, Russia's democratic awakening took both the Kremlin and the opposition completely by surprise. Putin had to come up with a new, convincing narrative that would legitimize his third presidency. The 'overwhelming majority' and the 'traditional value' have been attempts to create such a narrative. The narrative of Putin's first term in office was the salvation of Russia's statehood, the reinstating of vertical power and the dictatorship of law. The motto of his second presidency was to maintain the gains made during his first presidency. Dmitry Medvedev's presidency tried to present a narrative of the country's modernization when the financial and economic crisis shook people's faith in 'business as usual'. It was a failure. Stability, the magic word of the late 2000s, has enjoyed a happy comeback. And it has certainly achieved some results. Fear of a new period of unrest continues to haunt the population. By stoking this fear and presenting himself as the guarantor of peace, Putin has managed to neutralize the protests so far.

The events in Ukraine since mid-November 2013, the growing protest on the Maidan Square in Kiev, the killing of more than 100 people there on 20–21 February 2014, the following flight of President Viktor Yanukovich and the regime change in Ukraine altered things fundamentally. The Kremlin reacted to this direct threat to its own power in two ways: With a preventive ideological counter-revolution within the country and an increased anti-western political course in the outside world.

The revolution within Russia was directed primarily against all remaining islands of independent societal actors such as NGOs, but also the last parts of the free press, mainly the internet, independent scholars and the small number of oppositional politicians. Inside Russia, the anti-western course in foreign policy, culminating so far with the annexation of the Crimea Peninsula and the meddling in the eastern part of Ukraine did lead to a patriotic consolidation and further marginalized different opinions, and even made them in a way dissident again. For Russian NGOs, this development further narrows their space for manoeuvres. Once more, the whole concept of an independent civil society organization became suspicious. On 18 March 2014, in his address to the Federal Assembly to mark the annexation of the Crimea, President Putin made reference to a 'fifth column' or groups of 'national traitors' active inside Russia (Putin 2014).

All this points to the fact that those in power will most probably continue to try to gain control of the still-independent groups or will try to close them down, because they perceive them largely as a threat. The main danger in this scenario is that a further deteriorating situation in the country could lead to a radicalization of a broader part of the NGO community. It is not unlikely that those in power would react to such a radicalization by tightening political control and repression. As a result, NGO activists might regress to their earlier role of dissidents in a mainly closed society. If this were to happen, and the development turns in this direction, it will be very difficult to speak about the existence of a civil society in Russia at all.

Note

1 Brazil, Russia, India, China, South Africa.

References

Auzan, A. (2012) 'Zalozhniki nedoveriya', *Otechestvennye Zapiski*. Online. Available: www.strana-oz.ru/2012/2/zalozhniki-nedoveriya (accessed 3 February 2014).

Chechel, I. (2013) 'Vremya vpered? Preambula k diskussii o "podavlyayoshchem bolshinstve"', *Gefter*, 17 July 2013. Online. Available: http://gefter.ru/archive/9447 (accessed 4 March 2014).

ClosedSociety.org (2014) 'State Pressure on NGO's Monitoring'. Online. Available: http://closedsociety.org/en/ (accessed 22 April 2014).

Gudkov, L. (2012) 'Sozialnaya kartina i ideologicheskiye orientatsii', *Pro et Contra*, 3(55): 6–31.

Habermas, J. (1971) *Strukturwandel der Öffentlichkeit. Untersuchungen zu einer Kategorie der bürgerlichen Gesellschaft*, Berlin: Neuwied.

Levada Center (2011) Perspektivy grazhdanskogo obshchestva v Rossii. Online. Available: www.levada.ru/sites/default/files/levada_civil_society_2011_report.pdf (accessed 24 April 2014).

Luhmann, N. (2000) *Vertrauen. Ein Mechanismus zur Reduktion von sozialer Komplexität*, Stuttgart: Lucius & Lucius.

Memorial (2012) 'O zakone ob "inostrannykh agentakh". Zayavleniye, Mezhdunarodnogo Memoriala', 21 September 2012, Online. Available: www.memo.ru/d/129219.html (accessed 11 July 2014).

Putin, V. (2014) 'Address by President of the Russian Federation', 18 March 2014. Online. Available: http://eng.kremlin.ru/transcripts/6889 (accessed 23 April 2014).

Roth, R. and Rucht, D. (2008) 'Autonomie und die Politik der ersten Person', in Roth, R. and Rucht, D. (eds), *Die Sozialen Bewegungen in Deutschland seit 1945. Ein Handbuch*. Frankfurt am Main: Campus Verlag.

Siegert, J. (2011) 'Evolyutsiya grazhdanskoy aktivnosti', *Pro et Contra*, 15: 1–2. Online. Available: http://carnegie.ru/proetcontra/?fa=43952 (accessed 24 April 2014).

Tikhonova, N. (2014) 'Sozialnaya struktura Rossii: teorii i realnost', Moskva: Novyy Khronograf. Online. Available: www.isras.ru/files/File/publ/Tikhonova_Social_struktura_Rossii.pdf (accessed 16 June 2014).

Valdai Club (2013) 'Vladimir Putin Meets with Members the Valdai International Discussion Club'. Transcript of the Speech and Beginning of the Meeting, 20 September 2013. Online. Available: http://valdaiclub.com/politics/62880.html (accessed 28 February 2014).

World Bank (2014) 'Russian Economic Report 31: Confidence Crisis Exposes Economic Weakness', 26 March. Online. Available: www.worldbank.org/en/news/press-release/2014/03/26/russian-economic-report-31 (accessed 16 June 2014).

Zubarevich, N. (2012) 'Four Russias: Rethinking the post-Soviet Map', *Open Democracy*. Online. Available: www.opendemocracy.net/od-russia/natalia-zubarevich/four-russias-rethinking-post-soviet-map (accessed 24 February 2014).

11 Regional inequality and potential for modernization

Natalia Zubarevich

The issue of regional inequality is highly politicized in Russia with its vast and heterogeneous territory. Both politicians and public opinion are influenced by a number of settled stereotypes concerning the issue, for example it is claimed that 'Regional inequality is so deep that it becomes an obstacle to further development', or 'Inequality is growing in Russia, as opposed to the developed countries'. Another common view is that 'Inequality can be reduced by applying a policy of large-scale equalizing economic development level of the regions'. Some geographers and regional economists in Russia concur with these widely expressed views. However, consensus in the expert community has not yet been reached on the issue of the objective nature of inequality of spatial development and the role of regional policy.

There are still relatively few scientific studies of the causes of and trends in regional inequality in Russia. Instead, regions with extreme characteristics are compared, and the results are used to argue that regional differentiation in Russia is extremely high and ever growing. The first quantitative studies applying modern methodologies appeared only in the 2000s. These studies use econometric methods (Drobyshevskiy *et al.* 2005 Gaidar Institute 2007). Later Novosibirsk economists have used the decomposition method to identify the contribution of individual industries to the inequality of regions by per capita gross regional product (GRP) (Gluschenko 2010; Lavrovskiy and Shiltsin 2009). Another approach is to use the Gini coefficient to estimate the social and economic inequality of regions of Russia and countries in the post-Soviet space (see, for example, Maleva 2007; Zubarevich 2008; and for Russia, Kazakhstan and Ukraine, Zubarevich and Safronov 2011).

In contrast to the common sayings about inequality in Russia, quantitative studies from the mid-2000s show no sustained trend of divergence or convergence among the regions of Russia. The mixed results are understandable. First, the measurement period is too short: statistics of GRP, employment and income of the population did not appear until the mid-1990s. Second, Russia and other countries of the Commonwealth of Independent States (CIS) have experienced several crises and a period of growth, while various economic trends may have different impacts on regional disparities. Third, the reliability of regional statistics is rather low, especially for per capita money income and GRP. Fourth, the studies use different methods of measurement of regional inequality, which significantly affects their results.

The purpose of this chapter is to investigate the inequality between regions in Russia and the redistribution that has occurred between 1998 and 2012. First, the analysis focuses on a comparison of per capita GRP, the impact of redistribution of oil rent over the federal budget, social indicators and the Gini coefficient. The trend from these indicators shows that inequality has been declining in these indicators from the mid-2000s as a result of a number of different factors. The first and most significant is the huge redistribution of oil and gas rents via federal budget transfers. The second is the crisis of 2009 which had a negative influence on the more developed regions. In 2012–13, transfers from the federal budget were shrinking in nearly all of the less developed regions. Next, the chapter compares regional inequality between Russia, Ukraine and Kazakhstan, and shows that Russia has a trend of more convergence in equality between regions than the other countries in the 2000s. Finally, the chapter analyses heterogeneity in human capital, living conditions and the modernization of values between different parts of Russia using the centre–periphery model. This analysis allows conclusions regarding the heterogeneity of political views and strategies to adapt to economic and political change based on geographical factors and the level of living conditions.

The outline of the chapter is as follows: The first section gives a background of issues and literature in the area of spatial inequality. The second section analyses inequality between regions using standard indicators such as GRP per capita, federal budget transfers, employment and unemployment rates, the Gini coefficient and the Human Development Index (HDI). The third section compares trends in inequality in Russia, Ukraine and Kazakhstan. The fourth section analyses the heterogeneity of Russian regions with the centre–periphery model. The fifth section draws conclusions for regional policy for the different groups of regions and their problems in the medium and the long term.

Factors and trends of spatial inequality

Opportunities for mitigating economic and social disparities among regions are one of the most controversial topics in regional science. The tendency toward a concentration of economic activity in territories with favourable conditions for businesses was discovered by Myrdal (1957) in the mid-twentieth century. Core–periphery theory or the theory of polarized development, by Friedmann (1966), has become an important contribution to understanding spatial development patterns. The *new economic geography* established at the end of the twentieth century has applied quantitative methods to explain the causes of concentration of economic activity and workforce mobility.

In recent years, under the influence of 'the new economic geography', there has been a paradigm shift from a rigid equalizing policy to a more adequate vision of the range of opportunities to address this problem. A considerable contribution to the shift was made in studies devoted to economic geography by Krugman (1991),

Martin (2005), and the World Bank (2009). Competitive advantages of territories depend on the two groups of factors – *first* and *second nature* (Krugman 1993). Dominance of *first nature factors* is a characteristic trait of the post-Soviet countries. First of all, it is the abundance of mineral resources, oil, gas, and metals. *Second nature factors* in post-Soviet countries often take the shape of obstacles to development: the institutional environment continues to be unfavourable; investments in human capital are low; infrastructure is underdeveloped; agglomeration effects are rather weak, except in the largest Moscow agglomeration. The number of big cities with a population over 200,000 people is under 10 per cent, that is, only 91 out of 1,099 cities in Russia. The actual barriers to development are rather strong.

European experiences

The World Bank (2009) shows that in the developed European countries, regional inequality as measured by per capita GRP was the deepest at the end of the nineteenth century and the first half of the twentieth century, when rapid industrial development took place. Growth of inequality became slower by the end of the twentieth century due to the predominance of second nature factors. In the long run, the *second nature factors* tend to diminish the growth of economic inequality of regions.

The less developed countries of Western Europe that joined the European Union (EU) in the 1970s and 1980s have managed to close the development gap as measured by per capita GDP, which existed between them and the older EU members. But the price of success was the growth of regional inequality in the majority of these countries (Duro 2001). As shown by Martin (2005), divergent and convergent tendencies do not coincide for EU countries and their regions. The inequality of regions within a country increases because the business invests in the regions with competitive advantages. The investment priorities therefore polarize the country's economic space. However, differences among countries may at the same time decline because regions with competitive advantages provide higher returns on investments and, thus, make the whole country's economy grow faster. So, the European integration stimulates convergence at the level of countries but does not lead to a convergence of their regions, which is noticeable in less developed countries.

Those Central and Eastern European countries that have joined the EU during the past decade face the same tendencies. Companies make their investments, first of all, in regions close to capitals and to the western borders with older EU members. Investment strategies make it possible to use competitive advantages, such as the agglomeration effect and the short distance to markets, which reduces costs. As a result, regional inequality also grows in these countries and leaders leave peripheral regions far behind.

Development, human capital and institutions

In large developing countries, spatial economic inequality also grew at the end of the twentieth century. This is a consequence of the accelerated development of regions with explicit competitive advantages. In China, these are maritime regions; in Brazil, agglomeration; and in India, territories featuring higher human capital. This led to faster economic growth of these countries as a whole. Only in recent years has China begun to pay attention to the development of inner territories. The global experience shows that catch-up development always takes place and the regional polarity of space may become even stronger. For developing countries, the main priority is to promote economic development of territories with competitive advantages such as a favourable geographical location, an agglomerative effect, and the availability of natural resources.

The other aspect of the problem is social inequality, which is measured by a set of indicators, namely, differences in income and employment rates, as well as qualitative features, such as health and education. The social inequality of regions hinders the growth of human capital and the modernization of institutions. Therefore, its growth adversely affects the development itself. How does social inequality change in the long run? The World Bank (2009) shows that during the 1960s–70s, social inequality (measured by per capita income rates) decreased in many developed countries. One cause for this change is the effective targeted social policy of a state that is supporting low-income groups of the population. The European experience shows that income inequality of regions can be smoothed by an effective redistributive social policy, rather than by stimulating regional policy aimed at attracting investments and creating jobs in less developed regions.

Regional inequality in Russia

The problem of differences between the levels of economic development is viewed as paramount, but regional inequality, in fact, is exaggerated. Except for the main oil- and gas-extracting regions[1] and Moscow, at one extreme, and a few underdeveloped republics,[2] at the other extreme, there is no great difference estimated in per capita GRP between the levels of economic development of most Russian regions (Figure 11.1). Moreover, regional economic disparities have decreased through the 2000s: the ratio between the richest and the poorest regions, respectively the oil- and gas-extracting Tyumen Region and the underdeveloped Republic of Ingushetia, fell from about 30 times in 2005 to 13 times in 2010 (per capita GRP adjusted for price level differences). The reduction in inequalities was promoted by the huge growth of oil rent, the centralization of oil and gas revenues in the federal budget and large-scale redistribution by increased federal transfers to the less developed regions. In 12 regions,[3] federal transfers account for over half of all budget revenues, and in Chechnya and Ingushetia, they are close to 85–90 per cent. In the leading oil- and gas-extracting regions,[4] these industries play an important role in regional economies, creating well-paid jobs and providing large revenues for regional budgets. However, the domination of such segments and the formation of single-industry regional economies increase development risks due to the instability of oil prices and the depletion of natural resources in the long term.

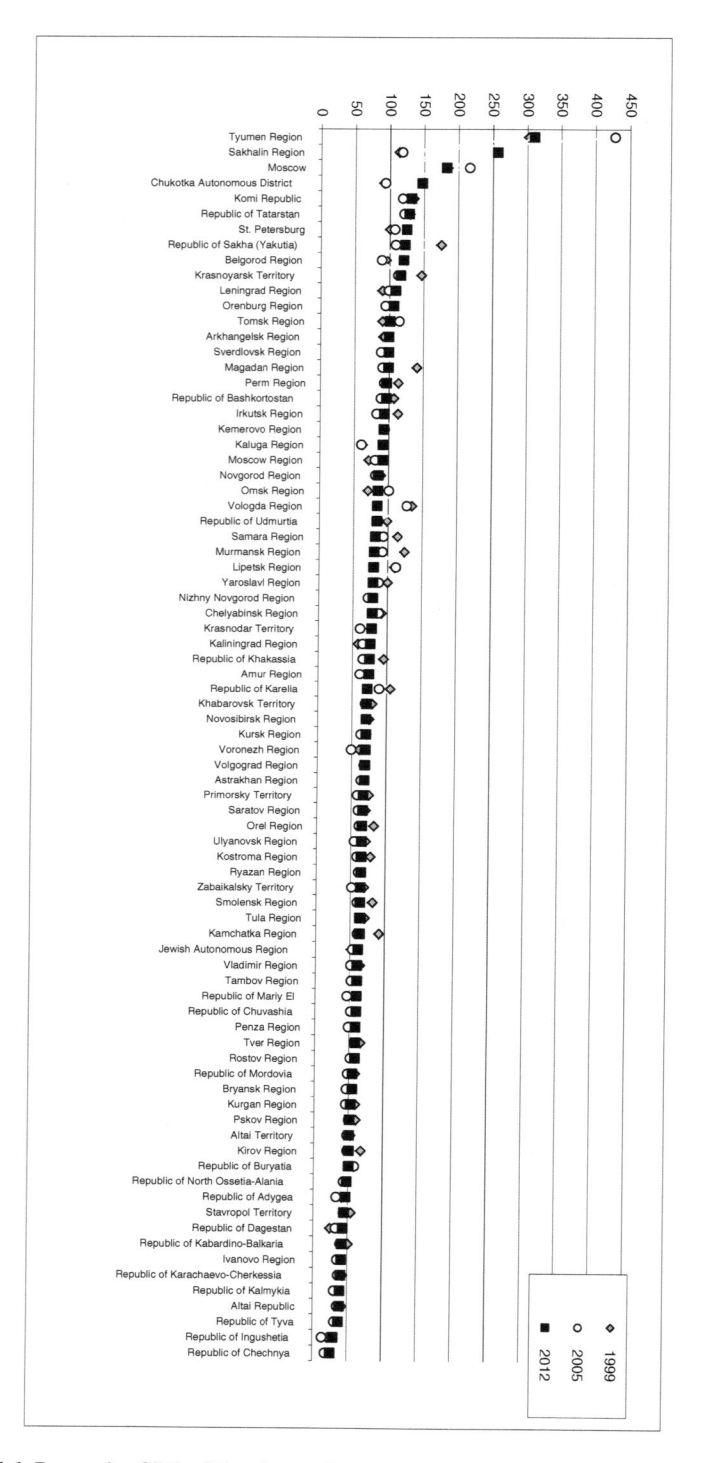

Figure 11.1 Per capita GRP of Russian regions as per cent of the national average (adjusted for regional prices differentiation).

Source: Rosstat database.

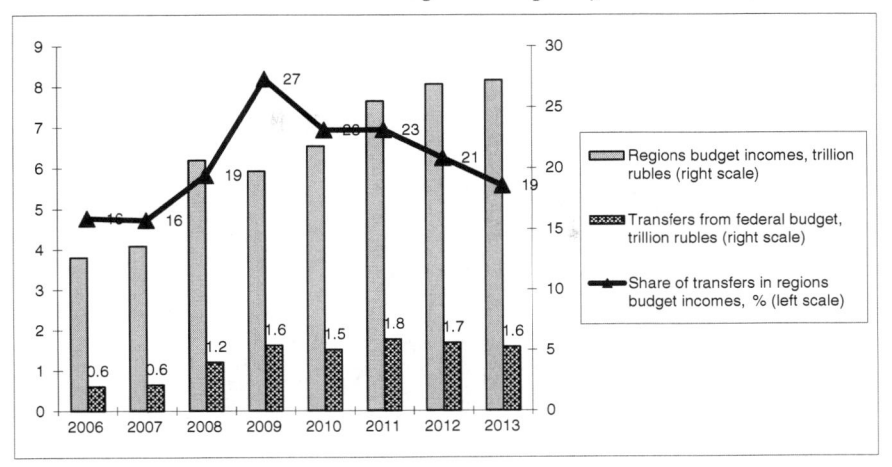

Figure 11.2 Russian regions budget revenues, transfers from federal budget and share of transfers in regions' budget revenues.

Source: Federal Treasury database.

It follows that positive levelling trends that are based on the redistribution of oil and gas rents are not stable. If the federal redistribution policy weakens, the economic disparities will grow. This process may be noted since 2012 as a consequence of the deteriorating economic situation in Russia. During the crisis of 2009, the federal budget increased transfers to the regions by 34 per cent and helped to minimise the negative effects. In 2009 there was a huge growth in federal transfers, but in 2012–13 the transfers from the federal budget and the share of transfers in regional budget revenues have been shrinking (Figure 11.2). This implies that there is a risk of change in the trends in economic inequality – from convergence to divergence – which may be emphasized by a growing role of regions' competitive advantages and investment spatial disparities.

The spatial inequality of investment has reproduced regional economic disparities. During the 2000s, investments were concentrated in the oil- and gas-extracting regions, the federal cities Moscow and St Petersburg and their agglomerations and to the regions where major federal projects were underway (Table 11.1). Per capita investment in the less developed republics and depressive regions were 2–4 times lower than the average in the rest of the country. In the crisis year of 2009 investments decreased by 16 per cent, and this decline in investment had still not been overcome by the end of 2013, neither in Russia as a whole, nor in half of the regions. The slow recovery in investment reflects the unfavourable investment climate and economic stagnation that began in 2013.

Public investments over the federal and regional budgets represent one-fifth of all investments in Russia and are divided roughly equally between the federal and regional budgets. Investment from the federal budget flows mainly to the regions of 'big projects'. For example, Krasnodar and Primorsky Territories

Table 11.1 Per capita investment in 1999–2012

Annual regional averages* in 2011 constant prices, *thousand RUR*

Leaders		Outsiders	
Oil and gas extracting regions		*Depressive regions*	
Nenets Autonomous District	1194	Kirov Region	25
Yamal-Nenets Aut. District	680	Republic of Mariy El	24
Khanty-Mansy Aut. District	293	Kurgan Region	23
Sakhalin region	260	Ivanovo Region	21
Republic of Sakha (Yakutia)	125	Bryansk Region	21
Komi Republic	111	Altai Territory	19
The largest agglomerations		*Less developed republics*	
Leningrad Region	104	Republic of Kabardino-Balkaria	24
Moscow	75	Republic of Dagestan	23
St Petersburg	59	Republic of North Ossetia	20
Regions of the "big projects"		Republic of Karachaevo-Cherkessia	20
Krasnodar Territory	75	Republic of Ingushetia	13
Republic of Tatarstan	73	Republic of Tyva	13

Source: Rosstat database.

Note: * Russia average = RUR 54 thousand.

received almost 20 per cent of all investments from the federal budget in 2011–12 to allow them to prepare them for the Winter Olympic Games in Sochi 2014 and the APEC[5] Summit, respectively, while Tatarstan received 5 per cent as it prepared to host the World Student Games. In total, in 2011 these three regions took a quarter of all investments from the federal budget. Another 10 per cent went to Moscow, which has its own huge budget. Only 10 per cent from the federal budget were invested in the North Caucasus republics. As a result, the federal investment policy has a poor equalizing effect.

Social indicators show the contradictory trends of regional inequality. The unemployment rate diminished from 10.6 per cent to 5.5 per cent in the period 2000–13 (labour surveys according to ILO methodology), but regional differentiation is still large enough: from 39 per cent in the Republic of Ingushetia and 26 per cent in the Chechen Republic to 2 per cent in Moscow and St Petersburg. The real money incomes of the Russian population grew by 2.6 times in the decade of economic growth (1999–2008) and regional inequalities, measured by average per capita income, have been in decline for the past decade.

For the more correct measuring of regional inequality trends, one may study the coefficient of variation and the Gini coefficient.[6] The Gini coefficient and the coefficient of variation were weighted by the population of the region to minimize the influence of the huge heterogeneity of Russian regions in terms of population (a population from 43–50 thousand in Nenets and Chukotka Autonomous Districts to 10.9 million in Moscow and 7 million in the Moscow Region). Calculations of the Gini coefficients for GRP per capita show the changing trends (Figure 11.3). The period of divergence (the first years of growth after the economic crisis of 1998 and the beginning of the boom in oil prices in 2004–5) has been alternating with the period of convergence as a result of redistributing interbudgetary policy growth in the 2000s and the crisis that began in 2008. However, the trend over the whole period is clear: there has been an increase in the economic inequality of regions in terms of per capita GRP.

The Gini coefficient for the variable 'money income per capita' shows a trend of a stable decline of regional inequality (Figure 11.3). Russian regions converging in terms of all living standard indicators: income, salaries and wages, poverty rate, and consumption, which is measured by the turnover of per capita retail trade. Recent successful years of economic growth and the increased redistribution of oil revenues resulted in the rapid growth of public sector employees' wages as well as social subsidies for low-income groups. The share of public sector employees is higher in underdeveloped regions because of the absence of other jobs, as well as the proportion of low-income groups. As a result, measures of social policy reduced regional income inequality. Increases in pensions, which took place in 2008–12, had the strongest impact on the money income of the population of semi-developed regions of the European Center and North-West, where the age structure of the population is the oldest. The consequence of this was a

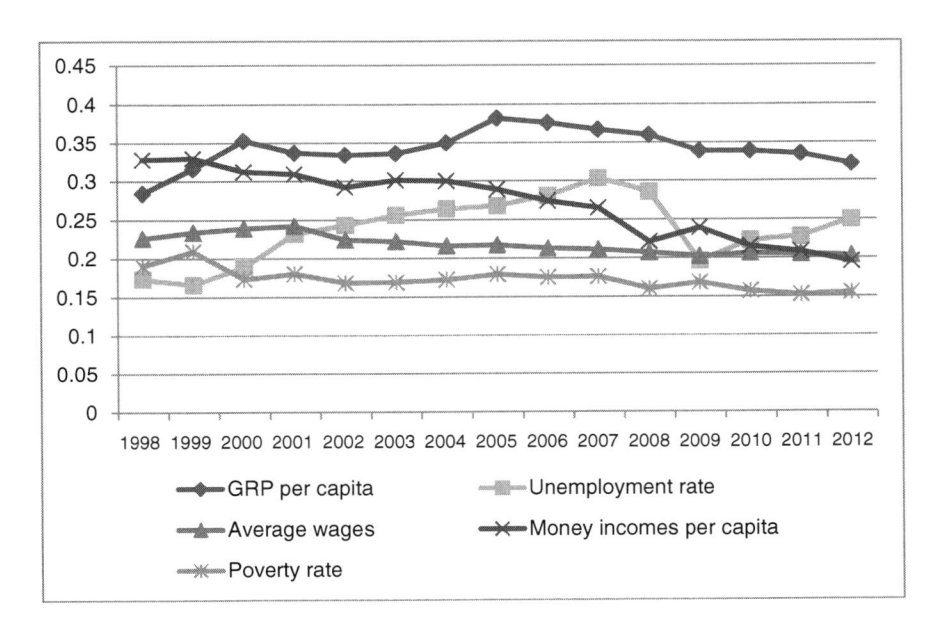

Figure 11.3 Inequality of Russia's regions: Gini coefficient for socio-economic indicators.

Source: Rosstat database.

significant drop in the Gini coefficient, because it is more sensitive to differences among medium regions of a certain range.

The growth of regional disparities in employment continued until the crisis of 2008. One of the main causes is low investments in the less developed regions (see Table 11.1) and the lack of new jobs, which reinforced the regional differences in unemployment rates. The change of trends under a transformation of the economic conditions corresponds to models of developed countries (Martin 2005). In regions with low unemployment, economic growth leads to faster job creation, and unemployment tends to decrease more rapidly, while it grows more quickly during the initial stage of a crisis. Underdeveloped regions with higher unemployment rates are more stable in any phase of the economic cycle.

These trends can be supplemented with a complex HDI, including indicators of life expectancy at birth, level of education and GRP per capita. The measurement of regional development using the HDI presents a favourable picture: during the 2000s the index rose substantially in all regions (UNDP 2013). A significant increase of life expectancy at birth had been an important social achievement over the period. The regional differentiation is almost unchanged, however: 20 per cent of Russia's population live in relatively prosperous regions (including 8 per cent in Moscow); about 10–12 per cent live in 'outsider', poorer regions, and more than two thirds live in regions with an average level of human development. These proportions have not changed during the 2000s and the inequality in human development is still high and stable.

Regional inequality in Russia, Ukraine, and Kazakhstan

Gini coefficient calculations show that the level of regional inequalities in three large post-Soviet countries – Russia, Ukraine, and Kazakhstan – differs, being at its highest in oil- and gas-extracting Russia and Kazakhstan and lower in Ukraine (Table 11.2). The general trend in the 2000s has been for a growth in economic inequality in the regions until the beginning of the crisis of 2008–9. This coincides with the trend in other developing countries. Only in Russia has the growth of economic inequality been less stable and in the mid-2000s it alternated with the trend of convergence under the influence of large-scale interbudgetary redistributing measures. In Kazakhstan and Ukraine, the trends of economic divergence of regions have been more explicit, which follows from a stronger oil and gas specialization of the economy in Kazakhstan, on the one hand, and a weak redistribution and investment policy under conditions of significant political instability in Ukraine (Zubarevich and Safronov 2011).

As noted above, the regional disparities in living standards decreased in Russia due to a social policy based on the redistribution of oil and gas revenues. This trend is similar to the dynamics of regional income inequality in developed European countries with a strong social policy, for example, France and other countries. However, the strengthening of the state does not always lead to a convergence of regional average money income. In Kazakhstan, the process of regional convergence has been noticeable only in terms of per capita money income and is not

Table 11.2 Regional inequality of Russia, Ukraine and Kazakhstan: Gini coefficient for GRP and money income per capita

	2000	2001	2002	2003	2004	2005	2006	2007	2008	2009	2010	2011	2012
GRP per capita													
Russia	0.353	0.337	0.334	0.336	0.350	0.382	0.376	0.367	0.360	0.339	0.339	0.335	0.322
Ukraine	0.184	0.226	0.228	0.235	0.248	0.248	0.253	0.271	0.268	0.258	0.263	0.254	0.258
Kazakhstan	0.336	0.336	0.364	0.376	0.387	0.410	0.430	0.390	0.396	0.382	0.391	0.375	0.361
Average wages													
Russia	0.239	0.242	0.224	0.222	0.216	0.217	0.213	0.211	0.207	0.202	0.206	0.205	0.203
Ukraine	-	-	0.085	0.081	0.091	0.092	0.100	0.108	0.117	0.126	0.126	0.123	0.136
Kazakhstan	-	0.269	0.266	0.27	0.266	0.272	0.236	0.233	0.243	0.239	0.231	0.217	0.208

Sources: Author's calculations from databases of Rosstat, State Statistics Committee of Ukraine and Statistics Agency of Kazakhstan.

present in terms of salaries and wages or poverty rate. This is a consequence of a less developed social policy and the lower standard of living among the rural population. In the rural households of the southern and western regions of Kazakhstan, which are the main recipients of social assistance, poverty is deeper than in Russia, and the birth rate is higher. As a result, social subsidies cannot lift poor households with many dependents above the poverty rate. Ukraine is the most striking example of divergence between regions by all social indicators, which is caused by a weak social policy.

A comparison of the trends in regional disparities in employment shows that in all three countries, the period of recovery growth after the 1998 crisis was accompanied by the divergence of regional unemployment rates, while the beginning of the crisis of the 2008 is characterized by convergence. These trends are also affected by economic cycles: in periods of economic growth, divergence prevails, while in times of crises, there is a decline in the regional differences in unemployment rates. However, in Kazakhstan there is a very high proportion of the self-employed, estimated to one third of all employed, and it is impossible to identify trends.

Thus, among the three large countries – Russia, Ukraine and Kazakhstan – Russia has shown the more explicit convergence trends in the social development of regions during the 2000s, although the initial differences were very high. Ukraine has displayed the opposite case: a divergence of regional social and economic development levels has taken place, whereas inequality was initially less pronounced. Kazakhstan lies in between these two countries in terms of the trends in regional disparities in social indicators. Although authoritarian regimes are more likely to exercise a policy of equalization, in Kazakhstan there is a synthesis of a relatively liberal social policy and dirigisme in the regional economic policy. In Russia, an authoritarian regime is more consistent: the redistributive paternalistic social policy and redistributive dirigisme of regional policy fit together. The reduction of differences between Russian regions in the 2000s, particularly with regard to inequalities in incomes and poverty levels, has played an important role in the stabilization of economic development and the stability of Putin's regime.

However, the role of regional policy should not be overestimated. The laws of spatial development are stronger than political regimes. Spatial development is inertial, with its factors and barriers being long term in nature. It is unlikely that any significant changes will take place over the next 10–15 years. The actual drivers and barriers will continue to influence the trends in regional inequality in the same way. This means that economic disparities among the regions will grow under the influence of objective factors such as comparative advantages and competitiveness. The development of regional disparities of economic and labour market indicators will continue to be impacted by economic cycles. This leads to a divergence in periods of growth and convergence in recessions. Russia has faced the new crisis cycle with visible trends of economic stagnation in 2013 and prospects of downturn.

From regional inequalities to the centre–periphery model

While the regional differences are great, they are generally not the most important ones. Things become very intuitive if we change the scale, and instead of one
Russia or 83 (the number of regions), we distinguish four parts of Russia (see also
Zubarevich 2013 for a similar analysis). This way, Russia's modernization can be
interpreted through the centre–periphery model. The country's population can be
divided into three roughly equal parts in accordance with the centre–periphery
model (Friedmann 1966), and a small and distinct fourth part can be added to them.
The centre–periphery model explains the hierarchical settlement pattern where settlements are arranged from most modernized urban areas to patriarchal rural areas.
Centre–periphery distinctions are typical of other countries, especially those characterized by 'catching-up development'. But they have their own peculiarities in
Russia, where the largest cities are well ahead of the rest of the country and industrial cities face diverse issues, but, most importantly, there is a vast deteriorating
and depopulating periphery. The centre–periphery model can be used to describe
Russia's internal heterogeneity. The populations of metropolitan areas, midsize
cities, small towns, and rural areas display different modernization potentials and
employ different adaptation strategies in times of economic and political change. In
December 2011, it was in the big cities, rather than in smaller settlements, that pro-
testors took to the streets after the Duma elections and demanded fair elections. The
regional elections held in 2013 also demonstrated that there are different Russias.

The first Russia

The first Russia primarily includes the big cities with a population of over or close
to 1 million, and containing approximately 21 per cent of Russia's inhabitants.
This means that one in five Russians lives in the 14 cities with populations of
around one million or more. The federal cities – Moscow and St Petersburg – are
at the top of this group and about one in nine of the population lives in just these
two cities. The advantages of life in two 'federal' cities are obvious. They are
at the heart of the post-industrial economy, enjoying a high level of economic
development. Moscow's economic indicators are all considerably higher than the
averages for Russia. In terms of spending power (PPP), Moscow's GRP translates
as USD 47,000 per capita and that of St Petersburg as USD 22,000, both of which
are comparable with the developed world. Both cities have the highest shares of
the middle class – up to 40 per cent of city residents, the most educated population
(39–43 per cent of city residents over the age of 15 have a higher education), as
well as the most diverse labour market and the highest-paid jobs, higher shares of
small business employees and widespread internet access. The inhabitants of both
cities have a higher standard of living than that elsewhere in Russia. But it is also
worth noting that the two cities have an older population, with about 25 per cent
of the inhabitants above retirement age.

The federal cities, especially Moscow as the capital, incorporate the financial
and human resources of the entire country. Political transformation is particularly

rapid here; protest sentiments and demands for regime modernization are also on the rise in these cities. The election data also point in this direction: for example, the opposition candidate won 27 per cent of the vote in the Moscow mayoral election, and less than half of the Muscovites voted for Putin in the 2012 presidential election. The results of this election were marred by greater electoral fraud in St Petersburg; nevertheless, the protest potential is also strong.

The past twenty years have also brought change to the other 'million-plus' cities.[7] The pace of transformation is faster in Yekaterinburg and Novosibirsk, since being macroregional centres of the Urals and Siberia works to their advantage. These cities also experience a more rapid transformation from an industrial to a post-industrial economy and major service industry centres. They attract more migrants and create more modern high-paid jobs. Patterns of employment have changed in all 'million-plus' cities: the proportion of white-collar workers has risen, there are more medium-sized businesses, and even in the public sector, there is greater demand for staff with high qualifications. These cities are the first to adopt the capitals' consumer lifestyle, although the salaries are substantially lower than in Moscow. It is here that you find the middle class, the 'angry urbanites' that came out on the streets in December 2011 – although it must be said that the majority of these live in Moscow. The smaller cities are much less active – since their middle classes are not large enough to make a difference. But probably this is just a question of time. Objectively speaking, the 'grapes of wrath' are ripening: migration in Russia is directed towards the largest cities, the only difference being that greater Moscow and St Petersburg and its contiguous Leningrad region attract migrants from all over the country, 60 per cent and 20 per cent, respectively, of all net migration in Russia, while for their growth, regional cities rely on an influx from their own regions, mostly young people going into higher education. The increasing concentration of active and well educated citizens in the big cities 'tolls the death knell of the "power vertical"'.

If cities with a population over 500,000 are added to this category, the number of people living in large cities reaches 31 per cent. Examples of such cities are Sochi, Kaliningrad and Tver. Practically all cities with populations over 500,000 are regional centres, which helps them to concentrate regional resources, especially human capital. On the whole, city size and high human capital concentration are key factors in modernization. Compared with the 'million plus' cities, cities with a population over 500,000 change more slowly, especially if their inhabitants have lower income and education levels, and higher percentages are employed in the public sector and the industry. But even here, the differences are vast.

About 9 per cent of the Russians live in cities with populations between 250,000 and 500,000, with most of these cities also being regional capitals. In Russia, being a capital makes for more sustainable city development but, in most cases, such cities lack the financial and human resources to modernize. This is a transition zone between the *first* and *second Russias*. These cities vary enormously, from an academic hothouse such as Tomsk with its academic specialization (one person in five is a student), independent TV channels and a flourishing cultural life, to much more traditional centres of some republics. The boundaries of the 'first Russia' will vary according to the criteria used: if one talks about the dynamics of change, then it stops at the 'half-million' cities; if the criterion is stability, then it includes towns with a population of over 250,000.

The share of large-city residents in Russia's population is growing steadily as a result of migration. It is in the large cities that Russia's 50 million internet users are concentrated, as well as the Russian middle class that is demanding change. This group's activism is not founded on a fear of imminent crisis, but the scary prospect of a long Putin's stagnation which will put the brakes on social mobility. The stimulus for protest in this 'first Russia' was not an economic crisis or a collapse in the price of oil, but rather a moral repugnance.

The second Russia

The second Russia encompasses smaller cities and towns with populations between 20,000 and 250,000, accounting for around 30 per cent of Russia's present-day population. Not all of these towns have retained their industrial profiles during the post-Soviet era, but Soviet values and way of life still remain strong. They have large numbers of blue-collar workers and public sector employees of lower qualifications. There is usually little in the way of small business, either because of low spending power of consumers or a high level of cronyism. There are, of course, exceptions; in Magnitogorsk, for example, there is a wide variety of small businesses, but they are critically dependent on its famous iron and steel works: if the steel workers' wages fall, then so does demand for their services.

A study by the Independent Institute for Social Research in Moscow shows that industrial towns, even the more successful ones specializing in the oil- and gas-extracting industries and metallurgy for the global market, are losing their attraction for residents (Zubarevich and Safronov 2013). At times of economic growth, wages there have risen more slowly than in regional centres; the government has been quick to raise public sector and managerial salaries on the back of enormous oil revenues, but the industrial sector has been unable to increase its wage bill to the same extent. During the 2009 economic crisis, wages also fell faster because of the slump in the industry. As a result, the population numbers in the vast majority of second Russia cities and towns are falling rapidly. Young people move to the larger cities and the capital for educational opportunities as well as more appropriate jobs, and they rarely come back.

The location of medium-sized towns, both industrial and post-industrial, is crucial. If they are close to large population centres then their future is assured: they will gradually be absorbed into the conurbation, and sustainable enterprises will emerge to service the metropolitan market. Towns situated on main arterial roads also have more of a future. All towns on the Moscow–Minsk motorway, the road to Europe, are gradually being transformed into logistics and handling centres for the Moscow agglomeration. However, if a town is less fortunately located, it is shrinking. The 2009 economic crisis hit metallurgic and heavy engineering company towns such as Magnitogorsk and Nizhnyi Tagil particularly hard. The government's main response was to protect jobs at any price, regardless of companies' viability. There was widespread recourse to reduced working hours and work creation programmes, and despite a huge fall in production, the employment levels were maintained thanks to large injections of government finance. A longer term support strategy, based on economic diversification, was not a success. The complex investment plans mostly remained on paper.

Those living in the second Russia do not like the political situation in the country either. The results of the 2011 Duma elections showed that the numbers of votes cast for United Russia in many industrial towns were as low as they were in larger regional centres (29–38 per cent). In the presidential election, however, the second Russia voted for Putin, since people living there place a high value on stability, stable employment and wages. Liberal ideals of political modernization are unlikely to take hold here, unless they are accompanied by strong social policies. The results of the presidential election provide more evidence of political cleavage. Should a new crisis arise, it is the second Russia that will be hit the hardest. The old problems have not gone away, and the last crisis confirmed that the industry is declining faster than other economic sectors. There are few alternative sources of work in these towns, and the local populace suffers from a lack of mobility and low levels of qualifications. Even if a new economic crisis does spark a mass protest, the second Russia will be fighting for work and wages, increasing the pressure on the federal and regional authorities to make concessions, but it will remain indifferent to the issues that rally the middle class. The Russian government recognizes the danger of social protest in the second Russia and will probably be able to calm the situation through economic and administrative measures as long as the federal budget can afford it.

The third Russia

The third Russia is the vast peripheral territory of villages, semi-urban villages and small towns that are home to around one-third of Russia's population. The third Russia lives off the land and is indifferent to politics. Depopulated small towns and semi-urban villages with an elderly population are scattered across the country, but there is a higher concentration in Central Russia, the north-west, and the industrial areas of the Urals and Siberia. Villages are most common in the south of Russia and the north Caucasus, where 27 per cent of the country's rural population are concentrated. The southern 'Russian' village is still a viable demographic unit that survives thanks to the intensive exploitation of the region's fertile black earth on its residents' individual smallholdings. Large-scale agribusiness is expanding in the most profitable and non-labour-intensive areas of production (grain and sunflower oil), depriving many locals of work, and young people are flooding out of the villages into the towns.

Third Russia is represented by the traditionalist and extremely passive rural periphery and semi-urban villages as well as by small towns of less than 20,000 people; cumulatively, they account for 36 per cent of Russia's population. The lowest levels of both education and mobility can be found here. Employment in the public sector and agriculture predominates and there is much involvement in the shadow economy. The periphery lies outside of politics and always votes for the regime. In addition, the third Russia is depopulating rapidly. Local conflicts are caused by ethnic clashes and occur primarily in the southern regions. They cannot spread over extensive territory and are quickly extinguished by the authorities.

The borders between the three Russias are blurred and rather tentative. It is quite evident that population concentration is not the sole factor in determining the pace of modernization. The fastest transformation of rural areas occurs within the boundaries of the Moscow agglomeration, where a lot of new jobs are unconnected with agriculture. And even in the villages around Moscow, many people have come from other regions, and migrants are always more energetic and adaptable. In the depopulated peripheral areas, the situation is more depressing. In the Pskov region, for example, 40 per cent of the female population are pensioners. The potential protest power of the third Russia is minimal, even if a crisis brought delays in the payment of pensions and wages.

The fourth Russia

The three previous Russias have been defined using the centre–periphery model, which explains social variations by the position in a hierarchy of settlements from the most modernized large cities to the patriarchal rural periphery. This model is perfectly valid for most of the country, but we need to abandon it to define a *fourth Russia*. This name can be given to the less developed republics of northern Caucasus and, to a lesser extent, southern Siberia, the Tyva and Altai republics, which are home to less than 6 per cent of the country's population. They differ substantially from the rest of the country: they are at an earlier urban transition stage; the demographic transition is still in progress; birth rates are high; the clan structure endures; and ethnic and religious tensions run high. The centre–periphery gradient is much weaker here. The cities have not yet digested the growing migration from the rural areas; an urban lifestyle and values are just beginning to be formed; and the modernized urban segment of society is small and grows slowly, since some educated and competitive young people leave for the largest Russian cities. Like the other 'Russias', the fourth Russia is not homogenous. For instance, the more urbanized North Ossetia and Adygea, where ethnic Russians predominate, are substantially more socially modernized than Chechnya.

In the fourth Russia, the rural population is rising in number and, in contrast to other regions, it is still comparatively young. Young people actively migrate from the villages to regional population centres, but few of them find work there. To get a job you need help from your clan, who will either buy you a legal public sector job, or find you one in the shadow economy. The fourth Russia is also the most corrupt, with fierce fighting between clans for power and resources and numerous ethnic and religious conflicts. It must be said that the populace of the cities of north Caucasus is undoubtedly less traditional in its thinking, but not to the extent of creating a trend towards modernization in the whole region. The fourth Russia will not break away, no matter how much that is presented as a threat, or a promise. The overwhelming majority of people in the north Caucasian republics consider themselves to be Russian citizens. The region has many problems and federal politics have an enormous role to play in their solution. At first glance, the policy seems to consist of throwing more money at places where there is unrest. In 2010–13, the republics of the northern Caucasus, home to just 5 per cent of Russia's population, received 10.6 per cent of all federal government subsidies given to the Russian regions. Of this figure, more than one-third of this went to Chechnya. However, federal aid to less developed areas is not spent rationally and transparently, which leads to increased corruption. This is a huge problem in the Caucasus, but the situation is not much better in other regions. The problems of the Caucasus can only be solved by governmental reform at the federal level.

Conclusions: regional inequality and regional policy

The priorities of spatial development in Russia have not yet been defined, regional policies are formulated in the framework of *dirigisme*: objective factors and barriers to regional development are not taken into account appropriately, which reduces the effectiveness of the decisions taken. As a result, these policies have almost no effect on regional disparities in economic development. Long-term development needs effective social and regional policy, taking account of the specificity of different regions of the Russian Federation. Several groups of Russian regions can be identified with particular combinations of development problems and priorities for addressing them. In other regions, the specifics of the problems are less clearly expressed, as they occupy an intermediate position between the groups. The identifiable groups and their problems are as follows:

- *Federal cities and their agglomerations.* Environmental and infrastructure problems caused by a rapid growth of vehicle and a large-scale inflow of migrants, social problems due to a high level of income inequality and the problem of migrants' adaptation.
- *Main resource extraction areas in the north and east of the country.* Acute environmental problems, a depletion of the resource base and long-term economic risks of reliance on a single industry, outward migration in most regions, strong income inequality, higher risks of unemployment.
- *Industrial regions of the Urals and Siberia.* Bad ecology, poor infrastructure and difficult living conditions, marginalization of people living in small industrial towns and rural areas, high risk of rising unemployment, particularly in single-industry towns.
- *Central and north-western regions.* Aging population and depopulation, low incomes, shrinkage of social services, degradation of rural areas, low investment attractiveness.
- *Regions of the Far East and the Trans-Baikal area.* Poor infrastructure, low incomes accompanied by an increasing cost of living, higher unemployment and long-term outward migration.
- *The least developed republics.* Dominance of the informal economy, low investment attractiveness, high levels of unemployment, poor education and health care.

Russian regional policy is, to a large extent, focused on support for the two most problematic groups of regions – those which are geographically remote and those which are the least developed. Federal programmes are being implemented for the development of regions in the Far East and around the Lake Baikal region, and also for the North Caucasus republics. The federal budget invests substantial sums in these programmes. The focus of regional policy on specific territories is insufficient; instead a broader institutional reform is needed. The institutional reforms, which are most required, are as follows:

- Deregulation and decentralization of management, the transfer of responsibilities and tax revenues to regions and municipalities. This approach involves risks: regional inequalities will increase and efficiency improvements will not be achieved everywhere, since the quality of management in different regions and municipalities differs. However, decentralization will facilitate the development of more developed regions and cities, particularly that of large regional centres.
- Improving the efficiency and transparency of the redistributive policy implemented by the federal government, increasing the share of transfers allocated through a transparent formula that takes account of the level of development and living conditions in the regions. Similar changes are a need for the redistributive policies, which regional authorities exercise towards municipalities in their regions.
- Social policy adaptation to regional conditions without using a single template for the whole country. Regions are able to create a variety of 'best practices', taking into account regional conditions. Federal government policy should encourage the spread of 'best practices' and reduce institutional barriers.
- Feedback to improve management quality, public assessment of management decisions. The best feedback mechanism could gradually be achieved by a direct election of mayors and governors.
- Russia desperately needs a two-stage decentralization that will first delegate authority and resources to the regions and then further down to the municipalities. Large cities, that is, the most modernized first Russia, stand to gain the most from this. To be honest, decentralization comes at a great cost. It will inevitably lead to territorial economic inequality growth and will create a political patchwork of territorial units ranging from principality and khanate-like regions to modernizing large cities.

Reducing the costs of decentralization will be an important objective. Regional development and social inequalities reduction can be addressed by measures of social and institutional policies, aimed at increasing human capital and population mobility, targeted social support to vulnerable population strata, and the modernization of institutions. These recommendations have become commonplace, but it is necessary to repeat them again and again, as at present the main barriers to the development of Russia are the bad institutions and the deterioration of human capital. For the future development of the country, it is necessary to alleviate the social disparities among regions. As shown by the experience of developed countries of the EU, one of the means to achieve this goal is a large-scale and efficient social policy, which becomes feasible with the growth of state revenues and the modernization of institutions. The second tool is the promotion of development zones in less developed regions, that is, zones featuring competitive advantages, to accelerate the development of a region as a whole. As shown by international experience, such a policy is rarely successful. However, success could be possible if effective institutions are in place. As a result, the circle closes: without modernizing institutions, the problems of regional inequality in Russia cannot be solved.

Notes

1 Tyumen region, including Yamal-Nenets and Khanty-Manti Autonomous Districts), Sakhalin region.
2 Republics of North Ossetia; Kabardino-Balkaria, Karachevo-Cherkessia, Dagestan, Kalmykia Ingushetia, Chechnya, Altay and Tyva.
3 All the less developed republics of the North Caucasus and Kalmykia, Siberian republics (Altay, Tyva) and the three Far East regions (Kamchatka territory, Amur region and Jewish Autonomous Region).
4 Tyumen and Sakhalin regions.
5 Asia-Pacific Economic Cooperation.
6 The Gini coefficient measures the inequality among values of a distribution, for example levels of income. A Gini coefficient of zero expresses perfect equality, where all values are the same (for example, where everyone has the same income). A Gini coefficient of one (or 100 per cent) expresses maximal inequality among values (for example where only one person has all the income).
7 Novosibirsk, Ekaterinburg, Nizhny Novgorod, Samara, Kazan, Ufa, Chelyabinsk, Perm, Omsk, Rostov-on-Don, Volgograd (Voronezh and Krasnoyarsk were added to the million cities in 2012–13).

References

Drobyshevskiy, S., Lugovoi, O. and Astafeva, E. (2005) *Faktory ekonomicheskogo rosta v regionakh RF*, Moscow: IEPP (Gaidar Institute for the Economy in Transition).
Duro, J.A. (2001) 'Regional Income Inequalities in Europe: An Updated Measurement and Some Decomposition Results', mimeo, Instituto de Anàlisis Economico, CSIC.
Friedmann, J. (1966) *Regional Development Policy*, Cambridge, MA: MIT Press.
Gaidar Institute (2007) *Ekonomiko-geograficheskie i institutsionalnye aspekty ekonomicheskogo rosta v regionakh*, Moscow: IEPP (Gaidar Institute for the Economy in Transition).
Gluschenko, K.P. (2010) *The Methods of Inter-regional Incomes Inequality Analysis*, Novosibirsk: Novosibirsk University.
Krugman, P.R. (1991) *Geography and Trade*, Cambridge, MA: MIT Press.
Krugman, P.R. (1993) 'First Nature, Second Nature, and Metropolitan Location', *Journal of Regional Science*, 33: 129–44.
Lavrovskiy B.L. and Shiltsin, E.A. (2009) 'Russia's Regions: Convergence or Stratification?', *Ekonomika i Matematicheskie Metody*, 45(2): 31–6.
Maleva, T.M. (ed.) (2007) *Obzor sotsialnoi politiki v Rossii: nachalo 2000-kh*, Moscow: NISP.

Martin, P. (2005) 'The Geography of Inequalities in Europe', *Swedish Economic Policy Review*, 12: 83–108.

Myrdal, G. (1957) *Economic Theory and Underdeveloped Regions*, London: Duckworth.

UNDP (2013) *National Human Development Report for the Russian Federation 2013*, Moscow: UNDP Russia.

World Bank (2009) *World Development Report 2009: Reshaping Economic Geography*, Washington, DC: World Bank.

Zubarevich, N.V. (2008) 'Socio-economic Development of Regions: Myths and Truth About Equalization', *SPERO*, 9: 7–22.

Zubarevich, N. (2013) 'Four Russias: Human Potential and Social Differentiation of Russian Regions and Cities', in Lipman, M. and Petrov, N. (eds), *Russia 2025: Scenarios For the Russian Future*, Basingstoke and New York: Palgrave Macmillan, pp. 67–85.

Zubarevich, N. and Safronov, S. (2011) 'Regional Inequality in Large post-Soviet Countries', *Regional Research of Russia*, 1(1): 15–26.

Zubarevich, N. and Safronov, S. (2013) 'Neravenstro regionov i gorodov Rossii: rost ili snizhenie?', *Obschestvennye nauki i sovremennost* (ONS), 6: 15–26.

12 Promoting sustainability in Russia's Arctic

Integrating local, regional, federal, and corporate interests

Robert W. Orttung[1]

In Russia's federal system of government, which player is more likely to have an interest in promoting sustainability in the Arctic's resource development regions and put such policies into practice? Within the Russian state, the key players are the federal government, regional governments, and local governments. In terms of society, the main players are corporations (both Russian and international) and civil society organizations (again both Russian and international). Each of these actors has a different set of interests and capabilities. Asking which of these actors is most likely to pursue sustainability is important because currently we see extensive development of Arctic resources, but little attention to key concerns, such as protecting the environment, preparing for climate change, or designing and implementing a coherent set of policies for stewardship of the north.

This chapter will examine which player is most likely to promote sustainability goals by focusing on a case study of the Yamal-Nenets Autonomous Okrug (YaNAO). While there are several Russian Arctic regions that deserve attention, YaNAO is important because it is the centre of Russia's natural gas industry and an area of burgeoning growth where 84.9 per cent of the population lived in urban areas in 2010. The high level of urbanization is important because it is at the city level that most decisions about sustainability are made. Cities, particularly cities in the north, concentrate large numbers of people and resources, so this is the point where human interaction with nature is most keenly felt (Rasmussen 2011).

The analysis reaches a disheartening conclusion: the players with the greatest interest in promoting sustainability often have the fewest resources to do so. The Russian federal government and various Russian and international corporations have the largest set of resources to promote sustainability, but they seem least inclined to do so. In contrast, local governments and Russian and international civil society organizations are the loudest advocates for sustainability causes, but have the least ability to influence policy-making. As the analysis here shows, the centralization of decision-making authority in Russia has shifted power from actors who are interested in promoting sustainability to actors who give such goals low priority.

Before proceeding to the analysis, it is necessary to explain what we mean by the term sustainability. As a concept sustainability often eludes precise definition, with many scholars and policy-makers conceptualizing it differently, leading to a cacophony of 'sustainababble' (Engelman 2013). For purposes of intellectual clarity, we rely on the original definition of the concept from 'Our Common Future,' the report of the World Commission on Environment and Development chaired by Gro Harlem Brundtland, as meeting 'the needs of the present without compromising the ability of future generations to meet their own needs' (World Commission on Environment and Development 1987). Long-term economic stability, a lower environmental impact from natural resource extraction, and a social sphere that meets the needs and aspirations of Arctic residents comprise the central elements of sustainability for the cities of the Russian North (Orttung and Reisser 2014).

For resource-producing centres, the sustainability discourse presents an additional problem, as the production of non-renewable resources is inherently unsustainable. The resource curse literature has demonstrated a strong connection between resource extraction and economic volatility (Ahrend 2005; Åslund 2005; Gelman 2010; Ross 2012). Moreover, the Arctic is deeply affected by climate change, with rising temperatures reducing sea ice and making it possible to extract resources while at the same time thawing permafrost is undermining the foundation for the very infrastructure needed to bring Arctic oil and gas to market (Anisimov and Reneva 2006; Streletskiy *et al.* 2012). Because energy extraction industries are the economic lynchpin of many northern regions, and indeed of much of the Russian economy as a whole, the concept of sustainability can be adapted to the Brundtland Commission's idea of socioeconomic sustainability. Within this definition, resource extraction activities can be considered sustainable as a way to increase the overall level of social and economic development as long as the environmental impact does not undermine the ability of future generations to meet their own needs (Langhelle *et al.* 2008). Because natural resource extraction is such a crucial component of the economy of the Russian North, any conception of sustainability must, at least under the current economic circumstances, integrate continued resource production with the social and environmental needs of northern peoples. At the same time, Russia should be working to overcome the Soviet legacy (Gaddy and Ickes 2013; Hill and Gaddy 2003) while also making provisions for a time when oil and gas are no longer the centrepiece of the economy.

The chapter will proceed as follows. First, it will lay out the interests and capabilities of the key players at the federal, the regional and local levels, and among corporations and social groups. Second, it will trace the evolution of centre–periphery relations between Moscow and the regions. Third, it will examine the evolution of decision-making in YaNAO. Fourth, it will lay out the outcome of some key policies in the region. Finally, it will draw conclusions about these political processes for sustainable development in the Arctic.

Defining the interests and capacities of the key players

The key players involved in Russia's Arctic policy-making and implementation can be divided roughly into two groups: state and society. Within the state, the key actors are the federal, regional, and local governments. In society it is corporations

Table 12.1 Key actors addressing sustainability in Russia: interests and capacities

Actor	Interests	Capacity
Federal Government	−	+
Regional Government	−	−
Local Government	++	−
Corporations (Russian, International)	−	+
International Organizations	+	−
Russian Civil Society	+/−	−

Source: The author.

and organizations, both international and domestic. Table 12.1 lists these actors and scores their interest in sustainability as either positive or negative and their capacity to implement their policy desires, again as either positive or negative.

Federal government

Even though the focus here is on the Arctic, Moscow is the key player in Russia's centralized political system. It generally makes Arctic policy with little regard for regional interests and scant participation from them (Wilson Rowe 2009a, 2009b). At the federal level, there are a variety of players with a wide range of interests. The key figure in the process for Russia's energy sector and Arctic policy is President Vladimir Putin. He sees energy development as central to maintaining the power and vitality of the Russian state and takes a personal interest in the development of the energy industry and the distribution of the money that it generates (Balzer 2006). He plays a personal role in all large deals and important decisions that are made (Gustafson 2012). Many of these decisions are made behind closed doors and for reasons that are not made public, in a system that Russians call 'manual control'.

Putin works closely with key figures in the energy industry in making decisions, including Igor Sechin, the chairman of Rosneft, Alexei Miller at Gazprom, and Gennady Tymchenko, who owns half of Novatek. Given the personalized nature of the process, normal market signals are less important in decision-making than they would be in a less centralized political economy, but economic reality still works in shaping what actually happens on the ground in the Arctic – the much-heralded Shtokman project has been delayed, for example (Emmerson 2013; Tamnes 2011). While a wide variety of federal agencies, such as the Ministry of Economic Development, Ministry of Regional Development, Ministry of Energy, and others, take part in policy formation, we will devote less attention to them since they are all dependent on the support of the president to influence policy-making.

The interests of the president in energy and the Arctic are focused on ensuring his continuing political power. In difficult economic times and under conditions where the president's popular approval has been bolstered mainly by nationalist rhetoric surrounding the Winter Olympics in Sochi and the use of military force and occupation of territory in Ukraine, the government needs a large and reliable source of money to support its current policies (Gudkov 2014). Since gaining the presidency in 2000, Putin has centralized power in the Kremlin, significantly reducing the ability of the regional governors and energy business leaders to act independently of the Kremlin (Orttung 2011). A key aspect of this centralization process has been to gain much stronger federal control over the financial flows generated by the energy industry and redirect them away from regional governments and independent private companies and into Kremlin control to be redistributed according to the priorities established by Putin and his closest advisers. Accordingly, any type of tax reform in the Russian energy sector that would change this basic system is unlikely as long as Putin remains in office. In particular, the government will want to maintain a high mineral extraction tax (MET) in order to ensure that it has the financial resources to support projects it deems important (Kryukov and Moe 2006; Kryukov *et al.* 2011).

In this sense, Russia's Arctic development programme fits into the larger pattern of Russian development, which focuses heavily on mega-projects. Today the most prominent effort is Russia's plan to pour resources into developing the Far East (Kinossian 2013). The Olympic-inspired redevelopment of Sochi and surrounding areas is another clear example. Development of the Arctic has much in common with these other mega-projects because the centralized, non-transparent process provides fertile grounds for corruption, giving the authorities a convenient way to redistribute money and lucrative contracts to their clients and thereby helping to perpetuate Russia's existing neopatrimonial system (Hale 2012; Orttung and Zhemukhov 2014).

Theoretically, the federal government could be the best actor to promote sustainability in Russia because it has the broadest perspective and can use Arctic resources to best serve the national interest. It also has the resources to think about 'big picture' issues, such as climate change. On the other hand, the Russian state has effectively been captured by a small group of individuals who use its assets for their personal enrichment. The result is an approach to governing that pays little attention to environmental and sustainability issues. For example, in the president's Strategy for the Development of the Arctic Zone, published 20 February 2013, there are some mentions of the environment and climate change, but they are well buried among other goals (Putin 2013). In short, the federal government has excellent capacity to address issues of sustainability, but little desire to do so.

Regional government

Russia's governors stand at the nexus between federal and local interests. On one hand, regional interests naturally oppose the centralization of resources and decision-making power in Moscow and try to bring as much back to the regional level as possible. While the federal government may see the Arctic as a source of income that can be redistributed throughout the country, the regional leaders there have an interest in retaining as much of the proceeds as possible at the regional level to improve the standard of living for residents there and to support their own client networks.

On the other hand, in Russia's highly centralized system, the regional governments have relatively little power on their own since the Kremlin tightly controls who serves as governor (appointing governors from 2004 to 2012 and strictly controlling the voting process after restoring gubernatorial elections in 2012). Additionally, Moscow controls most of the financial flows in the country. Because their ability to remain in office depends on the approval of the president, the governors must work closely with the federal government and relevant corporations while also trying to direct some of the profits from the resource development projects to their region. As Andre Schultz and Alexander Libman (2013) have pointed out, to be successful in their policy-making, governors must have strong local knowledge, namely a detailed understanding of the local elite and how to work with them, and good contacts in Moscow that ensure access to necessary resources. Since the governors are constantly seeking a balance between their constituent interests at the regional level and the necessity of maintaining good ties within the federal bureaucracy, they have little interest or capability to pursue environmental concerns unless either federal or local interests strongly demand it. At the interface between the two levels, their main interest is to maintain stability in their particular part of the country. They do not have the time or inclination to step back and examine the bigger picture.

Local government

Around 85 per cent of the Yamal-Nenets Autonomous Okrug's residents live in cities, making mayors key actors in the region. These city leaders have a much greater interest in promoting issues of sustainability than governors. Cities concentrate people and services in one place, making them an important area of interaction between human activity and the natural environment. In contrast to policy-makers working at the national level, city managers deal with direct trade-offs between economic growth and development, the quality of human life, and preserving and protecting the natural environment (Katz and Bradley 2013). In key ways, mayors can be crucial to pursuing important policy goals when national politics become dysfunctional (Barber 2013).

Despite Russia's centralized system, the reach of federal power should not be overestimated (Stoner-Weiss 2006). Even under conditions in which the central government maintains a large degree of policy control, regional policy has tangible effects on the development and sustainability of northern cities. The divergent evolution of power relationships between northern cities and their regional administrative centres demonstrates how important local policy can be. The cities of Gubkinsky and Muravlenko, similarly sized urban centres in the YaNAO, have experienced starkly differing outcomes chiefly due to the different policy models applied in each (Pilyasov 2013). In Muravlenko, the closer proximity to the administrative centre of Noyabrsk resulted in a governance framework primarily focused on interaction with the higher-level administration to the exclusion of local concerns. Gubkinsky's more independent policy situation allowed it to focus instead on its own development, noticeably improving local outcomes relative to Muravlenko. Small business growth, economic diversification, and cultural expenditures were all significantly stronger in the more independent Gubkinsky, while Muravlenko has continued to stagnate.

These trends reinforce the argument that efforts by distant administrative centres to hamper local decision making tends to result in ill-adapted policies, with negative consequences for economic and social sustainability. Mayors in Russia have comparably much less authority than do city executives working in developed democracies. In the Russian context, centralized control blocks local officials from taking action to promote sustainability, even though it is precisely these officials who have the greatest interest in it. Moreover, much of the future resource development in the Arctic will take place offshore, under federal rather than local jurisdiction. In the case of Sakhalin, where resource development is also taking place offshore, the federal authorities reneged on plans to share resources with regional and local levels of government (Bradshaw 2010; Graybill 2009).

Russian and international corporations

Both Russian and international energy corporations see the Arctic as a place to make large profits from developing resources; they have little interest in sustainability issues. The 2008 law on subsoil resources defines a category of 'strategic' hydrocarbon fields and allows only Russia's state-controlled energy national champions – Gazprom and Rosneft – to develop the lucrative offshore resources that are expected to provide the energy sources of the future (Adachi 2009). Nevertheless, the involvement of foreign energy corporations is key to Kremlin plans to develop the Russian Arctic. Although Gazprom's plans to develop the Shtokman off-shore gasfield have been put on hold, in April 2012, Rosneft signed an agreement with ExxonMobil, ENI, and Statoil to develop offshore oil sites. Gazprom is a monopolist in Russia, producing about 80 per cent of the country's natural gas, controlling all of its gas pipelines, and holding the only export license, while Rosneft is increasingly the favoured oil producer, now controlling more than 50 per cent of the market with the acquisition of energy assets from Yukos and TNK/BP (Åslund 2010; Lunden *et al.* 2013; Moe and Rowe 2009; Overland *et al.* 2013; Stern 2005; Victor and Sayfer 2012). Novatek is an independent gas producer that is active in YaNAO and is responsible for about 20 per cent of Russian gas production. Its key owner has close personal connections to Putin, who seems to use the company as a lever for exerting pressure on Gazprom. The tax revenues from Russia's oil and gas production provide a key source of revenue for the government.

Because output is dropping at the traditional gas-producing fields of the Nadym-Pur-Taz Basin and its three super-giant fields Medvezhe, Urengoy and Yamburg, corporate attention is now focused on the Yamal Peninsula and its vast untapped gasfields. Given the need to build new facilities north of previous production sites, all of the companies face rising production costs and naturally lobby the government to lower tax rates. Russian gas producers face a variety of challenges on international markets: they had hoped to sell gas into the U.S. market but those plans have been scrapped due to the development of shale gas supplies in North America; other producers are bringing on line capacity to ship more liquefied natural gas; an EU lawsuit is seeking to force Gazprom to change the way that it prices its gas for sale in Europe; and the ongoing fighting in Ukraine has called into question Russia's ability to ship gas supplies to Europe on a reliable basis. On the positive side, Russia hopes to open new markets to Asia, building on a pipeline deal signed with China in 2014, and to develop ways of using natural gas for the transportation sector.

In facing these challenges and opportunities, Russia's major energy companies focus on generating money, ultimately used for a variety of state and private purposes. While the corporations interact with all levels of government, they are typically more powerful than regional and local interests due to their strong connections within the federal government. Accordingly, it is only the federal government that can impose regulations on them. Given the various interests of the federal and corporate actors, the corporations have devoted few resources to pursuing sustainability goals.

Russian and international civil society organizations

Space constraints prevent a full examination of domestic and international civil society organizations. In short, we can observe that they have an interest in promoting sustainability issues, but little ability to affect policy. When Greenpeace sought to block Russia's offshore oil production in Arctic waters in September 2013, Russia arrested the protesters and detained them for four months. The Kremlin has similarly cracked down on local groups who act independently. In the Arctic region, the case of the Russian Association of the Indigenous Peoples of the North (RAIPON) is the most prominent example of a civil society organization that has faced official repression. Of course, Russian society is not monolithic and many people freely support the development of Arctic resources despite the risk to the environment. In this sense, the relationship between society and resource development is complex and deserves more careful further research.

Evolution of centre–periphery relations in Russia since 1991

Since the collapse of the Soviet Union, the relationship between the federal, regional, and local governments and Russia's largest corporations has evolved through a variety of stages. The result has been to reduce the power of the actors who have an interest in promoting sustainability while strengthening the hand of those who have other priorities. Understanding the current situation requires a sense of the evolution of centre–periphery relations. The main driver of change in this evolution is the strength of the federal government. Throughout most of the 1990s, the federal government was relatively weak and that allowed regional governors, corporations, and to some extent, mayors, to play a much more autonomous role. After Putin's election to the presidency in 2000, he was able to consolidate power relatively quickly and placed considerable constraints on lower-level officials and corporations.

While Yeltsin had allowed the citizens of each region to elect their governors beginning (with some exceptions) in 1996, Putin overturned the system in 2004 and restored the president's right to appoint governors. This reassertion of central control changed the fundamental political calculus in the thinking among Russian governors – no longer was their main aim to please their constituents to win re-election; now they sought to curry favour with the Russian president so that he would continue to allow them to remain in their posts. However, the longer Putin stays in power, the less popular he becomes with the electorate; the invasion of Ukraine revived Putin's rating, but this change is likely to be short-lived, as in the case of the 2008 war with Georgia. While declining popularity does not threaten his ability to stay in office, it does put into question his ability to rule effectively. In the wake of the December 2011 protests about the lack of fairness in the State Duma elections held that month, then President Medvedev announced that Russia would return to a system of electing governors. The first elections were held in five carefully selected regions in October 2012 followed by eight similarly stage-managed elections in September 2013. While the restored regional elections are far from free and fair, they suggest that some small amount of power is returning to the regions.

Control over the money flows between the federal government and the regional and local governments reflect a similar trajectory as the overall distribution of power. Accordingly, the situation of the regions depends heavily on the development policies adopted in Moscow, which determine how much money flows to which regions, the level of investments in those regions and the situation of the population (Zubarevich 2013). In simple terms, shortly after the Soviet collapse, the regional governments were able to control a substantial amount of the taxes generated on their territory. Through 2001, for example, the law on subsoil resources stipulated that the taxes collected from resource extraction would be divided so that 40 per cent went to the federal government, 30 per cent to the regional government, and 30 per cent to the local government of the resource-producing region (Kryukov *et al.* 2011: 265).

During the period when citizens directly elected their governors, regional leaders could play a relatively independent role negotiating among the federal government and corporations. In particular, they could favour one corporation over another by providing access to land rights, using their influence to direct more resources to the regional level. However, in the late 1990s, the federal government began to exert intense pressure on the regions. After 2001, tax and budget legislation, not the subsoil law, defined the distribution of resource rents between the federal and regional governments and since these were federally controlled, the distribution began to heavily favour the federal government. A new law in the late 1990s allowed Russian corporations to pay taxes in Moscow where their headquarters were located rather than the regions where they actually worked (Brie

2004; Colton 1995). This law had a major impact on the development of Russia because it drew money out of the regions and concentrated it in the capital. Beginning in 2005, federal law limited the rights of the autonomous okrugs, a change which required YaNAO to sign an agreement with Tyumen Oblast that allowed it to preserve its ability to work with its own budget while also transferring money to the oblast (Kulikov no date). The government introduced the mineral extraction tax in 2002. Initially, the federal government received 80 per cent of the revenue and the regional governments received 20 per cent. Over the 2000s, the regional share of this income dropped (Kryukov *et al.* 2011: 276). Since 2010 all funds from this tax flow directly into the federal budget. In order to compensate for this loss, Moscow began to provide subsidies to regions like YaNAO. While in 2010 this income almost fully compensated for the lost income, such compensation was being phased out over four years and will eventually end. As Natalia Zubarevich (2013) points out, the structure of the transfers from the federal budget to the regional governments and the criteria for making them are not transparent. YaNAO in 2011 was one of the largest recipients of the most opaque form of federal subsidy, in the category 'other grant income', receiving 15 billion roubles (11 per cent of its budget income). Also, at the same time that YaNAO started to lose the income from the mineral extraction tax, the authorities again changed the system of taxation for large corporations, requiring them once again to pay their taxes in the areas where they work rather than where their headquarters are located. This new law went into effect at the beginning of 2012 and is being gradually implemented over several years. Since Gazprom is one of the largest taxpayers, its payments in the YaNAO should increase while cities like Moscow, St. Petersburg, and Tyumen, the home of many head offices, will receive less income (BOFIT 2012).

Relations between corporations and regional governments have also evolved over time. Gazprom and YaNAO signed their first general partnership agreement in February 1995. Beginning in January 1997, bilateral annual agreements laid out the terms of their financial relations, including the level of Gazprom's tax payments. A November 1997 agreement obliged the company to pay the okrug government USD 51 million per month during 1998, up from USD 31 million the previous year. The agreement also allowed the okrug to sell USD 375 million worth of gas and oil on its own. Since these arrangements included barter deals, there were many dubious deals and the actual size of Gazprom's payments dropped in the late 1990s and early 2000s (Kusznir 2006). The two sides signed the agreement for 2013 on 25 November 2013 (Gazprom 2013). Over the six-year period 2008–13, Gazprom invested more than 1.6 trillion roubles in the region. According to recent agreements, Gazprom paid 35 billion roubles into the YaNAO budget in 2010, 45 billion in 2011, 53 billion in 2012, and more than 59 billion in 2013 (see Table 12.2). Once the Bovanenkovo development comes on line, Gazprom expects these payments to reach as high as 70 billion roubles a year (Gazprom 2012). Key priorities of the agreement are developing hydrocarbons in YaNAO, providing natural gas to residences in the region, and carrying out the programme to increase energy efficiency. YaNAO

Table 12.2 Gazprom contributions to the Yamal-Nenets Autonomous Okrug budget (bn RUR)

2010	*2011*	*2012*	*2013*	*Estimated future annual contributions*
35	45	53	59.2	70+

Source: Gazprom (2012; 2013). The 2012 figure is extrapolated from data for the first nine months of the year.

will provide tax benefits for organizations involved in developing, transporting, and processing hydrocarbons, gasification, and working on energy efficiency, and provide help in obtaining land rights for construction of industrial and socially important projects. Gazprom will make it a priority to hire local workers and indigenous people who have the necessary qualifications and build sport complexes for local children.

Evolution of Yamal-Nenets politics

The key player in YaNAO politics during most of the 1990s and the 2000s was Governor Yury Neelov. He had a long history in Siberian politics, working his way up through the Komsomol and Communist Party of the Soviet Union (CPSU). Yeltsin appointed him governor in 1994 and he subsequently won elections in 1996 and 2000. He long sought to have Yamal-Nenets secede from Tyumen Oblast so that it would have more independence (YaNAO has a confusing status in the Russian federal system in which it is simultaneously an independent region and a part of Tyumen Oblast). Although Neelov personally did not wield much political clout, he gained power by picking leaders to follow in Moscow (Orttung *et al.* 2000: 632–8). During the 1990s, he criticized Moscow's role in the regional economy, complaining that the federal government made it difficult to attract investment to develop the region's resources. He argued that the federal government abused its power to suppress the initiatives and activities of the regions.

Given the scope of its wealth and activities in the region, Gazprom plays a major role in YaNAO politics (Kusznir 2006). In the 1993 State Duma elections, the region voted for a candidate critical of Gazprom because the company at that time had not paid salaries or made its social contributions. In order to regain its footing, Gazprom backed Neelov, the newly appointed governor, and made him a member of the Gazprom board of directors. When Gazprom registered in Moscow and began to pay the bulk of its taxes there, the reduction in income angered Neelov and he began to favour other companies and give them licenses to work in the region. Accordingly, Neelov's relations with Gazprom soured and he was not re-elected to the Gazprom board in 1999. Instead, he focused his attention on oil companies, such as Rosneft and Sibneft, and small independent gas companies. In particular, Deputy Governor Iosif Levinson helped nurture the development of Novatek, which went on to become a major player. Neelov's victory in the 2000 gubernatorial election showed that he had a powerbase independent of Gazprom. After 2000

Gazprom bought up many of the other companies working in the region (including Sibneft), though Novatek remained independent. As a consequence of the Gazprom acquisition spree, the regional economy became dependent on the gas monopolist again, particularly as Gazprom's share of taxes to the budget comprised over 70 per cent of revenue in the mid-2000s. (Tax revenues from oil and gas production account for more than 90 per cent of regional revenue for YaNAO) (Kusznir 2006).

Putin's return to a system of gubernatorial appointments substantially reduced Neelov's leeway in appointing his own subordinates, and he had to dismiss Levinson. As Julia Kusznir has pointed out, the relationship between Gazprom and the governor is what determines the nature of the interactions between the other political and economic players. In short, between 1994 and 1999, Neelov cooperated with Gazprom; between 2000 and 2005, he tried to build relations with other companies, and between 2005 and 2010, the close ties between Gazprom and the federal government weakened the governor and expanded the influence of Gazprom in the region (Kusznir 2006).

Gazprom has strong representation in the regional legislature. From 2000–5 28.8 per cent of the deputies were directly associated with Gazprom. In 2005–10, the figure grew to 36.4 and fell slightly in 2010–15, to 30.0 per cent. Usually executive managers of regional subsidiaries represent the company in the regional parliament. In the current body, Novatek has one representative. Medvedev replaced Neelov as governor with Dmitry Kobylkin in 2010. By the time of his removal, Neelov had become a relatively reliable Gazprom ally in the region. Neelov resigned suddenly after being summoned to Moscow following the appearance of a petition from YaNAO residents warning that not appointing him to an additional term would lead to street protests (Plyusnina 2010). Medvedev largely cleared out the Yeltsin-era governors during his tenure in the Kremlin and particularly bristled at being put under pressure by regional groups.

Kobylkin, in contrast to Neelov, came out of the Novatek hierarchy, having been the director of Purneftegazgeologiya, a Novatek subsidiary at the time of his leadership tenure. From October 2005 to his appointment as governor, he served as head of the Pur Raion. While Medvedev did not explain why he appointed Kobylkin governor, analysts speculated that the appointment was an effort to boost Novatek in a region dominated by Gazprom. In any case, Kobylkin continued the late-Neelov policy of working closely with Gazprom and continued to sign the annual cooperation agreements with the monopolist. Perhaps the federal authorities supported him because he did not have the lobbyist contacts in Moscow that his predecessor had developed over time and therefore would be easier to manage from Moscow.

YaNAO is a donor region so its budget has its own sources of revenue and does not depend heavily on transfers from the federal government. Given the high level of energy production in the region, the main sources of revenue are the corporate profit tax (approximately one-third), income tax on individuals (approximately one-quarter), corporate property tax (one-quarter), and others. Table 12.3 lists the expenditures of the YaNAO budget, showing which areas it prioritizes. Direct spending on protecting the environment is particularly low.

Table 12.3 Expenditures in the YaNAO 2012 regional budget *(thousand RUR)*

National Economy (roads, agriculture, forestry, etc.)	28,479,707
Housing	20,623,037
Education	17,397,144
Healthcare	16,263,631
Subsidies to regions and municipalities	16,262,813
Social Policy	12,557,855
State Administration	3,307,183
National Security and Law Enforcement	2,350,453
Culture, Cinematography	1,907,648
Physical education and sport	1,422,602
Media	1,245,092
Protecting the environment	627,927
National Defense	17,326
Total	**122,462,418**

Source: YaNAO Legislative Assembly (2012). Budget figures 2012.

How are policies implemented on the ground?

Policy implementation in YaNAO is difficult because the economy is heavily dependent on the fluctuations in the price of oil and natural gas. The constant shifts in the energy sector create population flows in and out of the region and make it hard to develop coherent housing and education policies. Additionally, it is hard for the regional government to anticipate federal investment and social policies; changes in these policies, for example, could shift resources away from YaNAO to other regions (YaNAO Department of the Economy 2011).

YaNAO has many positive attributes. It boasts high income, low poverty, a young population and significant natural growth, as well as a well-financed social sphere thanks to strong budget revenues. On the negative side of the ledger, however, are an undiversified economy that relies heavily on the energy sector, a high cost of living, low provision of social infrastructure, such as schools and child care (a problem inherited from the Soviet era), and a poorly developed vocational education system (Kulikov no date). The population grew dramatically in the 1980s and then began to oscillate with the natural gas boom and bust cycles. Up to 1959, the entire population of the region was just 62,000 individuals. The development of the gas industry meant that the population grew rapidly from 1979 to 1989, swelling from 158,000 to 486,000. Half of the urban population is in the two largest cities – Novy Urengoi and Noyabrsk – which are focused on resource development. In the early 1990s, after the collapse of the USSR, many residents began leaving. In post-Soviet Russia, the population dynamics followed cyclical trends depending on the state of the gas industry. There was another great outflow in 1999 following the drop in gas prices, but then in-migration as prices rose in 2001–4. During the 2000s, the quickest growth took place in Novy Urengoi, Salekhard, and Noyabrsk. From 2005 there was an outflow, with people leaving and coming in approximately equal numbers.

The cycles of the energy sector make it hard to deliver services to the population. There are significant problems with the healthcare system in terms of old equipment and difficulty in gaining access to the system. There is also a shortage of qualified doctors. Many of the health problems in the region are concentrated among the indigenous population. In 2011, YaNAO was one of the regions with the greatest increase in healthcare spending. But Zubarevich questions how effective this spending has been, pointing out that the media is full of stories describing schemes for increasing the prices for medical equipment that is purchased and various forms of kickbacks (Zubarevich 2013).

Providing educational services is also a problem. There is a higher than average share of children in the population (21 per cent versus 16.1 per cent for all of Russia). As of 2010, there was a shortage of places for kids in pre-school (10 per cent more kids than spaces) and many have to go to the second shift for schooling. In 2011, YaNAO increased spending on education by 150 per cent.

Providing sufficient housing is a key problem because the housing industry is driven by the boom–bust cycle in the natural gas economy, which makes it extremely unstable from year to year. High gas prices in 2006–7 led to rapid growth in housing starts. However, the 2008 crisis cut housing construction in half (Kulikov, no date). Overall, YaNAO 'preserves the extremely expensive Soviet strategy of providing mass housing in resource-extracting regions located in extreme climactic conditions instead of developing the more economical shift-labour forms of employment. Such an approach makes sense in Khanty-Mansi, but that region benefits from milder climate conditions and there are larger cities with a more developed service sector' (Kulikov, no date). Approximately 15 per cent of the workforce have their permanent homes outside the region and live in camps when they are working in YaNAO (YaNAO Department of the Economy 2011). At the same time, less than 50 per cent of the residences are supplied with gas. Additionally, only 3 per cent of families receive housing subsidies, even though more than twice that many live in poverty (Kulikov no date).

Currently 9.6 per cent of the housing stock is dilapidated. This share is increasing, even though the YaNAO authorities are spending considerable sums to address the problem. Additionally, the authors of the strategic plan to develop YaNAO through 2020 complain that many pensioners are moving into the region, which puts an additional strain on the budget (YaNAO Department of the Economy 2011). The share of the population older than working age grew from 4.4 per cent in 2000 to 7.9 per cent in 2009.

Finally, the region faces important environmental problems as it starts to develop new fields in previously untouched territory. A key problem is the increased pressure on the water resources of the region. A major cause of the damage to the environment is the use of old technology for hydrocarbon development, which leads to flaring natural gas. Difficulties in transporting waste from both production and consumption sites also create problems (YaNAO Department of the Economy 2011).

The regional government has been able to attract financing from Gazprom to fund key development projects to address these problems. Under the Yamal Megaproject, several domestic development projects for YaNAO are being funded and led by Gazprom according to agreements between the company and the region. In exchange for continued tax benefits, Gazprom has allocated 7.5 billion roubles to run the Comprehensive Yamal Development Program, which includes the construction of school facilities, urban infrastructure, gasification of the region, and land reclamation projects. Additionally, Gazprom has assisted in the YaNAO government's effort to eliminate dilapidated housing stock by 2020 by building new housing and assisting other residents in relocation to other cities and regions.

Conclusion: Implications for Arctic urban sustainability

The central challenge for Russia's politicized economy is developing a political system that allows the various actors to better express their interests through effective policy-making. Overall, Russia's current system has a variety of state and societal actors that have an impact on its ability to promote sustainability goals. These include federal, regional, and local governments as well as Russian and international corporations and civic organizations. Despite the diversity of actors and interests, the evolution of Russia's political system since the collapse of the Soviet Union has shifted power from regional and local actors to the federal level. The result is that the groups that support sustainability goals no longer have much influence over the policy-making process while groups that have little interest in sustainability control the essential levels of power.

This process can be seen in detail in the YaNAO. The evolution of Russia's political system since the end of the Soviet Union has shifted considerable power from the local level to the federal level, making it hard for local officials to address sustainability issues on the ground. Current policy is aimed at producing resource rents from oil and gas development rather than making concern for the environment a top priority.

Russia's centralized system makes it possible for the federal government to exercise considerable control over the development of the Arctic. In theory, this oversight could provide for resource development policies that take into account the human needs of the population while limiting the impact of resource production on the environment to a minimum. However, the nature of the current government in Moscow places the top priority on the development of resources to ensure the ability of the current elites to stay in power. Resource rents are needed to fund Russia's neopatrimonial system, which drain resources away from other forms of investment.

While mayors and some civil society groups may have a strong interest in carrying out work to promote sustainability and otherwise improve the living standards of their residents, the system does not provide them with sufficient resources to be able to implement these kinds of policies. Of course, managing the trade-off between development and environmental preservation is difficult in any country. In the Russian case, the centralization of power and the incumbent elite's need to earn and distribute rents makes it even harder for the pro-sustainability voices in Russian society to influence policy than would be the case in more democratic countries.

Looking forward, there is little reason for optimism. As long as President Putin remains in power, there are few possibilities to change the political system in any fundamental way that would allow local or societal groups to have a greater say over policy. Similarly, there is no evidence that Putin himself will change in this direction in the future. Accordingly, Russia is essentially in a holding position in which the current status quo will remain in place until the country reaches a breaking point. Future research should investigate potential pressure points on the Russian political and policy-making system in order to better understand where potential sources of change might arise.

Note

1 I am grateful to The George Washington University Elliott School of International Affairs SOAR Project Initiation Fund for providing the seed money that helped launch this project. Additionally, I would like to thank the National Science Foundation for funding the Research Coordination Network-Science Engineering and Education for Sustainability: Building a Research Network for Promoting Arctic Urban Sustainability in Russia (award number 1231294). I would like to express my gratitude to my George Washington University colleagues Colin Reisser and Luis Suter, who provided invaluable research assistance supporting this chapter.

References

Adachi, Y. (2009) 'Subsoil Law Reform in Russia under the Putin Administration', *Europe–Asia Studies*, 61(8): 1393–414.

Ahrend, R. (2005) 'Can Russia Break the "Resource Curse"?', *Eurasian Geography and Economics*, 46(8): 584–609.

Anisimov, O.A. and Reneva, S. (2006) 'Permafrost and Changing Climate: the Russian Perspective', *Ambio*, 35: 169–75.

Åslund, A. (2010) 'Gazprom: Challenged Giant in Need of Reform', in Åslund, A., Guriev, S. and Kuchins, A.C. (eds), *Russia After the Global Economic Crisis*, Washington, DC: Peterson Institute for International Economics.

Åslund, A. (2005) 'Russian Resources: Curse or Rents?', *Eurasian Geography and Economics,* 46(8): 610–17.

Balzer, H. (2006) 'Vladimir Putin's Academic Writings and Russia's Natural Resource Policy', *Problems of Post-Communism,* 53(1): 48–54.

Barber, B.R. (2013) *If Mayors Ruled the World: Dysfunctional Nations, Rising Cities*, New Haven, CT: Yale University Press.

BOFIT (2012) 'New Laws Diminish Moscow's Tax Revenues', *BOFIT Weekly*, 35.

Bradshaw, M.J. (2010) 'A New Energy Age in Pacific Russia: Lessons from the Sakhalin Oil and Gas Projects', *Eurasian Geography and Economics*, 51(3): 330–59.

Brie, M. (2004) 'The Moscow Political Regime: The Emergence of a New Urban Political Machine', in Evans, A. and Gelman, V. (eds), *The Politics of Local Government in Russia*, Lanham: Rowman & Littlefield.

Colton, T. (1995) *Moscow: Governing the Socialist Metropolis*, Cambridge, MA: The Belknap Press of Harvard University Press.

Emmerson, C. (2013) 'The Arctic: Promise or Peril?', in Kalicki, J.H. and Goldman, D.L. (eds), *Energy and Security: Strategies for a World in Transition*, 2nd edn, Washington, DC: Woodrow Wilson Center Press.

Engelman, R. (2013) 'Beyond Sustainababble', in The Worldwatch Institute (ed.), *Is Sustainability Still Possible?*, Washington, DC: Island Press.

Gaddy, C.G. and Ickes, B.W. (2013) *Bear Traps on Russia's Road to Modernization*, London: Routledge.

Gazprom (2012) *Gazprom i YaNAO podpisali soglashenie o sotrudnichestve v 2013 godu*. Online. Available: http://gazprom.ru/press/news/2012/october/article146699/ (accessed 1 August 2014).

Gazprom (2013) *Gazprom i YaNAO podpisali soglashenie o sotrudnichestve v 2014 godu*. Online. Available: www.gazprom.ru/press/news/2013/november/article178513/ (accessed 1 August 2014).

Gelman, V. (2010) 'Introduction: Resource Curse and Post-Soviet Eurasia', in Gelman, V. and Marganiya, O. (eds), *Resource Curse and Post-Soviet Eurasia: Oil, Gas, and Modernization*, Plymouth: Lexington Books.

Graybill, J. (2009) 'Place and Identities on Sakhalin Island: Situating the Emerging Movements for "Sustainable Sakhalin"', in Agyeman, J. and Ogneva-Himmelberger, Y. (eds), *Environmental Justice and Sustainability in the Former Soviet Union*, Cambridge, MA: MIT Press.

Gudkov, L. (2014) 'V kakoi strane my zhivem: rossiiskoi obshchestvo ot noyabrya k martu'. Online. Available: www.levada.ru/books/prezentatsiya-doklada-lva-gudkova-v-kakoi-strane-my-zhivem-rossiiskoe-obshchestvo-ot-noyabrya- (accessed 1 August 2014).

Gustafson, T. (2012) *Wheel of Fortune: The Battle for Oil and Power in Russia*, Cambridge, MA: The Belknap Press of Harvard University Press.

Hale, H.E. (2012) 'Two Decades of Post-Soviet Regime Dynamics', *Demokratizatsiya: The Journal of Post-Soviet Democratization*, 20(2): 71–8.

Hill, F. and Gaddy, C.G. (2003) *The Siberian Curse: How Communist Planners Left Russia Out in the Cold,* Washington, DC: Brookings Institution Press.

Katz, B. and Bradley, J. (2013) *The Metropolitan Revolution: How Cities and Metros Are Fixing Our Broken Politics and Fragile Economy*, Washington, DC: Brookings Institution Press.

Kinossian, N. (2013) 'Stuck in Transition: Russian Regional Planning Policy Between Spatial Polarization and Equalization', *Eurasian Geography and Economics*, 54(5–6): 611–29.

Kryukov, V. and Moe, A. (2006) 'Hydrocarbon Resources and Northern Development', in Blakkisrud, H. and Honneland, G. (eds), *Tackling Space: Federal Politics and the Russian North*, Lanham, MD: University Press of America.

Kryukov, V., Tokarev, A. and Yenikeyeff, S. (2011) 'The Contest for Control: Oil and Gas Management in Russia', in Collier, P. and Venables, A.J. (eds), *Plundered Nations: Successes and Failures in Natural Resource Extraction*, Basingstoke: Palgrave Macmillan.

Kulikov, G. (no date) 'Yamalo-Nenetskii Avtonomnyi Okrug (YaNAO).' *Sotsialnyi atlas rossiiskikh regionov/Portrety regionov*. Online. Available: www.socpol.ru/atlas/portraits/Yam.shtml (accessed 1 August 2014).

Kusznir, J. (2006) 'Gazprom's Role in Regional Politics: the Case of the Yamalo-Nenets Autonomous Okrug', *Russian Analytical Digest,* 1.

Langhelle, O., Blindheim, B.-T. and Øygarden, O. (2008) 'Framing Oil and Gas in the Arctic From a Sustainable Development Perspective', in Mikkelsen, A. and Langhelle, O. (eds), *Arctic Oil and Gas: Sustainability at Risk?*, London: Routledge.

Lunden, L.P., Fjaertoft, D., Overland, I. and Prachakova, A. (2013) 'Gazprom vs. Other Russian Gas Producers: the Evolution of the Russian Gas Sector'. *Energy Policy,* 61: 663–70.

Moe, A. and Rowe, E.W. (2009) 'Northern Offshore Oil and Gas Resources: Policy Challenges and Approaches', in Rowe, E.W. (ed.), *Russia and the North,* Ottawa: University of Ottawa Press.

Orttung, R.W. (2011) 'Center–Periphery Relations', in Lipman, M. and Petrov, N. (eds), *Russia in 2020: Scenarios for the Future,* Washington, DC: Carnegie Endowment for International Peace.

Orttung, R.W., Lussier, D. and Paretskaya, A. (2000) *The Republics and Regions of the Russian Federation: A Guide to Politics, Policies, and Leaders,* Armonk, NY: M. E. Sharpe.

Orttung, R.W. and Reisser, C. (2014) 'Urban Sustainability in Russia's Arctic: Lessons from a Recent Conference and Areas for Further Investigations', *Polar Geography,* 37(3): 193–214.

Orttung, R.W. and Zhemukhov, S. (2014) 'The 2014 Sochi Olympic Mega-Project and Russia's Political Economy', *East European Politics,* 30(2): 175–91.

Overland, I., Godzimirski, J., Lunden, L.P. and Fjaertoft, D. (2013) 'Rosneft's Offshore Partnerships: the Re-Opening of the Russian Petroleum Frontier?', *Polar Record,* 49: 140–53.

Pilyasov, A. (2013) 'Russia's Policies for Arctic Cities', *Russian Analytical Digest,* 129: 2–4.

Plyusnina, M. (2010) 'Prezident vybral glavu raiona na post gubernatora Yamalo-Nenetskogo avtonomnogo okruga', *Kommersant,* 24 February. Online. Available: http://kommersant.ru/doc/1327163 (accessed 1 August 2014).

Putin, V. (2013) *Strategy for Developing the Arctic Zone of the Russian Federation and Guaranteeing National Security Through 2020.* Online. Available: http://sakha.gov.ru/node/102466 (accessed 1 August 2014).

Rasmussen, R.O. (2011) *Megatrends,* Copenhagen: Danish Ministry of Foreign Affairs in collaboration with the Nordic Council of Ministers.

Ross, M.L. (2012) *The Oil Curse: How Petroleum Wealth Shapes the Development of Nations,* Princeton, NJ: Princeton University Press.

Schultz, A. and Libman, A. (2013) 'Is There a Local Knowledge Advantage in Federations? Evidence from a Natural Experiment', Unpublished manuscript, Frankfurt School of Finance and Management.

Stern, J.P. (2005) *The Future of Russian Gas and Gazprom,* Oxford: Oxford University Press.

Stoner-Weiss, K. (2006) *Resisting the State: Reform and Retrenchment in Post-Soviet Russia,* Cambridge: Cambridge University Press.

Streletskiy, D.A., Shiklomanov, N.I. and Nelson, F.E. (2012) 'Permafrost, Infrastructure and Climate Change: A GIS-based Landscape Approach', *Arctic, Antarctic and Alpine Research,* 44(3): 368–80.

Tamnes, R. (2011) 'Arctic Security and Norway', in Kraska, J. (ed.), *Arctic Security in an Age of Climate Change,* Cambridge: Cambridge University Press.

Victor, N. and Sayfer, I. (2012) 'Gazprom: The Struggle for Power', in Victor, D.G., Kults, D.R. and Thurber, M. (eds), *Oil and Governance: State-Owned Enterprises and the World Energy Supply*, Cambridge: Cambridge University Press.

Wilson Rowe, E. (2009a) 'Conclusion', in Rowe, E.W. (ed.), *Russia and the North*, Ottawa: University of Ottawa Press.

Wilson Rowe, E. (2009b) 'Introduction: Policy Aims and Political Realities in the Russian North', in Rowe, E.W. (ed.), *Russia and the North*, Ottawa: University of Ottawa Press.

World Commission on Environment and Development. (1987) 'Our Common Future'. Online. Available: www.un-documents.net/our-common-future.pdf (accessed 1 August 2014).

YaNAO Department of the Economy (2011) 'Strategy for the social-economic development of the Yamalo-Nenets Autonomous District to 2020'. Online. Available: http:// de.gov.yanao.ru/component/content/article/263 (accessed 1 August 2014).

YaNAO Legislative Assembly (2012) 'Budget Figures 2012'. Online. Available: www. xn--80ansfm8f.xn--p1ai/control_activities/budget/ (accessed 1 August 2014).

Zubarevich, N. (2013) 'Monitoring of the Crisis and Post-crisis Development of Russia's Regions'. Online. Available: www.socpol.ru/atlas/overviews/social_sphere/kris.shtml#no21 (accessed 1 August 2014).

13 Russian regional resilience: cooperation and resource abundance

A case study of Khanty-Mansi Autonomous Okrug

Irina Ilina, Carol Scott Leonard and Evgeniy Plisetskiy[1]

This chapter examines regional financial resilience in Russia in the period following the global financial crisis. The level of risk continued to rise for several years after the financial crisis struck in 2009, as government emergency finance fell rapidly; the result was that some regions raised loans to cover even operational expenses. Most 'resource' regions, however, rebounded rapidly, despite having been severely affected by the crisis, particularly in relation to its impact on the Corporate Income Tax (CIT), the main source of regional revenue. This chapter examines the experience of one mineral resource-abundant region, Khanty-Mansi Autonomous Okrug (KhMAO), the largest 'donor' to the federal budget. It traces developments since the dramatic budget reforms (from the late 1990s to 2005), including the centralization of revenues and rationalized programme expenditure (Alexeev and Weber 2013). It assesses regional budget and debt management in response to pressures from the federal budget, the post-crisis withdrawal of subsidies, and the rolling out of new debt guidelines. It describes and explains KhMAO's stability and relatively flexible planning as part of the fiscal federalist regime, which support competitive regions and cooperative bargaining.

KhMAO is clearly an outlier in regard to revenue, as are most other resource-abundant regions, such as Orenburg Region, Yamalo-Nenetsk AO, Kemerovo Region, Republic of Sakha, Sakhalin Region and others. Its budget flexibility, investment potential, and per capita income, in particular, diverge from that of more typical less well-off regions. However, along with the enormous quantitative literature on aggregates in Russia's highly centralized fiscal federalism in the 83 regions (Spilimbergo 2007; Alexeev and Weber 2013a; Christenko 2002; Ilina *et al.* 2014), it is important also to examine outliers. Considering both budget and credit management, it would seem, in at least one region with steady growth potential, that regional finance is seemingly secure, even though, as a resource region, one would expect to find financial fragility as a consequence of price volatility. We ask: Why are some 'donor regions', which were more badly affected by the crisis than others, also possibly more resilient in the medium term? Is Russia's growth core of regions financially stable because of federal intervention? How vulnerable is the resource region to future oil price shocks? Our findings are tentative, since there remain questions about transparency and soft budget constraints (Plekhanov 2006). We shows that federalism is most supportive of competitiveness in oil regions, and this is in part because of cross-regional action to influence federal policy.

We use a case study approach for a number of reasons. Most important, although there is a considerable quantitative literature on Russia's fiscal federal system, it remains unclear how flexible regional budgets have become after more than a decade of reform. Our case is a snapshot of a particular group of regions with common economic structures. A case study approach, isolating for close examination either extremes in a trend or a typical case, is used widely for conceptual clarification prior to and during statistical analyses of large databases (Eisenhardt 1989). Since we examine the growth process rather than, for example, inequality, we choose to explore regional finance in a territory that is particularly vulnerable in term of its growth potential and not its general economic state.

The chapter is divided into subsections. This introduction is followed by a brief review of the large literature on fiscal federalism, with an emphasis on that analysis appropriate to oil-abundant federations. This is intended to establish a foundation for considering KhMAO in a comparative context. Russia's fiscal federalism is of scholarly interest both within and beyond the borders of Russia in large part because of intense and continuing effective reform through the 2010s, improving the delivery of both equity and efficiency. We use this literature about ongoing centralizing reform, however, to examine the continuing diversity still apparent in regional finance and regulatory regimes across the enormous country (Commander *et al.* 2013). We note in conclusion the importance of cooperation as well as competition among oil-abundant regions, although the exploration of cooperative federalism in any great detail is beyond the scope of our research. The final section is a conclusion.

Fiscal rigidity in Russia

There is widespread agreement among researchers about fiscal rigidity on the revenue side of Russia's federalism. Following the transformation of Russia's federalist system in the 2000s, revenues have been almost entirely centralized, with funds being allocated to cover federal social policy along with other expenditures. Revenues are collected centrally and allocated to regions according to a formula in the form of transfers, earmarked grants, subsidies and other allocations, which, in turn, are partially allocated to districts and municipalities (Alexeev and Weber 2013; Vartapetov 2011). Local government provides services in health, education and social welfare (Searle 2007). Reviewing the major budget reforms, Fitch ratings (28 September 2005) finds that:

> ... budgetary results showed increasing budgetary rigidity among the regions, the subordination of budgets to rapidly growing social spending and a lack of capital expenditure. Budget reforms have introduced a more structured

system of public administration, but regional governments now operate under considerable constraints of having revenue sources reduced through centralization and responsibilities increased by higher social welfare targeted expenditures. The vital indicator is economic development-related expenditure as a proportion to total expenditure. (Fitch 2005a)

The important constraint is not the collection of revenues but rather the access to them through shared spending authority. The spending side, for all regions, has been pressed by President Putin's 'May 7 decrees' in 2012, guaranteeing a standard of services, including a pay rise for government staff, and the provision of benefits to all citizens. Of course, these decrees were not only a constraint but a benefit, promising greater efficiency, the reduction of duplication and waste, and monitoring of the implementation of federal programmes (Prikaz 2012: N556n). Rigidity in the budget process, however, as Fitch points out, is important because it conflicts with another key priority objective: 'At the same time, there is a clear policy to reduce regions dependency on federal revenues and stimulate greater tax initiative and new local resources' (Fitch 2005a). In other words, excessive centralization will inhibit local initiatives in finding resources, which many economists find to be the key objective of intergovernmental fiscal policy. As Qian and Weingast maintain:

> The state must maintain 'positive' market incentives that reward economic success. When the government is tempted to take away too much income and wealth generated by the future success, individuals have no incentives to take risks and make effort today. In the terms of North (1990), this is the 'state predation' problem. The state must also commit to 'negative' market incentives that punish economic failure; if the government is tempted to bail out failed projects or continue costly, inefficient public programs, individuals have no incentives to avoid mistakes and waste. In the terms of Kornai (1986), this is the 'soft budget constraint' problem. (Qian and Weingast 1997: 84)

An incentive orientation is an argument for decentralization that among advanced countries has mostly replaced the former 'cooperative fiscal federalism' as the dominant approach in intergovernmental relations (Musgrave 1997: 65).

Russia's seemingly relatively inflexible budget rules, therefore, seem not to be aligned with current trends toward decentralization. The history of Russian budget reform offers one explanation of the situation. In order to end a decade of struggle with separatism, after 2000, the evolving post-Yeltsin state under President Putin sharply reduced the political autonomy of regions. Putin ended, briefly reinstated, and then ended, once more, direct gubernatorial elections. The government helped to forge a single dominant party and bring to heel 'regional authoritarianism', which was an obstacle to well-functioning political and market institutions (Golosov 2008; Stoner-Weiss 2006).

Centralization also brought economic reforms, which disadvantaged small and medium-sized enterprises. Concentration in economic activity increased, as nation-wide companies penetrated local markets. State intervention in the private sector has led, now, to its ownership of two-thirds of the market capitalization in the Russian stock market, which is limited to four industries – energy (oil, gas, and electricity), banks, defence industries and transportation. The government has also centralized investment-oriented economic policy (Ilina *et al.* 2014).

It is important to underscore that centralization has not resulted in the degree of uniformity or equalization that had undoubtedly been anticipated. Regional incomes, polarized in the 1990s, may be converging, but GDP per capita is not (Fedorov 2002; Gurev and Vaukulenko 2012). The regulatory environment remains diverse in the degree of enforcement of federal laws,

> ...substantial inter-regional variation in terms of the quality of the business environment. The differences are particularly large in the areas of competition from the informal sector, access to physical infrastructure, access to land and tax administration. (Commander *et al.* 2013: 43)

The reform of the historical regional revenue and expenditure system is described in detail in numerous articles (Siluanov *et al.* 2009; Vartapetov 2010, 2011; Siluanov 2011; Mamedov *et al.* 2013), and in the Oxford Handbook of the Russian Economy by Alexeev and Weber (2013b). Emphasis on key developments before 2002 can be found in Desai *et al.* (2005) and Lavrov *et al.* (2001). Briefly, to review Russia's budget reform history: under President Putin, the government eliminated most of the disadvantageous bilateral tax treaties between the federal government and the regions and much of the opacity, which stood in the way of further reform (Gurev *et al.* 2008; Martinez-Vazquez and Boex 2001; Solanko 2001).

The results are as follows: 100 per cent of the VAT was recentralized in the 1990s, along with 80 per cent of the oil and gas extraction tax, leaving by 2012 one quarter of the revenue base of regions from the corporate profit tax (including on resource industries) and personal income tax (28 per cent), approximately the same percentages as regional revenues from these sources in Canada. The property tax represents, on average, some 9 per cent of regional revenues in 2011, amounting to 1.9 per cent of GRP, roughly in line with property taxes elsewhere (0.5 to 1.5 per cent of GRP) (OECD 2014). Total regional tax revenues in Russia amount to roughly 11 per cent of GRP (Siluanov *et al.* 2009; Vartapetov 2010), again, comparable to other states (Canada 12.1 per cent, Australia, 4 per cent; Germany, 7.9 per cent; and the US, 5 per cent). As in other countries, expenditures are allocated by equalization grants (mainly for balancing the budget), earmarked grants (including unconditional grants for center-delegated spending (subventions) and earmarked matching grants (subsidies) for priority federal programmes, and compensation grants to adjust distribution of these allocations (Vartapetov 2011).

The main result of these reforms, we argue, is the standardization of Russia's budget process, which is 'partially centralized'. Revenue collections are centralized for efficiency of the collection process, an essential step in the evolution of Russian governance dating from the late 1990s. However, regions have tended to retain a steady share of total revenues (in the consolidated budget), which has varied between 38 and 51 per cent, since the start of reforms; in 2011, the regions' share was 46.8 per cent, within the range observed in other federations – from 34 per cent in the US to 44 per cent in Canada (Blöchliger and Rabesona 2009: 5). Budget rules have become increasingly transparent, although there remains some uncertainty in annual adjustments to the rules (Shleifer and Treisman 2005; CEFIR 2006; Hauner 2008; Kondrateva 2008; Siluanov 2011).

There are numerous advantages in centralizing revenues. By reducing the 'beggar-thy-neighbor' outcome and the misallocation of factors of production produced by autonomous budgeting, centralization can increase efficiency (Ahmad and Tanzi 2002; Broadway and Shah 1994). The federal level can best manage resources for equalization, especially where endowments are uneven, as in Canada, Russia and Australia. Taxes on energy production and export tend to be collected at the federal level, which can absorb the uncertainty and volatility of oil prices. Searle (2007: 11) summarizes: 'the usual starting point in an allocation of revenue sources between levels of government is that the level with the greatest fiscal capacity has the best tools for overcoming fluctuations in revenue collections.' Taking oil extraction revenues away from the regions is only one option, but slimmer budgets tend to make more efficient use by regions of the profit tax, or corporate income tax, to diversify expenditures (Cottarelli 2012). It may also diminish the influence that oil interests can have in the shaping of regional policy in resource regions (Freinkman and Plekhanov 2009). Centralization mitigates the curse, while guaranteeing comparable services at comparable taxation and providing 'insurance' for region-specific shocks (Otto 2001; Bishop and Shah 2011: 549). Finally, centralized revenues assist the federal level take responsibility for equalization (Mello 2000; Iimi 2005; Sepulveda and Martinez-Vazquez 2011; Hatfield and Miquel 2012; Alexeev and Weber 2013a).

Fiscal federalism 'best practice' is not well established, and there is a range among federations. In Australia, horizontal fiscal imbalance drives a strong trend toward centralization, with revenue sharing and allocations by formula (according to measures of regional fiscal capacity) in transfers, grants, subventions and subsidies to sub-national governments. By contrast, in Canada, problems of asymmetry have resulted in greater autonomy of regional revenues: mining royalties are allocated to the regions, for example, a considerable source of revenue from non-renewable resources that is missing in Russia's regional budgets. Furthermore, Canada removes restrictions on how provinces can raise money, while the federal level has taken over the unemployment programme. In Canada, mineral resource-abundant regions thus have considerably more autonomy than in the Russian Federation. The results of different regimes, however, are at best trade-offs: all of these federations experience political pressure from regions, some favoring more autonomy and some, more equalization.

In regard to spending, the region's role in the Russian Federation varies across the country. In 2012, for example, in Russia, officially recorded transfers from the federal to regional level at an average of 20.8 per cent of total income, but the range was from 86.4 per cent (Republic of Ingushetia) to 4.9 per cent KhMAO.[2] Among sources of support during the crisis for the regions in Russia has been the

Fund for Financial Support to regions with high deficits, and for social expenditures. It is difficult to determine the 'system' of allocations: rules exist, but they are not always public information (Siluanov *et al.* 2009; Vartapetov 2010). In general, these transfers consist of: (1) equalization grants, or formula-based grants aimed at building capacity to deliver country-wide a standard level of services; (2) earmarked unconditional grants to finance center-delegated spending and earmarked matching grants designed to co-finance regional expenditures that the federal government considers important; and (3) compensation grants, or one-off unconditional grants to adjust the above allocations (Vartapetov 2011).

Although centralization produces some rigidity, it has clear advantages in a federation such as Russia. For one thing, decentralization would not necessarily produce higher growth. Even in advanced economies, decentralization is not necessarily associated with higher rates of growth (Iimi 2005: 449). Under centralized systems, transfers can be used to promote growth. Clearly, KhMAO seems one of a few regions across Europe[3] that actually uses transfers to this effect: normally transfers will have a growth effect only where human capital is significant and institutions are strong (Becker *et al.* 2013). The one evident advantage of decentralization lies in community–government relations (Allers and Ishemoi 2011). In Russia, in other words, centralization has been beneficial in resolving both the inadequacy of some territorial administrations in the post-Soviet era and in uprooting deeply embedded informal networks, by which 'rentier' regions (those with mineral resource abundance) derived rent revenue from 'explicit and implicit taxation of extraction of mineral resources, primarily oil and gas' (Desai *et al.* 2005; Kumar *et al.* 2007). Finally, one may note that in Russia, there is a current expectation that the government will supply services and considerable public support for the May decrees, expectations that can best be met in the transforming economy by some centralization.

To summarize, by 2011, it was evident that after being rescued by budget equalization funds, regional fiscal stability passed a 'stress test' of sorts in the financial crisis (Vartapetov 2011). By 2013, the funds were dramatically cut back, however; for the first eight months of 2013, transfers were 7 per cent lower than in the previous year; corporate income tax also fell by 20 per cent less (Chernyavskiy 2013). Regions were now encouraged to rely on credit to cover deficits. Regions (and municipalities) began to borrow more heavily, albeit within strict limits, and some regions were allowed to do so on international capital markets (Martinez-Vazquez and Timofeev 2008). This helped by 2011-12 in reducing financial transfers to the weaker regions and fostered hope of ending regional 'dependency' on 'non-reimbursable (*bezvozmezdnye*)' federal subsidies (see Appendix Table 13.A1). In its review of the budget in 2012, however, the Accounts Chamber of the Russian Federation recommended more reform and further adjustments to budget rules, to resolve problems of regional indebtedness (Accounting Chamber 2013: 263–7).[4] Recommendations were in the direction of greater independence on the part of regions, encouraging local initiative in attracting investment resources, more competition for funds among regions, and greater budget efficiency (Siluanov 2011).

Case study: Khanty-Mansi Autonomous Okrug

Risk in oil-abundant countries is generally held as a potential curse, which can lower the rate of growth level over the long term and hollow out the non-oil sector (Sachs and Warner 2001; Papyrakis and Gerlagh 2007; Alexeev and Conrad 2009; Freinkman and Plekhanov 2009; Walker 2013). To be sure, Alexeev and Conrad (2009) argue that empirically in a survey of countries this threat is not borne out. In regions, the same kind of risk is not relevant, but oil is nevertheless important for regional budgets in producing opportunities as well as rents.

Resource regions in Russia

Resource regions have grown rapidly and steadily since the early 1990s and expanded their lead over other regions, on a per capita basis, in part because of their low population density. The pace of per capita growth of the ten leading regions in 1992 exceeded those in the slowest growing by 2.5 times; by 2000, the ratio was even greater, 3.2 times. The presence of oil – among opportunities offered – attracted federal cluster policies and funding in the mid-2000s for the attraction of non-oil investment and more skilled labor. Resource regions learned how to retain their budgetary surplus and low debts; KhMAO has an enviable standard of living. To what degree is this region vulnerable if the oil sector loses its productive potential and/or oil prices fall dramatically, followed by a plunge in the corporate and private income tax, the outmigration of highly mobile unemployed labor and the decreased productivity of fields and mines?

The vulnerability of resource regions lies, first, in their financial dependence upon the CIT. In the budget of KhMAO in 2012, this tax formed 40.6 per cent, and in 2013–15, 43.5 per cent of okrug revenues (Korosteleva and Kurbanova 2014). The large share of the CIT is characteristic for resource regions, with their significant endowments of globally traded natural resources. A second risk, however, for which insurance is required, are the unusually adverse natural and climatic conditions creating high transport costs, steep infrastructure (including transportation) requirements for production, low population density and extensive casual migrant labour. An exacting taxonomy of regions by vulnerability has been developed by Russian scholars, but most simply, they are grouped with little discussion of risk as attractors of investment and high-skilled, mobile labor (Polynev 2010; Demina and Vlasiuk 2012).

For a setting of regions similar to Khanty-Mansi, we select eight with production of oil land gas at over 40 per cent of GRP as in Table 13.1.

These regions have a substantially greater than average per capita income – for KhMAO, for example, indicators for living standards exceed even those for Moscow city. Located within but autonomous with respect to Tyumen Region – KhMAO is a so-called 'composite region', along with Yamalo-Nenetsk – and pays a subsidy to Tyumen for this special arrangement. KhMAO is among seven

Table 13.1 Oil- and gas-producing regions, 2012

Russian regions	Share of oil and gas production in GRP (%)
Russian Federation	**11.4**
Nenetskii Autonomous Okrug (located within Arkhangelsk Region)	78.5
Khanty-Mansiysk Autonomous Okrug (located within Tiumen Region)	67.2
Sakhalin Region	60.9
Tiumen Region	52.2
Yamalo-Nenetsk Autonomous Okrug (located within Tiumen Region)	48.3
Orenburg Region	36.9

Source: Rosstat (2013).

regions (including Moscow and St Petersburg) at investment-grade rating, and since two rating agencies have provided that assessment, it is allowed to obtain funds in international capital markets, where interest rates are considerably lower (8–10 per cent) and repayment extends over a longer period (3–5 years) than domestically. KhMAO is among three regions actually doing so (Vedomosti 2013a). Table 13.2 shows its relatively high standard of living at a level between that of Moscow city and that of the rest of Russia.

Population trends are stable in KhMAO, across periods of decline in oil extraction, which is not always the case in resource regions and shows its resilience in that regard (Ilina *et al.* 2014). Fundamentally, the reliance in this region is a sign of how its endowment has been used: in 2012 the profit tax from the oil and gas sector comprised some 95 per cent of KhMAO's operating income. In this year taxes from the major oil and gas companies comprised 52.1 per cent of total revenue (51.5 per cent in 2011) (Fitch 2013b). Falling extraction at major fields and a dip in the share of oil in GRP to less than half (43.6 per cent) is a cause of concern. The forecast without estimation of investment returns is that by 2030, according to the region's Energy Strategy, the annual production of oil will fall at a minimum from 260 to 222 million tons (mt), and, more likely, to 196 mt, as costs of extraction increase due to flooding and technological challenges (Ria Novosti 2013). It is not that technologies are unavailable to KhMAO producers—oil is a global industry. It is that these technologies, hydraulic fracturing, horizontal drilling, three-dimensional seismic modeling, are especially costly in the initial stages. This puts pressure on the region to attract more investment and, especially, exploration. Resilience requires special concern, under such conditions, for the stability of future income and well-being under volatile price conditions. Is there a threat here exceeding the capacity of current preparations to resolve it?

Table 13.2 Standard of living indicators, 2011, Khanty-Mansiysk Autonomous Okrug, Moscow city, Russian Federation average

	Average per household member, rubles per month						Average per household member, rubles per month		
	Disposable income	*Consumption*	*Expenditure on food*	*Expenditure on non-food items*	*Expenditure on services*	*Percent households on internet*	*Income poor households*	*Income extremely poor households*	*Minimum sustainable monthly income set by region*
Average Russian Federation	15,816	10,460	3,250	4,178	2,615	53	4,858	2,637	6,090
City of Moscow	25,629	21,145	4,720	8,220	6,900	82	8,287	NA	8,656
Khanty-Mansiysk AO	27,061	15,278	3,240	7,112	4,494	71	7,094	3,073	5,234

Source: Regions of Russia (2013).

Post-crisis finance in Russia's regions

There is a general optimism about long-run regional growth in Russia, as expressed in scholarship and at Davos 2014 (RIA Rating 2013; World Economic Forum 2014; Russia Beyond the Headlines 2014; Berkowitz and Dejong 2011). At the same time, however, accumulating regional government debt in the short term is also of widespread public concern (Vavulin and Simonov 2013: 32).[5] Professor Zubarevich, a regional expert at Moscow Lomonossov State University, writes:

> ...regional budgets are buckling. Revenues in the first half of 2013 decreased due to a 20 per cent decline in profit tax revenue and a 15 per cent cut in federal budget transfers. Meanwhile, spending grew 5 per cent to fulfill the president's promises to increase public sector wages. Budgets are running deficits in two thirds of all regions, and aggregate regional and municipal debt has surpassed 25 per cent of (tax and non-tax) revenue. The regions are reducing investment spending, but it's not enough... the decline in public sector employment is accelerating... Laid off workers have difficulty finding another job. (Vedomosti 2013b)

Total municipal and regional tax and non-tax debt is about 20 to 25 per cent of income of Russia's regions. Regional rating reports, carried out by RIA rating,

Fitch and S&Ps, and Ministry of Finance open access data show the importance of debt. RIA Rating (2013) reported that the total public debt of all subnational entities increased by 15.6 per cent in 2012 and on 1 January 2013 amounted to 1.335 trillion rubles. Similarly, S&P flagged its concern by reporting Ministry viewpoints as "excessively optimistic": a decline in the profit tax cast doubt on Ministry forecasts of 8–10 per cent growth of regional revenues over 2014–16. 'The regional deficit will rise to 3 trln roubles more than planned, double the current amount.' It goes on, 'the regional gap will widen and in half of the regions, debt will exceed 60 per cent of operational income (as it does now in 15 regions), and average debt service will reach 10 per cent of revenues and in half of the regions, over 15 per cent' (Finmarket 2013).

These fears bear little relevance, however, to the wealthiest regions, which have most of the outstanding regional bonds: Moscow, Krasnoyarsk, Nizhniy Novgorod, Samara and Moscow regions (64 per cent), regions that can easily cover their obligations (RIA Rating 2013). The term structure of obligations and debt service matter, and Russia's debt service is high, about 10 per cent of revenues compared with the US to an average of 5 per cent, a ceiling for state debt (Cherniavskii 2013; Dinopoli 2012). However, resource regions have a low level of debt to income, far below than the average, at 10 per cent (Granik and Samarina 2013). Russia's resource regions mostly have lower total debt figures than the average for the country and even by international comparisons (Table 13.3).

Regions with elevated debt include Mordovia (179 per cent), Vologda Region (92 per cent), and Riazan (91 per cent); ten others have debt over 70 per cent of their income; and 19 regions have debt ranging from 50 to 70 per cent. However, in sum, the average level of regional debt in 2013 is 26 per cent of GRP, and in the view of the Ministry of Finance, relatively low in a global perspective

Table 13.3 Debt in resource regions *(% of GRP)*

Region	2010		2013*	
	Debt, regional (% GRP)	*Debt, regional & municipal (% GRP)*	*Debt regional (% GRP)*	*Debt, regional & municipal (% GRP)*
Nenetsk AO			18.2	19.5
Orenburg Oblast	1.9	2.1	4.4	5.4
Tiumen Oblast	0.0		0.0	0.1
Khanty-Mansyisk AO	0.6	0.7	0.8	0.8
Yamalo-Nenetsk AO			0.3	0.7
Kemerovo Oblast	2.9	3.3	5.7	5.9
Republic of Sakha	4.0	4.4	5.4	6.0
Sakhalin Oblast	0.1	0.6	0.3	0.7

Source: Regions of Russia (2013).

Notes: *The gross regional product (GRP) for 2013 is estimated from forecasted annual growth rate 2005–10.

(Krizis-kopilka 2013; Newsland 2013; RIA Rating 2013). In regard to continued dependence on federal budgets, Orenburg and Sakha show greater dependence than KhMAO, which derives a very small percent of its budget from transfers.

What have reforms meant for budget rigidity? Looking at the ratio considered by Fitch as critical in regard to rigidity, economic spending to total expenses of the consolidated budgets. Protown.ru (2014) explains that economic spending supports infrastructure investment and science.[6] To summarize, what does a closer look at resource regions, in particular, at KhMAO, show in regard to resilience? One may begin with the impact of global financial crisis. The profit and income tax fell, in some regions (Chelyabinsk and Kemerovo) by 90 per cent. The well-off resource regions, including KhMAO, suffered most (Iandiev 2013a,b). However, it is those regions that suffered least, in part due to emergency federal support, that are now in a worse position. In the resource regions, the liquidity of banks quickly recovered and oil and gas firms' profits rose, once again boosting revenues.

Budget priorities for 2014–16 for KhMAO were ambitious, including repeated assurances of fulfilling the May decrees of 2012 and the creation of a fund for capital investment. Tax objectives for KhMAO are aligned with federal interest and long-run modernization and diversification; significant property tax breaks are now given to small and medium size enterprises, to incubators that promote them, to non-profits with socially oriented objectives, to production that reduces environmental risk, to organizations that rent property for affordable housing, and to firms producing gas by fracking (Rasporiazhenie 2014). Even more ambitious is the effort among resource regions to increase the regional share of corporate taxes allocated to regions and eliminate the federal share (of the 20 per cent tax 2 per cent is currently given to the federal government); a broad lobbying effort including Urals and Siberian governors has led to a law giving the regions the entire 20 per cent, which is making its way through the Russian parliament (Vd-tv.ru 2013).

Bargaining and informal arrangements (public/private and intergovernmental) are difficult to follow, as some regions seek amendments to legislation (Dahl 1961). It is at the level of the region and blocks of regions, however, that tax policies of enormous importance are made, lobbied and adjusted (Yakovlev *et al.* 2011). The case of one resource region by no means necessarily captures the overall dynamic. However, this study suggests that those regions which are most competitive are in no real danger from debt or instability; there will be no likely slimming of federal programmes and federal guidelines are observed in preparing the long-run budget, but there is considerable autonomy. Ensuring the stability of resource regions is a priority cooperation of regional governors and ministry officials and past and present representatives of the oil companies, who meet informally as a 'Board of Directors of Ugra', discussing, essentially, policy options for the country as well as the region (Vd-tv.ru 2013).

Conclusion

For the European Union (EU), there is a major investigative effort to discover factors in regional 'resilience', as illustrated in the October 2012, European Commission's brief on 'The EU approach to resilience', formulated for an EC action plan.

Russia's wealthiest regions exhibit that resilience in some of the regions hardest hit by the recent financial crisis 2008–9. Budgets show that some donor regions suffered a substantial decline in corporate and personal income tax receipts during 2009, but without taking on much credit, they re-established a surplus, while also covering the increased salaries and other obligations announced in President Putin's 'May decrees'.

The resilience in the instance of KhMAO, we have argued, is due to its financial flexibility in the fiscal federalist regime. KhMAO's stable finance can be attributed to relatively successful multi-year budgeting, which includes setting revenues aside in a reserve fund. Adaptability and representation of local interests are evident in fiscal management despite revenue centralization. The case illustrates that, at least in one critically important region, Russia's fiscal federalist regime is more cooperative than decentralized, and the budget process shows consideration of a wide range of stakeholder interests.

In the long run, per capita economic indicators show a steady rise and population growth, including in periods of volatile oil prices. KhMAO cluster policy has attracted industrial giants other than in the oil sector, and the business environment, which includes maintenance of a relatively high standard of living, is supported regional level by innovation-oriented budgets. Most fundamentally, there is evolving multi-region cooperation, groups of regions acting together to secure negotiated decisions on tax allocations and spending requirements and US style private/public partnerships in governance at the regional and national level. Our conclusion supports that of Chebankova (2008), who uses the term adaptive federalism; we apply it to budget reform. Not top-down federal intervention but cooperation and coalitions, as a fiscal federalist regime, help explain regional resilience.

Appendix

Table 13.A1 Tax structure in resource regions in Russia, 2005–11 *(% of total revenues)**

A1-1 Corporate Income Tax (CIT) (% of revenues)

	2005	2006	2007	2008	2009	2010	2011
Russian Federation	31.8	30.6	31.7	28.3	18.0	23.2	25.2
Nenetsk AO	39.5	32.5	21.9				
Orenburg Oblast	29.9	30.3	33.6	30.0	22.8	25.4	29.6
Tiumen Oblast	66.8	59.6	42.2	42.1	37.4	49.1	58.8
KhMAO	95.7	47.0	37.5	38.9	28.5	31.5	37.4
Yamalo-Nenetsk AO	40.8	32.9	27.5	29.5	23.1	32.5	34.4
Kemerovo Oblast	25.2	17.8	19.6	29.3	9.4	19.8	28.0
Republic of Sakha (Yakutia)	14.6	12.3	16.4	17.5	8.4	13.9	18.9
Sakhalin Oblast	15.5	17.2	17.1	19.9	34.4	29.9	31.6

A1-2 Personal Income Tax (PIT), % revenues

	2005	2006	2007	2008	2009	2010	2011
Russian Federation	23.6	24.5	26.2	26.9	28.1	27.4	26.1
Nenetsk AO	20.4	17.9	12.2	6.9	6.7	5.9	5.3
Orenburg Oblast	22.8	23.8	22.4	22.5	22.2	22.8	22.0
Tiumen Oblast	5.1	5.8	11.1	10.2	12.6	11.8	10.7
KhMAO	18.8	27.4	29.2	27.7	31.9	30.8	27.4
Yamalo-Nenetsk AO	24.1	25.7	29.0	29.1	29.5	26.2	23.1
Kemerovo Oblast	23.5	28.3	28.3	24.2	25.6	24.8	24.9
Republic of Sakha (Yakutia)	15.0	16.5	18.3	18.0	17.1	16.6	15.6
Sakhalin Oblast	35.6	33.4	28.3	22.3	24.5	27.4	27.7

A1-3 Property Tax (% revenues)

	2005	2006	2007	2008	2009	2010	2011
Russian Federation	8.4	8.2	8.5	8.0	9.6	9.6	8.9
Nenetsk AO	13.1	13.7	16.5	24.3	47.6	44.7	35.6
Orenburg Oblast	10.8	10.2	8.7	8.7	10.3	10.9	9.9
Tiumen Oblast	1.6	1.6	2.9	2.3	3.6	3.6	3.0
KhMAO	9.7	12.9	13.2	12.6	19.3	19.6	17.2
Yamalo-Nenetsk AO	17.5	21.6	22.7	22.1	25.3	24.4	20.8
Kemerovo Oblast	9.1	12.6	13.0	7.8	11.2	10.6	10.4
Republic of Sakha (Yakutia)	4.7	5.7	5.0	4.2	6.0	5.9	5.1
Sakhalin Oblast	6.1	5.3	3.9	2.7	2.8	3.5	3.7

A1-4. Transfers from Federal Budget (% revenues)

	2005	2006	2007	2008	2009	2010	2011
Russian Federation	14.7	15.9	13.4	19.4	27.3	23.1	23.1
Nenetsk AO	3.4	2.7	5.1	33.8	35.0	23.6	19.9
Orenburg Oblast	12.4	10.3	13.5	18.0	24.3	22.5	20.1
Tiumen Oblast	0.9	1.1	3.2	4.2	5.3	27.7	19.9
KhMAO	-42.8	-2.0	3.2	4.8	5.9	4.9	8.2
Yamalo-Nenetsk AO	2.7	8.3	4.0	6.3	10.3	7.0	13.6
Kemerovo Oblast	15.2	13.0	13.9	17.0	29.9	20.0	12.6
Republic of Sakha (Yakutia)	30.8	34.1	34.1	40.3	51.5	45.8	42.3
Sakhalin Oblast	19.9	23.2	27.3	30.5	21.4	23.8	14.6

Source: Regions of Russia (2013).

Notes: *Some revenues are not identified, and the total listed does not add up to 100.

Notes

1 This chapter is part of a larger project on governance and growth in Russia, which has received funding from the HSE Basic Research Program under grant agreement No. TZ-43 / D.95674.
2 Data regarding regional budgets are from the database of the Russian Federation Ministry of Finance and as reported by the Russian state statistical agency (Rosstat).
3 In the EU, some 30 per cent.
4 The Accounting Chamber of the Russian Federation recommended that regional allocations from taxes be increased in percent, that only regions be allowed to establish tax exemptions for firms (a loss in 2012 of some 200 billion roubles to the regions from federal regulations), and that – as soon as the cadastral survey was complete – individual property tax on expensive real estate be raised.
5 Debt was used to cover the impact of a simultaneous cut in subsidies and budget deficit from the rise in obligations from the 'May decrees'. It proved difficult to cover the cost of increased pay for teachers and doctors to the average level of regional salaries. According to the Ministry of Finance of the Russian Federation, by 2013, sub-national entities (excluding Moscow city and Moscow Region) needed in 2013 an extra 337.4 billion roubles are required, although allocations from the federal level rose only to 209.1 billion roubles. According to the Audit Chamber of the RF, the total regional debt just to pay salaries of administrators was 150 billion.
6 Expenditure commitments of the section 'national economy' are determined by Federal laws, decrees of the President of the Russian Federation, resolutions of the Government of the Russian Federation on extraction and use of mineral resources, development of agriculture, forestry and water economy, transport, road management, communications, science and scientific and technical policy, space activities, Federal target programmes, as well as international agreements and treaties.

References

Accounting Chamber (2013) 'Conclusion of the Accounting Chamber of the Russian Federation on the Draft Federal Law "on the Federal Budget for the Year 2013 and for the Planning Period 2014 and 2015 Years"', 5 October, Accounts Chamber of the Russian Federation, N 41K (874): 263–7.

Ahmad, E. and Tanzi, V. (2002) *Managing Fiscal Decentralization*, London: Routledge.

Alexeev, M. and Conrad, R. (2009) 'The Russian Oil Tax Regime: A Comparative Perspective', *Eurasian Geography and Economics*, 50(1): 93–114.

Alexeev, M. and Weber, S. (2013a) 'Russian Fiscal Federalism: Impact of Political and Fiscal (De)centralization', London, *Centre for Economic Policy Research Discussion Papers*, No. 9356.

Alexeev, M. and Weber, S. (2013b) *The Oxford Handbook of the Russian Economy*, Oxford and New York: Oxford University Press.

Allers, M.A. and Ishemoi, L.J. (2011) 'Equalising Spending Needs of Subnational Governments in a Developing Country: the Case of Tanzania', *Environment and Planning C-Government and Policy*, 29(3): 487–501.

Becker, S.O., Egger, P.H. and von Ehrlich, M. (2013) 'Absorptive Capacity and the Growth and Investment Effects of Regional Transfers: A Regression Discontinuity Design with Heterogeneous Treatment Effects', *American Economic Journal-Economic Policy*, 5(4): 29–77.

Berkowitz, D. and DeJong, D. (2011) 'Growth in post-Soviet Russia: a Tale of Two Transitions', *Journal of Economic Behavior & Organization*, 79(1–2): 133–43.

Bishop, G. and Shah, A. (2011) *Fiscal Federalism and Petroleum Resources in Iraq, Obstacles to Decentralization: Lessons from Selected Countries*, Cheltenham, UK: Edward Elgar.

Blöchliger, H. and Rabesona, J. (2009) 'The Fiscal Autonomy of Sub-Central Governments: An Update', *OECD Working Papers on Fiscal Federalism*, Paris: OECD.

CEFIR (2006) 'Analytical Report on Growth and Investment in Russia's Regions: "Unleashing the Potential"', *CEFIR Policy Series* 24. Online. Available: www.cefir.ru/download.php?id=321 (accessed 20 May 2014).

Chebankova, E. (2008) 'Adaptive Federalism and Federation in Putin's Russia', *Europe–Asia Studies,* 60(6): 989–1009.

Christenko, V.B. (2002) *Mezhbiudzhetnye otnosheniia i upravlenie regional'nymi finansami: opyt, problemy, perspektivy*, Moscow: Delo.

Commander, S., Plekhanov, A. and Zettelmeyer, J. (2013) 'Diversifying Russia: Harnessing Regional Diversity', London: EBRD.

Cottarelli, C. (2012) 'Fiscal Regimes for Extractive Industries: Design and Implementation', Washington, DC: IMF Fiscal Affairs Department. Online. Available: www.imf.org/external/np/pp/eng/2012/081512.pdf (accessed 20 May 2014).

Dahl, R.A. (1961) *Who Governs? Democracy and Power in an American City*, New Haven: Yale University Press.

Demina, O.V. and Vlasiuk, L.I. (2012) 'Effektivnye regiony: kriterii i klassifikatsiia', *Prostranstvennaya Ekonomika*, 1: 29–42.

Desai, R., Freinkman, L. and Goldberg, I. (2005) 'Fiscal Federalism in Rentier Regions: Evidence from Russia', *Journal of Comparative Economics*, 33(4): 814–34.

Dinopoli, T. (2012) 'Debt Impact Study: An Analysis of New York State's Debt Burden'. Online. Available: www.osc.state.ny.us/reports/debt/debtimpact2012.pdf (accessed 20 May 2014).

Eisenhardt, K.M. (1989) 'Building Theories from Case-Study Research', *Academy of Management Review*, 14(4): 532–50.

Fedorov, L. (2002) 'Regional Inequality and Regional Polarization in Russia 1990–99', *World Development*, 30: 443–56.

Finmarket (2013) 'Default Roams the Country: by 2015 Regional Debt Will Double', 11 December. Online. Available: www.finmarket.ru/main/article/3574451 (accessed 20 May 2014).

Fitch (2005a) *Fitch: Provisional 2005 Results Signal Rising Budgetary Rigidity For Russian Regions*, 28 September. Online. Available: www.fitchratings.com/creditdesk/press_releases/detail.cfm?pr_id=180771 (accessed 20 May 2014).

Fitch (2013b) 'Fitch prisvoilo Kyanty-mansiyskomu avtonomnomu okrugu RF reiting «BBB»', 8 October. Online. Available: www.fitchratings.ru/rws/press-release.html?report_id=804352 (accessed 20 May 2014).

Freinkman, L. and Plekhanov, A. (2009) 'Fiscal Decentralization in Rentier Regions: Evidence from Russia', *World Development,* 37(2): 503–12.

Golosov, G. (2008) 'Politics in the Russian Regions', *Democratization*, 15: 445–6.

Granik, I. and Samarina, L. (2013) 'Dolgi regionov prevysili ikh dokhody,' *Moskovskie novosti*, 12 March. Online. Available: http://mn.ru/business_economy/20130312/339615887-print.html (accessed 20 May 2014).

Gurev, S. and Vakulenko, E. (2012) 'Convergence Between Russian Regions', *CEFIR Working Paper 180*. Online. Available: www.cefir.ru/download.php?id=3469 (accessed 20 May 2014).

Gurev, S., Yakovlev, E. and Zhuravskaya, E. (2008) 'Interest Group Politics in a Federation', *CEPR Discussion Paper*, DP6671. Online. Available: http://ssrn.com/abstract=1140953 (accessed 20 May 2014).

Hatfield, J.W. and Miquel, G.P.I. (2012) 'A Political Economy Theory of Partial Decentralization', *Journal of the European Economic Association*, 10(3): 605–33.

Hauner, D. (2008) 'Explaining Differences in Public Sector Efficiency: Evidence from Russia's Regions', *World Development*, 36(10): 1745–65.

Iandiev, M. (2013a) 'Budgetary and Financial Sector of the Russian Federation: Results of the Past Decade (2000–2010)', *Acta Moraviae*, 12.

Iandiev, M. (2013b) 'Otsenka effektivnosti realizatsii tselevykh programm subektov Federatsii', *Finansy*, 2.

Iimi, A. (2005) 'Decentralization and Economic Growth Revisited: an Empirical Note', *Journal of Urban Economics*, 57(3): 449–61.

Ilina, I., Leonard, C.S. and Plisetskiy, E. (2014) 'Russian Regional Resilience: Finance, Cooperation and Resource Abundance (a Case Study of Khanty-Mansiysk)', *Higher School of Economics Working paper*, WP BRP 15/PA/2014.

Kondrateva, N.B. (2008) *Regiony Rossii i Evropeiskogo Soyuza na puti k stroitel'stvu obshchego ekonomicheskogo prostranstva*, Moscow: Institut Evropy RAN.

Korosteleva, V.V. and Kurbanova, T.A. (2014) 'The Role of Tax Revenues in the Budget of the Subject of the Russian Federation (by the Example of the Khanty-Mansiysk Autonomous District – Yugra)', *Sibac.Info*, Online. Available: http://sibac.info/index.php/2009-07-01-10-21-16/4315-2012-10-22-04-02-12 (accessed 26 May 2014).

Krizis-kopilka (2013) 'Regions of Russia Mired in Debt', *Krizis kopilka*, 23 February. Online. Available: http://krizis-kopilka.ru/archives/9618 (accessed 20 May 2014).

Kumar, M.S., Leigh, D. and Plekhanov, A. (2007) *Fiscal Adjustments: Determinants and Macroeconomic Consequences*, Washington, DC: IMF.

Lavrov, A., Litwack, J.M. and Sutherland, D. (2001) *Fiscal Federalist Relations in Russia: a Case for Subnational Autonomy*, Paris: OECD.

Mamedov, A., Nazarov, V. and Siluanov, A. (2013) *Problemy mezhbiudzhetnykh otnosheniy v Rossii*, Moscow: Institute of Economic Policy.

Martinez-Vazquez, J. and Boex, J. (2001) *Russia's Transition to a New Federalism*, Washington, DC: World Bank.

Martinez-Vazquez, J. and Timofeev, A. (2008) 'Regional-local Dimension of Russia's Fiscal Equalization', *Journal of Comparative Economics*, 36(1): 157–76.

Mello, L.D. (2000) 'Fiscal Decentralization and Intergovernmental Fiscal Relations: a Cross-country Analysis', *World Development*, 28(2): 365–80.

Musgrave, R.A. (1997) 'Devolution, Grants, and Fiscal Competition', *Journal of Economic Perspectives*, 11(4): 65–72.

Newsland (2013) 'Debts' Regions Exceeded Their Income', 12 March. Online. Available: http://newsland.com/news/detail/id/1140285/ (accessed 20 May 2014).

OECD (2014) Revenue Statistics-Comparative Tables. Online. Available: http://stats.oecd.org/Index.aspx?DataSetCode=REV (accessed 20 May 2014).

Otto, J. (2001) 'Fiscal Decentralization and Mining Taxation'. Washington, DC: World Bank Mining Group. Online. Available: http://siteresources.worldbank.org/INTOGMC/Resources/miningtaxationjotto.pdf (accessed 20 May 2014).

Papyrakis, E. and Gerlagh, R. (2007) 'Resource Abundance and Economic Growth in the United States', *European Economic Review*, 51(4): 1011–39.

Plekhanov, A. (2006) 'Are Sub-National Budget Constraints Soft: Evidence from Russia', Cambridge, UK, working paper.

Polynev, A.O. (2010) *Konkurentnye vozmozhnosti regionov: Metodologiya issledovaniya i puti ee povysheniya,* Moscow: KRASAND.

Prikaz (2012) 'O forme i sroke predstavleniya zayavki na perechislenie subsidii iz federalnogo byudzheta byudzhetu subekta Rossiiskoy Federatsii na sofinansirovanie raskodnykh obyazatelstv subekta Rossiiskoj Federatsii, voznikayuchshikh pri naznachenii ezhemesyachnoy denezhnoy vyplaty, predusmotrennoy punktom 2 Ukaza Prezidenta Rossiiskoy Federatsii ot 7 maya 2012. N 606 "O merah po realizatsii demograficheskoy politiki Rossiiskoy Federatsii", forme, poryadke i sroke predstavleniya otcheta ob ispolnenii predostavleniya ukazannoy subsidii' ot 29 noyabrya 2012, N 556n. Online. Available: www.isiarussia.ru/gretta.php?id=2577 (accessed 20 May 2014).

Protown.ru (2014) 'Analysis of Budget Expenditures on the National Economy in 2011–2013'. Online. Available: www.protown.ru/information/hide/6374.html (accessed 20 May 2014).

Qian, Y.Y. and Weingast, B.R. (1997) 'Federalism as a Commitment to Preserving Market Incentives', *Journal of Economic Perspectives,* 11(4): 83–92.

Rasporiazhenie (2014) 'Ob Osnovnykh napraveniyakh nalogovoy politiki Khanty-Mansiyskogo avtonomnogo okruga – Yugry na 2014 god i na planovyi period 2015–16', 9 August 2013, Pravitelstvo Khanty-Mansiyskogo avtonomnogo Okruga – Yugry, N 405.

Regions of Russia (2013) *Regions of Russia: Socio-economic Indicators. 2013,* Moscow: Rosstat.

Ria Novosti (2013) 'The Authorities of Yugra are Looking for Ways to Keep Falling Oil Production in the Region', 19 April. Online. Available: http://m.ria.ru/analytics/20130419/933482745.html (accessed 20 May 2014).

RIA Rating (2013) 'The Rating of Socio-economic Conditions of the Regions – 2013', 10 June. Online. Available: http://riarating.ru/regions_study/20130610/610567066.html (accessed 20 May 2014).

Rosstat (2013) *Rossiiskii statisticheskii ezhegodnik,* Moscow: Federal Statistical Service.

Russia Beyond the Headlines (2014) 'Davos Experts Urge Russia to Focus on Regional Development', 24 January. Online. Available: http://rbth.ru/business/2014/01/24/davos_experts_urge_russia_to_focus_on_regional_development_33491.html (accessed 20 May 2014).

Sachs, J.D. and Warner, A.M. (2001) 'The Curse of Natural Resources', *European Economic Review,* 45(4–6): 827–38.

Searle, B. (2007) 'Revenue Sharing, Natural Resources and Fiscal Equalization', in Martinez-Vazquez, J. and Searle, B. (eds), *Fiscal Equalization: Challenges in the Design of Intergovernmental Transfers,* pp. 371–401.

Sepulveda, C.F. and Martinez-Vazquez, J. (2011) 'The Consequences of Fiscal Decentralization on Poverty and Income Equality', *Environment and Planning C-Government and Policy,* 29(2): 321–43.

Shleifer, A. and Treisman, D. (2005) 'A Normal Country: Russia after Communism', *Journal of Economic Perspectives,* 19(1): 151–74.

Siluanov, A.G. (2011) *Mezhbydzhetnye otnosheniya v usloviiakh razvitiya federalizma v Rossii,* Moscow: Delo.

Siluanov, A., Kadochnikov, P., Nazarov, V. and Mamedov, A. (2009) 'Intergovernmental Relations and Subnational Finances in Russia in 2008, Russian Economy in 2008', Working papers, Institute for the Economy in Transition, 30: 31–47.

Solanko, L. (2001) 'Fiscal Competition in a Transition Economy', BOFIT Discussion Paper, 4.

Spilimbergo, A. (2007) 'Measuring the Performance of Fiscal Policy in Russia', *Emerging Markets Finance and Trade*, 43(6): 25–44.

Stoner-Weiss, K. (2006) 'Russia: Authoritarianism Without Authority', *Journal of Democracy*, 17(1): 104-18.

Vartapetov, K. (2010) 'Russia's Federal Fiscal Grants: Regional Equalisation and Growth', *Post-communist Economies*, 22: 471–81.

Vartapetov, K. (2011) 'Russian Fiscal Federalism under Stress: Federal Support of Regions during the Global Financial Crisis', *Eurasian Geography and Economics*, 52(4): 529–42.

Vavulin, D.A. and Simonov, S.V. (2013) 'Bond Loans as an Alternative Mechanism for Financing Deficit of the Regional Budget', *Finances and Credit*, 42(570): 32.

Vd-tv.ru (2013) 'The Profit Tax Will Be Given to Regions', 27 November. Online. Available: http://vd-tv.ru/news.php?12874 (accessed 20 May 2014).

Vedomosti (2013a) 'What's Next for the Four Russias?', 24 September. Online. Available: http://valdaiclub.com/politics/63661.html (accessed 20 May 2014).

Vedomosti (2013b) 'Fitch: Regions Need to Borrow Abroad', 6 December. Online. Available: www.vedomosti.ru/finance/news/19744291/ukazy-putina-oplatyat-inostrancy#ixzz2rckm3x76 (accessed 20 May 2014).

Walker, A. (2013) 'An Empirical Analysis of Resource Curse Channels in the Appalachian Region, Morgantown, WV', West Virginia University.

World Economic Forum (2014) 'Russia's Regions: Drivers of Growth project'. Online. Available: www.weforum.org/content/global-agenda-council-russia-2012-2014 (accessed 20 May 2014).

Yakovlev, A.A., Marques, I. and Nazrullaeva, E. (2011) 'From Competition to Dominance: Political Determinants of Federal Transfers in the Russian Federation', Working Papers. Moscow, WP BRP 12/EC/2011, Higher School of Economics. Online. Available: www.hse.ru/data/2013/02/22/1306748794/02.02.pdf (accessed 20 May 2014).

Index